WITHDRAWN

OAKY
MEMORIAL
LIBRARY

*In Eight Volumes. Crown 8vo. With Maps, etc.
Eight Shillings and Sixpence net each Volume.
The Complete Set £3, 8s. net.*

PERIODS OF EUROPEAN HISTORY

General Editor—ARTHUR HASSALL, M.A.
Student of Christ Church, Oxford.

THIS Series embodies the results of the latest investigations, and contains references to and notes upon original and other sources of information, thus forming a comprehensive and trustworthy account of the general development of European History.

No such attempt to place the History of Europe in a comprehensive, detailed, and readable form before the English public has previously been made, and the Series forms a valuable continuous History of Mediæval and Modern Europe, and also deals fully and carefully with the more prominent events in each century.

Period I.—The Dark Ages. A.D. 476-918.
By Sir C. W. C. OMAN, K.B.E., M.A., LL.D., Chichele Professor of Modern History in the University of Oxford. 8s. 6d. net.

Period II.—The Empire and the Papacy. A.D. 918-1273.
By T. F. TOUT, M.A., D.Litt., Hon. Professor of History in the University of Manchester. 8s. 6d. net.

Period III.—The Close of the Middle Ages. A.D. 1273-1494.
By Sir R. LODGE, M.A., LL.D., Formerly Professor of History in the University of Edinburgh. 8s. 6d. net.

Period IV.—Europe in the 16th Century. A.D. 1494-1598.
By A. H. JOHNSON, M.A., Late Fellow of All Souls' College, Oxford. 8s. 6d. net.

Period V.—The Ascendancy of France. A.D. 1598-1715.
By H. O. WAKEMAN, M.A., Late Fellow of All Souls' College, Oxford. 8s. 6d. net.

Period VI.—The Balance of Power. A.D. 1715-1789.
By A. HASSALL, M.A., Author of 'A History of Europe' and 'A Class Book of English History.' 8s. 6d. net.

Period VII.—Revolutionary Europe. A.D. 1789-1815.
By H. MORSE STEPHENS, M.A., Late Professor of History at the University of California, Berkeley, California, U.S.A. 8s. 6d. net.

Period VIII.—Modern Europe. A.D. 1815-1899.
By W. ALISON PHILLIPS, M.A., Lecky Professor of Modern History in the University of Dublin. 8s. 6d. net.

THE DARK AGES, 476-918

By Sir C. W. C. OMAN, K.B.E., M.A., LL.D., M.P., Chichele Professor
of Modern History in the University of Oxford.

Forming Volume I. of PERIODS OF EUROPEAN HISTORY.

'A thorough master of his subject, and possessed of a gift for clear exposi-
tions, he has supplied the student with a most valuable and helpful book.'—
Spectator.

'No better exponent of this era, so full of difficulties and complications,
could have been chosen.'—*Journal of Education.*

'Mr. Oman has done his work well. His narrative is clear and interesting,
and takes full account of recent research.'—*English Historical Review.*

'This volume will be valued by all historical students as supplying a real
want in our historical literature, and supplying it well. . . . His touch is
sure and his insight keen. For the accuracy of his facts his historical
reputation is a sufficient guarantee.'—*Times.*

THE EMPIRE AND THE PAPACY, 918-1273

By T. F. TOUT, M.A., D.Litt., Hon. Professor of History
in the University of Manchester.

Forming Volume II. of PERIODS OF EUROPEAN HISTORY.

'This admirable and impartial work. . . . A more trustworthy historical
treatise on the period and subject has not hitherto appeared.'—
Morning Post.

'One of the best of the many good historical text-books which have come
out of our universities in recent years.'—*Times.*

'Altogether Professor Tout has given us a most trustworthy adjunct to
the study of mediæval times, which all who may be called upon to interpret
those times to others may safely recommend and themselves profit by.'—
English Historical Review.

THE CLOSE OF THE MIDDLE AGES, 1273-1494

By SIR R. LODGE, M.A., LL.D., Formerly Professor of History
in the University of Edinburgh.

Forming Volume III. of PERIODS OF EUROPEAN HISTORY.

'The book is admirably written, it contains maps and genealogical tables,
an exhaustive index, and a bibliography which students will value as an aid
to the interpretation of the whole period as well as a clue to any part of it.'
—*Standard.*

'We are exceedingly thankful for the Series, and as we have already said,
to Prof. Lodge. There is no longer any excuse for English-speaking teachers
to be wholly ignorant of the history of Europe. The obligation lies on them
to purchase these volumes, and then read, mark, learn, and inwardly digest
them, so that they can supplement their teaching with intelligible comment.'
—*School World.*

'The book must be regarded as quite indispensable to all English students
of the late Middle Ages.'—*University Correspondent.*

'Professor Lodge's book has the supreme merit of clearness, not less than
that of conciseness.'—*Pall Mall Gazette.*

'A work of great value on one of the most difficult and at the same time
one of the most important periods of European history. The book is a
monument of skill and labour.'—*Aberdeen Journal.*

EUROPE IN THE 16TH CENTURY, 1494-1598

By A. H. JOHNSON, M.A.,
Late Fellow of All Souls' College, Oxford.

Forming Volume IV. of PERIODS OF EUROPEAN HISTORY.

'A singularly clear, thorough, and consistent account of the great move·
ments and great events of the time, and the volume may be accepted as one
of the best extant handbooks to a period as complex as it is important.'—
Times.

'In the present volume Mr. A. H. Johnson has made a useful and unpre-
tentious contribution to a Series of which it can be said more truly than of
most series that it supplies a real want. Mr. Johnson is well known as one
of the most experienced and successful teachers of history at Oxford, and the
book has all the merits which the fact of being written by a good teacher can
give it. It is clear, sensible, and accurate, and commendably free from fads
or bias.'—*Manchester Guardian.*

'There is certainly no other single book in English which covers the
ground so adequately.'—*University Correspondent.*

'Mr. Johnson's narrative is clear and accurate, and his grasp of the history
of his period wonderfully strong and comprehensive.'—*Journal of Education.*

THE ASCENDANCY OF FRANCE, 1598-1715

By H. O. WAKEMAN, M.A., Late Fellow of All Souls' College, Oxford.

Forming Volume V. of PERIODS OF EUROPEAN HISTORY.

'His story is no dry compendium, but a drama, each act and scene of
which has its individual interest.'—*Guardian.*

'Mr. Wakeman has produced an excellent sketch, both clear and con-
cise.'—*Oxford Magazine.*

'Mr. Wakeman's book is a sound, able, and useful one, which will alike
give help to the student, and attract the cultivated general reader.'—
Manchester Guardian.

'A thoroughly scholarly and satisfactory monograph.'—*Leeds Mercury.*

THE BALANCE OF POWER, 1715-1789

By A. HASSALL, M.A., General Editor of the Series.

Forming Volume VI. of PERIODS OF EUROPEAN HISTORY.

'Although it contains more than 400 pages, we felt as we read its last page
that it was too short. It is not, however, too short to prevent its author
dealing adequately with his subject according to the scheme of the whole
Series. There is little detail in it, and but little theorising, and ·what it
contains are clear statements of masterly summaries. . . . We may cordially
recommend this interesting and well-written volume.'—
Birmingham Daily Gazette.

'Treated with much accuracy, patience, and vigour.'—*Educational Times.*

'The author has struggled manfully with the difficulties of his subject, and
not without a distinct measure of success. He has availed himself of the
latest researches on the period, and his narrative is well ordered and
illustrated by excellent maps and some useful appendices.'—
Manchester Guardian.

REVOLUTIONARY EUROPE, 1789-1815

By H. MORSE STEPHENS, M.A., Late Professor of History at the University of California, U.S.A.

Forming Volume VII. of PERIODS OF EUROPEAN HISTORY.

'As a piece of literary workmanship can hardly be surpassed. . . . The result is a boon to students, and a serviceable book of reference for the general reader.'—*Daily News*.

'Mr. Stephens has written a very valuable and meritorious book, which ought to be widely used.'—*Manchester Guardian*.

'An admirable, nay, a masterly work.'—*Academy*.

'To say that Mr. Morse Stephens has compiled the best English text-book on the subject would be faint praise.'—*Journal of Education*.

'We are happy to extend a hearty welcome to this much-needed Series, which, if it throughout keeps on the same high level of this volume, will fill up a painful gap in our accessible historical literature.'—*Educational Times*.

'The volume contains one of the clearest accounts of the French Revolution and the rise of the First Napoleon ever written. In fact, it is the work of a real historian. The style of the book is strong and picturesque.'—*Western Morning News*.

MODERN EUROPE, 1815-1899

By W. ALISON PHILLIPS, M.A., Lecky Professor of Modern History in the University of Dublin.

Forming Volume VIII. of PERIODS OF EUROPEAN HISTORY.

'Remains the most readable general introduction to the history of the 19th century, and may be recommended for the period 1815-1876.'—*Times, August 6, 1914*.

An exceedingly difficult task has been accomplished, we may say without hesitation, to admiration. We have read the book with the keenest and quite unflagging enjoyment, and we welcome it as one of the very best histories that have been written within the last few years.'—*Guardian*.

'It has achieved, with a remarkable success, the difficult task of compressing into a compact space the long history of a time of extraordinary complications and entanglements; but—much more important—it has never lost vigour and interest throughout the whole survey. . . . The completeness of the book is really extraordinary. . . . The book is by far the best and handiest account of the international politics of the nineteenth century that we possess. . . . Should give Mr. Alison Phillips distinct rank among historians of the day.'—*Literature*.

'Altogether, the book offers a most luminous and quite adequate treatment of its subject, and makes a worthy conclusion of a Series that well deserves to be popular.'—*Glasgow Herald*.

'Mr. Phillips shows decided literary power in the handling of a not too manageable period, and few readers with any appreciation of the march of history, having once commenced the book, will be content to lay it aside until the last page is reached.'—*Manchester Guardian*.

EUROPE

IN THE

SIXTEENTH CENTURY

1494-1598

BY

A. H. JOHNSON, M.A.

LATE FELLOW OF ALL SOULS' COLLEGE, AND HISTORICAL LECTURER
TO MERTON, TRINITY, AND UNIVERSITY COLLEGES, OXFORD

PERIOD IV

TENTH IMPRESSION
SEVENTH EDITION

RIVINGTONS
34 *KING STREET, COVENT GARDEN*
LONDON
1928

All rights reserved

Printed in Great Britain by T. and A. CONSTABLE LTD.
at the University Press, Edinburgh

940.2
J66c

PREFACE

THE limits as to length imposed upon me by the Editor of the Series forced me to adopt one of two alternatives. I had either to content myself with a very slight sketch of the whole of European History during the period, or I had to exercise some principle of selection.

Unwilling to do over again that which has already been well done by Mr. Lodge in his *History of Modern Europe*, I have fallen back on the second alternative, and confined myself to the greater Powers of Western Europe.

Nor is such a selection without some justification; for it is the struggle for supremacy between these Powers which underlies the other issues, affects every movement (even the religious ones), and gives unity to this many-sided and involved period of the world's history.

My readers will therefore find no reference to the affairs of England, nor to those of the Kingdoms of Northern and Eastern Europe, except so far as in their foreign policy they affect the course of that great struggle.

My best thanks are due to Mr. Armstrong for help, more particularly in points of Spanish History, and to Mr. Fletcher, who has revised the proofs, and assisted with his kindly criticism.

OXFORD.

2/75

PREFACE TO FOURTH EDITION

I have only to thank my critics, and especially Mr. Armstrong and Mr. Fotheringham, for many helpful suggestions.

OXFORD.

NOTE TO SEVENTH EDITION

I have made a few corrections in this edition, and have placed in Appendix IV. those which could not be made in the body of the book.

OXFORD.

LIST OF MAPS

CONTENTS

BIBLIOGRAPHICAL NOTE [1]

GENERAL—

Cambridge Modern History, vol. i.

Lavisse et Rambaud, *Histoire Générale.*

Creighton, *History of the Papacy during the Reformation*, c. vii. to the end.

Philippson, *La Contre-Révolution religieuse.*

Ranke, *Fürsten und Völker von Süd Europa im 16ten u. 17ten Jahrhundert.*

Zur Kritik neuerer Geschichtschreiber.

Maps.—Spruner Menke, No. 8. Putzger, *Historischer School Atlas.* Clarendon Press Historical Atlas, No. 8.

N.B.—The Clarendon Press Maps, with Notes, can be purchased separately, the Spruner without Notes.

A chronological summary will be found in Hassall, *Handbook of European History.*

FRANCE—

Cambridge Modern History, c. xii.

Martin, *Histoire de France.*

Michelet, *Histoire de France.*

Grant, *The French Monarchy.*

---

[1] This list may be supplemented by reference to the following Bibliographies :—

I. *The Cambridge Modern History*, of which vol. i. has already appeared.

II. Armstrong, *Charles V.*

III. Monod, *Bibliographie de l'Histoire de France.*

IV. Dahlmann-Waitz, *Quellenkunde der deutschen Geschichte.*

V. Förster, *Kritischer Wegweiser durch die neuere deutsche historische Litteratur.*

VI. Pirenne, *Bibliographie de l'histoire de Belgique.*

VII. Lavisse et Rambaud, *Histoire Générale.*

Gasquet, *Précis des Institutions Politiques et Sociales de l'ancienne France.*

Chéruel, *Dictionnaire historique des Institutions, mœurs et costumes de la France.*

Cherrier, *Histoire de Charles VIII.*

Godefroy, Théod., *Histoire de Charles VIII. et Louis XII.* (a collection of Chronicles).

Müntz, *La Renaissance en Italie et en France à l'Époque de Charles VIII.*

Philippe de Commines, *Mémoires.*

Lettenhove : Commines, *Lettres et négoc. avec un Commentaire.*

Memoirs given in Pétitot, Michaud et Ponjoulat, especially *Fleuranges, Bayard, Tavannes, Condé, La Noue.*

Mignet, *Rivalité de François Ier et de Charles Quint.*

De Thou, *Historiarum sui temporis libri* cxxxviii. (translated into French).

Ranke, *Französische Geschichte* (translated *The Civil Wars in France*).

Armstrong, *Civil Wars in France.*

Baird, *The Rise of the Huguenots.*

Forneron, *Les Ducs de Guise.*

Aumale, duc d', *Histoire des Princes de Condé.*

Delaborde, *Coligny.*

Whitehead, *Coligny.*

Solden, *Geschichte des Protestantismus in Frankreich.*

Willert, *Henry IV.* (Heroes of Nations Series).

Mornay, Ph., du Plessis *Mémoires.*

Maps.—Spruner Menke, No. 54.

Clarendon Press Historical Atlas, Nos. 57, 58.

GERMANY—

Cambridge Modern History, cc. ix. xvi. xvii. xviii. xix.

Nitzsch, *Geschichte des deutschen Volkes.*

Krönes, *Handbuch der Geschichte Österreichs.*

Ranke, *Geschichte der romanischen und germanischen Völker* (translated.)

Bezold, *Geschichte der deutschen Reformation* (Onckens Series).

Alman, *Kaiser Maximilian I.*

Vehse, *Memoirs of the House of Austria* (translated).

Hutten, Ulrich von, *Schriften.* Ed. Bocking.

Strauss, *Ulrich von Hutten* (translated).

Geiger, *Renaissance und Humanismus in Italien und Deutschland* (Onckens Series).

Johann Reuchlin.

Erasmus, *Opera.* Ed. Le Clerc.

Froude, *Erasmus.*

Lamprecht, *Deutsche Geschichte* (good for the Social and Economic History).

Allgemeine deutsche Biographie.

Zeller, *Histoire d'Allemagne: La Réformation.*

Ranke, *Deutsche Geschichte im Zeitalter der Reformation* (part translated).

Janssen, *Geschichte des deutschen Volkes seit dem Ausgange des Mittelalters* (in course of translation).

Beard, *The Hibbert Lectures,* 1803.

Köstlin, *Martin Luther.*

Maurenbrecher, *Studien u. Skizzen zur Reformationszeit.*
         Geschichte der katholischen Reform.
         Karl V. und die deutschen Protestanten.

Armstrong, *Charles V.*

Baumgarten, *Geschichte Karls V.*

Garchard, *Life of Charles,* in *Biographie Nationale,* vol. iii.

Mignet, *Rivalité de François Ier et de Charles Quint.*

Sir Stirling Maxwell, *Cloister life of Charles V.*

Lanz, *Correspondenz des Kaisers Karl V.*
         Staatspapiere zur Geschichte des Kaisers Karl V.

Bradford, *Correspondence of Charles V.*

Garchard, *Correspondance de Charles Quint et d'Adrien VI.*

Brandenburg, *Moritz von Sachsen.*

Ranke, *Zur deutschen Geschichte vom Religionsfrieden bis zum dreissigjährigen Krieg.*

Wolf, G., *Deutsche Geschichte im Zeitalter der Gegenreformation.*

Köstlin, *Martin Luther.*

Kampschutte, *Calvin.*

Maps.—Spruner Menke, Nos. 43, 73, 74.
         Clarendon Press Historical Atlas, Nos. 37, 38, 39, 47.

BOHEMIA—

Palacky, *Geschichte von Böhmen.*

Map.—Clarendon Press Historical Atlas, No. 46.

SWITZERLAND—

Dierauer, *Geschichte der schweizerischen Eidgenossenschaft.*

Coolidge, *Article in Encyclopædia Brit.*

Map.—Clarendon Press Historical Atlas, No. 44.

ITALY—

Cf. *Cambridge Modern History,* cc. iv, v, vi, vii, viii, xvi, xvii, xviii, xix.

Gregorovius, *Geschichte der Stadt Rom*, vols. vii. viii. (translated).

Creighton, *Popes of the Reformation*.

Ranke, *Die römischen Päpste* (translated).

Pastor, *Geschichte der Päpste* (translated).

Sismondi, *Histoire des Républiques italiennes du moyen âge*.

Brown, H. F., *Kalendar of Venetian State Papers*.
      Venice.

Romanin, *Storia documentata di Venezia*.

Perrens, *Histoire de Florence*.

Guicciardini, *Storia d'Italia*.
      Considerazione intorno ai Discorsi di Machiavelli: opere
       inedite, vol. i.
      Storia Fiorentina. opere inedite, vol. iii.

Guido Capponi, *Storia della republica di Firenza*.

Capponi, G. A., *Storia del Reame di Napoli*.

Jovius, *Vitæ illustrium virorum · Elogia virorum illustrium ·
 Historia sui temporis*.

Burcardas Diarium. Ed. Thuasne, 1883-1885.

Giustiniani Dispacci. Ed. Villari.

Alberi, *La relazione degli Ambasciatori Veneti al Senato durante il
 Secolo* xvi.

Da Porto, *Lettere Storiche*.

Sanuto, 1 *Diarii*.

Symonds, *The Renaissance in Italy*.

Zeller, *Italie et la Renaissance*.

Burckhardt, *Die Cultur der Renaissance in Italien* (translated).

Geiger, *Humanismus und Renaissance in Italien und Deutschland*
 (Onckens Series).

Yriarte, *Venise*.
    César Borgia.
    La vie d'un Patricien de Venise.

Burd, *Machiavelli : Il Principe* (with Biographical and other Notes).

Machiavelli, *Storia Fiorentina* (French translation, Perier, 1842).
     Legazioni e Commissarii, vol. iii. of *Opere Discorsi*.

Morley, *Machiavelli* (Romanes Lecture).

Villari, *Niccolo Machiavelli* (translated).
    La Storia di G. Savonarola (translated).

Ranke, *Savonarola u. die florentinische Republik*.

Sarpi Paolo, *Istoria del Concilio Tridentino* (translated into French by
 Courrayer).

Maps.—Spruner Menke, No. 27.
    Clarendon Press Historical Atlas, Nos. 68, 69.

Markham, Sir C. R., *Life of Christopher Columbus.*
                   History of Peru.
Kretchmer, *Die Entdeckung Amerikas.*
Payne, *History of the New World called America.*
Peschel, *Geschichte des Zeitalters der Entdeckungen.*
Prescott, *History of Conquest of Mexica.*
           History of Conquest of Peru.
Winsor, *Narrative and Critical History of America.*
Maps.—Spruner Menke, No. 20.
        Clarendon Press Historical Atlas, No. 85.

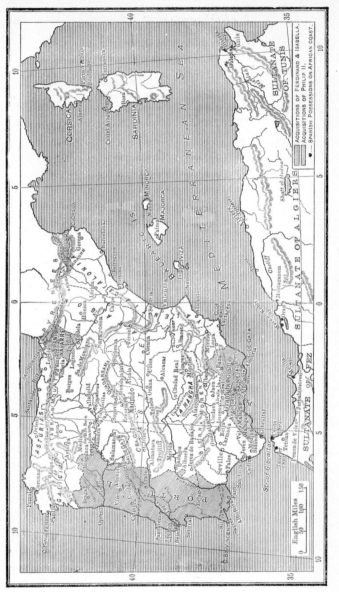

SPAIN, 1494-1598

English Miles
50   100   150

ACQUISITIONS OF FERDINAND & ISABELLA.
ACQUISITIONS OF PHILIP II.
SPANISH POSSESSIONS ON AFRICAN COAST.

INTRODUCTION

THE division of history into periods may be very misleading if its true purport be not understood. One age can no more be isolated from the universal course of history than one generation from another. The ideas, the principles, the aims of man change indeed, but change slowly, and in their very change are the outcome of the past. The old generation melts into the new, as the night melts into the day. None the less, just as the night differs from the day, although it is impossible to say when the dawn begins, and when the day, so does the Modern differ from that which has been termed the Middle age. This once granted, the importance of the later years of the fifteenth century may be easily grasped. The mediæval conception of the great World-Church under Pope and Emperor had by this time lost all practical power. The authority of the Emperor was confined to Germany, and was even there disputed, and, if the Papacy still retained its pretensions, they no longer had their old weight. Not only had they been resisted by the various powers of Europe in turn, they had even been severely criticised by two General Councils. Already the man was born who was to take the lead in the final overthrow of the unity of the Western Church. Meanwhile, the older society was breaking up: the links which in binding a man to his lord, his fields, his trade, or his town, bound him to his fellows, and his livelihood to him, were falling to pieces, and the 'individual' of modern

[marginal notes:] True meaning of the division of History into Periods.

Importance of closing years of the fifteenth century.

Break-up of mediæval idea of a World-Church.

Rise of Individualism.

life was emerging. To this change many things contributed. The movement of the Renaissance emancipated men from the somewhat narrow limits of mediævalism ; it opened to them the knowledge of the ancients, and gave them a glimpse of the worlds of thought beyond, of which the New World about to be discovered to the west seemed but a type. The economic revolution had a like effect. The break-up of the older organisation of trades under the system of close guilds, was accompanied by the rise of modern competition. In life, as in thought, the individual was asserting himself.

Amidst the clashing of rival interests which this revolution necessitated, a new principle of unity—that of nationality—
Growth of   arose. This conception, due to an appreciation
nationalities. of the identity of interest based on such things as common language, common religion, natural boundaries, common hopes and fears, was, if a less attractive one than that of the Holy Roman Empire, at least more capable of realisation, and alone seemed able to control the spirit of individualism from running riot. It was in France, Spain, and England that this new spirit of nationality had been most successful : but, if Germany was no more than a loose confederation of princes, the Hapsburgs had already laid the foundation of a monarchy of their own, while the Pope was becoming more and more the prince of a temporal kingdom in Italy. The first result of this triumph of nationality
The rivalries   was not surprising. When once a people have
of the   realised the identity of their interests, they are
nations   apt to be aggressive. This now occurred. Eng-
lead to
foreign   land indeed, isolated from the Continent and
wars.   absorbed in domestic questions, did not take much part as yet ; but the others began to look abroad, and Italy, where alone no political unity existed, offered fair hopes of spoil. No sooner had France made the first move in pursuit of her claims on Naples than their cupidity was aroused, and Western Europe was involved in a series of wars which continued, with but little intermission, until the Peace of Vervins,

1598. The circumstances of the age gave to this struggle its peculiar character. National consolidation had been accompanied by the triumph of the monarchical principle, after its long struggle with aristocracy —a struggle which of late had not been confined to the temporal sphere, but had been illustrated also within the Church by the conflict between the Papacy and the General Councils. It followed that the dynastic interests of the reigning families predominated. The monarchs, no doubt, represented the passions and aspirations of their subjects. Nevertheless, their policy was deeply coloured by their personal and family rivalries, and hence the wars were more prolonged than otherwise they might have been. To this also must in part be attributed the shifting combinations of alliances and counter-alliances, which change with the variety and rapidity of a kaleidoscope, and which make the period, so far as its wars are concerned, one of the most confused in history. In the struggle which ensued, the Romance and the Teutonic nations came into close though hostile contact; the theory of the Balance of Power became a guiding principle of politics; and diplomacy found its birth.

[marginal note: The triumph of monarchy.]

[marginal note: Rise of the theory of the Balance of Power and of Diplomacy.]

Before many years were passed, the unity of the Church of the West was broken by the Reformation. It was inevitable that the religious and the political questions should become involved. The struggle for supremacy in Europe, the internal politics of the several kingdoms, were deeply affected by the religious issues. The web of European complications became more confused than ever, and, if the interest of the period before us is thus enhanced, its difficulty is certainly increased. Into it all the problems of the Middle Age became absorbed, and out of it Modern Europe was to arise.

[marginal note: Political issues affected by the Reformation. The beginning of Modern Europe.]

CHAPTER I

THE ITALIAN WARS, 1494-1518

§ 1. *The Expedition of Charles VIII.*

AT the date of the Italian expedition, Charles VIII. had been eleven years on the throne of France. The monarchy to which he succeeded was, perhaps, less controlled by constitutional checks than any other in Europe. The crown had earned popularity as the leader in the struggle against the English—a struggle which had created the French nation; and as the patron of the middle classes against the feudal nobles. The Estates-General, the deliberative assembly of the kingdom, had never succeeded in vindicating its claims. The class divisions which divided it, as they did the people, had prevented united action. The third estate did not adequately represent the middle classes; the knights of the shire, those valuable representatives of the country districts, who had formed the backbone of the English House of Commons, did not exist. With these defects, the Estates-General had failed to

4

secure the command of the purse, or to control the legislation and administration of the country. All power accordingly lay with the Royal Council, a body of royal nominees who issued ordinances and levied taxes at their will, so long as they did not entrench on the privileges of the nobility to be free from all direct taxation beyond their feudal dues.

True, the 'Parlement' of Paris, the supreme judicial court of the realm, tried to exercise a power of veto by insisting on its right of registering, and therefore of refusing to register, the royal edicts. The King, however, could easily overcome this opposition by holding a 'Lit de Justice,'—that is, by summoning the members of the Parlement before the Great Council, and ordering them to register; and under a strong King, at least, the Parlement became the humble instrument rather than the opponent of the crown.[1]

As Charles was in his fourteenth year on the death of his father Louis XI. in 1483, a regency was not necessary according to the ordinance of Charles V. (1374). But Louis XI., conscious of the way in which he had from policy or from cynicism[2] neglected his son's education, had intrusted him to the guardianship of his daughter Anne, wife of the Sire de Beaujeu, who, on the death of his elder brother in 1488, became Duke of Bourbon.

Charles VIII. under the guardianship of Anne of Beaujeu, 1483-1492. Her successful policy.

Of Anne Louis XI. had said 'she is the least foolish woman in France.' But her conduct during the earlier years of Charles' reign belied his further remark that 'of wise women he knew none.' She had, in the interests of centralisation at least, though perhaps to the permanent loss of her country, successfully evaded the claims made by the States-General of 1484 to share in the government. She had defeated the repeated attempts of the nobility headed by Louis of Orleans, the heir-presumptive, to oust her from

---

[1] Cf. Appendix i.

[2] 'If he knows these five Latin words, *Qui nescit dissimulare nescit regnare*, it will suffice,' Louis XI. had said of his son.

power, and to restore feudal licence—a movement which had been supported by Francis II. Duke of Brittany, by Maximilian, then King of the Romans, by Richard III., and subsequently by Henry VII. of England.

On the death of Francis, Duke of Brittany (1488), she had interfered in the affairs of the duchy and won by arms the hand of Anne, the Bretonne heiress, for the young King. By the marriage-contract the autonomy of Brittany was indeed acknowledged, but it was agreed that the duchy should fall to the survivor, and the Duchess Anne bound herself, in the event of her husband dying before her without children, to marry the next possessor of the French throne. Thus the way was prepared for the final incorporation into the monarchy of the last great semi-independent feudatory state, so long a thorn in the side of France.

This brilliant triumph of diplomacy aroused all the enemies of France. Maximilian had a double affront to avenge. He himself had been married by proxy to Anne of Brittany, while Charles VIII. had at the Treaty of Arras, 1482, plighted his troth to Margaret, Maximilian's daughter. Thus, by Charles' marriage with the Breton Duchess, both the Emperor and his daughter were jilted. Stung by this twofold insult, Maximilian forthwith laid claim to Margaret's dower, Artois and Franche-Comté, and tried to enforce his claims by arms. Henry VII. attempted to prevent the union of Brittany with France, and Ferdinand of Aragon seized the opportunity to reclaim Roussillon, which had been ceded to Louis XI.

The claim of Maximilian to the dower of his daughter was a just one and could scarce be denied. But the cession of Roussillon should have been resisted at all hazards, while the interference of Henry VII. might have been answered by a resolute attempt to regain Calais and drive the English finally from the kingdom. Whether France was strong enough for so bold a stroke may perhaps be doubted, but at least her policy should have been devoted to the strengthening of her frontiers and the consolidation of the kingdom.

Unfortunately at this moment Charles had become infatuated with the idea of the Italian expedition. Being now old enough to act independently of his sister, he hurriedly yielded to the demands of his enemies. Henry VII. was bought off by the Treaty of Étaples, November 1492. Cerdagne and Roussillon were ceded to Ferdinand by the Treaty of Barcelona,

Charles bent on the Italian expedition makes peace with his enemies.

January 1493, and by the Treaty of Senlis, May 1493, the princess Margaret was restored to her father with Artois and Franche-Comté. Having thus evaded his difficulties near home, Charles hurried on his preparations for the Italian campaign.

After the fall of the Roman Empire, Italy had rapidly lost all national cohesion. In spite of fruitless attempts which were made now and again to establish a united kingdom in the Peninsula, the principle of dis- integration had finally triumphed. The Emperors of the West indeed had claimed supremacy, but, since the close of the thirteenth century, this had ceased to be a reality, and on the ruins of those claims, amidst numerous smaller states, five had risen to special prominence, and in all these, with the exception of Venice, civic independence had fallen before despots.

Condition of Italy in 1494.

In the centre of the plain of Lombardy stood Milan, which at the close of the thirteenth century had fallen to the Visconti. That cruel but capable family, while they destroyed the liberties, extended the domin-

Milan.

ion of the republic, and absorbed most of the smaller states of the plain which escaped the rule of Venice. The territory, which on the extinction of the male line of the Visconti was seized by the Condottiere, Francesco Sforza (1450), stretched from the river Adda, where it marched with the Venetian lands, to the Sesia, where it met Piedmont then under the Duke of Savoy, and the Marquisate of Montferrat. In 1476, the son of Francesco, Galeazzo Maria, had paid the penalty of his tyranny, lust, and cruelty at the hands of three Milanese nobles who, if tyrannicide may ever be defended, are worthy of the name of patriots. He left a widow Bona of Savoy, who ruled in the

name of her infant son Gian Galeazzo, aided by her husband's
wisest counsellor, Francesco Simonetta. Three years later,
1479, Ludovico 'Il Moro,' uncle of the young Gian, overthrew
her rule, caused Simonetta to be executed, and assumed the
regency. Ludovico, though ambitious, unscrupulous, and a
lover of intrigue, was not wantonly cruel as many of his predecessors had been, and, if his rule was a despotic one, he was
a liberal patron of the arts and kept his dominions contented
and at peace.

To the east of the Duchy of Milan stood the republic of
Venice. Once a democracy, she had by the close of the
thirteenth century become a commercial oligarchy.
At the close of the fifteenth century, not only did
the Great Council monopolise the electoral functions of the
state, but the Doge himself had become little more than an
ornamental figure-head.[1] Venice originally had concerned
herself little with the politics of the mainland. Entrenched
behind her lagoons, she had turned her attention to the
Mediterranean and the East, from whence came her commerce, the source of her wealth. At the commencement of
the fifteenth century, however, she had turned her eye westward to form a territory on the mainland.[2] In this venture
she had indeed met with great success, and, besides her
possessions on the east of the Adriatic, in the Morea, and
the Ægean Sea, she now ruled a large territory north of the
Po, which stretched westwards to the Adda and northwards to
the spurs of the Alps. But this policy had drawn her into the
troubled tangle of Italian politics, and aroused the jealousy of
the Italian states. Still Venice was formidable. By the treaty
of 1479, she had surrendered indeed Scutari, Negropont, and
most of her possessions in the Morea, but had retained her
commercial privileges, and secured a temporary peace with
the Turk. In 1488, she annexed, by a fiction of remarkable
ingenuity, the island of Cyprus.

The rule of her aristocracy was far less corrupt and far more

[1] Cf. Appendix iii.   [2] On this cf. p. 57.

consistent than that of other Italian states. The stability of
her Government and her immunity from those revolutions to
which the other states of Italy were ever subject excited the
envy of her neighbours. The leniency and wisdom with
which she governed her dependencies secured her the loyalty
of her subjects. Her riches were still great; her patronage
of art magnificent; and if the tone of private morality was low,
it was not lower than in the rest of Italy.

To the south and south-west of Venice lay the two
independent territories of Mantua and of Ferrara. Of these
Mantua, situated amid the marshy flats of the   Mantua and
Mincio, belonged to the warrior family of the   Ferrara.
Gonzagas, while Ferrara, commanding the mouths of the Po,
was ruled by the ancient house of Este.

Nestling under the Apennines, Florence held the watershed
of the Arno with her dependent cities of Volterra, Arezzo,
Cortona, Pistoja, and Pisa. To the north-west
and to the south of her lay the independent states   Florence.
of Lucca and Siena, long her deadly enemies.

Nominally a republic based on a system of trade-guilds,
Florence was practically in the hands of the Medici, who,
while they left the outward form of the constitution intact,
kept the government in the hands of their partisans. From
time to time a packed 'Parliament' of the citizens elected committees or Balías, under whose control the Signory and other
officials were selected. Finally, in 1480, a college of seventy,
practically nominated by Lorenzo, took for a time the place
of the Balías. This college not only nominated the Signory,
but elected the *Consiglio Maggiore*, the legislative body of the
republic, and thus became master of the city. A clever mani-
pulation of the taxes, by which they struck at the rich, gained
the Medici the support of the lower classes, while the confusion of the public treasury with the finances of their banking-
house gave them the final control of the administration.[1] The
rule of the Medici was a far more temperate one than that of

[1] Cf. Appendix ii.

the Sforza of Milan. Their power was the result of real political genius. By that alone they had succeeded in controlling the most restless, the most acute, and the most brilliant people the world had yet seen since the days of the Athenians. In Florence was concentrated the essence of Italian art and literature, and with it, alas, much of that immorality and licence which stains the glory of the Renaissance. Unfortunately, at this crisis of her history, Lorenzo the Magnificent, the type of a Medicean prince, died (April 1492), and, under the incapable rule of his son Piero, the authority of the family was being rapidly undermined.

Encircling the territories of Siena and Florence on the south and the east, and stretching across the centre of Italy from sea to sea, stood the Papal States, formed of the Patrimony of St. Peter, the Campagna, the Duchy of Spoleto, the March of Ancona and the Romagna.

The Papal States.

Of these territories all, except the two first, while acknowledging the suzerainty of the Pope, were practically independent, and in the Patrimony and in the Campagna, the powerful families of the Orsini and the Colonna were ever setting his authority at defiance. It had been of late the policy of the Popes to enforce their rule in these districts and to organise a strong temporal dominion, a policy definitely begun by Sixtus IV. (1471-1484). They are probably right who maintain that by this means alone could the Papacy hope to survive. The mediæval conception of the Holy Roman Empire had gone beyond recall. The idea of a united Christendom under one faith was no longer a reality. Largely, though by no means entirely, through its own deficiencies, the Papacy had lost its moral hold on Europe, and the attempt of Nicolas V. (1447-1455) and Pius II. (1458-1464) to regain the intellectual leadership of Europe had met with scant success. During the period of the captivity of Avignon (1309-1377), and the great Schism (1378-1417), the power of the larger Italian states, and the lust for further extension, had grown. Under these circumstances, if the Papacy was to save itself from falling as low as it had fallen in the tenth century, when it was the puppet of the neighbouring nobles, it must needs follow suit, and form a strong and united dominion. Yet the necessity cost it dear.   Sucked into the vortex of political intrigue, the Papacy prostituted its spiritual powers for these secular objects and shocked the conscience of Europe.   Unfortunately the Popes who ascended the papal throne at this moment were men of low principle. Sixtus IV. (1471-1484) was venal, and sacrificed everything for the advancement of his nephews.   Innocent VIII. (1484-1492), hopelessly corrupt and indolent, was the first Pope who openly acknowledged his children ; while of Rodrigo Borgia, who ruled as Pope Alexander VI. from 1492 to 1503, it is difficult to speak with moderation.   To enume-rate the charges which have been brought against him would exhaust the crimes of the decalogue.   Even if we dismiss those charges on which the evidence is not conclusive, it cannot be denied that Alexander was profligate beyond ordinary profligacy, contemptuous of the ordinary conven-tionalities of decency, avaricious and cruel, and in states-manship absolutely without scruple.

The desire of the Popes to form a temporal dominion was also injurious to Italy.[1]   Not strong enough to unite the Penin-sula under their own sway, they were determined to prevent its union under any other hands.   In this attempt to reconcile their interests as head of the Church with those of a temporal prince, they were ever ready to barter away their country's liberties.   They had more than once before this summoned the foreigner to their aid, and, if they were not responsible for the first invasion of the French, they went far to make the foreign dominion permanent.

The extremity of the Peninsula formed the kingdom of Naples, now in the hands of Ferrante I. (1458-1494), illegiti-mate son of Alfonso the Magnanimous, of Aragon ; while Sicily and Sardinia belonged, with Aragon, to the legitimate

[1] Cf. Machiavelli, *Discorsi*, Book i. c. 12.

branch represented just now by Ferdinand the Catholic (1479-
1516). Always the most disturbed of the Italian states,
Naples had in 1485 been the scene of a baronial revolt against
the tyranny of Ferrante. The King, indeed, by cunning and
ability had triumphed, but his faithlessness and inhuman
cruelties had made him most unpopular, and his rule most
insecure. He died in January 1494, to be succeeded by his
son Alfonso II. (1494-1495), who, according to the French
chronicler Commines, though not so dangerous, was a worse
man than his father, since 'never was any prince more bloody,
wicked, inhuman, lascivious, or gluttonous than he.'

The rivalry of these five states, mutually repellent, yet
unable to establish complete independence, was to cause the

*Rivalry
of these
states.*
ruin of Italy. Too equally balanced to allow of
the supremacy of one, too jealous of each other
and too divergent in the character of their peoples
and the form of their governments to unite in a federal bond,
they lost all sense of common national interest. The existence of numerous petty states between their frontiers, which
could only hope to survive by dexterous intrigue, excited their
cupidity and thickened the thread of treacherous diplomacy
which was now to call the foreigner into Italy.

But if the quarrels of these Italian rulers led to the first
invasion, and subsequently prevented any permanent coalition,

*Intellectual
activity and
moral degra-
dation of the
Italians.*
the condition of the people of Italy destroyed all
hope of successful resistance. In reading the
social history of Italy during the fifteenth century
two lessons are forced upon us: first, the fatal
effect of the loss of liberty, and of political faction on
the moral fibre of a people; secondly, the danger of luxury,
and of devotion to art and literature, if not chastened by the
religious spirit.

In states like Milan and Naples, where all political liberty
had been destroyed, the only weapons of the oppressed
were those the tyrant had taught them—intrigue and assassination. In cities like Florence, where constitutional forms

remained but the spirit had fled, and where the state was torn by deadly feuds which vented themselves in cruel proscription and exile of the defeated, the people were inspired by mutual suspicion and deep political hatreds. To lose power was to lose everything. Hence men became desperate, forgot the necessity for patience, the duty of a minority, and sought to overthrow their enemies by secret conspiracy or open revolt. In the smaller states things were worse. There was even less stability, the factions were more bitter, the chance of successful revolt greater. No doubt Venice and the Papal Dominions were more stable than the rest of the Peninsula, but even there intrigue, corruption, and conspiracies were not uncommon.

Amid such political circumstances as these, not only did all feeling of Italian nationality perish, but patriotism for city or kingdom died before the imperative instincts of self-preservation. The worship of success replaced devotion to principle and obedience to authority, while cleverness and selfishness flourished at the expense of morality. Moreover, to protect themselves or to pursue their schemes of conquest, the tyrants introduced the Condottieri. The republics, partly from indolence, partly from the difficulty of resisting the trained soldier with a half-disciplined militia, followed suit, and Italy became the victim of mercenaries. Of war these made a game : with no interest in the quarrels beyond their wage, or their individual ambitions, they loved the battlefield by which they lived, yet did not wish the battle to be decisive. Ever ready to change sides at the dictates of self-interest, or for higher pay, they set up and overthrew states and spread confusion around. Meanwhile the citizens forgot the art of war, and, when the moment of their trial came, finding themselves no match for the martial nations of the North, were frightened at the fury of their onslaught.

The rapid increase of luxury and the development of literature and art tended to the same results. Undue devotion to material comfort made the Italians cowardly, selfish, and indolent.

The revival of the critical faculty led to scepticism; the critic destroyed indeed, but had not the enthusiasm nor the faith to reconstruct. The return to classical ideals caused a revival of paganism, while the concentration of man's mind on the pleasures of art, on the sensuous delight in beauty of form and colour, led many on to sensuality. The history of the Renaissance stands as a warning that the æsthetic spirit is not necessarily religious or even moral. No doubt it is easy to exaggerate. No doubt there were to be found many who lived a pure and simple life. Perhaps the denunciations of an enthusiast like Savonarola[1] are too extravagant. But the contemporary evidence against the Italians is overwhelming. The literature of the time must have found readers. The cynical frankness with which Machiavelli disregards all moral scruples in his treatises on the art of government are without parallel in the history of political literature, and the carnival songs of Lorenzo are of themselves enough to convince us of the depths of degradation to which Italian morality had sunk. Thus Italy, without any sense of nationality or patriotism, and devoid of those more sterling qualities which might have rendered resistance possible, was to see her fair plains the scene of other nations' rivalries, and to fall eventually under the yoke of a foreign dominion which lasted till our own day.

The French claims on Italy were twofold, and were of long standing. The House of Orleans, in virtue of their

French claims on Italy.

descent from Valentina, heiress of the Visconti of Milan, looked upon themselves as the legitimate aspirants to the ducal throne, and considered the Sforzas usurpers. The House of Anjou disputed the title of the Aragonese kings of Naples and declared that Joanna II., who died in 1435, had left her territories to René, the head of their house. The claims of the House of

---

[1] Cf. Savonarola 'on the Contempt of the World,' given in Villari, *Life of Savonarola*, vol. ii. App. and his Sermons, *passim*.

Orleans were now represented by Louis of Orleans, cousin of
Charles VIII., who already held Asti, while those of the House
of Anjou had in 1481 fallen to the crown, together with Anjou
and Provence, according to the will of René I., the last Duke
of Anjou.   Louis XI. had contented himself with Anjou and
Provence, but his foolish and ambitious son, fascinated with
the dream of a southern kingdom which might serve as a
starting-point for a new crusade against the Turk, was eager
to enforce his claims in Italy.   Yet even Charles might have
hesitated if a quarrel between Milan and Naples had not
offered a tempting opportunity.

In 1435, Alfonso the Magnanimous, the rival of René of
Anjou for the kingdom of Naples, had warned Filippo Maria,
who then ruled Milan, that the French, once
masters of Naples, would seek to extend their *The Peace
of Italy
depended on
the Triple
Alliance of
Milan,
Florence,
and Naples.*
territories in the north.   Francesco Sforza, who
secured Milan shortly after Filippo's death
(1450), conscious that the legitimate claim to
Milan had passed with the hand of Valentina to
the French House of Orleans, needed no convincing.   The result had been a close alliance between these
two powers, which had been strengthened by the marriage of
Ippolita, Sforza's daughter, with Alfonso, Prince of Calabria.
Lorenzo, true to the traditional policy of the Medici, had
joined this league.   He hoped, by a triple alliance of Milan,
Naples, and Florence, to maintain the balance of power in
Italy, resist the desire for territorial aggression shared by
Venice and the Papacy, and, by keeping peace within the
Peninsula, deprive the foreigner of all excuse for interference.
Whether Lorenzo would have succeeded may well be doubted,
but certainly his death (April 1492) removed the only man to
whom success was possible.

Even before Lorenzo died, the alliance between Milan and
Naples had threatened to break up.   The *coup d'état* of 1479,
by which Ludovico 'Il Moro' had seized the reins of power
from Bona of Savoy, had received the approval of Ferrante of

Naples.   In the following year, however (1480), the death of
Ippolita, Ludovico's sister and wife of Alfonso, son of Ferrante,

Rupture of
the Alliance
between
Milan and
Naples forces
Ludovico to
call in the
foreigner.

broke the bond between the two families.   The
subsequent marriage of the young Gian Galeazzo,
with Alfonso's daughter, Isabella (1489), made
matters worse.   Alfonso became jealous of Ludovico's rule and wished to see his son-in-law, who
had in the year 1492 reached the age of twenty,
recognised as duke. This jealousy was shared by

Isabella, who was envious of the higher honours conferred on
her kinswoman, Beatrice of Este, the wife of Ludovico.

Piero de Medici, who had just succeeded Lorenzo at Flor
ence (1492), joined Alfonso in a secret league against Ludovico,
to which Ferrante of Naples was somewhat unwillingly prevailed upon to accede.   Thus the triple alliance of Milan,
Naples, Florence, upon which the safety of Italy depended,
was broken, and Ludovico was driven to look elsewhere for
support.   To Maximilian, who in 1493 was elected King of
the Romans, he gave the hand of his niece, Bianca, and
gained in return the investiture of his duchy, which had
hitherto been denied to the Sforza family.   Despairing of
more effective aid from that impecunious prince, he next turned
to France.   San Severino, Count of Cajazzo, who had been
exiled from Naples after the Barons' War, was sent to 'tickle
Charles, who was but twenty-one years of age, with the
vanities and glories of Italy, and to urge the right he had to
the fine kingdom of Naples' (Commines).

The policy of Ludovico has received undue condemnation.
Every Italian prince had called upon the French when it
suited his purpose.   Hitherto Ludovico had been the most
strenuous opponent of this policy, and when in 1485, Innocent VIII. had urged René II. of Lorraine to press the Angevin
claims on Naples, it was he who had prevented it.   Though
selfish, and a master of diplomatic treachery, he was by no
means the worst of the Italian princes of his day.   It was
the altered policy of Naples which drove him to the fatal step.
Moreover, Gian Galeazzo was an incapable man, and it seems

probable that Alfonso, who had an insatiable lust for power, hoped to make him his puppet. Ludovico neither desired nor expected the French to conquer Naples. Italians, indeed, had so often used the threat of foreign intervention that they had forgotten what it might mean. His appeal to Charles was but a move in the game of intrigue which all were playing, and all that can be said is that, while others had tried it without success, Ludovico succeeded, to his own ruin, and that of Italy. Nor was he the only one who at this moment called on Charles. His exhortations were supported by the Prince of Salerno, a Neapolitan fugitive, eager to avenge the cruelties which Ferrante, in violation of his promise, had exercised on the leaders of the revolt of the Barons in 1485. To these were added the solicitations of the Cardinal Julian della Rovere, the rival and deadly enemy of Borgia, who had just ascended the papal throne as Alexander VI. (August 1492).

'The question of the expedition,' says Philippe de Commines, 'was warmly debated, since by all persons of experience and wisdom it was looked upon as a very dangerous undertaking.' Anne of Beaujeu, her husband, and many others, did their best to dissuade the King, but 'Charles was foolish and obstinate,' and was supported in his obstinacy by his favourites, Stephen de Vers, once gentleman of the Chamber, now Seneschal of Beaucaire, and Briçonnet, Bishop of St. Malo ; the one hoping for lands in Naples, the other for a cardinal's hat, promised by the Milanese ambassadors. The younger nobles, eager for the spoils of Italy, joined in the cry, and Charles rashly started on an enterprise 'for which neither his exchequer, his understanding, nor his preparations sufficed.'

Charles decides on the expedition in spite of better advice

In August, the King, who had wasted the spring and early summer at Lyons, spending on festivities and on amorous intrigues the money he had collected or borrowed for his expedition, passed down the Rhone to Vienne, and thence crossed the Alps by the pass of Mont Genèvre (September 2). His army was

Charles crosses the Alps. Sept. 2, 1494.

not exclusively a French one, for German landsknechts and Swiss mercenaries also accompanied it. Thus it was a fit harbinger of those foreign invasions which were for the next hundred years to desolate the fair plains of Italy.

At Asti, where Ludovico met him, he was delayed first by his gaieties, then by illness, and it was not until the 6th of October that he left Asti for Piacenza. Here the question as to his future course was debated. He was now to leave the territories of his ally. Venice to the north-east was neutral. The Pope, had after some hesitation, decided to resist the French. In Florence, opinion was much divided. The citizens, true to their traditions, were for the French, and were strengthened in their views by the warnings of Savonarola that a scourge should chastise Italy. Piero, on the other hand, was in league with Naples. Finally, it was decided to choose the more western route by the Via di Pontremoli

Charles crosses the Apennines and advances on Florence. rather than the easier way through Bologna. Charles would thus avoid the Neapolitan Prince, Ferrante, who had been sent by his father, now King Alfonso, to hold the Romagna, and would maintain his communications with the sea which had been won by the victory of the Duke of Orleans over Don Federigo, the brother of the King of Naples, at Rapallo (September 8). Florence, moreover, it was hoped, would declare for France on the king's approach.

The pass was a difficult one, and the country through which it passed was so barren that it did not even supply forage for the horses. Had the French here been met with stubborn resistance they might never have penetrated into Tuscany, for Ludovico was beginning to repent of having called Charles into Italy. His suspicions of French designs on Milan were already aroused, and the death of his unfortunate nephew, Gian Galeazzo (October 1494), by poison, as was generally believed, removed the need of French assistance against Naples. But the divided counsels of the Florentines came to Charles' aid. The French were left to pass the defiles undisturbed, and after sacking the town of Fivizzano, sat down before the fortress of Sarzana. Hither Piero, terrified at the disaffection in Florence, hastened, and acceded to Charles' demands. He promised

Piero driven from Florence. Nov. 9, 1494.

a sum of money; he surrendered four of the most important cities: Sarzana, Pietra-Santa, Pisa, and Leghorn. These humiliating concessions still further irritated the Florentines. On Piero's return to Florence (November 8) the citizens rushed to arms, and he was forced to fly in disguise to Venice. The defection of Florence threatened the position of Ferrante in the Romagna and opened the way to Rome. Thither therefore Ferrante retired.

Meanwhile Charles, after granting to the Pisans freedom from their hated mistress Florence, a present which was not his to give, passed on to Florence. Disregarding the warning of Savonarola that he would only be victorious if he showed mercy, especially to Florence, and was not an occasion of stumbling, he entered the city 'with lance in rest' as if he came as conqueror (November 17). This

Charles enters Florence, and having with difficulty made terms, passes on to Rome.

threatening attitude was accompanied by extravagant demands. First, he asked for the recall of Piero. That being refused, he insisted that a French lieutenant should be left in the city, whose consent should be necessary for every act. As the Florentines still demurred, the king in anger said: 'We shall sound our trumpets.' 'And,' we answered, 'Capponi shall sound our bells.' Seeing that he might go too far, Charles abated his demands. The Florentines consented to pay 120,000 florins in six months, and to allow two representatives of the king to remain in Florence. But the Medici were not to be recalled,[1] and Charles promised to restore the cities ceded to him by Piero at the end of the war (November 27). Having thus settled the difficulty with Florence, Charles passed through Siena

---

[1] For four months, after which the question might be reopened.

which accepted a French garrison (December 2) and advanced on Rome.

Alexander VI. had done his best for the cause of Naples, but he now became seriously alarmed. His correspondence with the Turkish Sultan, Bajazet II., in which, in return for help, the murder of the Sultan's brother, Djem, then in Alexander's keeping, had been mooted, had fallen into Charles' hands. His enemies were crying for a General Council. Ostia had been seized by Fabrizio Colonna in the name of his enemy, della Rovere (September 18). He therefore determined to come to terms, and, securing a free retreat for Ferrante and his army, admitted the French within the walls of Rome, while he retired to the castle of St. Angelo. The Cardinals della Rovere and Sforza urged Charles to offer no further concessions, and to summon a General Council which should depose the Pope and proceed to reform the Church. But Briçonnet did not wish for a breach which might endanger his hope of a cardinal's hat; Charles was scarcely the man for a reformer; the bribes of Alexander had their effect; and finally a compromise was effected. The Pope agreed to surrender Civita Vecchia, Terracina, and Spoleto, for safe keeping till the conclusion of the war, to pardon the rebellious cardinals, and to deliver up Prince Djem. He also conferred on the bishop of St. Malo the coveted cardinal's hat, and ordered his son, Cardinal Cæsar Borgia, to accompany Charles as a hostage. No sooner had the king left Rome for the south than Cæsar slipped away, and Djem died. The death of the latter, popularly attributed to poison administered by Alexander, was probably due to natural causes; but Cæsar's disappearance warned Charles that no trust could be placed in the promises of the Pope.

Alexander comes to terms. Jan. 15, 1495.

The success of the French had been so extraordinary, that Alfonso might well feel dismay.[1] He knew that his subjects hated him with a deadly hatred, and, with the cowardice so common to cruel men, he now became a victim of superstitious

Alfonso resigns his crown and goes to Sicily. Feb. 3, 1495.

[1] See Appendix iv.

terror. Declaring that 'the very stones and trees cried France,' he resigned his crown to his son and fled to Sicily (February 3, 1495).

His son, Ferrante II., showed more spirit and joined his army at San Germano. Here a mountain pass and the river Garigliano offered a favourable opportunity for defence ; but the news of the savage conduct of the French at the storming of Monte San Giovanni spread terror among his troops, and they fell back on Capua. A revolt at Naples recalled Ferrante, to find that his general, Trivulzio, had made terms with Charles. Naples now rose again,[1] and the luckless King, declaring that he suffered for the sins of his fathers, not his own, and promising to come to the aid of his faithless subjects, should the barbarity of the French cause them to wish for his return, left for Sicily (February 21). On the following day Charles entered Naples, and within a few weeks all the country, with the exception of one or two fortresses, was in his hands.

Charles enters Naples. Feb. 22, 1495.

'The success of Charles,' says Commines, 'must be considered the work of Providence.' Almost without breaking a lance, he had traversed the length of Italy and won a kingdom. It seemed as if his boast, that he would lead a crusade against the Turks and conquer Constantinople, would be fulfilled. But his triumph was short-lived, and 'his fortunes changed as suddenly as the day rises in Norway.' The French, puffed up by their success, 'scarce considered the Italians to be men,' and alienated them by their cruelties and licence. Charles took no steps to secure his conquest, but betook himself to his pleasures. No pains were taken to conciliate the Neapolitan nobles ; all offices were conferred on Frenchmen, and the promised remission of taxes was never fulfilled.

Reaction against the French.

Meanwhile a storm was gathering in the North. Ludovico had long repented of his rashness in inviting the French, and feared that Louis of Orleans might lay claim to Milan ; the

[1] See Appendix iv.

Pope dreaded a General Council, and was only too glad to raise up enemies against the King; Venice, which had at first

laughed at the expedition, became seriously alarmed; Ferdinand the Catholic had already remonstrated with Charles, and began to apprehend an attack on Sicily; the dignity of Maximilian was ruffled by the preponderance of the House of Valois. Negotiations between these powers had long been going 'on at Venice. The conquest of Naples brought matters to a climax, and on March 31, they formed the League of Venice, ostensibly to defend their territories and to prepare for war against the Turks. Guicciardini asserts that they secretly engaged to drive the French from Italy. Their object was more probably to protect themselves against further French aggression. Florence alone refused to break faith with the French, hoping to regain Pisa through their help.

With incredible folly, Charles delayed till May, in the vain hopes of receiving the papal investiture of Naples. Then

hastily receiving the crown at the hands of the Archbishop of Naples, he began his retreat with scarce 10,000 men (May 20). The Count of Montpensier, 'a good soldier,' says Commines, 'but with little wisdom, and so indolent that he did not rise till mid-day,' was left as viceroy. Stephen de Vers, now Duke of Nola, was made governor of Gaëta and controller of the finances, and Stuart d'Aubigny, the best soldier of them all, governor of Calabria. As Charles approached Rome, Alexander fled to Orvieto; and thence to Perugia. Arrived in Tuscany, Charles found all in confusion. Siena, Lucca, and Pisa had formed a league against Florence, and pleaded for French assistance. The Florentines, who had reformed their government after the advice of Savonarola, demanded the restitution of the cities temporarily ceded to the King. Charles, incapable of decision, put them off with negotiations, and leaving French garrisons in the ceded towns, crossed the Apennines, June 23.

But the French were not to escape from Italy without a

battle. Their fleet on the west coast for the moment protected
them from the attack of Venetian or Spanish ships,[1] but on the
mainland the forces of Milan and of Venice under   The Battle
the Marquis of Mantua met them at Fornovo   of Fornovo.
on the Taro.   The army of the League had the   July 6, 1495.
advantage of numbers and position, and had they shown
determination, might have inflicted a decisive defeat.   But
the Italians were little eager to bring the French to bay, and
Charles, wisely wishing to pursue his march, pushed on his
vanguard   It was met by the Milanese troops under the
Count Cajazzo, but the attack was feeble and easily
repulsed.   This, according to Guicciardini, was due to
Ludovico.   Fearing that too complete a victory might place
him in the power of the Venetian troops, which were far
more numerous than his own, and that too crushing a defeat
might draw on him the vengeance of the French, he had
ordered his captain not to press the French too closely.
Meanwhile the assault on the centre and rearguard[2] was far
more vigorous, and Charles was in momentary danger.   He
was, however, saved by the enemies' want of discipline;
many of the Italians turned to plunder his camp, the reserves
did not attack, and the French king, with loss of baggage but
not of prestige, was able to pursue his way.

At Asti, Charles was delayed by the question of Novara.
Louis of Orleans had occupied that town in June, only to be
besieged by Ludovico.   In vain, Louis begged for instant aid.
Charles would not stir till reinforcements came, and meanwhile
solaced himself with amorous intrigues.   Fortunately Ludovico
was anxious to get the French out of Italy, and in October
came to terms.   Louis surrendered the town, but   Treaty of
Ludovico, breaking with the League, promised   Vercelli.
to give free passage to the French, and even to   Oct. 10, 1495.
assist them whenever they might march against Naples.   This,
however, seemed unlikely for the present.

No sooner had Charles turned his back on Naples than his
conquests began to melt away.   The Neapolitans, according

<hr>

[1] [2] See Appendix iv.

to Guicciardini, were the most inconstant people of Italy, and
the follies of the French reminded them of Ferrante's words.

Charles leaves
Italy and his
conquests
melt away.

Ferrante accordingly returned at the end of
May, aided by troops sent by Ferdinand the
Catholic under Gonzalvo de Cordova, the most
brilliant of the Spanish generals.   Defeated by
Stuart d'Aubigny at Seminara, and driven to Messina, he
directed a second attack on Naples.   The city rose, the gates
were opened, and Montpensier took refuge in the castle (July 7),
which he was forced to evacuate shortly after.   The Venetians,
in return for money, were allowed to occupy Monopoli, Otranto,
Brindisi, and Trani.   Montpensier struggled on for some time
longer, hoping for reinforcements from France.   But Charles
was immersed in pleasure ; Louis of Orleans, who was heir-
presumptive to the throne, refused to leave France, and finally
Montpensier capitulated at Atella (July 21, 1496).   D'Aubigny,
though sick with fever, held out a little longer, but by the close
of the year 1496, all was lost to France.   Ferrante did not live
to see the end.   He died in September, and his uncle Federigo
quietly succeeded him.   Thus five kings had sat on the throne
of Naples within three years.

Of Charles' acquisitions, the only traces which remained
were the cities ceded to him by Florence.   These should
have been restored on his retreat, but in hopes of return,
Charles had evaded his promise, and the officers he had
left in command proceeded to violate it entirely.   Leghorn
was indeed surrendered in September, but Sarzana was
sold to the Genoese, Pietra-Santa to Lucca, and the citadel
of Pisa to the Pisans.   Of these Pisa was only regained
in 1509, after a prolonged struggle which exhausted the
republic and contributed materially to its fall, Pietra-Santa
not till the Medici had been restored in 1513, and Sarzana
not at all.   Thus the ally of France was the one to suffer
most.

Charles VIII. survived the Italian expedition scarce three
years.   Always indulging in dreams of a renewed attack on

Naples, he was at first too much engrossed in his pleasures
to carry them into effect.   During the last few months of his
life he had, according to Commines, 'resolved   Death of
within himself to live a more strict and religious   Charles VIII.
life.' If so, death anticipated him.   While staying   April 7, 1498.
at the castle of Amboise, which was being embellished by
Neapolitan artists, he struck his head against the lintel of a
door, and died at the age of twenty-seven of a fit of apoplexy
which resulted from it (April 1498).

Contemptible in mind, though with great bodily strength,
inspired with chivalrous ideas which he had not the capacity
to execute, a victim to profligacy, it is strange that he should
have played such a leading part in history, and yet it does
not seem altogether unfit that those Italian wars, which caused
such infinite misery in Italy, and were so disastrous to the
best interests of France, should be associated with his name.
His children had all died in infancy, and the crown accordingly passed to his cousin and brother-in-law, Louis, Duke of
Orleans, then a man of the age of thirty-six.

§ 2. *Savonarola and Florence.*

A month after the death of Charles VIII., the Friar
Savonarola, who had done so much to give an air of mystery
to the Italian expedition, fell a victim to his enemies.

This remarkable man was born at Ferrara in 1452.   Having
gradually won a reputation as a preacher of wonderful power
and zeal, he was in the year 1491, elected Prior   Savonarola,
of the Dominican Convent of San Marco in   Prior of
Florence.   In spite of the independent attitude   San Marco, 1491.
which he here assumed, Lorenzo showed him no ill favour,
and even summoned the friar to his deathbed to ask a
blessing.[1] In all probability, however, Savonarola would have
remained a great revivalist preacher and nothing more, had it

---

[1] For the question as to the true account of the interview, cf. Creighton,
The Papacy, Appendix vii.

not been for the expedition of Charles VIII. The constant theme of his sermons had been that the scourge of God should visit Italy to punish her for her sins and purify her by fire. The French invasion, and the rapid success of Charles were looked upon as the fulfilment of his prophecy, and Savonarola became one of the leading men in Florence.

In the overthrow of the Medici he did not take an active part, but on Piero's flight (November 1494) he was sucked

Savonarola and the revolution of 1494.

into the politics of the city. Supported by his powerful advocacy from the pulpit in the Duomo, and guided by his advice, the popular party, to which he naturally belonged, was able to introduce and carry a reform of the Constitution. By the decree of December 23, the government was to be as follows :—

A permanent Great Council (*Consiglio Maggiore*) was to be composed of all eligible 'citizens,' that is, of all citizens of the age of thirty whose father, grandfather, or great-grandfather had been elected to the greater offices of state. This Council, numbering some 3000, was to elect out of its own members a 'senate' (*Consiglio degli ottanta*), holding office for six months, and forming with the Consiglio Maggiore the legislative body of the city. Further, the Great Council was to nominate the Signory and other magistrates out of a list presented by a body of nominators, themselves elected in the Council, and to hear appeals on criminal cases. The Signory remained as it was before, composed of the Gonfalonier and the eight priors : it was to be elected every two months, while the Ten of Liberty and Peace (*Dieci di Liberta e Pace*), in whose hands lay the conduct of foreign affairs, were to hold office for six months.

The constitution can scarcely be called a democratic one, for at least 7000 citizens were disenfranchised. In common with most theorists of his day, Savonarola admired the stability of Venice, and vainly thought to secure this for his native city by establishing a closed and permanent electoral and legislative body, the Consiglio Maggiore, after the

Venetian type. Nevertheless, the government was preferable to the old system, by which the city, a republic in name, had fallen into the control of a single family and their clique.

Savonarola did not content himself with this. From his pulpit he insisted on moral reformation as the necessary basis of true liberty, and pressed for a general amnesty which might allay the dangers of party strife. In thus becoming a politician, Savonarola protested that he acted unwillingly. In his sermon of December 21, 1494, he declared that he had pleaded with God to be excused from meddling with the government, but had been bidden to go on and establish a holy city, which favoured virtue and looked to Christ as its master.

That Savonarola was sincere we may well believe. None the less the interference in politics was a fatal error. Thereby he became closely associated with a party, responsible for its faults, and dependent on its success. This weakened his position as a reformer, while his adherents had henceforth to count as enemies all those who disliked his attempts at a reform of morals. A serious opposition was thus aroused. The Bigi (the Greys) worked for the restoration of the Medici; the Arrabiati (the enraged), while casting off the Medici, objected to the changes in the Constitution; the Compagnacci (companions) disliked the preacher's interference with their pleasures. These three groups, working at first with very different aims, were eventually united together in common opposition to the Piagnoni (weepers), the followers of the friar. But if Savonarola's interference in the politics of the city weakened his position in Florence, the attitude of his party drew down upon him the enmity of foreign statesmen. The desire to regain Pisa was an overmastering passion at Florence, and there was nothing she would not suffer to attain that end. She had refused to join the League of Venice, in the hopes of regaining Pisa from the hands of Charles. These hopes had been disappointed. Still the adherents of the friar headed by Francesco Valori,

Savonarola becomes associated with a political party and arouses enmity at home and abroad.

clung fondly to the dream that Charles would once more
enter Italy, and at last fulfil his promise.   In these expectations
they were supported by the preaching of Savonarola, who
announced that Italy must yet suffer much, but that eventually
Florence should after much tribulation be saved by God.
By thus refusing to join the League, Florence drew down
upon her the enmity of Ludovico, of Maximilian, of Venice,
and of the Pope.   The three first in turn supported the
Pisans with arms, and, in October 1496, Maximilian himself
came to Italy.   But mutual jealousies prevented united
action, and the expedition of Maximilian ended in a fiasco.

The opposition of the Pope was to prove more serious.
Alexander vi. cared but little for the denunciation of the
Alexander VI. reformer against the vices of the times, but his
interferes. interference with politics he would not brook.
Sept. 1495. Accordingly, in September 1495, he had suspended him from preaching.   Savonarola at first obeyed, and
was silent during the following Advent.   But, in the Lent of
1496, the Signory, then composed of the friar's partisans,
ordered him to resume his preaching.   He complied, and in
the Carnival of 1496, the enthusiasm of the Piagnoni broke
forth in religious processions.   The children swept the streets
in thick array, bearing olive-branches in their hands and
chanting hymns.   This disobedience Savonarola justified, by
declaring that no papal prohibitions should move him from
his duty, and that if they contradicted the Law of Love set
forth in the Gospel, they must be withstood, since 'a Pope
that errs does not represent the Church,' of which he claimed
to be a loyal son.   Even this bold conduct did not immediately
rouse Alexander—nay, some would fix this as the date when
he tried to win the friar by the offer of a cardinal's hat.   If so,
Savonarola contemptuously rejected the offer, and the Pope
was driven to take further measures.

The Tuscan congregation of the Dominican order had,
at Savonarola's request, been separated from that of Lombardy.   This had given him a position of exceptional
independence, which aroused the jealousy of many of his order.

Alexander now united the convent of San Marco with a new formed Tusco-Roman congregation (Nov. 7, 1496). This was clearly within the competence of the Pope, it was popular with the order generally, and the Pope hoped to strike at the friar through a superior of his own brotherhood. Savonarola, however, refused to obey, and was supported by some 250 of his brethren of San Marco. The Carnival of 1497 followed. Here the enthusiasm of the Piagnoni reached its highest pitch. The children going from house to house begged for ' vanities.' Cards, trinkets, immodest books, pictures, works of art, were handed up, and these, heaped promiscuously in one common pyre, were solemnly burned in the Piazza. These and other extravagances, which unfortunately cannot be denied,[1] disgusted many, and added to the number of the friar's enemies. The reaction was seen in the election of Bernardo del Nero, a secret adherent of the Medici, to the office of Gonfalonier, March 1497 ; in the unsuccessful attempt of Piero to regain Florence in April, and in a riot in the Duomo, raised by the Compagnacci, while Savonarola preached, on Ascension Day, May 4. *Reaction against Savonarola.*

Influenced, perhaps, by the knowledge that Savonarola was losing ground, Alexander now decided to strike. After a vain appeal to the Florentines, in which he even promised to regain Pisa for them if they would join the League, a promise which they prudently distrusted, he declared that they were being misled by the prophecies of a chattering friar, and proceeded to excommunicate him, May 1497. The Signory meanwhile had attempted to stay the excitement in Florence by forbidding all preaching either from Savonarola or his opponents, and things remained more quiet for a time. *The Pope excommunicates him. May 1497.*

The elections of July, however, again gave the Piagnoni a majority in the Signory; and in August, the city was startled by the news that five of the leading citizens stood accused of complicity with the Medicean plot of the preceding April. On condemnation, they were refused *The Piagnoni regain power.*

---

[1] Savonarola, however, was no enemy to literature and art. Cf. Villari ii. 133.

their right of appeal to the Great Council, contrary to the express provision of the new Constitution, and executed. The condemned belonged to Savonarola's opponents, and some of them, notably Bernardo del Nero, had lately held office. Their execution therefore, for a time, materially strengthened Savonarola's position, and from this date until the ensuing March the Signory was filled with Piagnoni.

Accordingly, on Christmas Day, Savonarola celebrated the Mass in San Marco. In the Carnival another pyre of vanities was burnt; and on invitation by the Signory to resume his preaching, the friar mounted the pulpit of the Duomo with Consecrated Host in hand, called on God to strike him dead if he deserved excommunication, and declared that if the instrument by which God ruled the world withdrew himself from God, he was but broken iron, and need not be obeyed.

But Savonarola had at last miscalculated his strength. Religious enthusiasm is avowedly subject to relapses, and such a relapse now came on Florence. The extravagances of his followers, and his own, had swelled the number of his enemies. Many originally well disposed towards him were shocked at his open defiance of the Pope, and at his daring to administer the sacrament when excommunicated. The Franciscan order, always jealous of the Dominicans, now redoubled their attacks, led by Savonarola's old rival Fra Mariano de Genazzano. Even the majority of the Dominicans outside San Marco declared against him. Of this reaction his enemies were quick enough to take advantage. Accordingly the Signory of March, 1498, only counted three of his adherents among its members. Still many of the Dieci, who having been elected for six months did not leave office, were in his favour. When therefore Alexander threatened the city with an interdict, unless Savonarola ceased preaching and came to Rome for absolution, the Government adopted a middle course; they persuaded the friar to cease preaching, yet would not force him to leave for Rome.

Final reaction against Savonarola.

It is doubtful whether in any case Alexander would now have stayed his hand, for Savonarola had begun to speak of a General Council, and it was known that Charles VIII. was likely to support the cry, while the opponents of Savonarola, more especially the Franciscans of Santa Croce, were open-mouthed for his destruction.   In any case the fatal suggestion of the ordeal by fire precipitated the crisis.   This, whether first suggested by the Franciscans or no, was eagerly taken up by them.   'I believe I shall be *The ordeal by fire.* burned,' said the Franciscan, Francesco da Puglia, 'but I am ready to die to free this people.   If Savonarola does not burn, you may hold him to be a true prophet.'

Savonarola himself declined to thus tempt God, but Fra Domenico da Pescia, his most faithful follower, declared his willingness to stand his champion.   Savonarola could scarcely refuse; the Signory after much debate consented; and on April 7, an eager crowd assembled on the Piazza to witness the ordeal.   It may be questioned whether either party expected that the ordeal would really be essayed; in any case it was the Franciscans who raised objections.   Declaring that they feared magic on Savonarola's part, they first demanded that his champion should lay aside his chasuble and his vestments; they then objected to his bearing the crucifix, and finally insisted that he should not carry the Host into the fire.   Here at last Savonarola refused compliance. Meanwhile the day wore on.   It began to rain, and finally the Signory postponed the trial.   The mob was now mad with disappointment, and next day the Compagnacci seized the opportunity to attack San Marco (April 8).   Francesco Valori, the firmest supporter of Savonarola, who had often held office as Gonfalonier, was slain among others.   The brethren, however, stood firm at San Marco until the Signory intervened and arrested Savonarola and his two chief supporters, Fra Domenico and Fra Silvestro.

Alexander now demanded that the friar should be handed over to him for trial.   After much negotiation it was agreed that the Pope should send two commissaries to judge of the spiritual offences, while the Florentine commissioners should decide on the offences against the city. At the same time, Alexander granted to Florence a tax of three-tenths on ecclesiastical revenues. 'Three times ten makes thirty,' said a Piagnone; 'they have sold our master, as Christ was sold, for thirty pieces of silver.' Meanwhile Savonarola had been put to the torture, and was said to have confessed that he was no true prophet. But it is acknowledged that confessions extorted under torture are not worthy of the slightest credit; there is good reason, moreover, to believe that his depositions were falsified. His enemies were determined on his ruin. All that was necessary to secure their final triumph was that the elections of May should return a Signory hostile to the friar. This was attained by excluding 200 Piagnoni from the Great Council. A Signory of Arrabiati was thus secured. Savon-

Execution of the Friar. May 23, 1498. arola and his two followers, found guilty of heresy by the papal commissaries, and of treason to the State by his fellow-citizens, went to their death with all the constancy of martyrs, May 23, 1498.

Contemporaries were much divided in their opinions on the merits of Savonarola, and the contest rages still. 'The thing I shall be most anxious to know when I get into Heaven,' said a later Pope, 'is whether Savonarola was a righteous man or no.' Those who denounce him as a hypocrite, pretending to believe in divine guidance, and in the gift of prophecy to attain his ends, are surely ignorant of the subtle influences under which religious leaders have ever acted; men who carry with them into life a profound conviction of the divine ruling of the world. Those who lightly dismiss him as a fanatic, have never felt the burning shame of sin which consumes the reformer's soul. That he was led to think that God had intrusted him with a mission and had used him as the trumpet of His warnings we may well believe; that he was betrayed into some extravagances will only convict him of ordinary human frailty

As has been stated above, his real mistake lay in trespassing on the sphere of politics. Had he confined himself to the work of a moral reformer, he perhaps would not have risen so high ; yet he would have escaped from many contradictions, and never have fallen so low. The office of the preacher and that of the statesman are not easily reconciled. When once he had associated himself with the fortunes of a political party, nothing but complete supremacy could save him from disaster. For the rest, the work of Savonarola must not be confused with the later Reformation. He had no idea of breaking from the Church, or of disputing her doctrines. His mind was set in a mediæval mould. He belongs to the long list of those great reformers who, like St. Francis of Assisi, strove to bring the life of man into closer harmony with Christian teaching as then understood, but did not dispute the accepted interpretation of that teaching. He stands forth as the opponent of that godless pagan spirit which marred the movement of the Renaissance, to rebuke the moral turpitude of his country, which was surely working her ruin.

§ 3. *Louis XII. The War of Milan and Naples.*

The accession of Louis XII. was popular. He had in his earlier years led the opposition against Anne of Beaujeu, and for that had suffered imprisonment, but of late he *Internal* had been the loyal supporter of King Charles. *policy of* Careless and fond of pleasure as a young man, he *Louis XII.* had, while retaining his generous and chivalrous spirit, now become more serious. Declaring at his accession that 'the King did not remember the wrongs done to him as Duke,' he showed favour to Anne of Beaujeu and her husband, whom he had once so bitterly resisted. On the marriage of their only child, Susanna, with the young Charles, Count of Mont-pensier, he annulled the decree of Louis XI. which had declared that, in the default of male issue, the dominion of Bourbon should fall to the crown. By this act of generosity, he postponed the incorporation of the last great noble domain in France.

The reign was inaugurated by several useful measures. The 'taille' [1] was reduced; the sale of judicial offices forbidden; an attempt was made to check the venality of the magistrates. Provence and Normandy were given local *Parlements* or courts of justice, which might serve as a counterbalance to the *Parlement* of Paris, while the extravagant privileges of the University of Paris in the matter of jurisdiction were curtailed. Political interest may by some be held to justify Louis' divorce from his first wife Jeanne, daughter of Louis XI., and his marriage with Anne of Brittany, widow of Charles VIII.; for Jeanne was childless, and Brittany threatened to break away again from France. But, in the negotiations with the Pope concerning the divorce, the King acted meanly, and the stipulation insisted on by Anne of Brittany, that her duchy should not be united to the crown of France, might have led to further trouble, had not Francis of Angoulême, subsequently King Francis I., married Claude, the issue of the marriage. In a word the home policy of the King might justify his title of 'Father of his People,' had not his ambition led him

Louis determines to attack Milan.

to follow in the steps of Charles and seek for conquests in Italy. If his chivalrous spirit demanded war, the renewed attempt of Maximilian to regain Burgundy and the lands on the west of Flanders, which he still claimed as the heritage of his son, the Archduke Philip, would have fully justified Louis in taking the offensive, and adding Franche-Comté to his dominions. But his eyes, like those of Charles, were dazzled with the fair skies and plains of Italy, and Italy alone would satisfy French ambitions. Milan, however, and not Naples, was the first object of Louis' attack.

The invasion of Charles VIII. should have taught the Italians the necessity of union. But this was not to be.

---

[1] The 'taille' was a tax levied on land and income. It was first imposed by the Estates of Orleans, 1439. The nobles, clergy, the officials of the sovereign courts, and other royal officials were exempt. It therefore fell exclusively on the lower classes. Cf. Appendix I., p. 456.

Even in the League of Venice, the aims of Italian statesmen had been purely selfish, and the common danger once removed, their old rivalries returned and broke up the coalition.

Savonarola had been 'sacrificed by the Pope, because Florence would not join the League'—yet no sooner was he gone than Alexander vi. deserted it himself. The chief aim of Alexander's pontificate was to strengthen the temporal dominion of the Papacy. Following in the steps of Sixtus iv., he hoped to gain his end through his family. His eldest son, the Duke of Gandia, was first chosen as his instrument. He designed to make him Lord of the Patrimony of St. Peter and crush the Orsini, who had given him a pretext by supporting the cause of Charles viii. But the Orsini had proved too strong. The attempt had failed, and the mysterious murder of the duke in June 1497, seemed for the moment to ruin his hopes. The Pope, however, was not a man easily dismayed. He shortly resumed his scheme, and now looked to his third son, the notorious Cæsar Borgia. Cæsar, unfortunately, was both deacon and cardinal ; but in August 1498, his father released him from his ecclesiastical vows 'for the good of his soul.' Having thus removed this primary obstacle, the Pope at first designed to marry him to Carlotta, the daughter of Federigo of Naples, whereby Cæsar might some day gain a claim to the throne of that kingdom. Baulked in this hope by the refusal of Federigo, Alexander turned to France. In return for the papal bull sanctioning the divorce of his first wife Jeanne, and a cardinal's hat for George of Amboise, his chief adviser, Louis xii. invested Cæsar with the counties of Valentinois and Diois, and the title of duke. Subsequently he bestowed upon him the hand of his niece, the beautiful Charlotte d'Albret (May 1499), and promised to assist him in his designs on the Romagna. Thus Alexander was detached from the League.

The relations between Venice and Ludovico had never been cordial. At the battle of Fornovo, the duke had played it

Alexander and Venice desert the League of Venice and ally themselves with France.

false, and ordered his troops not to press the French too closely.   Shortly after this the Pisan War led to further disagreement.   Angry at the refusal of Florence to join the League of Venice, Ludovico and Venice had both supported Pisa in her struggle for independence.   But the lust of conquest soon began to tempt them, and, as both could not hold Pisa, a quarrel was inevitable.   At first Ludovico called upon the Emperor Maximilian to secure that city, hoping eventually to wrest it from his hands; but the expedition had failed (October 1496), and Ludovico, rather than see the city fall under Venetian control, deserted the Pisan cause, and aided the Florentines with men and money (May 1498).   Venice accordingly turned a ready ear to Louis' offers, and in the Treaty of Blois (February 1499), agreed to support his claim to the Duchy of Milan with arms: Louis, on his side, promising her Cremona and the Ghiara d'Adda, a small district on the left bank of that river, as her share of the Milanese spoil.

Thus Louis had succeeded in breaking up the League, and Ludovico was left without an available ally.   Ferdinand of Spain was already thinking of seizing Naples for himself, and had no mind to interfere in Lombardy; Federigo of Naples was trembling for his throne, and was in no position to lend him aid; while Maximilian, at this time engaged in a war with the Swiss, and at variance with his Diet on questions concerning the Imperial Constitution, could not render any assistance.   In his despair Ludovico stirred up the Turks, and Bajazet II. sent an army to ravage the Venetian territories in Friuli, an act which did not materially assist him, and still further irritated his enemies.

In August 1499, the French army crossed the Alps commanded by three redoubtable leaders: the Lombard Trivulzio, who had deserted the cause of Alfonso of Naples and adopted France as his country, a man of whom Ludovico said, 'a halter awaits him as soon as caught'; Stuart d'Aubigny, who had already earned a

Desperate position of Ludovico.

The French enter Italy. August 1499.

reputation in the war of Naples; and Louis de Luxembourg, Count of Ligny, the patron of the Chevalier Bayard, whose chivalrous exploits in the coming campaigns remind us that the Middle Age had not yet departed. The Duke of Savoy gave them free passage through Piedmont. At Asti they were joined by a contingent of 5000 Swiss, sent by the Cantons, who had made a treaty with Louis. The advance on Milan met with scant resistance. The village of Annona, fortified by Ludovico, indeed held out, but was taken by assault on the second day, and the garrison put to the sword. Terrified by their fate, and beguiled by the promises and the bribes of Trivulzio, castles and cities opened their gates. Alessandria, evacuated by the Milanese army under Galeazzo di San Severino, who was probably bribed by the French, made submission, but was cruelly pillaged, and the French crossed the Po.

Meanwhile the Venetian army from the east occupied Caravaggio, and advanced to Lodi. Ludovico now saw that his cause was lost. Warned by a riot in Milan that the capital could not be trusted, he despatched his two sons and his treasure to Germany, threw provisions into the castle of Milan, and fled to seek assistance of Maximilian at Innsbruck (September 2). Ludovico gone, the citizens of Milan hastened to offer the keys of the city to the French. On September 14, the citadel itself was sold to the French by its commander; Genoa followed suit, and thus within a month, the French and Venetians found themselves masters of the Milanese, without having had to fight a single important battle. But they were not to hold their conquest without another struggle. The rapidity of the French conquest, like that of Naples by Charles VIII., illustrates the weakness of Italy. The treachery and cowardice of the soldiery was the result of the evil traditions of Italian condottier warfare. The army once gone, the citizens could scarcely have resisted if they would, and they would not if they could. Devoid of all sense of patriotism or loyalty,

[margin note:] The Venetians advance on Lodi.

[margin note:] Ludovico flies to Innsbruck. The French and Venetians occupy the Milanese. Sept. 1499.

they feared the vengeance of the French, and listened easily to their promises of milder government, and lighter taxation.

Reaction against the French.

These indeed Louis attempted to fulfil, but extravagant expectations had been raised, and the choice of Trivulzio as Governor of Milan was an unfortunate one. A Lombard himself, he became a party man; his severity alienated the lower classes, while the pride and insolence of the French soon lost them the affection of their new subjects.

A few months sufficed to disillusionise the Italians, and when, in February 1500, Ludovico returned with an army he had

Ludovico returns. Feb. 1500.

collected in the North, the French were forced to evacuate Milan and surrender their conquests as quickly as they had gained them. All seemed lost, when in April the French army, reinforced from France, again

The French evacuate Milan, but take Ludovico prisoner at Novara, April 5, and re-occupy the city.

moved forward to relieve the citadel of Novara, which, with the castle of Milan, alone held out. The motley character of the army of Ludovico, composed as it was of mercenaries from Franche-Comté and Switzerland, Albania and Lombardy, would in any case have rendered victory doubtful, but the chances of battle were never tried owing to the treachery of the Germans and the Swiss. The latter pleaded as an excuse that they could not fight against their countrymen who were serving the French with leave of the Confederation. The only pretext the Germans could find was arrears of pay. Allowed by the French to retire, these honourable companions in arms did not even insist on the same terms being granted to their Milanese comrades, or to the Duke. When therefore the Milanese troops attempted to retreat, they were cut down by the French. The Duke was discovered among the Swiss in the disguise of a friar, and on April 17, the French re-entered the capital. The rich Duchy of Milan was now theirs, with the exception of the strip of country to the east of the Adda, which fell to the Venetians, and the district round Bellinzona, which was seized by the Swiss in the pay of Louis, and which they retain to this day.

The Sforza family suffered cruelly for Ludovico's fatal act in first calling the French into Italy and for his subsequent breach of faith. The Duke, who had vaunted himself on his cleverness, ended his days in the dungeons of Loches in Touraine (1508). His brother, the Cardinal Ascanio, and Francesco, son of the unfortunate Gian Galeazzo, also fell into French hands. Ascanio was released in 1503, but died in 1505. Francesco was forced to become a monk and died in 1511, and the only important representatives of the male line of the Sforza who remained were the two sons of Ludovico, Maximilian and Francesco Maria, who were hereafter for a period to regain the duchy.[1]

Fortunes of the Sforza family.

The collapse of the power of Ludovico is a signal illustration of the insufficiency and untrustworthiness of mercenary troops. Caring nothing for the cause they had momentarily espoused, they were ever open to bribes, or ready to desert when desertion served their turn.

For the rest, the policy of Venice in thus calling the French for the second time into Italy, was as short-sighted as it was blameworthy. The Venetians pleaded as a pretext their fears of the ambitious schemer Ludovico, yet he was never likely to be so formidable as the French, and, as Machiavelli well observes, 'in their desire to win two districts in Lombardy they helped Louis to become master of two-thirds of Italy.'

Short-sighted policy of Venice.

Louis once master of Milan hurried on his preparations against Naples. The only opponent who was likely to be formidable was Ferdinand the Catholic. He had helped to restore the Aragonese dynasty after the retreat of Charles, and might well put in his claim, if the illegitimate branch of his house were to be excluded. 'But how,' said his envoy, ' if you were

Treaty of Granada between Louis and Ferdinand. Nov. 11, 1500.

[1] Three other sons of Galeazzo Sforza, one legitimate, the other two illegitimate, were also taken prisoners and died in captivity.

to come to some agreement with us respecting Naples as you did with Venice about Milan?' The suggestion was welcomed by Louis, and in November 1500, the secret Treaty of Granada was signed. An excuse for that shameless compact was found in the alliance which Federigo in his distress had made with the Turk. After deploring the discords of Christian princes, which weakened them before the Turk, the preamble asserts that 'no other princes, save the Kings of France and Aragon, have any title to the crown of Naples, and as King Federigo has excited the Turk to the peril of Christendom, the two powers, in order to rescue it from this danger and to maintain the peace, agree to compromise their respective claims, and divide the kingdom of Naples itself.' The northern provinces, consisting of the Abruzzi and the land of Lavoro, with the title of king, were to go to Louis; the Duchy of Calabria and Apulia in the south as a dukedom to Ferdinand. That there was danger to be apprehended from the Turks was true enough; not only had they ravaged Friuli in the autumn of 1499, they had also defeated the Venetian fleet off Sapienza, and taken Modon and Navarino in the Morea. That the cry of a crusade was not a mere pretext is proved by the treaties made by Louis in the spring of 1500 with Ladislas, King of Bohemia and Hungary, and with the King of Poland; by the fleet despatched by Ferdinand to aid the Venetians in the siege of St. George in Cephalonia (September 1500), and by the French attack on Mitylene in 1501. It is even possible, that the conquest of Italy from the north alone saved that country from falling before the Turk, but the advance of the Sultan might have been more successfully opposed by a joint European coalition, and, as events showed, lust of conquest was the primary motive of the allies.

The treaty of Granada was 'the first open assertion in European politics of the principles of dynastic aggrandisement; the first of those partition treaties by which peoples were handed over from one Government to another as appendages to family estates.' Not only was the treaty of

Granada a crime, it was also a fatal blunder on the part of Louis. 'The French,' says Machiavelli, 'have little skill in matters of State, for whereas before, Louis was sole umpire in Italy, he now entertained a partner, and whereas Louis might have made the king of Naples his pensioner, he turned him out and put the Spaniard in his place, who turned out Louis himself.' The compact was at first kept secret, and Federigo still hoped for assistance from Ferdinand. In June 1501, however, when the French army under D'Aubigny entered Rome on its southward march, Pope Alexander publicly ratified the treaty, declared Federigo deposed as a traitor to Christendom, and invested Louis and Ferdinand with his dominions.

Federigo, despairing of his cause, did not dare to meet the French in the field. Capua, which alone stood out, was taken by assault on July 23, and handed *Federigo* over to a brutal soldiery who massacred the men *abdicates* and outraged the women. To save his country *and retires* from further misery, the unfortunate King capitu- *to France.* lated, and, accepting the terms of Louis, retired to France, to *August 1501.* live till 1504 a pensioner, with the title of Duke of Anjou.

The southern part of the kingdom made a somewhat more vigorous resistance to the Spaniards. They would have preferred, they said, the French as masters. But on the fall of Taranto in March 1502, Ferrante, the young Duke of Calabria, surrendered, and, in violation of a promise that he might retire whither he would, was sent to Spain to die in 1550.[1] Thus in less than two years the two families, whose quarrels had first invited the foreigner into Italy, had been driven from their country.

Naples and Milan conquered, Western Europe found itself dominated by two great leagues, that of Louis XII., *Quarrel be-* closely allied with the Pope and some of the *tween Louis* German princes, and that of the Austro-Spanish *and Ferdinand.* houses. The latter was a family league cemented by the

[1] For the fate of the other children of Federigo, cf. Sismondi, *Hist. des Rep. Italiennes*, ix. 295.

marriage of the Archduke Philip, son of the Emperor Maximilian, with Joanna, eldest daughter of Ferdinand and
Isabella,[1] and included England and Portugal. At this moment there seemed a prospect of these two leagues coalescing.
In 1501, it had been agreed that Charles, the young son of the
Archduke Philip, should marry the Princess Claude, daughter
of Louis XII. The children were yet young, but the joint
conquest of Naples by the Spanish and the French seemed a
guarantee of their future friendship, and that the marriage
would eventually take place. Had this compact stood, Europe
would have been united as it had never been before, and, if
there was some danger that this powerful league would have
destroyed the political balance, and ridden rough-shod over
the smaller princes, at least a crusade to check the advance of
the Turks, or even to drive them from Europe, might have been
possible. The dream, however, was soon to be dispelled by
the quarrel of Louis and Ferdinand over their spoil in Naples.
In the original treaty of partition no definite mention had
been made of the Basilicata,[2] the Capitanata, and the two
districts of the Principati. These furnished an easy cause of
dispute, which was further complicated by the claim to the
tolls paid on the sheep-flocks as they passed from their
summer pasture in the Abruzzi to their winter quarters in the
Capitanata. The quarrel might possibly have been com-
promised had it not been fomented by the internal factions of
the country. The old partisans of Anjou were strongest in
Apulia, while the Spaniards found many adherents in districts
held by the French.

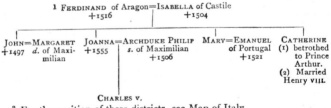

1 FERDINAND of Aragon = ISABELLA of Castile
        +1516   +1504

JOHN = MARGARET	JOANNA = ARCHDUKE PHILIP	MARY = EMANUEL	CATHERINE
+1497 *d.* of Maxi-	+1555 *s.* of Maximilian	of Portugal	(1) betrothed
milian	+1506	+1521	to Prince
			Arthur.
			(2) Married
			Henry VIII.

CHARLES V.

2 For the position of these districts, see Map of Italy.

These dissensions soon led to an open rupture, and in July 1502, the war began. The ensuing struggle is famous in the history of chivalry, which gleamed forth for the last time in these Italian wars, and is well depicted in the picturesque pages of the life of Bayard. On the French side, we find Imbercourt, 'to whom, wherever there was a battle to fight, the heat of the Italian noontide seemed like the cool of morning'; the aged La Palice, who in the *mêlée* forgot his age; and Bayard himself, the soul of knightly courtesy and valour. On the side of Spain, stood Diego de Paredes, whose feats of extravagant daring furnish the theme for many a Spanish romance; and Pedro de Paz, a squinting dwarf, who scarce could be seen above the head of his charger, yet had the heart of a lion; while Gonzalvo de Cordova, the 'Great Captain' himself, added to his masterly qualities as a general the chivalrous courtesy and manners of a knight-errant. These, and many others, fought, not so much for victory, as for honour. Not content with the opportunities offered by the regular military operations for the display of their prowess, they challenged each other to jousts and tourneys, which, though fought *à l'outrance*, were conducted with all the punctiliousness, and all the ceremony of the lists. As we read the history of their combats, we fancy that we are present at a tournament of the Middle Ages—the contest, one for knightly prestige, the prize, some guerdon awarded by lady's hand.[1] But the real issue was not decided by these feats of personal valour. On the declaration of hostilities, the French had the advantage in numbers and in the quality of their troops, as well as the command of the sea.

In December 1502, the victory of D Aubigny at Terranova,[2] over a force which had just landed from Spain, gave him the whole of Calabria. Gonzalvo de Cordova, the Spanish

The War of Naples. July 1502.

[1] Cf. especially, Le Combat singulier entre Bayard et Don Alonzo, and Le Combat des treize contre treize, *Les tresjoyeuse Histoire des gestes du bon Chevalier*, c. xxii.-xxiii. Ed. Petitot, vol. 15.

[2] See Appendix iv.

commander-in-chief, unable to keep the field, assumed the defensive attitude, and threw his troops into the fortified towns
of Apulia. Of these, Barletta was the most impor-

D'Aubigny's
victory at
Terranova,
Dec. 15, 1502.

tant. Here the Spanish general entrenched himself, and patiently waited for reinforcements from
Sicily and Spain; but Ferdinand was remiss in
sending aid; while a French fleet, holding the sea, prevented

Siege of
Barletta.

troops or supplies being shipped from Sicily. The
distress was so severe that Gonzalvo de Cordova
had great difficulty in preventing a surrender, and had the
French general, the Duc de Nemours, shown more energy,
the Spaniards might have been driven from the country.

In April 1503 there seemed a chance of peace. The
Archduke Philip, as he passed through France, visited
Louis XII. at Lyons, and there made a treaty by which it was

Treaty of
Lyons.
April 5, 1503.

agreed that Naples should eventually go to the
young Charles and the Princess Claude, who, in
1501, had been betrothed. Until the children
should be old enough to marry, the French portion of the
kingdom was to be administered by a nominee of Louis, the
Spanish, by the Archduke Philip, or some deputy appointed
by Ferdinand. Whether Ferdinand had allowed these negotiations to be entered into merely to gain time, as the French
declare, or whether, as seems more probable, Philip, who was
not on good terms with his father-in-law, had exceeded his
instructions, the results to France were fatal.

The treaty signed, Louis countermanded the embarkation
of reinforcements from Genoa, and ordered a suspension of
hostilities in Naples. Meanwhile the position of the Spaniards

Hostilities
renewed.

had materially improved. In February, their
general, taking advantage of the foolish movement
of the Duc de Nemours to recover Castellaneta, which had
just revolted to Spain, made a sortie from Barletta, captured
Ruvo, and took La Palice prisoner. In March, the defeat of
the French fleet gave the command of the sea to Spain.

Now strengthened by reinforcements, Gonzalvo de Cordova
openly repudiated the treaty of Lyons, and at last assumed

the offensive. So overwhelming was the superiority of the Spaniards that two battles fought within eight days of each other sufficed to make them masters of the country.

The defeat of D'Aubigny at Seminara by the Spanish General, Fernando de Andrada, on April 20, and his surrender which shortly followed, gave them Calabria. On the 27th, the Great Captain at last leaving Barletta, where he had lain entrenched so long, sought the French at Cerignola (April 28). Here taking up a strong position, with his front protected by a ditch, which he filled with pointed stakes and strengthened with a rampart, he awaited the onslaught of the French. The Duc de Nemours, true to that cautious strategy which had hitherto prevented him from taking full advantage of his superior strength, was for postponing the attack. Stung, however, by the reproaches flung at him by Ives d'Allègre, one of his officers, he rashly ordered an advance as evening was already closing in. 'Now,' said he, 'perhaps those who vaunt the loudest will be found to trust more to their spurs than to their swords.' The event justified the taunt. In vain, the French flung themselves with desperate valour on the ditch and ramparts. They were exposed to the concentrated fire of the enemy and beaten back. The Duc de Nemours himself, and Chandieu, the leader of the Swiss contingent, were slain. The explosion of a Spanish powder magazine caused more confusion to the French than to the foe, and Gonzalvo de Cordova, seizing the moment, ordered a general advance. The French, wearied by their long struggle, broke and fled.

French defeated at Seminara, April 20, 1503; and Cerignola, April 28.

Henceforth, the advance of the Spaniards was unchecked. The French proved the truth of the Italian saying that, 'while in their attacks they were more than men, they were less than women in their retreats.' In one day, thirty castles surrendered to the 'Great Captain.' On the 13th of May, Naples opened its gates, and Gaëta, Venosa, and Santa Severina remained the only important places in French hands.

The French driven from Naples.

Louis XII. made desperate attempts to retrieve his disaster. Three large armies were raised : one to penetrate into Spain by the way of Fontarabia ; the second to invade Roussillon and seize Salces on the frontier ; the third to re-enter Italy. Two fleets were also equipped, one in Genoa, the other in Marseilles ; the first to support the invasion of Naples, the other to co-operate with the attack on Roussillon by threatening the coast of Catalonia. But fortune did not smile upon his efforts. The invasion of Spain was delayed by the supineness or the treachery of the commander, Alan d'Albret.[1] The fleet intended for Catalonia was driven back by heavy weather. The attack on Roussillon was equally unfortunate. The fortress of Salces, strengthened by Pedro Navarra, the best engineer of his day, was too strong to be taken by assault ; and in October, Ferdinand, marching to its relief with a superior force, drove the French over the frontier. Disheartened by these reverses Louis XII. consented to a truce of five months (15th November), which was subsequently extended. Curiously enough, the unfortunate Federigo of Naples was called upon to act as peacemaker between the two robbers who were still quarrelling over the kingdom they had dispoiled him of. For Naples was not included in the truce, and thither the third French army had marched in July 1503, under the leadership of La Trémouille.

Renewed attempts of Louis XII.

But the death of Pope Alexander, on August 18, caused delay. The papal tiara had long been the aim of Cardinal d'Amboise, an ambition favoured by Louis XII. Under the idea that the presence of the army might influence the election, it was ordered to halt within a few miles of Rome. The cardinals were indignant at this attempt to overawe them, and the movement of a Spanish force from the south, as well

Death of Alexander VI., Aug. 18, 1503, and election of Pius III.

[1] His son John d'Albret, king of Navarre in right of his wife, had allied himself with Ferdinand, fearing the claims on Navarre of the younger branch, then represented by Gaston de Foix, nephew of Louis XII.

as the presence of Cæsar Borgia with his troops in the Castle of St. Angelo, made them fear lest the matter might lead to a conflict. D'Amboise therefore allowed the army to depart. Shortly after, despairing of success, he supported the election of Cardinal Piccolomini who, on September 22, became Pope Pius III. This delay of a month was fatal to the French cause. The expedition was postponed to the autumn and winter, which proved to be exceptionally wet and cold. La Trémouille fell ill and resigned his command to the Marquis of Mantua, an inferior general, and time was given to Gonzalvo de Cordova to obtain reinforcements.

Even as it was, however, the French were superior in numbers, and the 'Great Captain' found it necessary to abandon the siege of Gaëta, which still held out for the French, and to drop back on the river Gariglıano. The French, after a desperate conflict, succeeded in throwing a bridge over the river (November 6), but failed in dislodging the Spaniards from their position about a mile to the rear, which had, as usual, been strengthened by Don Gonzalvo. Finally, throwing up an earthwork to protect the bridge, they dropped back to their old position. Seven weeks of inaction followed, broken only by partial skirmishes and personal combats.

Battle of the Garigliano, Dec. 28, 1503.

Meanwhile the weather, which had been wet, grew worse. From this, owing to the lowness and swampiness of their position, the Spaniards suffered much. Yet Gonzalvo de Cordova succeeded in imparting to his men his unconquerable determination to hold the position at any cost. Urged to retreat he answered, 'I would not fall back a step to gain a hundred years of life.' The effect on the French was far more disastrous. In spite of their being on higher, and therefore drier ground, the troops and the horses did not endure the wet and cold so well. The country and even the roads became so sodden, that the movements of the cavalry, and still more those of the artillery, the two forces in which the French excelled, were seriously impeded.

Under such depressing circumstances, insubordination, the chief evil of the French armies of those days, began to show itself, and finally vented itself against the Marquis of Mantua, their general. Pleading ill-health he resigned, to be succeeded by the Marquis of Saluzzo. This led to the desertion of some Italian troops, insulted at the treatment of their countryman. Thus, time was fighting for the Spaniards; and when at last, recruited by the Orsini, whom he had cleverly succeeded in conciliating, he felt strong enough to assume the offensive, he met with but faint resistance. On the night of December 28, the troops who guarded the river were overwhelmed and the passage of the river effected. The French, surprised in their scattered cantonments by the suddenness of the attack, were unable to concentrate, and forced to retreat. In spite of numerous deeds of valour, the retreat soon became a rout, and the remnants of the army fell back in confusion on Gaëta. Here after one more struggle they capitulated (January 1, 1504), on the condition that they should retire unmolested, and that all prisoners in Spanish hands should be released. The few remaining strongholds speedily surrendered, and the Neapolitan kingdom was won for Ferdinand.

The French finally lose Naples, 1504

The victory of the Spaniards was due to their possession of Sicily, whence they could draw support, and to the failure of the French to retain the command of the sea, so that reinforcements could come from Spain; to the exceptional inclemency of the winter, which seems to have been more severely felt by the French than the Spaniards; in great measure to the unpopularity of the French, the result of their licence and overbearing conduct; largely to the quarrels of the French generals; but, above all, to their inferiority when matched against the 'Great Captain.' Cautious, where caution was necessary, he refused to be drawn from his position till the right moment came; but, when he saw his opportunity, struck with decision and rapidity. Never despairing under the most gloomy circumstances, he was able to communicate his fortitude, and impart his cheerfulness to his soldiery. Gracious and conciliatory, he earned the love of his army, yet knew how to be severe when discipline was threatened. A master of diplomacy, as well as of war, he succeeded, as no other foreign general had, in winning over enemies, and in settling the factions of that most factious country, Italy. Courteous in manner, and splendid in his style of life, he won the hearts of the giddy Neapolitans. Nor was Gonzalvo de Cordova above learning from his foe. To the short sword and buckler, the national weapons of the Spaniards, so effective for attack at close quarters, he added the long German spear, whereby their power of defence was materially increased. Indeed, he may be said to have made the Spanish infantry, which, re-armed by him and reduced to discipline, became for a time the most formidable force in Europe.

§ 4. *Alexander VI. and Cæsar Borgia.*

While the struggle between the French and Spaniards was being decided in Naples, events of importance to Italy and Europe were happening in the centre of the Peninsula. Need of French help in his designs on the Romagna had been the motive of Alexander's alliance with Louis XII. at the date of the Milanese expedition. To the realisation of these schemes he and his son now eagerly turned.

Alexander VI. and the Romagna.

The Romagna, once the old Exarchate of Ravenna, a district of somewhat indeterminate limits, lay on the eastern slopes of the Apennines, stretching to the Adriatic on the east, while to the north it was bounded by the territories of Venice, to the south by the march of Ancona. This country is said to have been originally granted to the Pope by Constantine. The gift was confirmed by Charles the Great, and all claims to it were definitely surrendered by Rudolph of Hapsburg in the thirteenth century. The Emperor, however, had granted but an empty title. The country was in the hands of numerous families who acknowledged indeed the nominal supremacy of Rome, but were practically independent.[1]

The possession of these petty states had been long coveted by Milan, Florence, and Venice. Venice indeed had already encroached on the territory of Ferrara (1484), and under the new aspect of affairs caused by the French invasion, the absorption of many of them by one or other of these powers seemed inevitable. This Alexander hoped to obviate by re-asserting the papal supremacy, which had never been formally denied, and by reducing the district to obedience.

The pretext for the overthrow of these principalities was that they had not paid the yearly dues which they owed the Pope as his vicars, and no sooner had the French entered Italy in the autumn of 1499, than Cæsar proceeded to execute the papal decree of confiscation.

Louis XII., in pursuance of his promise, sent 300 lances under the command of Ives d'Allègre, while 4000 Swiss infantry were hired as mercenaries. With these forces Cæsar marched against Imola and Forli (Nov. 9). The two cities did not make any resistance, but the castles held out longer, especially that of Forli, which was defended by the brave but masculine Caterina Sforza, and did not surrender till January, 1500.

The conquests of Cæsar in the Romagna. Nov. 1499-April 1501.

---

[1] The most important of these petty states in Alexander's time were the Duchy of Ferrara in the hands of Ercole, Marquis of Este.

Bologna,	,,	Giovanni Bentivoglio.
Imola and Forli,	,,	Caterina Sforza, niece of Ludovico il Moro, and widow of Girolamo Riario, nephew of Sixtus IV.
Rimini,	,,	Pandolfo Malatesta.
Faenza,	,,	Astorre Manfredi.
Pesaro,	,,	Giovanni Sforza, distant cousin of Ludovico and first husband of Lucrezia Borgia.
Camerino,	,,	Giulio Cæsare Varano.
Duchy of Urbino,	,,	Guidobaldo di Montefeltro.
Sinigaglia,	,,	Francesco Maria della Rovere, a boy.

A few such as Ancona were still republics, but were weak and obscure.

The return of Ludovico to Milan in February (cf. p. 38) necessitated the recall of the French contingent, and Cæsar was forced to postpone further hostilities until the ensuing September. Then, reinforced once more by French assistance, and holding the title of Gonfalonier of the Church, just bestowed upon him by his father, Cæsar speedily reduced Pesaro and Rimini. Faenza, happy under the mild rule of the young Astorre Manfredi, offered stout resistance, and did not fall till April, 1501. In violation of the terms of capitulation the unfortunate Astorre was sent to Rome, and in the following June was found drowned in the Tiber. By whose order the deed was done, no one knew, but all men not unnaturally suspected the hand of the Borgias.

Fortune now seemed to favour Cæsar. Created Duke of Romagna by Alexander, he had been enrolled a member of the Venetian nobility by that proud republic, which hoped thus to gain papal aid against the Turk. He had in his pay the best of the Italian condottiers, and the remaining cities of the Romagna were trembling. Dazzled by his rapid successes, his views expanded. He now aspired not only to complete his conquest of the Romagna, but to interfere in the affairs of Florence, if not eventually to make himself master of all Tuscany. For a time, however, his ambition was checked. Bologna and Florence were both under French protection, and Louis ordered him to stay his hand. The Pope became alarmed, and Cæsar was forced to content himself with a sum of money paid by Florence, and an agreement to take him into her service for three years. Leaving therefore his army to take Piombino, which surrendered in September, he joined the French expedition against Naples (July). In September he returned to find his sister Lucrezia betrothed to Alfonso, the son of Ercole of Este.

Cæsar created Duke of Romagna, April 1501. Admitted a member of the Venetian oligarchy.

Louis XII. forbids Cæsar to attack Bologna and Florence.

This beautiful woman,[1] whose character has been the

---

[1] The best account of Lucrezia Borgia is to be found in Gregorovius' *Cæsar Borgia*, a work which has been translated into French.

subject of almost as much controversy as that of Mary Queen
of Scots, and who has been accused, probably unjustly, of
Lucrezia   the most unmentionable crimes, seems rather to
Borgia.   have been a person of colourless disposition who
was made the puppet of the schemes of her father and
brother. She had already been married twice. From her first
husband, Giovanni Sforza, Lord of Pesaro, she had been
divorced to wed the Duke of Biseglia, an illegitimate son of
Alfonso II. of Naples (August 1498). At that date the Pope
desired an alliance with Naples, but two years afterwards
the papal policy had changed. The second invasion of
Naples by Louis XII. was about to take place, and the friendship of Naples was no longer needed. Personal antipathies
widened the breach, and in August 1500, the Duke was
murdered by Cæsar's orders. Now, barely a year since the
foul deed, a new husband was found for this girl of twenty-one.

Alexander's motives, as before, were political. The alliance
of Ferrara was valuable. It protected the Romagna from the
North, and threatened Bologna. The results were not so great
as had been hoped, but the marriage was a happier one than
might have been expected ; and Lucrezia in her Ferrarese
home found peace and a refuge from the slander which had
hitherto assailed her.

Meanwhile the quarrel between France and Spain offered
new opportunities to Cæsar, since Louis needed papal
Further   support and was in no position to thwart him
successes   overmuch. He had indeed to surrender Arezzo,
of Cæsar.   which had in June rebelled against Florence and
called in Vitellozzo Vitelli, one of Cæsar's captains. But
in January 1502, Fermo ; in June, Urbino ; in July, Camerino
had been occupied, while Pisa, which still held out against
Florence, offered to recognise him as its lord. Finally in
August, he obtained the leave of Louis to attack Bologna.

At this moment a revolt of his captains threatened to overwhelm him. The rapid success of Cæsar had awakened
the apprehensions of these men. Once master of the

Romagna, he would no longer need their help, and might turn against them; indeed, his negotiations with Florence at this time lead one to suspect that he had already made up his mind to destroy them. The chief conspirators were Vitellozzo Vitelli of Città di Castello, Oliverotto da Fermo, the Duke of Gravina and Paolo, both Orsini, and Gian Paolo Baglioni of Perugia. These gained the adhesion of Cardinal Orsini, Giovanni Bentivoglio of Bologna, and others. They met at Magione (October 9, 1502), near Lake Thrasimene, where they swore to be true to one another, and applied to Florence for aid. A rebellion was stirred up in Urbino, from whence Cæsar's troops were driven, and another contingent of his was defeated at Fossombrone (October 17).

The Conspiracy of Sinigaglia.

A terrible retribution was, however, soon to fall upon the rebels. Louis sent Cæsar aid. The opportune death of the wealthy Cardinal of Modena, whether poisoned or no, enabled Alexander to appropriate his possessions to Cæsar's military needs. Florence feared the hostility of Cæsar and would not help, and Venice, in spite of the exhortations of Ferdinand to seize the opportunity of freeing Italy from the tyrant, was too cautious to move.

The confederates began to hesitate. They were unable to raise any more troops, and were divided amongst themselves. Listening therefore to the fair promises of Cæsar and the Pope, they made their peace on October 28, abandoned the cause of Bologna, and, as an earnest of their goodwill, marched against Sinigaglia. The town surrendered, but the castle refused to yield to any one but the Duke. Cæsar accordingly came to Sinigaglia (December 31), and, beguiling his captains with gracious words, suddenly pounced upon them. Oliverotto and Vitellozzo were strangled that night, the first accusing Vitellozzo of tempting him to rebel; Vitellozzo imploring Cæsar to obtain a plenary indulgence for him from the Pope. Paolo Orsini and the Duke of Gravina were executed shortly after. Cardinal Orsini was seized at Rome to die in prison, probably of poison.

The Massacre of Sinigaglia. Dec. 31, 1502.

The conspiracy put down, nothing seemed to stand in the way of the papal ambition. Urbino was again reduced; Città di Castello and Perugia submitted; most of the Orsini strongholds fell; and Alexander was playing off Spain against France, in the hopes of gaining the assistance of one or another in support of the still more magnificent scheme of making Cæsar King of Tuscany, when father and son were suddenly struck down by an illness, to which Alexander succumbed on August 8. It was popularly believed that they had fallen victims to a poisoned cup, which they had intended for one of the cardinals. The story needs confirmation, but this and others of the kind are at least an indication of the popular opinion, which thought no crime too horrible, or too improbable, to be imputed to the Borgias.

Further successes of Cæsar suddenly stopped by his illness, and the death of Alexander. Aug. 8, 1503.

The fate of Cæsar now depended on the choice of the cardinals. If he could secure the election of one who would support him, he might yet hold his own. Of late Louis XII. had shown an inclination to desert the Borgia alliance. Cæsar therefore from his sick-bed intrigued to get one of the Spanish cardinals chosen, but in this he failed. Louis had hoped to obtain the papal tiara for the Cardinal D'Amboise; Giuliano della Rovere was determined to prevent the election of a Spaniard, and hoped to succeed himself. Foiled in the first instance, Giuliano concurred in the choice of an Italian cardinal, Piccolomini, who, in memory of his famous uncle Pius II., took the name of Pius III. But, in October, Pius died, and della Rovere, coming to terms with Cæsar, secured the votes of the conclave by promises and bribes. Machiavelli, who however exaggerates Cæsar's influence in the College of Cardinals, blames his shortsightedness, because, ' if he could not procure the election of his own nominee, he might have prevented that of della Rovere.' The new Pope, Julius II., had long been the enemy of the Borgias. He had instigated Charles VIII. to invade Italy, and urged

The election of Julius II. fatal to his cause. Nov. 1, 1503.

him to summon a council to depose Alexander, and although of late he had acquiesced in the inevitable, and affected reconciliation, he was not the man to forget past injuries. Fear of the designs of Venice on the Romagna caused him to support Cæsar for a moment.   But Julius was determined to win the Romagna for the Papacy, not for the Borgia family, and no sooner did Cæsar attempt to act independently than he ordered him to return to Rome (November 29).   Cæsar's captains, however, refused to surrender the places which they held without his consent, and Cæsar would not consent except at the price of freedom.   After long negotiation the agreement was concluded, and Cæsar, free once more, set out for Naples to seek the aid of Spain (April 1504).

Ferdinand was at first inclined to listen, till, convinced by the Pope that Cæsar would only disturb the peace of Italy, he ordered his arrest on May 26, 1504, as *The end* the Duke was on the point of sailing for the *of Cæsar's* Romagna.   In violation of a safe-conduct given *career.* him by Gonzalvo, he was shortly sent to Spain, where he remained a prisoner till November, 1506.   Escaping at last, he found refuge with his brother-in-law, now King of Navarre, to die in the succeeding March (1507), in a skirmish with a rebel vassal of the King.

Thus, at the age of thirty-one, ended the career of the man whom Machiavelli in his *Prince* holds up as a pattern, in all but his ill-fortune, to him who would attempt to form a united kingdom of Italy.   No doubt Cæsar had many of the qualities requisite for success.   Clever and versatile in conception, rapid and resolute in action, and a master of diplomacy, he had in a high degree the quality of 'virtù,' that compound of force and intellect, which we find praised not only by Machiavelli, but by Commines and other writers of the day, as the essential characteristic of the ruler.

We must, alas! allow that private morality is not always the accompaniment of good statesmanship.   Although Cæsar was absolutely without scruple in his treatment of the petty princes of the Romagna, it may be questioned whether the independence of these petty principalities was worth preserving. Ruled by despots, no question of political freedom was involved. With a few exceptions, such as that of Urbino, they illustrated the evils without the advantages of the larger tyrannies, and their history is one tangled tale of faction, murder, and intrigue. The country too, it must be confessed, was well governed under him, and his rule was not unpopular. But, when all is said, we cannot believe that a kingdom founded by such cruelty, and maintained by such villany and treachery, can really be a solid one. That Machiavelli, dazzled by the temporary good fortune of Cæsar, should boldly hold him up as a model to be copied, only makes one realise the cynical despair of the Italians as to the possibility of success in their country by any other means, and the depth of degradation to which the people had fallen.[1] Nor, finally, do we believe that the idea of thus founding a temporal dominion of the Papacy was likely to succeed. Had Alexander lived longer, it might, perhaps, have ended in the establishment of another petty kingdom in Italy. But the state would have been founded in the interest of the Borgia, not of the Papacy, and would have only added one more enemy to the advance of the temporal dominion. If the papal authority in the Romagna was to become a reality, it must be based on a firmer foundation than that of papal nepotism. This Julius II. saw. Most of the cities held or threatened by Cæsar fell at once into his hands, with the exception of Rimini, Faenza, and Cesena, which were seized by Venice, to be secured, however, by Julius in the war of the League of Cambray. Meanwhile Perugia and Bologna were gained by Julius in 1506, while the Duchy of Urbino fell to his nephew, Francesco della Rovere, who was adopted by Guidobaldo, its late Duke. These territories were incorporated into the papal dominions; the

[1] For a review of Cæsar's character, and of Machiavelli's treatment of him, cf. Creighton, vol. iv. 64; Burd, *Machiavelli*, introduction, pp. 22, 28; Villari, *Machiavelli*, ii. 154; Symonds' *Age of the Despots*, p. 275.

history of their semi-independent princes came to an end, and Julius II., rather than Alexander, established the papal dominion in the Romagna.

§ 5. *The League of Cambray.*

The pretext for the invasion of Italy by France and Spain had been the necessity of securing a base of operations for a crusade against the Turk. This had been prevented by the quarrel of the robbers over their spoil. They were now to prove by their attack on Venice—the only power which had seriously attempted to check the Moslem advance—that the idea, even if ever seriously entertained, had been definitely abandoned.

The hostility with which that republic was viewed by the rest of Italy dates from the beginning of the fifteenth century, when she definitely began to aim at establishing a dominion on the Italian mainland. A quarrel between Milan and the Carrara of Padua enabled her to overthrow that family, to seize Padua, then, step by step, Vicenza and Verona, and to advance to the Adige (1405). In 1427 and 1428, she wrested Brescia and Bergamo from the hands of Filippo Maria Visconti, Duke of Milan, and after his death secured Crema (1454). Meanwhile she had acquired the district of Friuli from the Patriarch of Aquileia (1420), and in 1441 had added Ravenna, hitherto an independent state under the Polentani, to her conquests. In 1484, the peace of Bagnolo, which closed the Ferrarese war, gave her Rovigo and the Polesine. In 1499, she gained Cremona and the Ghiara d'Adda from Louis XII., as the price of her assistance against Ludovico. On the death of Cæsar Borgia, she had occupied Faenza, Rimini, and Cesena; while in Apulia, she held the four towns, Trani, Otranto, Gallipoli, Brindisi, which she had acquired at the date of Charles VIII.'s expedition. Thus, within the space of some hundred years,

[sidenote:] Jealousy against Venice, the result of her advance on the mainland.

Venice had completely altered her character. The island city had gained a large territory on the mainland, which stretched to the neighbourhood of Milan, Florence, and the Papal States. The change of policy has usually been attributed to the advance of the Turk, which threatened her possessions in the Ægean Sea, and on the coast of Greece. This no doubt was one of her motives at a later date. But as her first advance on the mainland occurred in 1405, some years before the Turk seriously menaced her, we must look elsewhere for the primary cause. This is to be found in the danger to be apprehended from the growing power of Milan. As long as the plain of Lombardy and the approaches to the Alpine passes were in the hands of petty princes, she could hope to purchase, or to extort, an outlet for her commerce to the north; but, if these were to fall into the hands of the powerful and aggressive Dukes of Milan, they might be closed against her. An alternative route no doubt remained. She might have threaded the Straits of Gibraltar and reached the north of Europe by the Atlantic and the English Channel. But, though of late a Flanders fleet had yearly sailed from Venice, this route was not developed. It could, and probably would, have been closed by Spain. Nor would such a policy have saved her from Milan, which, if she became too powerful, might cut off her food supplies, surround her, and drive her into the sea.

The attempt, then, to form a state in Lombardy appears to have been inevitable; nor was it so selfish as her enemies declared it to be. Her treatment of the cities under her rule was not only infinitely superior to that of Milan, but compared most favourably with that of Florence. She left them as much local autonomy as was compatible with the main tenance of her supremacy; she did not tax them heavily. It was the aim of Venice to secure the affection of her subjects, and their loyalty in the days of her troubles, proved that she had succeeded. With equal injustice the policy of Venice towards the Turk has been denounced as faithless to the cause of Christianity. No doubt, despairing of the aid of Europe, she was anxious to keep on friendly terms with the Turk, and would, if possible, have avoided war ; but this policy was forced upon her by the refusal of European states to sink their common jealousies and join heartily in a crusade. Venice, after all, was the only power which seriously attempted to check the advance of the Moslem, and the coalition against her is the best proof of the hollowness of the cry of a crusade on the part of her spoilers. But though the advance on the mainland seems to have been inevitable, and is capable of justification, it was none the less a fatal step. Had it been possible for Venice to conquer Milan, and to have secured the whole of Lombardy before the date of the French invasion, she might some day have become the capital of a united Italy, and the history of the Peninsula might have been a happier one. But for this her resources were not sufficient, nor is it likely that the European powers would have acquiesced. Failing this, her vain attempts to find a strategic frontier only added to her enemies, and earned her the name of the most selfish and grasping of the Italian states ; while in her endeavour to protect her commerce by friendly treaties with the Turk, she added to her crimes the charge of treachery towards the cause of Christendom.

The real fault of Venice has not been so often noted by historians. Her interests imperatively demanded that the foreigner should be excluded from Italy. As long as the Peninsula was left to itself, she was strong enough to hold her own ; but she was no match for the more powerful kingdoms of the north. Her vacillation at the date of the expedition of Charles VIII. she had in part redressed by forming the League of Venice and driving him from Italy, although her occupation at that date of the Apulian towns eventually earned her the hostility of Ferdinand. The good work was, however, again undone by her foolish alliance with Louis XII. in his war against Milan. By this short-sighted policy she earned with some justice the accusation of territorial greed; irritated Maximilian, who did not relish being excluded from Lombardy; and established on her western frontier the ever-grasping power of France. Thus, by the close of the fifteenth century, Venice had incurred the enmity not only of the petty Italian states, but of the chief powers of Western Europe.

Maximilian desired to recover Friuli; Louis XII. wished to extend the frontiers of the Milanese; Florence feared that Venice might cross the Apennines; Ferdinand was determined to recover the cities in Apulia. Above all, Pope Julius was bent on humbling the proud republic. Her acquisitions in the Romagna interfered with his darling scheme of establishing the papal rule in that district. Between France in Milan, and Spain in Naples, Julius might hope to hold the balance, and to establish the temporal dominion of the Papacy, but Venice, or indeed any strong Italian power, would strenuously oppose it. In this Julius only followed the traditional policy of his predecessors in the papal chair, that of inveterate hostility to the growth of a strong native state in Italy. Moreover, the independent attitude of the republic in matters of church government,[1] illustrated at this moment by her refusal to allow him to nominate to the vacant bishopric of Vicenza, angered the haughty prelate.

European combinations leading to the League of Cambray.

They wish to treat me as their chaplain,' he said, 'let them beware lest I make them humble fishermen as they once were.'

Under these circumstances the sole hope for Venice lay in the mutual jealousies of her enemies. From these she had profited hitherto, but when they ceased her day of reckoning would come. Hence it is necessary to treat in some detail the relations of the European powers at the opening of the sixteenth century.

At the close of the Neapolitan war, the alliance between the houses of Hapsburg and Spain, based on the marriage of the Archduke Philip, son of Maximilian, with Joanna, the daughter of Ferdinand of Aragon and Isabella of Castile, threatened to break up. By the deaths in 1497, and 1500, of John, the eldest son, and of Michael of Portugal, the grandson of the

[1] Cf. *Cambridge Modern History*, vol. i. p. 267.

Spanish monarchs, Joanna became the heiress of Castile and
Aragon,[1] and, in the event of Isabella's death, would become
Queen of Castile to the exclusion of her father.   This at
once aroused the jealousy of Ferdinand against her husband
the archduke.   The temporary division of Castile and
Aragon would arrest the unification of the Peninsula ; while
the prospect of Spain eventually falling to the Hapsburg was
equally distasteful to him.

Ferdinand had accordingly rejected the treaty of Lyons
(April 1503), concluded between Philip and Louis XII. for
the settlement of the Neapolitan quarrel.   By that   Treaty of
treaty, it had been agreed that the kingdom of   Lyons, April
Naples should one day fall to Claude, the infant   5, 1503; and of
                                                   Blois, Sep. 22,
daughter of Louis XII., who had already, in 1501,   1504.
been betrothed to Charles, the young son of the archduke.
Philip, abandoned by his father-in-law, clung all the closer
to the French alliance, and was supported by his father,
Maximilian, who hoped by this marriage treaty to realise
his most magnificent dreams.   In September 1504, at Blois,
Louis XII., influenced by his wife, Anne of Brittany, who had
no son, promised Milan, Genoa, Asti, Brittany, and Blois, as
Claude's dower, to which Burgundy was to be added in the
event of his own death without male heirs.   In the following
year, Maximilian actually proposed, with the approval of the
French Queen, that the Salic Law should be repealed, in order
that Claude might succeed her father on the French throne.

Thus there seemed a prospect that the young Charles
would some day unite the kingdoms of Castile, Aragon,
France, the Milanese, and the kingdom of Naples, with the
hereditary dominions of the House of Hapsburg.   Had
this ever come about, the rest of Germany must have submitted, and the descendants of the poverty-stricken Frederick
III. would have found themselves masters of an empire over

---

[1] FERDINAND of Aragon＝ISABELLA of Castile

JOHN + 1497	EMANUEL of Portugal＝ISABELLA + 1498	JOANNA＝ARCHDUKE PHILIP
	MICHAEL + 1500	

most of the Teutonic and Latin races of the continent.
But the day dream was not to last. In November 1504,
Isabella died, and Ferdinand, determined to retain his hold
as regent of Castile, made haste to conciliate Louis XII.
At Blois, in October 1505, he agreed to marry Germaine

Second Treaty
of Blois.
Oct. 12, 1505.

de Foix, the niece of the French king. To her
the French claims on Naples were to be resigned,
which, however, were to revert to Louis XII. in
default of her having issue by Ferdinand. Ferdinand further
promised to Louis a sum of money, and an amnesty to
the French party in Naples. In the June of the following
year, 1506, Ferdinand was indeed obliged to surrender the
regency of Castile to Philip and Joanna; but in September
the Archduke Philip died at Burgos; the unfortunate
Joanna was declared to show signs of madness,[1] and
Ferdinand, by the help of Cardinal Ximenes, secured,
though with difficulty, the government of Castile. Thus the
quarrel between Louis XII. and Ferdinand was temporarily
accommodated, and Ferdinand was secure in Spain and in
Naples.

Meanwhile, in France the national hostility to a foreigner
had been aroused. The Estates-General at Tours (May 1506)
prayed the King to abandon the intended match between
Claude and Charles, and to marry her to Francis of Angoulême, the heir-presumptive to the crown, who was 'entirely a
Frenchman.' Maximilian, irritated at the failure of his
schemes, now broke with Louis. In 1507, he summoned the
Diet to Constance, and passionately demanded help of the
empire. 'The King of France,' he said, 'wishes to rob the
Germans of the Imperial crown, the highest dignity of the
world and the glory of our nation.' In return for a promise
to reorganise the Imperial Chamber, he received a contingent
from the Diet; he also took a body of Swiss mercenaries
into his pay. Crossing the Brenner, he reached Trent in

---

[1] On the question of Joanna's madness, cf. authorities at page 104,
note.

February, 1508, and there, with the consent of the papal legate, declared himself Emperor-elect.

But as usual the pretensions of Maximilian outran his abilities to a ludicrous extent. The Venetians, fearing his designs on Friuli, refused him free passage, and enforced their refusal by arms. His attempt on Vicenza failed. The Duke of Gueldres, stirred up by Louis XII., threatened the Netherlands, and the would-be ruler of Western Europe was forced to accept the terms of the insolent republic and retire. Burning to revenge himself, he pocketed his pride, and at Cambray, December 1508, came to terms with Louis XII. Peace was made with the Duke of Gueldres, and Maximilian promised, in return for money, the investiture of Milan to Louis XII. and his descendants. Their quarrels thus accommodated, the King and Emperor agreed to partition the Venetian territory. All princes who had any claims on Venetian lands were asked to aid in checking her intolerable selfishness and greed by recovering their lost possessions. Ferdinand and the Pope shortly joined, the latter with some misgivings, and only after Venice had refused to restore to him Rimini and Faenza ; a number of petty Italian princes followed suit, and Venice found herself face to face with one of the most shameful of coalitions in history. Ferdinand, however, was engaged in wars against the Moors of Africa. The penniless Maximilian was not ready for a fresh campaign ; and the French, and papal troops, assisted by the Duke of Ferrara and other Italians, alone took the field.

The League of Cambray. Dec. 10, 1508.

The wisest policy for Venice would probably have been, as Pitigliano urged, to avoid pitched battles, and to play a waiting game. If the war were prolonged, the robbers would be sure to quarrel. But rasher counsels prevailed. Neglecting the movement of the papal troops in the Romagna, the Venetians turned against the French and attempted to stop their attack at the frontier. As the two armies were manœuvring in the valley

Battle of Agnadello or Vaila. May 14, 1509.

of the Adda, it came about that the rear-guard of the Venetian army, under Bartolomeo d'Alviano, came within striking distance of the French advanced guard.   Alviano, a condottier with more valour than discretion, thought it more honourable to be beaten than to retreat, and at once ordered the attack. The Venetian army was a curious medley of Italian condottiers and peasants, Greek light horse from the Peloponnese and the Ægean isles, and half-savage archers from Crete.   Nevertheless it fought well, more especially the Italian infantry, composed of peasants from the Lombard plain and the slopes of the Alps and Apennines.   But it was exposed to the attack of the whole French army,[1] aided by a large body of Swiss.   The van, under the Count of Pitigliano, whether from jealousy, or because it was too far distant, did not co-operate; and, after a desperate struggle, the Venetian army turned and fled, leaving Alviano a prisoner, and most of their infantry dead on the field.   As is often the case with mercenaries, the defeated army soon became a mob.   The cities refused refuge to the fugitives, and opened their gates to the victors.   The French met with no opposition till they reached Peschiera, which they took by assault.

At Venice meanwhile, the Senate were debating their future policy amidst the wildest consternation.   Deciding to bow to the storm and to abandon their subject cities, they authorised them to surrender.   Verona, Vicenza, and Padua forthwith sent their keys to Louis, and on his chivalrous refusal to accept their submission, since they did not fall to his share, they turned to Maximilian.   In the Romagna, the Pope occupied Ravenna, Rimini, and Faenza.   The Duke of Ferrara entered the Polesine; the Marquis of Mantua seized the territories of which Venice had deprived him; and the Apulian towns surrendered to Ferdinand.

Venice had now lost all her acquisitions made during the fifteenth century, and seemed doomed to be confined again to her lagoons; nay, Maximilian even spoke of taking the city itself and dividing it into four districts among the

[1] See Appendix iv.

confederates.   But the Emperor as usual counted without his host.   Neither Ferdinand nor Julius were willing to press matters so far; they stayed their hand, while Louis, having attained his object, withdrew to Milan, and then to France.   In the conquered territories, more especially in those claimed by Maximilian, a reaction now took place in favour of the republic of St. Mark.   The nobles had easily deserted Venice, but now the lower classes in town and country rose in her defence.   The Senate regained courage.   By a majority of one vote it was decided to resume the offensive, and, on July 17, Padua was re-taken.   The law which forbade the Venetian nobility to serve on the mainland was revoked, and one hundred and seventy-six young nobles, headed by the sons of the Doge, Loredano, marched to the defence of the recovered city.   Maximilian at last determined to come in person, and laid siege to Padua with a large army composed not only of Germans, but of Spanish auxiliaries, and reinforced by a French contingent.   But the French and Germans were not on the best of terms.   The French knights, when ordered to storm the breach on foot, demanded that they should be joined by the German men-at-arms, and not be left to fight side by side with low-born lansquenets, and the German knights refused to serve on foot at all.   At last Maximilian, passing as was his wont from overweening confidence to blank despair, raised the siege, October 3, 1509, and recrossed the Alps, to hear that Vicenza had also revolted, and recalled the Venetian troops.

Venice saved by the loyalty of her subject lands and the dissensions of her foes.

Unable to defeat the Venetians in open battle, or to take their cities, Maximilian ordered their territories to be ravaged, and a cruel war of pillage and of massacre went on in Friuli throughout the winter of 1509-10.   On one occasion, six thousand men, women, and children were suffocated in a cave near Vicenza.   Such cruelties could only serve to convince the people of the superiority of the Venetian rule.

PERIOD IV.   E

Venice was now to be saved by the dissensions of her enemies. Julius II. had hitherto been the most bitter of her foes, and had supported the League not only by arms, but by excommunication. Yet he had always declared that Venice had driven him to this step by her refusal to recognise the just claims of the Papacy, spiritual and temporal. 'But for this,' he had said, 'we might have been united and found some way to free Italy from the tyranny of the foreigner.' Why should this not now be done? The lands he claimed were in his possession, and Venice was prepared to acknowledge his spiritual pretensions. Moreover, the overwhelming predominance, which France had gained, might be more dangerous to papal interests than the Venetian republic. Thus by joining Venice there was an opportunity, not only of furthering the papal cause, but also of realising that dream of every patriotic Italian, the expulsion of the foreigner. Julius, however, did not show his hand at once. It would be rash to do so until he could be sure that Venice was strong enough to resist her foes; hence his long refusal to listen to her prayers. When, at last, in February 1510, he admitted the city to his peace, it was only on the severest terms. Venice acknowledged the justice of the excommunication; renounced her claims to tax her clergy, and to nominate to her bishoprics; promised that clerics should be tried by ecclesiastical courts, and declared the navigation of the Adriatic free to citizens of the Papal States. The Council of Ten indeed entered a secret protest against these concessions as having been extorted by force, and subsequently repudiated them, but for the moment the Papacy had triumphed.

It was now the aim of Julius to drive the French and Germans from Italy by the assistance of Venice, and of the Swiss, who had broken with Louis. The Swiss alliance for the time failed him. Nevertheless he met at first with transient success. The neutrality of Ferdinand was secured by the investiture of Naples and Sicily, hitherto refused by the Papacy (July 1510). Modena, belonging to the Duke of Ferrara, and Mirandola, were conquered; the first by the nephew of the Pope, the Duke of Urbino; the second by the warlike Julius himself, who, rising from a bed of sickness, crossed the trenches on the ice, and took the city by storm (January 1511). But here his success ended.

On May 13, 1511, the French under Trivulzio captured Bologna, aided by treachery within the city, and in September, Louis summoned a general council at Pisa, which had been at last reconquered by Florence two years before. The council was a failure, for Europe was not prepared for another schism. But it was evident that the French were not to be easily driven from Milan. Julius, therefore, determined to be avenged on France, now turned to Ferdinand. The wily Spaniard had long lost interest in the League. Having regained the Apulian towns, he did not care to see Venice further humbled, and dreaded the increase of French power in Lombardy. Moreover, a quarrel in Italy would give him a pretext for seizing Navarre, which he had long coveted. Ferdinand accordingly gladly welcomed the offers of the Pope; and on October 5, 1511, the Holy League was formed between the Pope, Ferdinand, and Venice. The ostensible object of the League was the protection of the Church, the recovery of Bologna, and the restoration to Venice of her territories. The real aim of the confederates was to drive the French from Italy, while a further stipulation in the treaty, that the Pope should confirm the Spaniards in any conquest made outside Italy, pointed clearly to Navarre. The allies also gained the support of the young Henry VIII. of England, who was anxious to revive his claims to Guienne, and to strengthen his alliance with his father-in-law. Against this formidable coalition, Louis was at first successful. The French army was commanded by Gaston de Foix, the king's nephew and brother of Ferdinand's wife. The young man—he was twenty-three, 'a great general without having served as a soldier'—who by the rapidity of his movements earned in

(margin note:) The Holy League. Oct. 5, 1511.

this campaign the title of the Thunderbolt of Italy, first threw himself into Bologna (February 4), and forced the army of the League, under Raymond de Cardona, viceroy of Naples, to retire. Hearing of the revolt of Brescia, he hurried thither, took the town by assault, mounting the ramparts with bare feet to improve his hold on the steep slopes (February 18), and killed so many of the defenders 'that the horses could not put foot to the ground for the corpses that covered it.' Then, speeding back to Bologna, he forced his enemies to retire, and, pressing on to Ravenna, attempted to take the town by assault (April 19).

Cardona was anxious to avoid a pitched battle. Time, he knew, was on his side, for Maximilian was on the point of joining the League; the Swiss were preparing to pour down into the Milanese; and the projected invasion of France by Henry VIII. would prevent Louis from sending efficient reinforcements. He had accordingly retired to Faenza, but, fearing that Ravenna would fall if not relieved, was forced to return. Even then his tactics were defensive. His camp was protected on the left flank by the river; in front, by some of the numerous ditches which intersect the marshy country. Strengthening this further by his artillery, and by waggons with scythe-like implements mounted on them, he awaited the French attack.

Battle of Ravenna. Easter Day, 1512.

The position of Cardona was indeed a strong one, but in numbers his force was slightly inferior, and, if France was to win, the victory must be won at once. Gaston, therefore, decided rightly to tempt fortune once more, and on Easter Day at 8 A.M. he ordered the attack. He had hoped to dislodge the enemy from their strong position by means of his artillery, which had been brought to a condition of high efficiency under the Duke of Ferrara. In this he was disappointed. The fire of the Spaniards was nearly as effective as his own, and, although the cavalry of the League suffered as severely as that of the French, the Spanish infantry protected themselves by lying on the ground, a movement which French ideas of military honour forbade. After three hours' furious cannonade, the impatience of the cavalry of the League, and of the French and German infantry, could no longer be restrained, and while the former charged the French cavalry, which stood opposite to it, the latter attacked the Spanish foot. Thus cavalry was opposed to cavalry, and infantry to infantry. In the shock which followed, the French horse under Ives d'Allègre, after half-an-hour's struggle, carried all before them ; but their foot, with the German lansquenets, in spite of heroic efforts, found the position too strong, and were already being driven back, when a detachment of their horse, returning from the charge, took the infantry of the League in flank. The French and German infantry now rallied, and forcing their opponents back, finally drove them from their camp. The battle was already won, when Gaston, attempting to check the retreat of some two thousand Spanish footmen, rashly threw himself across their path, followed by a handful of men-at-arms. Though unhorsed he still fought on, 'rivalling the feats of Roland at Roncesvalles,' till at last he fell pierced by wounds. Thus ended the most bloody battle of the war, which had lasted from 8 A.M. to 4 P.M.

The graphic account, given by the biographer of Bayard, helps us best to realise its peculiar character. The shock of the men-at-arms, the thrust of pike and short sword, the arquebuses and 'hacquebutes,' or mounted arquebuses, belong to the Middle Age, but the efficiency of the guns reminds us that we are on the threshold of the sixteenth century.

The victory lay with the French. Pedro Navarra, one of the best of the Spanish generals, the young Marquis of Pescara, and the Cardinal de Medici, legate of the Pope, soon to become Pope Leo x. himself, were prisoners. 'The Spanish loss was such that an hundred years could not repair it,' and Ravenna at once surrendered. Yet, never was victory more dearly bought, or more useless. Though the Spanish troops had suffered most, the losses amongst the officers were more severe on the side of the French and Germans, and many a knight who had distinguished himself in Italy had bit the dust. More serious still was Gaston's death. Had he lived, he might have pressed on to Rome, and brought the Pope at once to terms. His death, however, caused delay, and delay was ruinous. The cruelty of the French had made them hated by the Italians; the richness of the booty, at Brescia and Ravenna, demoralised the troops, and many returned to France.

Maximilian had come to terms with the League just before the battle, but too late to prevent his lansquenets from taking

Maximilian and the Swiss join the Holy League. part and rendering most efficient help to the French. Now, in hopes of securing the Milanese for himself, or for his grandson Charles, he recalled his troops and openly broke with France. Deprived of their support, the French could hardly keep the field. It was, however, at the hands of the Swiss that they were to be driven across the Alps. In the previous wars, these mercenary mountaineers had been of the greatest service to Louis; but the cantons had been alienated by his refusal to increase the subsidy, and still more by his stopping their trade with the Milanese, whence they drew their corn and wine and oil. A strong anti-French party accordingly arose in Switzerland, headed by Mathias Schinner, Bishop of the Valais, the implacable enemy of France, and, in May 1512, a Swiss army, no longer as mercenaries, poured down on Milan. La Palice, who, on the death of Gaston, had succeeded to the command, felt too weak to resist them with an army deprived of the German contingent, and demoralised

The French recross the Alps. by its excesses. He accordingly withdrew to Pavia. Trivulzio, the governor of Milan, followed him, and shortly afterwards the French recrossed the Mont Cenis. With the exception of the castle of Milan, and a few others, their conquests rapidly melted away. Genoa drove out the French and elected Giano Fregoso as its doge. All the Romagna returned to the obedience of the Pope. The Duke of Ferrara indeed held out, but lost Reggio. Bologna was regained, and even Parma and Piacenza seized, while Julius claimed all the territory south of the Po.

In August 1512, representatives of the League met in congress at Mantua. Florence first demanded their attention. Since the death of Savonarola, the position of that republic had been most weak. The constitution established in 1494 had not worked well. It was too oligarchical to be popular, while the partisans of the exiled Medici did all they could to discredit it. In 1502, to strengthen the executive, the office of Gonfalonier had been made a life appointment, and Piero Soderini had been elected; in 1506, at the suggestion of Machiavelli, a militia had been formed. But these measures did not mend matters much. The long struggle to regain Pisa, which was only ended in 1509, exhausted the revenues of the state, and the intrigues of the Medici grew more active. Clinging to the French alliance, the city had refused the offers of the League; yet, in the pursuit of a policy of feeble neutrality, had given no help to Louis XII., when help might have saved him. Her turn was now to come. The confederates demanded that Soderini should retire from office, and that the Medici should be allowed to return as private citizens. The Florentines agreed to admit the Medici, but, over-confident in their new-formed militia, declined to depose Soderini. Accordingly, on August 12, 1512, Raymond de Cardona attacked the town of Prato, which lay a few miles to the north of Florence. The militia, although far more numerous than their enemies, did not justify the confidence which had been placed in them, and fled as soon as a breach was made; possibly there was treachery within the walls. In any case, the Spaniards entered the town without further opposition, and put it to the sack with such brutality that the memories of it are said to have disturbed the last moments of Giovanni, the future Pope, Leo x. This cruelty at least did its work. Soderini, an amiable though weak man, whose 'silly soul' the indignant epitaph of Machiavelli

The Medici restored to Florence. Sept. 1, 1512.

sentences to the limbo of infants, at once resigned rather than expose Florence to further woes; and, on September 1, the Cardinal Giovanni entered Florence. The Medici[1] returned nominally as private citizens, but the constitution of 1494 was swept away, and the government, restored as it had been under Lorenzo, was completely under their control. Although the revolution was effected with moderation, the partisans of the old government naturally lost office. Machiavelli, who had been secretary to the Council of Ten (Dieci di Liberta e Pace), and who had taken an active part in the diplomacy of the republic, was driven from public life, and devoted himself to writing *The Prince*, and *The Discourses*,[2] the former of which treatises has given him such an unenviable notoriety. The city under its new rulers abandoned the French alliance and joined the League.

The confederates then turned to the question of Milan. Maximilian was eager to secure this for his grandson Charles. But he was not acceptable to the Pope, the Venetians, or the Swiss, or even to Ferdinand. All dreaded the addition of the Milanese to the vast possessions present and reversionary of the young prince. Finally, it was agreed to recall Maximilian, the son of Ludovico il Moro, who had since his father's fall been brought up in the imperial court. On the 29th of December, Maximilian received the keys from the Swiss and entered the city. In return, 'their puppet duke' ceded to the confederates the Val Maggia, Locarno, and Lugano; and to their allies, the Rhætian League (later the canton of the Grisons), Chiavenna,

Milan granted to Maximilian Sforza. Dec. 29, 1512.

---

[1] The leaders of the Medici at this time were as follows:—

  1. Giuliano, Duke of Nemours, and Cardinal Giovanni, subsequently Leo X., both sons of Lorenzo.
  2. Giulio, nephew of Lorenzo, subsequently Cardinal and then Pope Clement VII.
  3. Lorenzo, Duke of Urbino, son of Piero, grandson of Lorenzo.

[2] On the purpose of the *Prince*, cf. Burd, *Il Principe*, Introduction. *Cambridge Modern History*, c. 6.

Bormio, and the Valtelline. This, added to the Val Leven-
tina, acquired 1440, and to Bellinzona, granted by Louis XII.
in 1503, gave the Swiss, and their allies, complete command
over four of the most important passes of the Alps, the St.
Gothard, the Splugen, the Maloia, and the Bernina, and
extended their territory to the Italian lakes of Como, Lugano,
and Maggiore.[1] Thus at the close of the year 1512, the
Medici and the Sforza found themselves again in power as
they had been at the invasion of Charles VIII.

Meanwhile France had been threatened by a joint attack
on Guienne—on the part of Ferdinand and Henry VIII. The
English indeed landed at Bayonne, but fortunately for Louis,
the attention of Ferdinand was called off to Navarre. That
kingdom, which sat astride of the Pyrenees, was at this
moment under the rule of Catherine de Foix and her husband, the Frenchman, John d'Albret. But her title had
always been disputed by the younger line, represented by
Gaston de Foix, the nephew of Louis XII. On his death at
the battle of Ravenna, his claims passed to his **Ferdinand
conquers
Spanish
Navarre.
July 1513.** sister Germaine, wife of Ferdinand, and these
Ferdinand now proceeded to press. Catherine,
the reigning queen, no longer afraid of France,
sought the alliance of Louis XII. This gave Ferdinand
the pretext he sought. He demanded a passage through
Navarre for his attack on France, and on being refused, invaded the little kingdom. He was supported by a powerful
faction, headed by the Beaumonts. The timid John fled.
'Wert thou queen and I king, the realm would not be thus
lost,' said Catherine, but was forced to follow her cowardly
husband, and, by the end of July, Ferdinand occupied all the
territory on the Spanish side of the mountains. That portion
of the country which lay on the French slope of the Pyrenees,
continued an independent kingdom, to be absorbed into France
in the sixteenth century, by the accession of Henry of Navarre

---

[1] Chiavenna, Bormio, and the Valtelline, were held till 1797. The
others since 1803 have formed the Swiss canton of Ticino.

to the French crown.   The English, irritated at Ferdinand's failure to co-operate with them, and attacked by disease, due to the hot climate, the incessant rain, and the heavy wine of the South in which they indulged too freely, withdrew from Bayonne, and France was relieved from immediate danger on that side.

At the beginning of the year 1513, it was pretty evident that the Holy League would not last.   The Venetians, finding

Break-up of the Holy League.

that the Emperor was coveting the share of their territory originally meted out to him by the League of Cambray, were looking again to France. At this moment, Julius II., one of the chief movers in that League, passed away.   The objects of this ' fiery personality '[1]

Death of Julius II. Feb. 20, 1513.

had been : first to conquer the Romagna, and establish the papal dominion there on a sound footing ; secondly, if possible, to free Italy from the foreigner.   Of these, the first had been the dominant aim, and he had attained it.   'For good or for ill, Julius is the founder of the Papal States.'   We may deplore the secular-ising influence of the temporal dominion on the spiritual character of the Papacy, but at least the scheme of Julius is infinitely preferable to that of Alexander VI.   Alexander had tried to establish his family ; Julius won territories for the Papal See.   But in gaining this, his primary aim, he sacrificed his second.   By the League of Cambray, he finally destroyed the political life of Italy, and called the foreigner to his aid ; and, when, in the Holy League, he attempted to undo the work, and to drive the French, the chief instru-ments of his previous policy, across the Alps, he found that he could only do so at the price of changing masters.   In his last days, indeed, he hoped to reconcile Maximilian by some small concessions, and then, with the help of the Venetians and the Swiss, to drive the Spaniards from the peninsula.   But the dream was an idle one.   Julius had riveted the chains of Italian slavery, and done much to advance the power of that formidable Austro-Spanish House

[1] See Appendix iv,

which was shortly to become so dangerous a menace to
Europe, and to control the destinies of Italy till our own
day.   None the less, the name of Pope Julius will always live
as the founder of the Papal States, as the last representative
of that great semi-political, semi-religious Church, whose
claims to universal supremacy over western Christendom were
on the point of being overthrown ; as the patron of Bramante,
Michael Angelo, and Raphael, the authors of those supreme
efforts of Renaissance art, the Cathedral of St. Peter,[1] and
the frescoes of the Sistine Chapel, and of the Vatican.

Of all the schemes of Julius II., few had more influence
on the immediate history of Italy and of the Papacy than
the restoration of the Medici to Florence.   He
had been led to it by the obstinate adherence of
the republic to Louis XII.   But the policy was a
mistaken one.   The republic was weak and could not have
had much influence, whereas, under the Medici, allied as
they were with Spain, Florence was likely to become formidable again.   Julius, however, could hardly have foreseen that
a family, which had only just been restored from exile, would
furnish his successor on the papal throne ; for the election of
the young Cardinal Giovanni de' Medici—he was only thirty-
eight—surprised every one.

*Election of
Leo X.
March 11, 1513.*

Giovanni, the second son of Lorenzo the Magnificent,
appointed a cardinal before he was a man, had indeed shown
himself a capable politician by the leading part he had taken
in the restoration of his family to Florence.   He was not,
however, otherwise noteworthy, and his election was due
mainly to the desire of the young cardinals for some rest
after the political activity of the pontificates of Alexander VI.
and Julius II.   This they hoped to gain by the election of the
pleasure-loving Medici, who represented the Renaissance in
its shallower aspects, loved magnificence, and dallied with
literature and art ; but had no serious purpose in life beyond

[1] Bramante began St. Peter's under Julius II., Michael Angelo added the
dome under Leo. X.

a desire to establish his family at Florence, and, for the rest, to be ever on the winning side.

But though, by the death of Julius II., the Holy League was robbed of its most earnest member, the change of Popes did not for the moment improve the prospects of peace. On the one hand France and Venice, united by common interest,

Treaty of
Mechlin.
April 5, 1513.

formed an alliance; on the other, the young Henry VIII. of England and his ambitious minister Wolsey, anxious to win a place in European counsels, pined for a new league of partition against France. This was signed at Mechlin, in April, between Maximilian, Henry VIII., Leo. X., and Ferdinand; although the last named was at the same moment making a secret treaty with the French King.

Threatened thus on all sides, France seemed likely to be overwhelmed. In Italy, her attempt to reconquer the Milanese,

Battle of
Novara.
June 6, 1513.

by the aid of the Venetians, was foiled by the disastrous battle of Novara. Here the Swiss, who looked upon Maximilian Sforza as their *protégé*, without cavalry or artillery, decisively defeated a French army three times as numerous as themselves, and well provided with both guns and horse.

Meanwhile Henry VIII., with the needy Maximilian in his pay, invaded France; laid siege to Terouenne; put a

Battle of
Guinnegate.
Aug. 16.

French relieving force to flight at Guinnegate with such ease, as to earn for the combat the name of 'the Battle of the Spurs'; and took Terouenne and Tournay. In September, the Swiss actually invaded France and extorted a treaty from Louis XII. In the

Flodden.
Sept. 9.

same month, James IV. of Scotland, as he sought to make a diversion in favour of his French ally, lost the flower of the Scottish nobility, and his own life, on the field of Flodden.

It looked as if France, the country which at first had gained most from the partition of Venice, was likely to be partitioned herself. But, as ever, the mutual jealousies of the European

powers prevented any lasting combination. Neither Ferdinand
nor Leo X. wished to see France too weak.   Leo thought
that his own interests and those of his family
would be best secured by balancing the powers   France once
of Spain and France in Italy, and hoped to secure saved
French assistance for his scheme of establishing   by dissen-
Giuliano his brother in Naples.   He accordingly   sions of her
became reconciled to the French King, and par-   foes.
doned the French cardinals, who had taken part   Ferdinand,
in the schismatic council of Pisa (November,   the Pope, and
                                                    Henry VIII.
                                                    are reconciled
                                                    to France.
1513). Ferdinand was above all things anxious to prevent the
undue aggrandisement of the House of Hapsburg.   He had
already made a secret treaty with Louis, and he now intrigued
to detach the Emperor from the English alliance.   Henry was
determined not to be thus left in the lurch.   He was irritated
at the treachery of Ferdinand, and the incurable shiftiness of
Maximilian, 'the man of few pence,' who would do anything
to gain a little money, and accordingly made his own peace
with Louis (August, 1514).   It was agreed that his sister
Mary, who had just been betrothed to Charles, the grandson
of Maximilian, should marry the French King.   The disparity
in their ages was serious.   The bridegroom was a widower
of fifty-two, and Mary was but sixteen.   But the scruples
of the maiden were overcome by the promise that, if she
would this time sacrifice herself to her brother's interests,
she should next time follow her own inclinations ; and peace
was concluded between France and England.   Thus France
escaped from her danger, and England, under the guidance
of Wolsey, had secured for herself an influential position in
Europe.

Of the folly of Louis' Italian policy, there cannot be a
doubt.   His three capital errors are thus described by
Machiavelli : 'He increased the power of the Church ; he
called the Spaniards into Italy, a foreigner as puissant as
himself ; he ruined the power of the Venetians, his best allies.'

The mutual jealousies of the other powers, indeed, saved

France itself from dismemberment.   But her resources were
terribly strained ; Spain had seized half of Navarre ; Tournay
had been lost to England ; and the attempt to hold Italy had
only proved the truth of the adage that 'Italy is the grave of
the French.'

Had Louis lived, Europe might possibly have had peace.
But the unfortunate man succumbed in three months in

Louis XII.
succeeded by
Francis I.
Jan. 1515.

his attempt to play the bridegroom, 'dining at
eight when he was accustomed to dine at midday,
and retiring to bed at midnight when he was wont
to sleep at six,' and was succeeded by his ambitious
cousin, Francis of Angoulême, who had, in 1514, married the
king's daughter, Claude, heiress through her mother to the
Duchy of Brittany.

The young king, now in his twenty-first year, is thus described by Sir Robert Wingfield, the ambassador of Henry VIII.
at the court of Maximilian : 'He is mighty insatiable, always
reading or talking of such enterprises as whet and inflame
himself and his hearers.   His common saying is, that his
trust is, that by his valour and industry the things which have
been lost and lettyn by his ignoble predecessors shall be
recovered, and that the monarchy of Christendom shall rest
under the banner of France as it was wont to do.'   Encouraged
by his mother, Louise of Savoy, who was bent on the exalta-
tion of her 'Cæsar,' he was no sooner on the throne than

Francis de-
termines to
invade Italy.
His treaties
with Venice,
England, and
Charles.

he resolved to plunge into Italy and wipe out the
disgrace of Novara.   In the spring and summer,
he renewed the treaties with Henry VIII. and
Venice, and concluded an alliance with the young
Charles, who, although only fifteen, had just been
called to assume the government of the Netherlands, and who, under the guidance of Croy, the Lord of
Chièvres, had adopted a conciliatory attitude towards France.
Francis also hoped to gain the support of Leo x.   In February,
he sanctioned the marriage of Giuliano de' Medici, the brother
of the Pope, with Philiberta of Savoy, sister of his mother

Louise, and held out hopes of some day establishing him in Naples.

The fickle Pontiff, however, was as usual playing double, and in the same month joined the counter-league against France, which was composed of the Emperor, Ferdinand, Florence, the Duke of Milan, and the Swiss. Had the allies been united it might have gone ill for Francis, but they were bent on their own interests, and divided their forces. Counter-
League
against
France. Francis, finding that the outlet of the passes of the Mont Cenis and Mont Genèvre were guarded by the Swiss, pushed his way across the Alps by the Col de l'Argentière, a new and difficult route, and reached Saluzzo unmolested. He then surprised Prospero Colonna, who commanded the Milanese forces at Villafranca, and completely turned the position of the Swiss at Susa. The Swiss dropped back on Milan, and the French advanced to Marignano, a place between Piacenza and Milan. Here, late on a September afternoon, they were attacked by the Swiss. Francis
crosses the
Alps,
Aug. 1515.
Victory of
Marignano,
Sept. 13. The intrepid mountaineers had been stirred by the eloquence of Mathias Schinner, the Cardinal of Sion, the life-long enemy of the French. With only a few Milanese cavalry to support them, and scarcely any guns, they trusted to the weight of their famous phalanx, and push of pike. The French they despised as 'hares in armour.' Disencumbered of their caps, and with bare feet to give themselves firmer footing, they dashed upon the enemy, hoping to repeat the exploit of Novara. But they underrated their opponents, who were led by the flower of French chivalry, the Constable of Bourbon, La Palice, the Chevalier Bayard, Robert de la Marck, the son of the 'devil of the Ardennes,' himself dubbed 'L'Aventureur,' and the Milanese, Trivulzio, who had fought in seventeen pitched battles. Pedro Navarra, the Spanish general of artillery, was also there. He had been made prisoner at the battle of Ravenna, and since the niggardly Ferdinand had refused to pay his ransom, he had taken service with the French.

The struggle which ensued was declared by Trivulzio to be a battle of giants, compared with which, all that he had ever been engaged in were but child's-play. When darkness came upon the combatants, they lay down to sleep 'within cast of a tennis ball of each other.' With the dawn the combat was renewed, and continued till midday. The Swiss had divided their forces in an attempt on the rear-guard, when d'Alviano attacked them in the rear with the Venetian contingents. This decided the matter, and Francis, knighted on the battle-field by the Chevalier Bayard, remained the master of the field. Yet though defeated, the Swiss retreated in good order, bearing their wounded with them.

The battle of Marignano gave Milan to the French. Maximilian Sforza abdicated his dukedom, which he had held for three years, and died some years after, a pensioner in France. By his victory, Francis shattered the military prestige of the Swiss, who had of late deemed themselves invincible, commanded the destinies of Lombardy, and 'tamed and corrected princes.' Never again did these mercenaries exercise an independent influence in Italy. Thus Francis had attained at one stroke the pinnacle of military glory, and, had he pressed his advantage, might have reduced the Pope and regained the kingdom of Naples. But for this he was not prepared, and, contrary to expectation, the battle for a moment promoted the cause of peace. Leo, eager to join the winning cause, hastened to come to terms. He ceded Parma and Piacenza, while Francis promised to support Lorenzo in Florence, and to sanction the papal attack on the Duchy of Urbino, whence Francesco della Rovere, the Duke, was driven. A short time afterwards, Francis gave Lorenzo a wife connected with the royal family, Madeleine de la Tour d'Auvergne.

Having thus settled their political affairs, Pope and King proceeded, by the concordat of Bologna, to share between them the liberties of the Gallican Church. The traditional privileges of the Church of France had been confirmed and

Results of the victory.

extended by Charles VII. in the Pragmatic Sanction of Bourges (1439). By it, the free election to bishoprics and abbacies had been secured to the chapters; the papal claims to first-fruits had been rejected, as well as the right to nominate to benefices by way of 'reservations' and 'expectancies'; appeals to Rome had been restricted, and the superiority of General Councils over the Pope had been declared. The independence thus gained by the Church of France had been distasteful, not only to the Pope, but to Louis XI. himself, who had attempted, though unsuccessfully, to repeal the Pragmatic Sanction. Now Francis had his opportunity, and was met half-way by Leo X. The Concordat of Bologna restrained indeed the appeals to Rome, and declared papal 'reservations' and 'expectative graces' abolished. But it restored the first-fruits to the Pope, omitted the assertion of the superiority of General Councils over the Pope, and gave to the King the right of nomination to bishoprics and archbishoprics, subject only to the papal confirmation and institution. A few years later, the King gained the same privilege with regard to the abbots of French monasteries. This serious attack on the constitutional liberties of the Church of France met with resolute opposition from the ' Parlement' and the University of Paris. But the ' Parlement,' after an ineffectual resistance, was forced to register it *de expressimo mandato regis*, the University was overawed by royal threats, and the Concordat became the law of France. Henceforth the French Church became the servant of King and Pope. The power, which the crown obtained by control of these nominations, may be estimated by remembering that in France at that time there existed ten archbishoprics, eighty-three bishoprics, and five hundred and twenty-seven abbacies. This right of nomination was almost exclusively exercised in favour of men of noble birth. Hence the mischievous distinction between the higher clergy who were nobles, and, for the most part, courtiers, and the *curés*, who were not. Under these circumstances, the

The Concordat of Bologna. Aug. 1516.

position of the Church formed a counterpart to the social condition of the country, with its sharp and disastrous division between the noble and the *roturier*. On the other hand, the right of veto enjoyed by the Pope on the royal nominations caused the higher clergy and the aspirants for office to look to him. Thus the Church of France, once the most independent of the European churches, became one of the most servile and ultramontane, whilst its rulers lost all touch with the middle classes.

Meanwhile, the policy of Ferdinand had changed. Since the death of the Archduke Philip, the King of Spain had been jealous of his grandson Charles. He feared lest he might reclaim the regency of Castile, and disliked the prospect of his eventually joining Austria, the Netherlands, and Spain under one rule. His hostility even led him to entertain serious thoughts of dividing his inheritance on his death between Charles and his brother Ferdinand. Now, fearing that France might become too powerful, he changed his will and bequeathed all to Charles. In January, 1516, the wily old diplomatist, who had so adroitly schemed to establish his undivided authority in Spain, and to balance the powers of Europe, died, and Charles found himself, at the age of sixteen, the ruler of Spain, the Netherlands, the kingdoms of Naples and Sicily, and the New World.

Death of Ferdinand the Catholic, Jan. 23, 1516. Charles King of Spain.

It was now the aim of Wolsey, who had gained his cardinal's hat in the previous year, to oppose the predominant power of France by an alliance between Charles, Maximilian, the Pope, and the Swiss. But Leo for the present preferred the French alliance, and Charles was not yet prepared for a struggle with Francis. His position was by no means secure; his succession in Spain was disliked by many of the Spaniards; the Netherlands lay exposed to the attacks of the Duke of Gueldres, and of Robert de la Marck, the Lord of Bouillon, both ever glad of a pretext for war. Finally, with all his titles, he was sadly in need of money. He was therefore in no position to contest the possession of Milan, and, following the advice of Chièvres, he concluded the Peace of Noyon with the victor of Marignano (August 13, 1516). Charles was betrothed to Louise, the infant daughter of Francis; the French retained Milan, but surrendered all claims to Naples; Charles promised to restore Spanish Navarre to the line of Albret; Venice agreed to offer 200,000 ducats to Maximilian for Brescia and Verona, but in the event of his refusing, the two Kings might adopt what policy they liked with regard to Venetian affairs.

Charles makes Peace of Noyon with Francis, Aug. 13, 1516, which Maximilian accepts.

The Peace of Noyon was a blow to Wolsey. In vain did he try to form an alliance with Maximilian, the Venetians, and the Swiss. The Emperor was ever ready with fantastic projects calculated to deceive the simple Sir Robert Wingfield, Henry's representative at his court, who was an ambassador of the old generation, and did not fathom the wiles of the new diplomacy. But Richard Pace, Wolsey's special agent, warned his master against the credulity of the good knight, whom he humorously describes as 'Summer will be green,' and against the shiftiness and money greed of Maximilian. Eventually, in December, Maximilian accepted the terms of the treaty of Noyon, and surrendered Brescia and Verona to Venice. Nor was Wolsey more successful with the Swiss. In November, in return for gold, they made a 'perpetual peace' with the French at Friburg. England seemed to be isolated once more. But the desire of Francis to recover Tournay, which had been seized by Henry VIII. in 1513, gave Wolsey an advantage, and by the Treaty of London (October, 1518), Henry surrendered that town. The alliance between the two countries was confirmed by the usual marriage arrangements. The English princess Mary, a child of two, was betrothed to the dauphin, who was not yet one year old. Thus England had at least saved herself from isolation, and Europe was at peace.

Henry VIII. makes Treaty of London, Oct. 1518. Europe for the moment at Peace.

The Pope, when he dissolved the Lateran Council in the March of the preceding year, had declared that schism had been ended, that the necessary reforms in the Church had been accomplished, and that he had good hopes that Europe, now at peace, might unite against the Turk. The powers of Europe openly professed their intention so to do ; indulgences were promised, and papal collectors attempted to raise money. Yet Europe was on the threshold of a renewed struggle between the Houses of Hapsburg and of Valois, which was to last with some slight pauses for another eighty years ; and already Luther had affixed his famous ' Theses' to the church door at Wittenberg, which were to lead to a schism such as Rome had never dreamt of.

The series of treaties just mentioned may be said to have closed the desultory war which had commenced with the League of Cambray. It is often said that the League ruined Venice, yet we find that she still retained almost all her dominions on the mainland, with the exception of the Apulian towns and a few districts surrendered to the Pope, and that the Adda still remained her boundary on the west. The long war had no doubt severely strained her resources and her exhausted finances, but these might have been restored. We must therefore look elsewhere for the causes of the decline of Venice. In the first place, the condition of politics had changed. The great monarchical states of Europe, more especially France and Spain, had become consolidated. Venice could no longer hope to compete with them ; her resources on the mainland were not sufficient to cope with the armies which these powerful nations could put into the field ; and in any case she must have contented herself with a subordinate position. We must also remember the strain of the Turkish wars. Europe, ever ready to accuse Venice of treachery to the cause of Christendom, turned deaf ears to her earnest entreaties for assistance. Thus Venice was left almost alone to face the

Marginal notes:

Effect of the Wars of the League of Cambray on the decline of Venice.

Real causes of the decline of Venice.

Turk. During the struggle, which continued with some few intermissions throughout the sixteenth and seventeenth centuries, Venice slowly lost ground. She had to surrender Cyprus in 1571, and Candia in 1669, after a desperate defence of four-and-twenty years. The expenses of these wars, added to those she had just incurred, would have been difficult to meet, even if her trade had been left to her. But even this was slipping away. Her wealth had depended chiefly on her commerce with the East and on her carrying-trade between East and West. The old routes of Eastern commerce had been mainly three. First, from Central Asia to the Black Sea, and thence to the Mediterranean; secondly, by the Persian Gulf and the Euphrates Valley, to the Levant; and lastly, to Cairo and Alexandria from the Red Sea. Thence goods were shipped in Venetian galleys to Venice, and were sent over the Alps, generally by the Brenner Pass, to the Inn, the Danube, the Maine, and the Rhine, and thence to Bruges, or were conveyed round by sea in the 'Flanders galleys.' But at the beginning of the sixteenth century, the Eastern routes to Venice became closed. The Turks, after their conquest of Constantinople, in 1453, cut off her trade with the Levant, while the advance of the Portuguese on India destroyed the trade through Egypt.

The old routes of commerce altered by discovery of route round the Cape.

The Genoese had been the pioneers of exploration on the western coast of Africa. They had rediscovered the Canaries and the island of Madeira, which had been known to the Carthaginians. But their attention had been directed to the Mediterranean, their strength exhausted in struggles with their Venetian rivals, and in the fourteenth century the Portuguese had reoccupied these islands. The great period of Portuguese discovery dates from the time of Prince Henry the Navigator (1394-1460). This son of John I. of Portugal built an observatory at Sagres, on Cape St. Vincent, the extreme south-west promontory of Europe, and devoted himself to the scientific study of

Discoveries of the Portuguese.

geography, and to the encouragement of discovery. Other motives were not wanting; the desire to avenge himself on the Moors, the hereditary foes of his country, and greed for gold dust, and the profits of the slave-trade, in which the Prince was the first to engage. In one expedition no less than two hundred and sixteen negro slaves were brought to Portugal, of whom one-fifth were assigned to Henry as his share; 'of which,' says the chronicler, 'he had great joy because of their salvation, who otherwise would have been destined to perdition.' Under his influence, the Portuguese planted colonies at Porto Santo and Madeira, discovered the Azores, and the Cape de Verde Islands, and began to creep down the western coast of Africa. In 1442, Prince Henry obtained from Pope Martin v. a grant of all kingdoms and lordships from Cape Bojador to India. The hopes of reaching India spurred him on. In 1479, Ferdinand of Spain, still occupied at home with the Moors of Granada, agreed not to interfere with the exclusive right of the Portuguese to traffic and discovery on the western coast of Africa, while claiming the Canary Islands. The agreement was confirmed by the bull of Alexander vi., which gave to Portugal all newly found lands east of a line one hundred—subsequently, in 1494, extended by treaty to three hundred and seventy —leagues west of the Cape de Verde Islands.

Eight years before this bull, Bartholomew Diaz rounded the Cape, to which he gave the name of Stormy, but which his more sanguine sovereign, John ii. of Portugal, called the Cape of Good Hope. In 1498, Vasco da Gama, again sailing round the Cape, crossed the Eastern Ocean, and set foot on the Malabar coast at Calicut. Shortly after, Emmanuel, King of Portugal (1495-1521), assumed the title of 'Lord of the navigation, conquest, and commerce of Æthiopia, Persia, Arabia, and India,' and sent Almeyda to India with the title of viceroy, although he did not yet possess a foot of territory there. The Portuguese now pushed steadily up the western coast of India, defeated the princes who opposed them, and

began to monopolise the trade.   In 1505, the first Portuguese
ships appeared at Antwerp, offering eastern wares at a cheaper
rate than they could be got at Bruges, the market for the goods
which came overland from Venice.   This advance seriously
threatened the Venetian trade through Egypt, then chiefly in
the hands of Arabian and Moorish merchants.   Accordingly,
in 1509, the Sultan of Cairo, in answer to an appeal from
some of the petty princes of the Malabar coast, despatched
an expedition from Suez against the Portuguese, which the
Venetians, conscious that their interests were involved, assisted.
But in February 1509, three months before the battle of
Agnadello, the expedition was defeated by Almeyda in the
harbour of Diu.   His successor Albuquerque fixed the centre of
the Portuguese rule at Goa, and occupied Ormuz,   Defeat of
an important port on the Persian Gulf.   Hence-   Egyptian
forth the advance of the Portuguese was un-   fleet by
checked.   By the close of the sixteenth century   at Diu.
not only did they control the commerce of the   Feb. 1509.
coasts of Africa, Arabia, and the western coast of India, but
they had planted themselves at Ceylon and in Bengal, had
opened up a trade with China and Japan, and, above all, had
occupied the true 'Spice Islands' which cluster round Borneo
and Celebes (1546).

Thus the same spring witnessed the fall of the Venetian
military power in the battle of Agnadello, and the destruction
of their trade with the East.   The caravans no longer came to
Cairo.   The eastern goods were shipped round the Cape.   The
mediæval trade-routes were revolutionised, and the carrying
trade passed from the Venetians to the Portuguese, shortly
to be followed by the Dutch and English, while Antwerp
took the place of Bruges as the 'entrepôt' in the North.
Finally, the conquest of Egypt by Selim I. (1516) destroyed
what remained of the Egyptian trade.   This loss of commerce
prevented Venice from recovering from her financial straits,
and was the chief cause of her decline.

The effect on the internal politics of the city was also fatal.

The nobility, who had hitherto enriched themselves by trade, either took to banking, which could not last without the aliment of commerce, or invested their savings in land, and became an idle class.   Poverty increased, and the aristocracy of Venice was weakened by internal feuds.   The rich monopolised the administration, while the less fortunate, with a majority in the Great Council, were ever attempting to overthrow their power by agitation, or by intrigues and plots, often with foreigners. Thus Venice, which had long been the admiration of Europe for the stability of her government, and the honour and patriotism of her nobility, became the victim of selfishness, corruption, and conspiracy.   It is this which explains the growing power of 'The Ten.'   This executive committee, an excrescence on the original constitution, first organised for temporary objects in 1310, assumed more and more the character of a committee of public safety, and with the three inquisitors, created in 1539 to deal more efficiently with treason, gave to the government a character of mystery, suspicion, and cruelty, hitherto unknown.   A loss of moral tone accompanied this decline.   As the wealth of the state decreased, the extravagance, both public and private, grew. At no date were the public pageants so magnificent, or the private luxury so unbridled.   In more vital questions of morality, though Venice had never maintained a high standard, even for Italy, she now fell lower, and private crime went almost unpunished.   It would be absurd to attribute this degradation entirely to the loss of her prestige and power, but that it was increased thereby no one can doubt.   Yet Venice still survived.   Protected by her impregnable position, and served by her clever diplomatists, who resided at every court and carefully steered the country through the mazes of European intrigue, she continued the Queen of the Lagoons, if no longer of the Mediterranean, 'The admiredst citie of the world' for her buildings, her blue lagoons, and azure skies.

In the domain of art she had something still to give the

world.   The sixteenth century is the age of Titian (1477-1576), Tintoret (1512-1594), and Paolo Veronese (1532-1588), in whose works painting reached its climax of technique, of elaborate and harmonious grouping, and of gorgeous, if somewhat sensuous, colour; while to the Aldine Press we owe some of the earliest triumphs of the art of printing.

In her struggle with the Papacy, in the later decades of the sixteenth and the first of the seventeenth centuries, Venice showed the world once more, as she had in days gone by, that though she accepted her religion from Rome, she was determined and powerful enough to maintain her independence in matters of church government.

Finally, in her long contests with the Turk, notably in the wars of Cyprus (1570-1571), and of Candia (1645-1669), she displayed a heroism which recalled the greatness of her past, and which, but for the abominable selfishness of Europe, might have checked the advance of that Power which could conquer, but knew not how to rule, or to develop the resources of subject lands.

CHAPTER II

Administration of Cardinal d'Amboise—Union of Crowns of Castile and
Aragon—Policy of Ferdinand and Isabella—Ximenes—Spanish Conquests
in Africa—Discovery of America—Character of Isabella and Ferdinand—
Results of their Policy—Maximilian and the Empire—Diet of Worms—
Attempted reforms—Opposition of Maximilian—Diet of Augsburg—
Compact of Gelnhausen—The Landshut Succession—Results of attempts
at reform—The Swiss Confederation—War with Maximilian—Peace of
Basel—Policy and character of Maximilian.

§ 1. *France.*

THE most important events in the internal history of France
during the reigns of Charles VIII. and Louis XII. have
already been mentioned. The nation, engaged
in war abroad, enjoyed peace at home. The
nobles, reduced in number, found, in the Italian
wars, satisfaction for their ambition, and did not disturb the
country with their feuds. Under the administration of the
Cardinal, Georges d'Amboise, the minister of Louis XII.
(1498-1510), the country prospered. Population increased
rapidly and towns grew. One-third of the land, we are told,
was again restored to cultivation. In a word, France, having
at last escaped from the disastrous English wars, showed her
marvellous power of recuperation. Nor was she behindhand in art. In the reign of Louis XII., the domestic architecture of the early Renaissance style reached, perhaps, its
highest point of excellence before it became over-refined and
overloaded with ornament : witness the eastern façade of the
chateau of Blois, and part of the chateau of Amboise ; while
so renowned were the glass painters of France that Julius II.
sent for the artists, Claude and William de Marseille, to help
decorate the windows of the Vatican.

*Internal
condition
of France.*

Louis earned the title of Father of his People, and the popularity of the cardinal is illustrated by the proverb, 'Leave things to Georges.' Nothing, indeed, was done to strengthen the constitutional liberties of the country. The Estates-General won no extension of their privileges. Although Louis forbade the sale of judicial offices, he really extended the evil system by openly applying it to the financial offices. Yet, if the government was despotic, it was at least kindly; and if the taxes were heavy, the poor were not oppressed. Indeed, if we confine our view to the domestic policy, we should not perhaps be wrong in holding that the popularity was well earned. If Louis had only refrained from the Italian wars, his reign might have been a turning-point in the history of his country, and in a few years she might have become the richest and most powerful country in Europe.

But if the internal history of France during the period we have covered is uneventful, far different is the case of Spain and Germany.

§ 2. *Spain.*

By the accession of Isabella to the throne of Castile in 1474, and of her husband, Ferdinand the Catholic, to that of Aragon in 1479, not only did these two countries escape from a long period of internal anarchy, but the rivalry hitherto existing between Castile and Aragon was put an end to, and, while the *Union of the Crowns of Castile and Aragon.* autonomy of the two governments was preserved, the policy which guided them was one. In their determination to increase the power of the crown at home and the prestige of their nation abroad, Isabella and Ferdinand were in singular agreement. The most startling events of their reigns either occurred before the beginning of our period, or have been already mentioned. In 1492, Granada had been conquered from the Moors; and the expulsion of the Jews, the establishment of the Inquisition, even the discovery of Hispaniola by Columbus, had also occurred before the Italian wars.

At this time, the policy of Ferdinand and Isabella was mainly devoted to the formation of a great European alliance

The Policy of Ferdinand and Isabella. Marriage Alliances. based upon the tie of marriage, whereby they might at once strengthen themselves against the formidable power of France, and contribute to the further consolidation of the Spanish Peninsula.

With this end in view, their eldest daughter, Isabella, was given in marriage to Alonso, the Prince of Portugal, and on his death to his kinsman, Emanuel, who ascended the Portuguese throne in 1495. To this period also belongs the betrothal of Catherine, their youngest daughter, with Arthur, Prince of Wales (1496), an alliance which brought England into intimate relations with Spain for the first time since the days of John of Gaunt. More important was the double marriage treaty with the House of Hapsburg. It was agreed that John, the heir to the Spanish kingdom, should marry Margaret, the daughter of the Emperor Maximilian, and that the Archduke Philip, the son and heir of Maximilian, should marry Joanna, second daughter of the Spanish monarchs. The hopes founded on these marriages by Ferdinand and Isabella were not, however, realised. By the death of their only son John in 1497, and by that of Don Miguel, only son of Isabella of Portugal, in 1500, all hopes of uniting Portugal to Spain were destroyed; and Joanna, the wife of the Hapsburg prince, and mother of Charles v., became heiress of Castile and Aragon. Thus an alliance which had been originally made to protect the balance of power against France, was eventually to destroy that balance in the interest of the House of Hapsburg.

In their internal policy, Ferdinand and Isabella consistently pursued the principles adopted from the commencement of

Their internal Policy. their reigns. In no countries in Europe perhaps were privileges so strong, the crown so poor, or the royal prerogative so limited, as they were in Castile in the fifteenth century.[1] A direct attack on these ancient privileges would have been dangerous among so proud a people. The sovereigns left, therefore, the outward forms of the constitution intact, and indirectly pursued their aim by concentrating the machinery of government in the royal hands, and by strengthening the personal authority of the crown. They took advantage of the disinclination of the nobles to attend the Cortes; they omitted to summon them to it, or even to call them to their councils, and deprived the hereditary officers of state of many of their powers.

One of the most efficient instruments for keeping the nobility in check was the 'Hermandad.' This association, which had been originally organised by the principal cities of Castile to protect themselves at once against the crown and the aristocracy, had, in 1476, been reorganised under royal control. In every city of importance a court was established for the trial of highway robbery and other acts of violence. From these city courts, appeal lay to a supreme court of the whole kingdom. The courts had in their service a force of mounted police, which was maintained by a contribution levied on householders. The regulation of affairs was placed in the hands of provincial assemblies acting under a supreme 'junta,' which passed laws relating to justice, and often trenched upon the privileges of the Cortes itself. So effectual was the work of this reorganised 'Hermandad' that in 1495 its powers were considerably curtailed. A few subordinate functionaries alone were retained for the execution of justice, and these were placed under the appellate jurisdiction of the ordinary law-courts.

During this period also, the resumption of grants of royal lands to the nobility was persistently pursued, while the policy of annexing the mastership of the powerful military orders to the crown, first begun in 1487 with that of Calatrava, was completed. In 1494, the mastership of Alcantara, and in 1499, that of St. Iago of Compostella, were assumed by Ferdinand. It was not until the reign of Charles v. that

[1] For a description of the constitution of Castile and Aragon, cf. *Cambridge Mod. Hist.*, vol. i. 348 ff.

a Bull of Adrian VI. finally accorded the papal sanction to
this measure, but Ferdinand and Isabella reaped the practical
fruits of the policy.   Not only was the royal prestige thereby
materially increased, but the crown gained complete control
of wealthy and powerful organisations, which had long been
a menace to its authority, as the Hospitallers and Knight
Templars had been in other European kingdoms during the
Middle Ages.

In the kingdom of Aragon the opportunities of the crown
were not so great.   The Cortes had more extensive powers,
the nobles were more regular in their attendance, and there
were no military orders whose masterships might be annexed.
Above all, the peculiar privilege of the 'Justiza' formed a
serious obstacle to royal encroachment.   This notable officer,
elected by the Cortes, claimed the right of hearing all appeals,
of inquiring into the legality of any arrest, of advising the
King on constitutional questions, and of sharing the executive with him.   Even here, however, Ferdinand excluded his
nobles as far as possible from political power, ruled with the
aid of commoners whose fidelity could be more safely relied
upon, and introduced the Castilian Hermandad.

The Catholic sovereigns also turned their earnest attention
to church reform.   The relations between Church and State
had always been close in Spain.   The long Crusades against
the Moors had given the crown a peculiar position of which
it had taken advantage.   It was the aim of Ferdinand and
Isabella to subordinate still further the Church to the royal
will, and use it as an engine at once for extirpating heresy,
and increasing the royal authority.   Having, in 1482, gained
from Pope Sixtus IV. the right of exclusive nomination to the
higher dignities of the Church, the sovereigns proceeded to
make excellent use of their prerogative.   The sees of Spain
were filled with men of energy and devotion, and the work
of reform begun.   Cardinal Mendoza, Talavera (the first confessor of the queen), and, above all, the famous Franciscan
friar, Francisco Ximenes de Cisneros, were the chief agents
of the royal policy.

Ximenes was first appointed confessor to the Queen in 1492 at the instigation of Cardinal Mendoza, Archbishop of Toledo, and on the death of his patron (1492), was nominated as his successor to this, the richest see of Europe, as well as to the post of High Chancellor. The very elevation of this remarkable man was a blow to the privileged classes, since the see of Toledo had hitherto been exclusively reserved to men of noble birth. The appointment was even contrary to the wish of Ferdinand, who had hoped to secure the coveted position for his natural son, the Archbishop of Saragossa. The confidence of the Queen was not misplaced. The proud Castilian nobles learnt to quail before the inflexible integrity of this Franciscan friar, whom no terrors, no blandishments nor bribes could turn from his purpose. Nor were the energies of Ximenes confined to secular matters. Appointed Provincial of the Franciscans in 1494, he had zealously pressed for reform of his Order, which of late had departed from its primitive severity, owned large estates, and lived in luxury and indolence. He now extended his view, and aimed at a general reform, not only of the Franciscans, but of the monastic orders and the secular clergy in his province. In the face of much opposition, not only on the part of the General of the Franciscans, who in vain visited Castile, but of the Pope himself, the efforts of Ximenes succeeded. A Castilian writer of the following century asserts that the clergy, the monks, and the friars of Castile, once the most lax in Europe, could then compare most favourably with those of other countries. The energies of the Archbishop were also devoted to the promotion of theology and scholarship. He insisted on compliance with a papal Bull of 1474, by which stalls were to be reserved in each chapter for men of letters, canonists, and theologians. He reformed the old universities, founded and richly endowed the University of Alcala, started other schools, and caused the famous polyglot Bible to be published. This was an edition of the Scriptures in the ancient

Administra- tion of Ximenes.

languages : the Old Testament in the Hebrew original, the Septuagint version, and the Chaldaic paraphrase with Latin translations thereof; the New Testament in the original Greek, and the Vulgate of Jerome. Under his influence there arose in Spain a school of Catholic Humanists free from the taint of heresy, and it is mainly due to the efforts of the Cardinal and his royal patrons, that Protestantism gained no hold in the country, and that Spain became the centre of the future Catholic reaction.

Unfortunately, the zeal of Ximenes was not confined to these excellent objects. He burned also to be the extirpator of heresy. By the terms of the capitulation of Granada in 1492, considerable privileges had been promised to the Moors. Freedom of worship and of education, as well as personal freedom, had been secured to them. They were to live under the Mahometan laws, administered by their own judges, and to be tried by mixed tribunals. Content with their position, the Moors had settled down in tranquillity, and many had been converted by the energetic but conciliatory policy of Talavera, Archbishop of Granada. But his measures were not stringent enough for the fiery Ximenes. The promises were violated. The Arabic copies of the Koran and other theological treatises were collected and consigned to the flames, and terror was called in to further the work of proselytism. A series of revolts ensued during the years 1500-1501, revolts which seriously taxed the military energies of Castile and embittered the relations of the two nationalities. Finally in 1502, on the suppression of the rebellion, a decree was issued offering the alternative of baptism or exile to the unfortunate Moors. Meanwhile, the Inquisition assailed the Jews and any Spaniard suspected of heretical views.

Mahometanism thus nominally driven from the Peninsula, it was natural that the Spaniards should cast their eyes across the narrow channel which divided them from Africa. The ravages of Moorish pirates on the Spanish coasts, the desire of national aggrandisement, jealousy

Conquests in Africa.

at the notable advances of the Portuguese on the eastern shores of Africa, the crusading spirit engendered of their past history, all these motives urged the Spaniards to extend their dominion in the north of the great dark continent. And we cannot be surprised to find that Ximenes, true Castilian as he was, eagerly advocated such a policy. At his instigation Mazarquiver, a nest of pirates on the Barbary coast, was taken in September, 1505. In 1509, the far more important reduction of Oran followed, while, in the following year, Algiers and Tripoli submitted to the Spanish arms.

But although these African exploits fill the pages of the Spanish chroniclers, the expeditions of Columbus and his followers, which received much less support from the royal exchequer, and which attracted far less attention, were destined to play a far greater part in the future of Spain and of Europe.

That the discovery of America was so long delayed will not surprise us if we remember the following facts. The Cartha-ginians, who had done something to explore the islands off the coast of Africa, had been overthrown in their struggle with Rome. The Romans were not a seafaring people; Europe *The discovery of America. Why so long delayed.* was large enough to monopolise their energies, and for the rest their gaze turned naturally enough to Africa, or to the East, which was inseparably bound up with their traditions. After the fall of the Roman Empire it was long before her Teutonic conquerors were strong enough, or consolidated enough, to think of foreign enterprise. When that time arrived, it was only natural that they too should look eastward. The East was the birthplace of their religion, and Palestine was in the hands of the Saracens and subsequently of the Turks; the East was the fabled treasure-house of riches and of luxury. Eastward therefore the adventurer, the trader, and the pilgrim turned, and found in the Mediter-ranean their natural pathway.

Besides all this, as a glance at a physical atlas will show, the winds and the currents of that part of the Atlantic which lies in the latitude of central Europe, are not favourable to western enterprise. There westerly winds prevail throughout the year, and with greater force than those winds which occasionally blow from the north and east. Moreover, the great ocean current known as the Gulf Stream sets continuously eastwards. To the north and south of these latitudes the conditions are different. In the north, the great arctic current runs southward from Davis' Straits to Greenland, and thence to the North American shore. In the south, the equatorial current sweeps from the shores of Africa to Brazil; while immediately north of the Equator, the trade winds blow to the south-west, and south of the Equator to the north-west, continuously. It might therefore have been predicted that America would not be discovered until the northern or southern latitudes had been occupied by some seafaring nation with sufficient resources, and sufficient knowledge of navigation, to brave the unknown perils of the ocean.

In the tenth century, indeed, the Norsemen had discovered Labrador, Newfoundland, and even the mainland of North America, which they called 'Wineland.' But their numbers were insufficient, Europe offered plenty of scope for their inroads and for settlement, and the memories of Wineland remained in their sagas alone. In the southern latitudes there was little opportunity for such enterprise until the close of the fourteenth century. Then, however, as shown at p. 85, the Genoese, and subsequently the Portuguese, had begun to creep down the African coast. The primary aim of the Portuguese in their expeditions had been to seek an oceanic route to India and the east, which since the appearance of the remarkable work of Marco Polo at the end of the thirteenth century, had assumed a new importance as an earthly paradise of gold and spices.

The African mainland, it was then believed, did not reach south of the Equator. But, as the continent continued to expand before the explorers in its endless length, these ideas faded away, and hopes were entertained of seeking Asia across the Atlantic. For, that the Atlantic washed the eastern shores of Asia, was a belief which gained strength in mediæval Europe. This idea, guessed at by some of the ancients, was first definitely revived by Roger Bacon, the Franciscan schoolman of Oxford, in the thirteenth century. From him it was adopted by Peter d'Ailly, the chancellor of the University of Paris, in his treatise *de Imagine Mundi*, written early in the fifteenth century. *The idea of reaching India by the Atlantic, abandoned by the Portuguese, is taken up by Columbus.* It seemed to receive confirmation from the tradition of islands lying out far in the Atlantic, and from drift-wood carried to European shores on the Gulf Stream, and was definitely asserted by Paolo Toscanelli, a Florentine astronomer, in a letter to a monk of Lisbon, dated June 25, 1474. By that time, however, the Portuguese had made a notable advance down the western shores of Africa, and finally the discovery of the Cape of Good Hope by Bartholomew Diaz in 1486, caused them to concentrate their efforts on the eastern route.

The idea thus abandoned by the Portuguese was now to be taken up by Christopher Columbus. To appreciate the exact position of this remarkable citizen of Genoa in the history of discovery, we must remember that he had no idea of discovering a new continent. To find a shorter way to the Indies was his sole aim. His views in this respect were not beyond his age. His knowledge was based on the authorities above mentioned; and he is marked out from his contemporaries only by his determination to sail due west until he should reach the continent of Asia. With this intention, and furnished with the treatise of D'Ailly, a copy of Toscanelli's letter, and a chart given him by the author, he first applied to the court of Lisbon, where he had already settled with his brother Bartholomew. But John II. of Portugal, intent on the circum- *Columbus approaches various courts, and finally gains the support of Spain.* navigation of Africa, declined his offer, and, if we may believe some accounts,[1] his attempts to obtain assistance from Venice and Genoa were equally unsuccessful. He now, in 1484, turned to England, and to Spain.

His brother Bartholomew sailed for England, but unfortunately fell among pirates in the English Channel. Returning to Portugal, he accompanied Diaz on his expedition which reached the Cape, and though he subsequently sought the court of Henry VII., where he was well received, it was then too late: Christopher had already entered into negotiations with Ferdinand and Isabella. The affair was indeed long delayed. The Spanish Monarchs listened to his tempting scheme; but the financial strain of the war of Granada, then in progress, was severe, and the terms of Columbus were high. He demanded the hereditary office of royal admiral and viceroy in all the lands and islands he might discover, and the privileges enjoyed by the high admiral of Castile. One-tenth of all treasures—gold, or otherwise—was also to fall to his share. On the conquest of Granada, however, the contract was at last signed (April 1492), and, in the following August, Columbus left the roadstead of Palos on his memorable voyage, with three carracks, one hundred and twenty souls, and provisions for twelve months. He carried with him a letter from the Catholic sovereigns to the Khan of Cathay, and announced his intention, not only of opening the riches of the Indies to Spain, but of leading a new crusade against the infidel. The details of his voyage we must leave to others, and content ourselves with the briefest summary.

In his first expedition, after a sail of five weeks due west from the Canaries, he touched land at one of the islands of the Bahama group, and shortly after reached Crooked Island and Long Island. Understanding from the signs of the natives that gold was to be found to the south-west, he reached the shores of Cuba, and from thence the island of Hispaniola or Hayti. Here, on the night

His first expedition, 1492.

---

[1] These supposed visits to Genoa and Venice are very doubtful.

of Christmas Eve, his ship struck on the sands and became a
wreck. Pinzon, one of his subordinates, had deserted him,
hoping to be beforehand in announcing the news in Spain ;
and Columbus, leaving the crew of the wrecked *Santa Maria* in
Hayti, returned to Spain in the *Nina*, his sole remaining ship.

In his second voyage, 1493, he discovered Jamaica, and
some of the Antilles group. In his third voyage, he at last
touched the continent, and explored the coast of His later
Venezuela. This was in 1498, the same year in voyages, 1493.
which Vasco da Gama, rounding the Cape, had reached
India by the eastern route. In 1502, Columbus landed on
the coast of Honduras. But although Columbus had thus
discovered the continent of America, he had been really
forestalled in this by his compatriot John Cabot, who started
from Bristol in the pay of Henry VII., reached the coast
of North America, near the mouth of the St. Lawrence,
in 1497, and traced the coast possibly as far south as Cape
Cod. Columbus therefore was not the first to touch the
continent, and, moreover, to the day of his death believed that
Cuba was part of the mainland of Asia, and that Hispaniola
and the other islands he had found lay in the Asian Archipelago.

Meantime, his governorship of his colony in Hispaniola
was so unsuccessful that he had been removed by the command of his royal masters in 1498. Although His failure as
Ferdinand and Isabella may be open to the a Governor.
charge of some ingratitude in their treatment of one who had
done so much for the cause of Spain, Columbus had certainly
shown himself incapable as a ruler, and it was out of the
question that they should fulfil all the promises originally
made to him. He had, indeed, been the unconscious
instrument in the discovery of South America, but the
determination he displayed in his first voyage forms his best
title to fame, and the true importance of his discovery was
left to be appreciated by his successors.

In 1500, Vincent Pinzon, one of the original companions
of Columbus, sailing farther southwards reached Cape St.

Agostino, at the northern extremity of the future Brazil, and
explored the coast to the north-west between that point and

Further
discoveries.

Venezuela. In the same year the Portuguese
Cabral, on his way to the Cape, was driven
to the westward and again reached Brazil, which was then
claimed by Portugal, as falling within the limits of the line
drawn by the Treaty of Tordesillas (p. 86). In the succeeding year, 1501, the country was more completely explored by
Amerigo Vespucci. This Florentine, who was once in the
employ of Spain, but had deserted to the service of Portugal,
now traced the coast line down as far as Rio de Janeiro—a
point far to the southward of any yet reached—and by a
curious literary freak was destined to give his name to this
New World. The 'New World,' however, was still supposed
to be either a huge promontory of Asia, or a large island
lying in the Atlantic. Five years later, Columbus died in
Spain, in obscurity, and almost forgotten. After his death the
discoveries continued apace.

In 1512, Ponce de Leon, a colonist of Hispaniola, discovered or explored Florida. Shortly after, the Gulf of Mexico
was again entered, and the continuity between North and South
America demonstrated. In 1513, Vasco Nuñez de Balbao
crossed the Isthmus of Darien, and from the summit of the
Cordilleras gazed on the waters of the Pacific. So strong, however, was the belief in the Columbian hypothesis, that this great
ocean was still believed by many to be but an inland sea.[1]

The final explosion of this idea was probably due to the
Portuguese advance in the East. During the early years of

America
discovered
to be a new
Continent
by Magellan,
1519.

the sixteenth century they had gradually crept
round the shores of Asia. Fernan de Andrade
explored part of the Asian Archipelago, and, in
1517, reached Canton. In some of these Portuguese expeditions Magellan had taken a part.
It was the knowledge thus acquired of a great sea to the

[1] On this point cf. Ruge, *Geschichte des Zeitalters der Entdeckungen*,
p. 458 ff.

east of Asia which led him to conceive his great exploit of seeking a western approach through the newly discovered world of America to Asia. Piqued by the refusal of Emmanuel of Portugal to increase his pay, he entered the service of the young Charles v., and in September 1519, started on his notable voyage. After thirteen months' sail, he discovered the Straits which are known by his name. It took him three months more to reach the Philippines. On the 27th of April, 1521, the intrepid seaman was unfortunately slain on one of the Ladrone islands in an attempt to aid a native Christian convert against his enemies, and eventually only one of his fleet of five ships returned to Spain (September, 1522). At last the globe had been circumnavigated; and though it took two centuries to work out the precise size of America and its relation to Asia, it had at least been proved to be a 'New World' in a sense hitherto never dreamt of. Meanwhile Mexico had been conquered by Cortes (1519-21), and in 1524 Pizarro began the conquest of Peru.

Some twenty days after the return of Columbus from his last voyage, the great Queen of Castile had passed away (November 26, 1504), in the fifty-fourth year of her age, and the thirtieth of her reign. No queen of Spain, and few queens in Europe have ever enjoyed such a reputation. She represents in a striking way the virtues and weaknesses of her times Of genuine and unaffected piety; affable, yet dignified; stern in the execution of her duty; gifted with rare fortitude, magnanimity, and disinterestedness, and with a true insight into the needs of her kingdom, she was admirable as a woman, and every inch a queen. The only blemish in her otherwise fine character is to be found in her persecuting spirit. The establishment of the Inquisition, the expulsion of the Jews, and subsequently the violation of the terms promised the Moors at the capitulation of Granada, these all met with her full approval. But in justice to Isabella it must be remembered that she shared this spirit of intolerance

Death of
Isabella,
Nov. 26, 1504.
Her character.

with the best men of the age, and that the time had not yet come when toleration was thought of, or perhaps was possible.

Her husband Ferdinand, who survived her twelve years, was not nearly so fine or attractive a character. Crafty, in an Character of age remarkable for its diplomatic faithlessness, he Ferdinand. prided himself on often having deceived others without himself ever having been duped. Suspicious, and often ungrateful to those who had served him best, with a cold and calculating heart which was rarely stirred by any generous emotion, he seemed unworthy of his wife. Yet it must be remembered that state-craft was then looked upon as virtue in a prince; that his contemporaries, if less successful in their falseness, were not more honest; and that his statesmanship was guided on the whole by a true insight into the needs of his country. He supported, and for the most part originated, the schemes for the consolidation of the royal authority, and, as long as Isabella lived, worked heartily for the union of the two kingdoms.

After her death, he seemed at times to waver in his policy. In the autumn of 1505, he married Germaine de Foix, in the His policy hopes of having a son by her who might succeed after the death to Aragon, hopes which, if realised, would have of Isabella. destroyed that union of the two kingdoms for which he had hitherto worked. Jealousy of the House of Hapsburg was, however, the explanation of this move. By the death of Isabella the crown of Castile had fallen to Joanna. As she had already begun to show signs of madness,[1] Ferdinand claimed the regency. This was, however, disputed by her husband, the Archduke, and eventually, in June 1506, Ferdinand had to yield. The death of Philip on the following September 25, removed, indeed, Ferdinand's more immediate apprehensions, yet transferred the claims of the Archduke to

---

[1] The madness of Joanna has been denied by Bergenroth, *State Papers*, London 1868, supplement to vol. i. 11. But cf. Gachard, *Sur Jeanne La Folle*, Brussels, 1869; Rösler, *Johanna die Wahnsinnige*, Vienna, 1870 ? Ranke, *Latin and Teutonic Nations*, Bk. II. ch. ii., note.

his young son Charles. Disappointed in his hopes of a male heir by his second wife, the King in his later years is said to have thought of leaving his dominions to Ferdinand, his younger grandson. The old diplomatist foresaw the danger both to Spain and Europe involved in the consolidation of so wide a dominion in Charles' hands. Had he had his will, he would have secured Italy and Spain for Ferdinand, Charles' younger brother, and thus balanced the power of Austria by that of Spain and France. But the victory of Francis at Marignano (September, 1515) aroused once more his apprehensions of French supremacy. The counsels of Ximenes prevailed, and on his death (January 23, 1516), the whole of the magnificent inheritance passed on unimpaired to Charles of Austria.[1]

The reigns of Ferdinand and Isabella form the turning-point in the history of Spain. Succeeding to their respective possessions after long periods of anarchy and civil discord, they had re-established order, and bridled the turbulence of the nobility. Their kingdoms, which had been divided by long-standing national rivalries, were united, never to be again dismembered. The confines of their territory had been extended by the conquests of Granada and Spanish Navarre, and now comprised the whole of the Peninsula with the exception of Portugal. To this had been added the conquests in Italy and on the north coast of Africa, while the discoveries in the New World were soon to give Spain a dominion upon which the sun never set. The infantry and artillery, reorganised by Gonzalvo de Cordova, and Pedro Navarra, had already become the terror of Europe, and Spain had definitely, and for the first time, established her position as one of the leading powers of Europe.

Importance of the reigns of Ferdinand and Isabella.

Yet amidst all these appearances of outward greatness, signs of coming trouble might have been detected. The union of the kingdoms was not more than a personal one. No constitutional unity had been effected, and the national rivalries were deep-seated. The nobility had been kept in

[1] Isabella had left Castile to Joanna, and after her to Charles, and Ferdinand did the same with Aragon. But Ximenes proclaimed Charles king conjointly with his mother ; and her madness made Charles practically sole king.

control, but their power was not gone, and the absence of all real constitutional liberty was to lead to the revolt of the 'Communeros' under Charles v. Above all, the bigotry which had led to the establishment of the Inquisition, the expulsion of the Jews, and the proscription of the Moors, was soon to destroy all liberty of opinion. The greed for the precious metals which accompanied the discovery of the New World, had already led to an inordinate belief in their value, and to a neglect and even a proscription of trade which was shortly to ruin the commercial prosperity of the country.

§ 3. *Germany.*

The history of Germany during the period we have covered (1494-1519), comprises almost exactly the reign of the Emperor Maximilian I. Elected King of the Romans during the lifetime of his father, Frederick III., he had of late practically controlled affairs, and, on Frederick's death in 1493, he quietly succeeded him. Our attention throughout the reign must be mainly directed to a consideration of those attempted reforms of the imperial constitution which, in their origin, and in their comparative failure, illustrate forcibly the weakness of Germany, and the fatal conflict of interests which prevailed.

Internal history of Germany during the reign of Maximilian, 1493-1519.

While the other kingdoms of northern Europe were becoming consolidated under the strong rule of a monarch, it was otherwise with Germany. The Holy Roman Emperor, in theory at least the temporal head of Europe, and still enjoying considerable prestige on that account, was, so far as his actual authority in Germany went, the weakest monarch in Europe. The office was considered too dignified a one to become hereditary, and, like that of the Pope, the spiritual head of Europe, was elective.[1] The

The Imperial Constitution.

---

[1] On election he assumed the title 'The King of the Romans.' But coronation by the Pope was then held necessary for the assumption of the title 'Holy Roman Emperor.' Frederick III. was, however, the last Emperor crowned at Rome; Maximilian in 1508, assumed the title of

electoral privilege was vested in seven Electors; the three Archbishops of Mainz (Mayence), Trier (Trèves), and Köln (Cologne), the Duke of Saxony, the Margrave of Brandenburg, the Count Palatine of the Rhine, and the King of Bohemia. Of these seven Electors all, with the exception of the King of Bohemia, who took no part in the legislative affairs of the Empire, formed the first college of the Diet. Below it stood two other colleges; that of the Princes, spiritual and lay; and that of the Imperial Cities, which had only lately obtained a place. The Diet deliberated on imperial questions, passed laws with the assent of the Emperor, and issued the ban of the Empire against the recalcitrant. But the rivalries between the three colleges, and between the Diet and the Emperor, prevented effective legislation, and it was still more difficult to get laws obeyed, or ban enforced.

The Diet was in no real sense a representative assembly. With the exception of the deputies of the Imperial Cities, who were few in number and played an unimportant part, the members sat in their own right,[1] while the lesser nobility, the Imperial Knights, were entirely excluded. This numerous and influential class claimed to hold immediately of the Emperor, and refused to pay the taxes levied by the Diet. Owners, perhaps of one, perhaps of several villages, they entrenched themselves in their strong castles, levied tolls and exercised other rights of petty sovereignty, and, profiting by the old German privilege of private war, disturbed the country with their quarrels and their raids. Nor was the system of imperial justice in any better plight. This lay with the court of the Emperor, called, since 1486, the Imperial Chamber (*Reichskammergericht*). But its jurisdiction was disliked as

'Roman Emperor elect' with the assent of the Pope; and after Charles v., who was crowned at Bologna (1529), no Emperor sought for coronation from the Pope.

[1] Besides the Princes who enjoyed an individual vote (*Virilstimme*), there were three collective votes (*Curiatstimmen*)—that of the Prelates who were not princes, and those of the Suabian and Wetterabian Graves and Barons.

being too much under the control of the Emperor. The Electors claimed to be free from its jurisdiction, except on appeal for refusal of justice, and in the other states it was impossible to get its verdicts enforced.

The weakness of the imperial system was also displayed in its military organisation. The imperial army was levied by a requisition of men from each Elector, Prince, or City. But the summons was often neglected, and if obeyed, resulted in the collection of a mob of ill-armed and ill-drilled soldiery, with no united organisation or even common commissariat. In a word, if we except the few occasions when the national spirit was really stirred as against the Turk, the imperial army was the laughing-stock of Germany and of Europe.

While the imperial authority, once—in theory at least—the centre of unity and control, had become a cipher, no efficient substitute had taken its place. So complete was the failure of the imperial constitution to maintain order, that Germany had of late protected itself by forming leagues. These were usually confined to one class or estate. In 1488, however, a union of the various existing leagues was established in Suabia. Joined by Cities, Knights, and Princes, it organised a common army, held a common purse, and regulated its affairs by a federal assembly consisting of two colleges. This famous Suabian League was favoured by Frederick III.; it maintained some order in the district, hitherto one of the most disturbed of Germany, and its authority was far more real than that of the Diet itself.

The reign of Frederick III., however, had witnessed a remarkable attempt on the part of the Electors to meet the most serious evils of their country. That attempt had failed; it was now to be revived. The aims of this party of reform, now led by Berthold Archbishop of Mayence, John of Baden the Archbishop of Trèves, Frederick the Wise of Saxony, and John Cicero of Brandenburg, were briefly these:

Attempted Reform of the Empire.

1. To establish and enforce 'The Public Peace' and put an end to the system of private feuds.
2. To establish a federative Court of Justice, freed from the absolute control of the Emperor, for the settlement of disputes, and the maintenance of peace.
3. To organise a more equal system of Imperial taxation under the control of the Diet.
4. To extend and complete the system of 'The Circles' for administrative purposes.
5. Finally, to establish a more effective Central Council of the Empire which might control the administration, and act as a check on the Emperor himself.

In a word, the Electors aimed at substituting a more effective system of justice, and a government freed from the irresponsible rule of the Emperor, and representing a new unity, based on a federative organisation of Germany.

Such were the reforms which the Electors demanded of Maximilian when, at the Diet of Worms, 1495, he sought the aid of the Empire for his expedition to Italy. Whether it would have been well for Germany if these reforms had been effected, is a matter much disputed.[1] Certainly they are wrong, who attribute the cry for reform solely to a selfish desire on the part of a few Electors for personal aggrandisement and independence. Yet who can doubt that the movement, if successful, would have resulted in the establishment of an aristocratic federation, primarily in the interest of the Electors and greater Princes— a federation which would have been unpopular with the smaller Princes, the Knights, and the other classes below them? Whether such a federation would have stopped the tendencies towards separation, and given Germany a new centre of unity, must ever remain doubtful. Yet the history of Germany from henceforth inclines one to believe that the cure of German evils was not to be found in this direction.

[1] Cf. *Cambridge Mod. Hist.*, vol. i. 299 ff.

In any case, the opposition of Maximilian was natural enough. He had indeed shown some sympathy with the Opposition of movement during his father's lifetime, and was not Maximilian. averse to reforms, so long as they did not weaken his own authority. Now, however, he saw more clearly their true import. Not only would they circumscribe his imperial prerogative, they would also seriously hamper his designs for the aggrandisement of his House. For although the highly romantic mind of the Emperor was not unaffected by the splendour of the imperial title, his policy was really dynastic, rather than imperial. The Empire he hoped to make practically, if not theoretically, hereditary in his family. The dignity of the office was to be enforced by the resources of the house of Hapsburg, and to be used meanwhile to further Hapsburg interests. To secure the Netherlands, to regain Hungary, and if possible, Bohemia, to reassert his claims on Italy, to overthrow the threatening power of France, these were his present aims ; while from time to time, day-dreams of an universal Empire in the future, based on a succession of brilliant marriages, and on an enlarged hereditary dominion, floated before his eyes. Thus might the anagram of his father A E I O U, 'Austriæ est imperare orbi universo,' be realised in part.[1]

With aims thus fundamentally different, real harmony between Maximilian and the Electors was impossible. Of all the projected reforms, those with regard to taxation alone met with his hearty approval, as likely to replenish his ever empty exchequer, and enable him to form a more efficient army for the prosecution of his own designs. Yet this was the one reform which the Electors cared for least. Whether therefore they would carry their projects depended on the fortunes of Maximilian. As long as he needed their assistance in men and money, something might be extorted from his weakness, but when success smiled upon him, he grew cold and opposed or postponed their schemes.

[1] This is the usual interpretation. But Ottokar Lorenz, *Deutschland Geschichtsquellen im Mittelalter*, ii. 280, reminds us that this solution is not found in the Emperor's 'Diary.' Cf. *Kollarii Analecta Monumentorum Vindobonensia*. ii. p. 675.

When in March 1495, he met the Diet of Worms, he was in need of help that he might join the League of Venice, just formed to prevent the undue extension of French influence in Italy. In return for the establishment of the Common Penny (*der gemeine Pfennig*)—that is, a tax upon all property throughout the Empire, and a poll-tax on those of small means,—he allowed the Diet to proclaim the public peace, and make it perpetual. Those who broke it were to be under the ban of the Empire.

To remove all pretext for private war, the Imperial Chamber was to be reorganised. The Emperor was to retain the right of nominating the President, the sixteen Assessors were to be elected by the Diet. The court was not to follow the Emperor, but was to have a fixed place of session, and was to be supported by imperial taxation. It was to have supreme jurisdiction in all cases arising between states of the Empire, and to hear appeals on all causes arising in their courts, except where the Prince enjoyed the *privilegium de non appellando*; and it could pronounce the ban of the Empire without the Emperor's consent. Maximilian also consented to an annual meeting of the Diet, and conceded to it the right of appropriating the proceeds of the Common Penny.

The demand for a Council of Regency (*Reichsregiment*) to control the central administration he rejected, as trenching too seriously on his prerogative. Yet five years afterwards, at the Diet of Augsburg, 1500, his difficulties were so great, and his need of help so imperious, that he yielded even on this point. His Italian expeditions of 1495 and 1498 had failed. On the day on which the Diet met, Ludovico Sforza had been taken prisoner, April 10, 1500 (cf. p. 38), and Milan was once more in French hands. Diet of Augsburg. April 1500.

The system of the Common Penny had failed, owing to the difficulty of collection. The Diet therefore ordered a levy of men for six months. Every four hundred inhabitants were to furnish one soldier, the Princes to provide the cavalry; a tax was also laid on those who did not serve. In return, the

Emperor consented to the establishment of the Council of Regency (*Reichsregiment*). This standing Council of the Empire was to be formed of a President, one Elector, one Bishop, one Prince, one Count, and sixteen representatives of the States. It was to summon the Diet, of which it served as a standing committee, to nominate the members of the Imperial Chamber, to collect taxes, to maintain order at home, and decide on questions of peace and war. Although under the presidency of the Emperor or his Stadtholder, nothing of importance could be done without its leave, and thus it shared the executive power with him.

Maximilian, however, had no intention of seeing his authority thus controlled, and this abortive Council only lasted a few months. Henceforth, disappointed at the niggard support which his concessions had produced—for the levy voted at Augsburg was never fully furnished—he determined to lean upon his own resources. 'As King of the Romans,' he said, 'he had only experienced mortification. He would for the future act as an Austrian Prince.' Accordingly, in 1502, he fell back on his imperial right of holding Courts of Justice (*Hofgerichte*), and erected a standing Court or Aulic Council (*Hofrath*), entirely under his own control, to which he referred matters pertaining to his own territories, and cases which he was called upon to adjudicate in his capacity of overlord.[1] He even thought of instituting a Council of his own to take the place of the Council of Regency. The Electors on their side entered into a solemn compact at Gelnhausen (June 1502) to unite themselves as one man against the dangerous innovations of the Emperor; carried on negotiations with Louis XII. on their own account; and, in 1503, even spoke of deposing Maximilian and electing his rival, the French king, in his stead.

1502. Opposition of Maximilian.

Compact at Gelnhausen. June 1502.

At this moment the position of Maximilian began to improve. He found himself supported by many of the literary men who cherished the memories of the Empire, by many of the

[1] The Aulic Council was also to act as a supreme administrative body.

Princes, the Imperial Knights, and others who dreaded the power of the Electors, and, in 1504, the question of the Landshut succession gave him an opportunity of humiliating his chief enemy, the Elector Palatine, Frederick the Victorious, or the Wicked, as his opponents called him. On the death of Duke George, the Rich, of Landshut (December 1503), without direct heirs, three claimants appeared: Rupert, the second son of the Elector Palatine, and son-in-law and nephew of George, who claimed under the will of his father-in-law; and the two Dukes of Bavaria, Wolfgang and Albert, who urged their claim as his nearest agnates. Maximilian supported the cause of Bavaria; called on the princes who were jealous of the Elector Palatine; with their help, defeated his forces in a battle where Rupert, his son, was killed, and forced the Diet of Cologne, in 1505, to divide the territories of Landshut between the Dukes of Bavaria and himself; while the son of Rupert was fain to content himself with the small district of the upper Palatinate on the north of the Danube.

1504. Success of Maximilian in the Landshut succession question.

By this defeat of a prominent Elector, the prestige of Maximilian was much enhanced. Moreover, the death of John of Baden the Elector of Trèves, and of Berthold of Mayence during the year, 1504, seriously weakened the party of reform. The Emperor's position abroad also seemed magnificent. The Treaty of Blois (September 1504) promised a brilliant match for his grandson Charles (cf. p. 61), a match which was not only to bring Brittany, Burgundy, and the French possessions in North Italy to the Hapsburgs, but might even, so Maximilian hoped, end in uniting the crowns of the Empire and of France. In the ensuing November, the death of Isabella made Joanna, his daughter-in-law, Queen of Castile; and the old age of Ladislas, of Bohemia and Hungary, gave prospects of the speedy fulfilment of the agreement, made by that King fifteen years before, by which Hungary was to fall to the Hapsburg house in the event of his dying without male issue.

1504. Death of Berthold of Mayence and of the Elector of Trèves.

Improved position of Maximilian.

PERIOD IV.

H

While Maximilian indulged in wild projects of universal empire, he was not in a mood to listen to further demands,

End of the attempted Reforms.

nor were the Electors in a position to enforce them. Here therefore the attempts at reform may be said to have practically ceased. The hopes of Maximilian were not indeed fulfilled. Accordingly, in 1507, at Constance we find him once more demanding men and money against the perjured Louis XII., in return for a promise to revive the Imperial Chamber, which had held no sittings for three years. Supplies were granted, no longer by the Common Penny, or by assessment by parishes, but by a matricula or roll on which the separate states were rated, according to their resources, a system which emphasised the independence of the separate states. Thus furnished, Maximilian once more invaded Italy, only to fail even more ludicrously than before (cf. p. 65); and the Diets of the years, 1509 to 1512, are taken up with mutual recriminations—the Emperor bitterly remonstrating with the Diet for refusing adequate support, and for attempting to weaken his prerogative; while the Diet retorted that his alliances and his wars had been entered into without its consent, and that he had prevented the execution of the reforms which had been enacted.

At the Diets of Trèves and Cologne(1512), something indeed was done. The organisation of the Empire into six circles,[1]

[1] The idea of dividing Germany into circles dates from the reign of Albert II. The four then instituted were now increased to ten—

1. Franconia.

2. Suabia, including the Duchy of Wurtemberg, the Margraviate of Baden, and 32 imperial cities.

3. Bavaria, with the Archbishopric of Salzburg.

4. The Upper Rhine, including Lorraine.

5. Lower Rhine, composed of the three Ecclesiastical Electorates.

6. Westphalia, Julich, Cleves, Berg, the County of Oldenburg, and numerous Bishoprics.

7. Upper Saxony, formed of the Duchies of Saxony, and Pomerania, the Margraviate of Brandenburg.

8. Lower Saxony, composed of the Duchies of Brunswick, Luneburg, and Holstein (held by the King of Denmark), Meckle burg, the Arch-

hitherto only used for elections to the Council of Regency, and of the Assessors to the Imperial Chamber, was extended, and the administrative and military work of the districts placed in their hands. Even then the Diets refused to allow Maximilian the privilege of nominating the Captains of the circles, or of appointing a Captain-general who should be supreme, or nominating a council of eight, who were to act as a Privy Council under his control. In short, the eternal conflict continued ; Maximilian, though not averse to reforms which might make the executive and judicial work of the Empire more efficient, refused to allow his prerogative to be touched, and the Diet would only sanction those which secured them some control. The measure therefore was still-born, the Captains were never elected, and the establishment of the circles was not finally effected till 1521, three years after Maximilian's death.

1512. Establishment of the Circles.

Of the reforms thus attempted during the reign of Maximilian, the Common Penny, and the Imperial Council of Regency were revived again under Charles v., soon to be abandoned for ever ; and though the Imperial Chamber (*Reichskammer*), the Aulic Council (*Reichshofrath*), the circles, the system of taxation, and the levy by matricula were destined, with certain modifications, to last as long as the Empire itself, they did not succeed in saving the Empire from the continuation of weakness and intestine disorder. Not only were they disliked by the Emperor in the shape in which they were passed, but they received lukewarm support from most of the Princes, and were opposed by the Imperial Knights ; while the Cities, which

Permanent results of the attempt at Reform.

bishoprics of Magdeburg and Bremen, and the towns of Hamburg, Lubeck, and Goslar.

9. Austria.

10. Burgundy, including the Netherlands and Franche-Comté.

N.B.—Bohemia did not form part of any circle.

The duty of police and administration were to be in the hands of a captain (*Hauptmann*), with two assessors elected by the circles.

feared increased taxation as likely to fall chiefly upon their citizens, complained that they had no representatives among the assessors of the Imperial Chamber. The failure of these reforms confirms the opinion that the idea of reconciling imperial unity with the establishment of an aristocratic federation was a hopeless one, and that two alternatives alone were practicable : either the consolidation of Germany into a strong concentrated kingdom under an hereditary Monarch ; or the overthrow of national unity, and the dismemberment of the Empire into a number of petty states, practically sovereign and independent.

The condition of the separate states formed a counterpart to that of the Empire. The more powerful Electors and Princes, who wished to establish a strong govern-

Condition of States of the Empire.

ment, met with the same opposition from their vassals, their cities, and even their peasants, which they themselves offered to the Emperor ; their provincial Diets were torn with the same dissensions as those which disturbed the Imperial Diet. Yet here, more surely than in the Empire, the authority of the ruler was asserting itself, based upon that principle of independent territorialism which was eventually to triumph.

The Imperial Knights, enemies of the Princes whose power they dreaded, were the chief opponents of such consolidation, and the Emperor was not ashamed at times to lean upon these questionable allies, who ruined commerce by their raids, and welcomed the wolves as their comrades. 'Good luck, my dear comrades,' cried an Imperial Knight to a pack of wolves which he saw fall on a flock of sheep ; 'good luck to us all, and everywhere.' The condition of the peasants under such a state of things was probably a more miserable one than in any other country, and led to frequent revolts and conspiracies, such as that of 'The Bundschuh' (peasant's shoe)—risings which, however, were put down with cruelty. Germany, in a word, was suffering the throes of dissolution. The old institutions were falling into decay, the new ones had not yet been established, and soon the religious troubles were to add one more element of discord and weakness.

But if Germany at the close of the fifteenth century was in a condition of anarchy political and social, it is a mistake to suppose that she was in a condition of barbarism. Many a prince—nay, the Emperor Maximilian himself—was a patron of art and literature; while the cities at least formed an exception to the prevailing anarchy. They protected themselves with some success from the raids of the knights by their strong walls, their sturdy burghers, and their leagues; and, although not free themselves from violent ferments between the governing bodies of the towns and the unprivileged classes, who sought for entrance into the town councils, this civic turbulence, as is often the case, did not ruin the trade by which many towns and burghers enriched themselves.

Social and economical condition of Germany.

The cities also were the home of education, of literature, and of art. At the close of the fifteenth century sixteen universities existed, of which nine had been recently founded. Hence came the humanist scholars, Agricola, Erasmus, Reuchlin, Melanchthon, and a host of others, who revived the knowledge of the ancient languages, and enriched their own mother-tongue with their pens. In the cities too, the arts of printing, etching, metal-working, and painting flourished—witness more especially the names of Holbein, Albert Dürer, and Peter Vischer, the metal-worker of Nuremberg. In a word, Germany was in a condition of transition, of unrest, of political dislocation, and yet of much intellectual ferment, which was preparing her to take the lead in the Reformation.

The reign of Maximilian witnessed also an actual loss of territory to the Empire, for it was then that Switzerland practically established its independence. The Swiss Confederation was originally one of those numerous leagues formed in Germany for self-protection as the Empire

The Swiss Confederation.

fell into decay. In the year 1291, the three Forest Cantons of

1291. The Everlasting Compact of the three Forest Cantons.

Uri, Schwytz, and Unterwalden, lying at the head of the lake of Lucerne, formed 'The Everlasting Compact,' to protect themselves more especially against the powerful Counts of Hapsburg, who, with their castle of Hapsburg on the lower Aar, held large possessions, and enjoyed considerable political authority within, and around these districts.

The struggle with the House of Hapsburg.

Henceforth, for some two hundred years, opposition to this aggressive house forms the clue to the history of Switzerland. By the victories of Morgarten, 1315, and of Sempach, 1386, they freed themselves from all claims to political control or jurisdiction

Battles of Morgarten, 1315, and Sempach, 1386.

on the part of the Hapsburgs and of any other power except the Emperor. In 1468, Sigismund of Tyrol ceded to them all the lands he held in Switzerland, with the exception of the Frickthal in the

Their wars with Charles the Bold.

Aargau. By their famous war with Charles the Bold, Duke of Burgundy, 1474-1477, they not only established the reputation of their formidable infantry, but gained a footing in the French-speaking territories belonging to the House of Savoy.

The primitive Confederation of the three Forest Cantons had, by the date of Maximilian's accession, increased its num-

Condition of the Confederation at the accession of Maximilian.

bers to ten, and ruled over a stretch of country roughly bounded by the Jura and the lake of Neuchâtel on the west, the Bernese Alps on the south, and the Rhætian Alps, the lake of Constance, and the Rhine on the south-east, east, and north.[1] The city of Constance was a free imperial city, and was not a member of the Confederation.

---

[1] List of Cantons in 1499, with date of their admission to the league :

1291. { Three Forest Cantons	{ Uri, Schwytz, Unterwalden.	1335. Zurich. 1352. { Glarus. Zug.	1353. Bern. 1481. { Fribourg. Solothurn.
1332. Lucerne.			

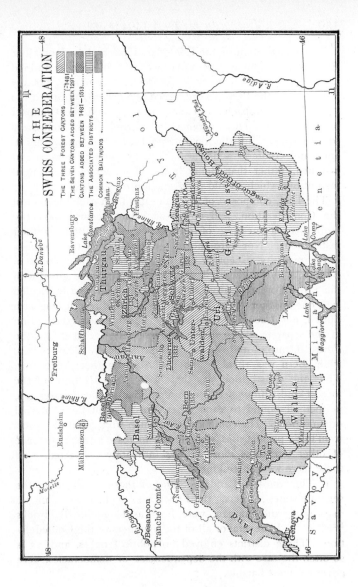

THE
SWISS CONFEDERATION

THE THREE FOREST CANTONS..........1291
THE SEVEN CANTONS ADDED BETWEEN 1291-1481
CANTONS ADDED BETWEEN 1481—1513...
THE ASSOCIATED DISTRICTS.............
COMMON BAILIWICKS.....................

The constitution of the Confederation was based on 'The Everlasting Compact' of 1291, which had been confirmed and expanded by subsequent compacts, notably the Parson's ordinance (*Pfaffenbrief*) of 1370, the Sempach ordinance of 1393, and the Compact of Stanz, 1481. These agreements referred almost exclusively to questions of jurisdiction and police, and of mutual assistance and common action with regard to foreign powers, and assumed, rather than defined, the character of the central institutions which should give sanction to these compacts.

The Diet, composed of two delegates from each member of the Confederation, and one from each 'Socius,' was little more than a meeting of envoys, strictly limited by their instructions. Nor were the minority bound by the decisions of the majority, except in matters concerning the 'Common Bailiwicks.' Although all the Confederates were allied with the three Forest Cantons, they were not necessarily leagued with one another—thus Bern had made no direct league with Zurich, nor Lucerne with Glarus. The internal constitution of the separate states also varied infinitely. Some, like the Forest Cantons and Zurich, were practically democracies, while Bern was ruled by an exclusive burgher aristocracy. Thus the constitution was that of a 'Confederation' of the loosest kind, a union between communities practically sovereign, neither all bound to each other, nor alike in their internal organisation. The complications, which were certain to result from these peculiarities, were further increased by the existence of other territories more or less intimately connected. Of these there were three kinds:

1. The 'Subject Lands.' Some of these belonged to the separate states; others, 'the Freie Orte,' such as the Thurgau and Aargau, were held as Common Bailiwicks by several or all of the members of the Confederation. These districts enjoyed no political rights, and, as is so often the case with the dependencies of democracies, were governed most harshly.

2. Secondly came the 'Associated Districts' (*Zugewandte Orte*). Of these, three indeed, the abbot, and town of St. Gall and the town of Bienne (Biel), on the lake of that name, were admitted as 'socii' with one vote each in the Diet. The Associated Districts.

But the far more numerous class, the 'Confœderati,' were not admitted to the privileges of full membership, and yet were bound to obey the orders of the Confederation in matters of peace and war.[1]

3. Lastly came the 'Protected Districts,' where the tie was still more loose. The Protected Districts.

The extraordinary complications and conflict of interests thus caused had from time to time led to serious disputes, both internal and 'external. They were now to involve the Swiss in a war with the Empire.

As long as the imperial title was in other hands than those of the hated Hapsburg, the Swiss had remained faithful to the Empire, although practically free. But in 1440, the election of Frederick III. reawakened their apprehensions. They feared lest he should use his imperial authority to regain his power over them. On the cession of most of the family possessions Causes of the War with the Empire. by Sigismund of Tyrol (cf. p. 118), a brief period of friendship ensued, which was strengthened when, by 'The Everlasting Compact' of 1475, he confirmed his renunciation, and promised help against Charles of Burgundy. But the startling successes of the Swiss had caused the Emperor and Sigismund to desert their cause, and the old jealousies revived. The Confederation looked with dislike on the formation of the Suabian League (1488), to the north of them, a dislike which was embittered by the open contempt shown by the German nobility for these upstart Swiss. The claim made by the imperial city of Constance to

---

[1] List of 'Confœderati' before 1497—

The league of Wallis, or Valais	Schaffhausen	Rothweil
	Mülhausen	Appenzell.
1497, The Grisons.	1498, The League of God's House.	

jurisdiction over the district of the Thurgau, which had been mortgaged to it by Sigismund, caused further friction. After the death of Frederick III. matters grew worse. The reforming party among the Electors were eager to bring Switzerland under the jurisdiction of the Imperial Chamber, and to force the Confederation to bear its share of the taxation imposed on the Empire by the Diet of Worms (1495). Maximilian here attempted to play double. He hoped that by allowing the Diet to make these claims he might frighten the Swiss, while by refraining from enforcing them he might gain the aid of the Confederation against the French. In this he made a double blunder. The Electors, anxious to make the imperial organisation a reality, insisted on the execution of the decrees of the Diet, and the Swiss looked upon his policy as a dishonest attempt to revive the claims of his house. They had long been practically, although not legally, free from all imperial jurisdiction and taxation. They had no representative in the Diet, and their consent had not been asked. The tax of the Common Penny they declared to be a scheme on the part of the princes to tax the peasants. In short, their view of the matter was singularly like that of the American Colonies when, in the eighteenth century, England attempted to tax them. The Swiss, however, not only refused to comply themselves, they even claimed independence for their ally St. Gall. This at least could not be sanctioned, and, in 1497, St. Gall was placed under the ban of the Empire. Maximilian still continued his double dealing. He delayed the execution of the ban in the vain hope of influencing the Swiss to make a personal arrangement with him, and serve him in his wars. Meanwhile, other differences precipitated the crisis. Of several leagues which had grown up around that of the Swiss Confederation, some of the most important were the three Rhætian Leagues: the League of God's House, 'Gotteshausbund,' round about Chur, from the cathedral of which it took its name; the 'Grauer Bund,' or Grisons, on the Upper Rhine; and the League of the Ten

Jurisdictions in the Prättigau and the valley of Davos. The succession of Maximilian to the possessions of the cadet branch of his family in Tyrol on the death of Sigismund (1496), not unnaturally aroused the fear of these Leagues, the more so because Maximilian also about this time gained part of the Prättigau. Accordingly in 1497, the Grauer Bund, and in 1498, the League of God's House, entered into an alliance with the Swiss and became associates (Confœderati). The Swiss Confederation was thus drawn into the interminable disputes as to possessions and jurisdictions, which existed between these two Leagues and Tyrol. Finally, the occupation of the Münsterthal—one of the valleys which joins that of the upper Adige—by the authorities at Innsbruck, led to hostilities (1499).

The war was at first carried on by Maximilian as Archduke of Austria, assisted by the Suabian League, and was not taken up by the Empire until the follow- Outbreak of ing year. The best policy on the Emperor's part War, 1499. would probably have been to concentrate his attack, and try to outmanœuvre the Swiss and crush them in one decisive battle ; for the Swiss army, organised according to the states in which it had been levied, was better fitted for detached enterprises, and its leaders were always somewhat deficient in strategy. Instead of this, Maximilian divided his forces and thus played into the hands of his enemies. The Swiss, advancing in a dense column, or in phalanxes in echelon of three divisions, with four rows of pikemen in front armed with pikes eighteen feet long, supported in the rear by Defeat of halberdiers with halberds (a combination of the Suabian battle-axe and spear), proved more than a match League and of for the German landsknechts. The French king Maximilian. sent money and artillery ; even the Venetians contributed money, unwilling to see Hapsburg influence increase in these parts. Ludovico Sforza, Duke of Milan, Maximilian's only ally, was at this moment driven from Milan (September 2). The Suabian League was defeated at Bruderholz and at

Dornach, near Basel. Maximilian himself was worsted at Frastenz in the Tyrol, and again at the gorge of the Calven in the Münsterthal, and on September 22, 1499, was forced to come to terms.

By the peace of Basel all matters in dispute between Maximilian and the Rhætian Leagues were referred to arbitration. All decisions of the Imperial Chamber against the Confederation were annulled, and though nothing definite was said as to its future relations with the Empire, no attempt was ever again made to subject the Swiss to imperial taxation, jurisdiction, or military levy. Though still nominally a member of the Empire the Confederation enjoyed practical independence, which was finally recognised at the peace of Westphalia, 1648.

The Peace of Basel, 1499.

In 1501, for the purpose of strengthening their northern frontier, the Swiss admitted Basel and Schaffhausen to the Confederation ; and the addition of Appenzell, in 1513, brought up the number of the Confederate States to thirteen, a number which was not increased till the present century. The Swiss continued to be the mercenaries of Europe, and in 1502, and 1512, gained, as we have seen, further possessions to the south of the Alps (cf. p. 72). One thing at least Maximilian learnt from his defeats. He copied the arms, and to some extent the organisation, of the Swiss, and thus did much to form that formidable infantry which did Charles v. good service in Italy. Yet even this had its disadvantages ; for the German landsknechts, finding themselves in request, sometimes adopted the mercenary habits of the Swiss, and took service with the enemies of their country.

In spite of Maximilian's attachment to the imperial name it may be said of him, as it was of an earlier Emperor, Charles iv., that he was 'stepfather' of the Empire. Further, it was his aim to humiliate the Electors. He had robbed the Palatinate of the succession to Landshut (cf. p. 113). He defrauded the Elector of Saxony of his claim

The Policy of Maximilian towards the Empire and his Hapsburg territories.

to Berg and Julich by securing the succession, through
marriage, to the Duke of Cleves, and of the tutelage of
Philip of Hesse, by declaring the young Landgrave of age
when only fourteen; and though he supported the house
of Brandenburg (Hohenzollern) by approving of the election
of Albert, a cadet of the house, to the Grand Mastership of
the Teutonic Order in Prussia (1512), he irritated him by
confirming the peace of Thorn of 1466, by which the knights
had been forced to cede Western Prussia to Casimir of
Poland, and to hold East Prussia as a fief of that king. To
this he was induced by family reasons: Lewis,[1] the nephew
of Sigismund, the reigning King of Poland, had recently
married Maximilian's granddaughter Mary, while Anne, the
sister of Lewis, married his grandson Ferdinand, with the
promise of succession to Hungary and Bohemia, should Lewis
die without heirs. In short, the policy of Maximilian was
mainly dynastic. To increase the power and the future
prospects of his house was his main aim,—by the aid of the
imperial position, if possible; if not, by conquest, His success
by policy, and by successful marriages. His as a Haps-
success in this design will be best realised by burg Prince.
contrasting the position held by his house in 1485 with
that which it enjoyed at his death in 1519.

In 1485, one year before Maximilian was elected King of
the Romans, Mathias Corvinus not only held Hungary and
Bohemia, which had belonged to the Hapsburgs from 1437 to
1457, but had driven Frederick III. from Vienna. The Tyrol
and Alsace were in the hands of Maximilian's cousin Sigismund. Styria and Carinthia were being ravaged by the Turk,
and Maximilian himself, now that his wife Mary of Burgundy
was dead (1482), was deprived of the government of the

[1] Casimir iv. of Poland, 1445-1492

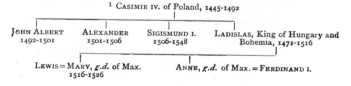

| John Albert 1492-1501 | Alexander 1501-1506 | Sigismund i. 1506-1548 | Ladislas, King of Hungary and Bohemia, 1471-1516 |

| Lewis = Mary, *g.d.* of Max. 1516-1526 | Anne, *g.d.* of Max. = Ferdinand i. |

Netherlands, and even of the education of his son Philip. Far different was the state of things in 1519. Not only had all Austria proper been regained, but on the death of Sigismund, 1496, the Emperor reunited in his own hands all the Hapsburg possessions, and the ravages of the Turks had for the time ceased. If he had lost Switzerland, and if his attempt to restore his authority in Italy had ludicrously failed, these were losses to the Empire rather than to his house.

It is, however, in his marriage alliances that Maximilian met with most success. The marriage treaties with Ladislas His Marriage and his son Lewis, mentioned just above (p. 125), Alliances. were shortly (1526) to restore Hungary and Bohemia to the Hapsburgs. His wife Mary, daughter of Charles the Bold, had brought him most of the possessions of the powerful House of Burgundy, and Philip, the issue of this match, had wedded Joanna of Spain. Already in 1516, Charles, their son, ruled in the Netherlands and in Spain and in Naples.[1]

In spite of his long struggle with the electors, and the failure of his Italian wars, Maximilian was not unpopular His with the Germans. Indeed, he must have been Character. an attractive character, if rather an irritating person to deal with. Although not handsome—for his complexion was pale, and he had a snub nose rising above a grey beard—his countenance was manly, and his activity and strength extraordinary, as his feats in pursuit of the chamois prove. His intellectual activity was not less remarkable; well educated, speaking seven languages or dialects; with wide interests, quick sympathies, a chivalrous and highly imaginative mind, and inexhaustible energy, his many-sidedness won him admirers among all classes. No doubt, some of these qualities stood in the way of his success. Fond of indulging in magnificent schemes, many of them incapable of realisation, his very versatility and resource opened him to

---

[1] The success of these and other marriages of the Hapsburgs is commemorated in the lines :— ' Bella gerant alii, tu felix Austria nube,

Nam quæ Mars aliis, dat tibi regna Venus.

the reproach of being indecisive and changeable. 'What he says at night he holds of no account on the morrow,' said Louis XI. of him. His self-confidence taught him to be impatient of strong men; 'to refuse the advice of any, and yet to be deceived of all,' says Machiavelli. His overweening ambition led him into financial straits, and these to humiliating shifts, more especially in his dealings with foreign powers who called him 'the man of few pence,' and treated him as an importunate beggar, to be pensioned or bought off at will. But at least, Maximilian was not self-deceived. In his epic of 'Teuerdank,' the adventurous knight of 'glorious thoughts,' who sets out to seek his bride and finally wars against the Turk, he depicts himself, and introduces us to self-conceit and the desire of adventure as the two great dangers which, with envious intrigue, beset him. This attractive, lovable, impracticable, exasperating man of dreams, of nervous, though ill-directed energy, is a fit representative of that period of transition which may be said to be covered by his reign.

With the accession of Francis in 1515, and with the death of Maximilian in 1519, we are definitely introduced to a new period. It is an interesting fact that Italy, the home of that papacy which had guided the Teutonic barbarians out of barbarism, had nursed their earlier days and introduced them to the priceless legacy of Roman law, government, and civilisation, should have been the stage upon which the scenes were shifted.

The death of Maximilian, 1519, marks the beginning of a new period.

It was in the Italian wars that the kingdoms of Europe first showed full consciousness of their national identity. In them, notwithstanding their deadly rivalries, they learnt that their fortunes were necessarily bound together as members of the European commonwealth of nations. Thence the system of the balance of power, the birth of modern diplomacy, the foundation of a system of international law. In short, during this period, that political system of Europe was established which still survives. Further, in the Italian wars the nations found it necessary to keep large armies on foot, and the art of war was revolutionised by the more extensive use of gunpowder.

Italy indeed suffered terribly.   At no date was the selfishness of nations more flagrantly exhibited than in these Italian wars.   The peninsula became the spoil of the foreigner, never to regain her independence till our own day.   Yet in the midst of her supreme agony, she had bestowed a priceless gift on Europe.   The revived knowledge of Greek art and literature, the highest perfection of painting, the new style of architecture, the knowledge of man, and the spirit of criticism—these were to be her final legacies to Europe in the movement of the Renaissance, which was so peculiarly Italian.

Henceforth the main interest of European history will no longer lie in Italy.   The struggle for her fair plains is not indeed over.   The papacy will still demand our atten tion, in its relations to the Reformation and to the Empire. But Italy falls back into a subordinate position.   The Mediterranean ceases to be the highway of commerce between east and west.   Our gaze is directed north of the Alps to follow the great struggle between the Hapsburg and Valois houses, and the momentous issues which were involved in the Reformation.

CHAPTER III

The Imperial Election—Preparations of Charles and Francis for war, which is, however, delayed—The Revolt of the Comuneros—The Diet of Worms —The Council of Regency—The Renaissance and the Reformation— Erasmus and Luther—The Imperial Ban—War between Charles and Francis—Their Alliances—Successes of Imperial Troops—Adrian VI. succeeds Leo X.—His quarrel with Charles—Battle of Bicocca—Treaty of Windsor—Luther and the Council of Regency—Diet of Nuremberg— The Knights' War—Congress of Ratisbon—Battle of Pavia—The Peasants War.

§ 1. *The Imperial Election.*

ON the death of Maximilian in January 1519, the destinies of Europe fell into the hands of three young Monarchs, all of them of marked individuality and of great ambition. Of these Henry VIII., now in his twenty-eighth year, was the eldest. The profound impression made on foreigners by his personal appearance is probably in part to be attributed to the fairness of his complexion, always much admired on the Continent ; but although in after life he became very corpulent, his high colouring, his massive head and wide-set eyes, his tall, powerful, yet active frame must have been striking enough. When to this is added his prowess in games and in the joust, his proficiency in music and languages, and, above all, his masterful character, we shall probably not think the estimate exaggerated.

The three candidates for the Imperial throne.

Francis I. was only three years younger. Nearly as tall as Henry, his dark complexion, his corpulence and thin legs especially struck contemporaries. A patron of art, a lover of pleasure, he was a true son of the Renaissance in its shallower aspects. With little foresight, prudence, or statesmanship—a bad King and a bad man—he was bold to rashness, fully as ambitious as his rivals and yet was gifted with a certain chivalrous spirit which was wanting in Charles, and which formed the redeeming feature of his otherwise worthless character.

Of Charles little was at that time known, and little expected. He was only nineteen, and was completely under the control of his Flemish counsellor, William de Croy, 'le Sieur de Chièvres.' Of middle height and slouching gait, his fine forehead and powerful aquiline nose were spoilt by the underhanging jaw of the Hapsburg, and small bad teeth. The troubles of his early life, the quarrels between his father and his grandfather Ferdinand, the jealousy which Ferdinand had subsequently shown him, the madness of his mother, had made him reserved and grave, and perhaps destroyed the enthusiasm of youth. These qualities gave the impression of stupidity; yet he was soon to show the world that, beneath that impassive exterior, lay a clear-headedness, a business capacity, and a determination which, coupled with indifference to sentiment, was to prove him the ablest statesman of the three.

These young Kings were the most important candidates for the imperial throne vacant by Maximilian's death, the election to which now monopolised the attention of Europe. Maximilian had squandered money and promises to win the Electors, and fondly believed that he had secured the votes of five of them for his grandson; but no sooner was he dead, than they repudiated their engagements, and began to chaffer again for bribes. Henry was scarcely a serious candidate; of the other two, the chances of Francis seemed at first the best. The victory of Marignano, and his ambition for military renown, pointed him out as the most likely leader of that Crusade of which Europe was ever talking, though never undertaking; and Francis vowed that, if elected, he would be in Constantinople within three years. Leo x., although unwilling to declare himself, hoped to see Francis elected The possession of Milan by the French made their friendship necessary if the Medici were to be secure in Florence, and it was the traditional policy of the Popes to prevent Naples and the Empire from falling into the same hands. 'Do you know,' said Leo, 'that it is only forty miles from Rome to the Neapolitan frontier?' The Electors, more especially Frederick the Wise of Saxony, and Joachim I. of Brandenburg, had many of them been irritated by Maximilian's opposition to reform, and by his general policy towards them (cf. p. 110 ff). The Rhenish Electors—that is, the three Archbishops of Mayence, Trèves, and Cologne, and the Elector Palatine— feared the vengeance of Francis if they refused their votes and Richard Greifenklau, the Elector of Trèves, was an ally of the Duke of Gueldres, the inveterate enemy of the Hapsburgs.

Francis, moreover, was determined to obtain the coveted title. 'And he spent three millions of gold,' he said, 'he would be Emperor'; and the bribes he offered to the Electors were higher than Charles had to give. So poor indeed did the prospects of Charles appear that he was urged by some to retire in favour of his brother Ferdinand, an alternative which Charles rejected with warmth, as fatal to the interests of his house, though promising that, if elected, he would prevail upon Germany to accept his brother as his successor. He then instructed his agents, for he himself was in Spain, to spare no pains and to refuse nothing whereby his election might be secured. Thus the dishonourable traffic continued with the Electors, who were at the election itself to swear that they gave their votes free from all promise, engagement, or earnest-money.

How the matter might have ended, if it had been left to the Electors, it is impossible to say. But, as the day of election drew near, the sentiment of Germany began to show itself unmistakably. Not only did the literary men declare for Charles, but the Suabian League also began to move. This powerful League had, in the previous May, driven Ulrich, Duke of Würtemberg, from his duchy on account of his cruelty and misgovernment, and was in a position to enforce its views. The League was commanded by Duke William of Bavaria,

German sentiment declares for Charles.

whose sister had been brutally treated by her husband, the Duke Ulrich, and by Franz von Sickingen, the famous imperial knight, who was already in the pay of Charles. The army of the League now proclaimed that it would not submit to the election of Francis, and was joined by the Swiss. The Confederates were generally the opponents of the Hapsburgs, and in 1499, by the peace of Basel, which closed their last war with Maximilian, had gained their freedom from imperial laws, justice, and taxation (cf. p. 124). Yet, influenced by Mathias Schinner, the Cardinal of Sion, they now supported the cause of Charles.

In the north, too, the Duke of Brunswick-Wolfenbüttel threatened to take up arms for the German candidate. This strong expression of German sentiment naturally influenced the Electors. They therefore lowered their demands, and accepted smaller sums and promises from Charles than Francis offered; while the Fuggers, the Rothschilds of that day, refused to honour the bills of the French King. Leo, too, seeing 'that it was useless to run his head against a brick wall,' abandoned his opposition to Charles.

The most important suffrage to be gained was that of the Archbishop of Mayence, the brother of Joachim of Brandenburg. His vote would certainly carry with it that of the vacillating Hermann von der Wied, Archbishop of Cologne, and he might have some influence on his brother, although that 'father of all avarice' was deeply pledged to support the French King. The Archbishop had been offered 120,000 florins and the perpetual legateship of Germany by Francis. Nevertheless, after much haggling, he accepted Charles' smaller promise of 72,000 florins and the legateship, and championed his cause in the electoral college which met on June 18. Here the Elector of Trèves, who had dipped

The Electors finally elect Charles. deeply into French money-bags, urged the claims of Francis, and suggested, that if he were not acceptable, they should elect some other German prince likely to be less dangerous than Charles—the Duke of

Bavaria, the Margrave of Brandenburg, or the Elector of Saxony. This had been the final move of Francis. The Elector of Saxony was the only one who had honourably refused all bribes, and so great was the reputation of his virtuous and godly life, as also of his singular wisdom, that, had he been willing, he might have been chosen. Too shrewd, however, to accept so dangerous a position, and patriotic enough to wish it conferred on a German, he declined the offer, and declared for Charles. His conduct decided the matter. Lewis, the young King of Bohemia, had married Mary, sister of Charles, and voted for his brother-in-law. Hermann von der Wied, Archbishop of Cologne, followed the lead of Mayence; the three remaining Electors, the Archbishop of Trèves, the Elector Palatine, and the Margrave of Brandenburg, followed suit, and Charles was unanimously elected Emperor. The papal confirmation was no longer thought necessary for the assumption of the title of Emperor, and, though Charles was subsequently crowned by the Pope at Bologna (1530), he at once assumed the title, not of King of the Romans, but of Emperor Elect. Thus ended the most memorable of the elections to that imperial dignity, which was fast becoming a mere shadow—an election which surpassed all others in the shameless corruption and intrigue which accompanied it, and which Henry's agent Pace declared to be 'the dearest merchandise which ever was bought.'

The desire of Francis to attain the title is a proof of his want of statesmanship. His success would have been disastrous to his country; the hostility of Germany, and probably of the whole of Europe, would have been aroused, and the resources of France would have been exhausted in a struggle in which she was not really interested.

By the election of Charles, the magnificent dreams of Frederick III. and of Maximilian were in part realised. The house of Hapsburg now ruled over Germany, the Netherlands, Spain, Naples, and a large part of the New World, and held once more the title of the Holy Roman Emperor.

And yet it may be questioned whether the imperial dignity
was really a source of strength. As a price of his election
Charles had to sign the 'Capitulations,' which henceforth
were demanded of every Emperor Elect. These 'Capitulations' well illustrate the views of the German Princes. The
The
Capitulations. fear of the Spanish and Flemish parentage of
the new Emperor is seen in their demands that
German or Latin should be the official language, that imperial
offices should be reserved for Germans, that the States should
not be subject to any foreign jurisdiction, and that no foreign
troops should serve in imperial wars without the consent of
the Diet. The opposition to papal claims prompted the
Princes to insist on the abolition of every innovation introduced by the court of Rome, in contravention of the concordat made with Germany after the Council of Constance
(1418). Finally, determined to maintain their privileges, they
demanded that Charles should confirm their sovereign rights
and appoint a standing Council which should take a share in
government. These last demands were of serious import,
and led to serious controversies. For the rest, as the sequel
will show, Charles' numerous and ill-assorted possessions and
claims led to difficulties, before which at last he succumbed.

That the election of Charles v. would lead to war was
almost inevitable. The fears of the French were not un-
War
inevitable. naturally aroused by the union of the Hapsburg and
Spanish claims in his person, while the personal
vanity of Francis had received a deadly affront by the election
of his rival to the Empire.

Under these circumstances, it was not difficult to find
occasions of quarrel. The terms of the treaty of Noyon (1516)
(cf. p. 83), had not been carried out on either side. Francis
could complain that Spanish Navarre had never been restored
to Henry d'Albret, while Charles asserted that Milan belonged
to him, as an imperial fief, and demanded the restoration of
the Duchy of Burgundy as part of his Burgundian inheritance.
Nevertheless, it was clearly to the advantage of Charles that

the war should be postponed. Now, as throughout his reign, the very extent of his dominions and the number of his titles were a source of weakness. Spain, indignant at the rule of the Flemings, was on the point of rebellion; Germany, which Charles had not yet visited since his election, for he was still in Spain, was annoyed at his continued absence; the Diet had to be reckoned with; and the question of 'the little monk Luther' demanded immediate attention.

Charles wishes to put off the war.

Francis on the contrary, with less extravagant pretensions, was master of a consolidated kingdom. He enjoyed a prerogative far less controlled, more especially with regard to the finances and the army, than his rival. He held the central position, and, as long as he retained Milan, cut off the Emperor from all communication by land between his German and Italian territories. Under these circumstances Chièvres was probably right, apart from the particular interests of the Netherlands, in wishing, at least, to postpone the commencement of hostilities. France, on the other hand, should have begun the war at once. But the treasury had been exhausted by the extravagance of the King, by the expenses incurred in the last war, and in the canvass for the Empire, and the addition of fresh imposts would cause discontent. Above all it was thought desirable, if possible, first to secure the alliance, or at least the neutrality, of England. Charles, too, realised the importance of English aid; and the two rivals were so evenly matched that an opportunity, such as had never occurred before, was opened to England to hold the tongue of the balance.

The opportunity was eagerly seized by Wolsey. To continue friends with both sides without offending either; to keep both asunder by fostering mutual suspicion; to prevent either from declaring war lest the aggressor might find England arrayed against him, and thereby to prevent if possible, if not to delay, the outbreak of hostilities; meanwhile, to gain for England the proud position of arbiter of Europe—this was

Attempt of Wolsey to keep the peace.

the aim of Wolsey, a policy which for nigh two years met with such success that the two most powerful monarchs of Europe became the humble suitors of the Cardinal and his master.

In May, 1520, Charles hurried from Spain to meet Henry VIII. at Sandwich, an act of condescension on the Emperor's part which excited the astonishment of Europe. Immediately afterwards (June 7), followed the interview between Henry and Francis at the 'Field of the Cloth of Gold,' near Guisnes in the Pale of Calais—again, be it noted, on English ground. The importance attached to this famous interview is not only attested by the magnificence of the display, by the feats of arms in which even the kings them-selves took part to the discomfiture of Francis, but by the attention it received from the artists and the writers of the day. Thence Henry VIII. passed to a second interview with Charles at Gravelines (July 10). The actual results of these meetings are doubtful;[1] but it is probable that Wolsey declined any definite agreements, since his policy was to avoid declaring himself on either side.

Thus the negotiations dragged on, much to the indignation of the Pope, Leo X., who had made treaties with both, yet was anxious that war should begin without delay in order that he might see who was likely to prove the winner before he com-promised himself too far.

At the close of the year 1520, however, the diplomacy of Wolsey began to break down. Francis determined to take the offensive, and accused Wolsey of betraying his secret to the Pope; while Charles, who had long been hesitating whether to carry out the proposed match with Mary of England, or to marry the Infanta of Portugal, attempted to implicate Henry in a war with France and demanded that he should fulfil his promises. Wolsey, however, was not thus to be entrapped, and recalled Tunstal, his agent at the Emperor's court. Yet Charles was in no position to declare war, and the actual outbreak of hostilities was accordingly postponed till 1521.

The diplom-acy of Wolsey fails to avert the struggle.

[1] Cf. *Cambridge Modern History*, ii. 416.

Meanwhile the troubles in Spain, the difficulties with the Diet, and the question of the condemnation of Luther, demanded the attention of the Emperor.

§ 2. *The Revolt of the Comuneros*

The troubles in Spain had commenced immediately on the death of Ferdinand. In spite of the temporary success which had accompanied the policy of that King Discontent and his consort, the work of consolidation was in Spain. by no means complete. Not only were the kingdoms of Castile and Aragon independent of each other, but even Valencia and Catalonia, although dependencies of Aragon, had their separate Cortes and characteristic institutions. This outward variety of constitutional machinery was but the symbol of deep and essential differences—differences which were the outcome of the physical peculiarities of the various countries, their racial differences, and their past history. The rivalries between Castile and Aragon were of old standing, and no sharper contrast is to be found in Europe than that which existed between the primitive and poverty-stricken population of the Asturias, the proud Castilian noble, and the busy trader of Barcelona, the democratic capital of Catalonia. Nor was there more unity within the separate kingdoms themselves. The social divisions were deepest in Castile. There the nobles enjoyed numerous exclusive privileges, notably that of freedom from taxation. The revenues derived from their wide domains were so great as to exceed in several instances those of the crown itself. Living in proud isolation, they despised the burghers of the towns and their struggles for the constitutional rights of the Cortes, the meetings of which they themselves had long ceased to attend.

In Aragon the nobles were less isolated. They were still represented in the Cortes, and joined with the deputies of the clergy and the towns in common defence of their political rights. Even here, however, the social cleavages were deep,

while in Valencia things were nearly as bad as in Castile.
But if Spain was the victim of national and class jealousies
and divisions, she was not on that account less tenacious of

The discon-
tent reaches
its climax on
the accession
of Charles,
especially in
Castile.
her privileges, and the change of rulers gave
her an opportunity of reasserting them. When
therefore Charles came to Spain a year after his
grandfather's death (1517), he had met with considerable opposition. The Cortes of Aragon only
consented to acknowledge him as King in conjunc-
tion with his mother after he had sworn to confirm their liberties,
and in Catalonia and Valencia he met with similar difficulties.

Meanwhile, in Castile matters were even worse. The Cas-
tilians had been irritated by the rule of the Fleming, Chièvres
—the 'goat' as they called him in allusion to his name—who
had administered affairs till Charles came to Spain. When
their new King did arrive he hurt their pride by his ignorance
of their language, excited the indignation of many by his heart-
less treatment of Ximenes, who was rewarded for his faithful
services by being dismissed to his diocese to die (November
17), and alienated all by conferring the dignities which had
been held by the Cardinal upon his hated Flemings. The see
of Toledo was given to the Bishop of Tournay, the nephew of
Chièvres; and Sauvage, another Fleming, succeeded him in
his office of Chancellor of Castile. Accordingly the Cortes
of Valladolid, in 1518, while acknowledging Charles and his
mother as co-rulers, and voting him a 'servicio' or money
grant, for two years, demanded that no foreigners should be
given office; that no gold, silver, or horses should be exported
from Spain; that Charles should speedily marry; and that his
brother Ferdinand should act as his representative until he
should have children. These demands, if ever granted, were
not complied with. Meanwhile, the imperial election increased
their apprehensions. The Emperor, they said, would rarely be
in Spain, and they would have to pay the expenses of the
honour as they had of the election. Charles, anxious to leave

Spain to meet Henry VIII. at Sandwich, and to be crowned at Aix-la-Chapelle (Aachen), consented to call another meeting of the Cortes before leaving the country. He, however, avoided the larger towns on account of their disaffection, and summoned it to Santiago (March 31), in Galicia, and subsequently (April 25) transferred it to Corunna that he might be near his ships. Here he extorted a sum of money by promises to return again in three years, on the faith of a King, to appoint no foreigners to office, and to spend the 'servicio' only in the interests of Castile. The Cortes, however, was by no means a full one; the deputies of Salamanca had been excluded, and some, such as Toledo, had refused to send any. Even so, the vote was only carried by a narrow majority.

The city of Toledo had special cause for indignation. The appointment of Chièvres' nephew as Archbishop had been looked upon as a special insult, and the envoys sent to remonstrate with Charles, had been refused an audience. The citizens therefore rose, headed by two nobles, Don Pedro Laso de la Vega, and Don Juan de Padilla, son of the Commendador or Governor of Leon, whose intrepid wife had forced him into a career for which he was ill fitted. They seized the government in the name of the king and queen, drove the royal Corregidor from the town, and formed a 'Communidad' of deputies from the parishes of the city (April 21).

Toledo rises. April 21, 1520.

Charles was now to experience for the first time, but not the last, the conflict of those jarring interests which resulted from his anomalous position. As King of Spain, his presence there was imperatively needed, yet his European interests necessitated his departure. Henry VIII. had promised to meet Francis in May or early in June, and, if the conference at Sandwich was not to be abandoned (cf. p. 136), no time was to be lost. Accordingly, on the 19th of May, he left Spain almost as a fugitive, having appointed Adrian, his old tutor, regent in Castile, Don Juan de Lanuza, viceroy in Aragon, and Don Diego de Mendoza, in Valencia.

The departure of the King only served to increase the discontent. The Spaniards felt that henceforth their country

Charles' departure from Spain, May 19, is followed by the revolt of Castile.

would no longer be the centre of his interests, but only a province of his wider Empire. The revolt therefore spread rapidly. At Segovia the deputy who had voted for the 'servicio' was murdered. Salamanca, Zamora, Madrid, Burgos, and many other towns rose ; and finally Valladolid, then the seat of government, took up arms. Meanwhile, in Valencia, a social war was raging between the nobles and the commons, although the disturbances there had no connection with those in Castile. At the end of July, the movements in Castile, hitherto isolated, coalesced under the leadership of the citizens of Toledo, and a 'Junta' of deputies from the insurgent towns

The Junta set up Joanna. August, 1520.

was formed at Avila. In August, Padilla, marching on Tordesillas, not far from Valladolid, seized Charles' mother, Joanna, who was now completely imbecile, and established the revolutionary government in her name. With this formidable revolt, Adrian was quite unable to cope ; he had been left without adequate resources in troops or money, and had not even been intrusted with full powers. After a fruitless attempt to quell the rebellion, he fled to Medina de Rio Seco, and hastily wrote to Charles demanding his own recall, and urging him to come quickly or Spain would be lost. Charles, however, was in no position to comply with his request, or to send reinforcements. He therefore bade Adrian temporise. He was to summon a Cortes, to offer to abandon the 'servicio' and promise to govern Spain according to the ancient laws ; yet in no way to touch the prerogatives of the crown. At the same time, Charles appointed Don Fadrique Henriques, the High Admiral, and Don Inigo de Velasco, the High Constable of Castile, as co-regents, hoping by this act to gain the support of the nobles. Meanwhile the 'Junta,' after vainly attempting to prove

Joanna sane, and to put her on the throne, proceeded to draw up a charter of their liberties. They called upon Charles to return to Spain, to marry the Infanta of Portugal, to reduce his expenses, and to live like his fore- fathers, and passed the following decrees. No foreigner was again to hold office; the taxes were to be reduced, and the exemptions of the nobility abolished; the crown lands, which had been alienated, were to be resumed, and future alienations were declared illegal; finally a Cortes, fully representative of the three orders of nobles, clergy, and burghers, was to meet once in every three years. These decrees were declared to be fundamental laws, which could never be revoked by King or Cortes, and Charles' acceptance of them was made the condition of his return.

The Junta present their Charter.

Hitherto the nobles had displayed extraordinary apathy. They had been irritated at the policy of Ferdinand and Isabella, and if, with few exceptions, they had not taken any active part in the rebellion, they had given Adrian no assistance. But now their fears began to be aroused; some of these decrees touched their privileges, and the movement in Castile threatened to follow that of Valencia, and to assume the character of a social revolt. Moreover, the appointment of two of their number as co-regents indicated a change in the policy of the government, and had done something to conciliate them. The hostility of the nobles once awakened, the position of the 'comuneros' became critical, and their chances of success were further jeopardised by the internal dissensions which now broke out.

The nobles declare against the rebels.

The citizens of Burgos, the capital of Old Castile, became jealous at the leading part assumed by Toledo, the capital of New Castile, while Pedro Laso, the President of the Junta, who represented the more moderate party, was opposed to the more extreme views of Padilla. The Regents, seizing the opportunity, managed to detach Burgos from the Junta (October 1520), and in

Jealousies weaken the rebels' cause.

December, the Count de Haro, son of the Constable, retook Tordesillas and gained possession of Joanna. Yet in spite of these successes the danger was by no means over. The nobles showed their want of union, and even the Constable and the Admiral quarrelled. The rebels, on the other hand, received the valuable support, not only of the Count de Salvatierra, a powerful noble of the north, but also of Acuña, the Bishop of Zamora. This clever and ambitious ecclesiastic attempted to give to the movement a wider significance, and to establish a democracy, while he hoped to gain for himself the Archbishopric of Toledo, just vacant by the death of the nephew of Chièvres. In these designs he obtained the support of Francis, and even the neutrality of the Pope. Inspired by these notable

Renewed vigour of the comuneros. March, 1521. additions to their party, the 'communeros' displayed renewed vigour. Padilla, marching on the town of Torrelobaton near Valladolid, took it and put it to the sack (March 3, 1521); and the city of Burgos, enraged at the refusal of the royalists to confirm their promises, again took up arms. Once more the King's cause seemed to be lost. The rebels had a short time before refused the concessions offered them by his Regents, and determined to win all or lose all. Charles therefore fell back upon his previous policy of letting things take their course, while he refused to surrender a jot of his prerogative.

This policy of obstinate inactivity met with a success it did not deserve. It is the common fate of all rebellions, *Failure of the rebellion.* when not guided by leaders of strong individuality, to fall to pieces of themselves. This now happened in Spain. The leaders of the revolt were men of no real strength. Padilla was an unpractical enthusiast, and the Bishop of Zamora a dishonest, self-seeking man. There was a complete absence of statesmanship or self-sacrifice. The Junta lost all control. Pedro Laso, the President, digusted at the turn things were taking, began to waver, and was followed by many who feared that anarchy would ensue.

The nobles, at last thoroughly alarmed, laid aside their quarrels, and showed a unanimity which, if displayed at first, would have nipped the revolt in the bud. Finally, the Count de Haro, reinforced by troops sent by the Count de Najera from Navarre, advanced against the army of the 'communeros,' which since the fall of Torrelobaton had remained idle. Meeting them on the plain of Villalar, as they attempted to retreat to Toro, he won a decisive victory. The rebels outnumbered, especially in cavalry, fled, leaving their commander Padilla in the enemy's hands. *They are defeated at* On the following day he was executed. The *Villalar.* defeat of Villalar, and the loss of their leader, *April 23, 1521.* sufficed to end the matter. The Bishop of Zamora was seized as he attempted to fly to France, and having murdered the governor of the prison was hung. Town after town capitulated, and on April 27, 1521, the viceregents entered Valladolid.

In Toledo, the first city to rise, Donna Maria Pacheco, the intrepid widow of Padilla, still held out. But in October, finding it impossible to keep the citizens in control, she fled to Portugal, and the city and citadel opened their gates. Shortly afterwards the revolt in Valencia was put down, chiefly by the nobles themselves.

The cause of the failure of this serious revolt may be summed up in one word—disunion. The rebellion had been confined to the kingdom of Castile. Neither *Causes of* Aragon nor Catalonia had moved, and the rebels *failure of the* of Valencia fought for their own cause and gave *Revolt.* no support. Nor were the 'comuneros' of Castile of one mind. They were divided in their aims, and showed no power of concentrated action, while their cause was further weakened by the incapacity and the jealousies of their leaders. The prestige of the monarchy, enhanced as it had been by the policy of Ferdinand and Isabella, was too great to be thus overthrown. Indeed, but for the European difficulties of Charles, and the lukewarmness of the nobles —an attitude which is largely to be attributed to their discontent—the revolt would either never have occurred, or would have been crushed out at once.

Charles did not come to Spain till the year 1522. A few of the rebels were executed, the estates of others were con-

Subsequent measures of Charles.

fiscated. He then summoned a Cortes in which he ordered that the 'servicio' should be granted before grievances were heard, and forbade all discussion in the absence of the President, who was to be his nominee. In future, deputies were nominated by the government and frequently bribed; and so valuable did a seat in the Cortes become, that in 1534 we find a deputy giving 14,000 ducats for his seat. The nobles, still insisting on their privilege of exemption from taxation, continued to be excluded from the Cortes, and rapidly lost all political influence. After the decline of the military power in Spain, the higher nobility, the 'ricos hombres,' relapsed into luxurious idleness; the lower nobility, 'the hidalgos,' and the knights or 'caballeros,' pressed into the service of the Crown, and became its creatures, while the commoners sought for titles of nobility that they might share the emoluments of office, and enjoy the other privileges of nobility. Nor was the Church more independent. The Crown made use of its power of nominating to benefices, filled them with its adherents, and kept it in a condition of servility. The Inquisition, however, was the most efficient weapon in the hands of the Crown. It was entirely under the King's control; the property of the condemned fell to the Crown, and no subject, cleric or lay, was free from its jurisdiction. Charles did not indeed directly tamper with the constitution of Castile, and was even more cautious in his treatment of Aragon. The meetings of the Cortes still continued, nor did Charles refuse to listen to their petitions. Nevertheless, the power of the bureaucracy of the Crown increased, and Spain, exhausted by the wars of Charles, was being prepared for the despotism of Philip.[1]

[1] On this point cf. Armstrong, *Charles V.*, II. c. iii.

§ 3. *The Diet of Worms*, 1521.

Charles had been forced to let the revolt of the 'comuneros' in Spain run its course because of the serious problems in which he was involved by his position as an Austrian Prince and as Emperor. After his interview with Henry VIII. at Gravelines in the beginning of July, he had passed on to Germany to be crowned. Partly owing to need of money, partly because of an outbreak of the plague at Aix-la-Chapelle (Aachen), this was delayed till October, and it was not till the following January, 1521, that he met his first Diet at Worms. Meanwhile he had settled the fate of the Austrian dominions. He had at first thought of keeping at least a portion of these lands in his own hands. Finally, however, while retaining the Netherlands and Franche-Comté, he granted to his brother Ferdinand the whole of the hereditary Austrian lands; to which were added the claims on Hungary and Bohemia, based on Ferdinand's marriage with the Princess Anne. Thus Spain and Austria, which had been in Charles' hands for two years, were once more divided, never to be again united. The questions which came before this important Diet were mainly three :

The Diet of Worms. Jan. 1521.

(1) The settlement of the Imperial Constitution.
(2) The war with France.
(3) The attitude to be adopted towards Luther.

1. The question of the reform of the Imperial Constitution revived those controversies, of which we have treated in speaking of Maximilian, and with very similar results. Charles had promised in his 'Capitulations' (p. 133) that the Council of

Regency (*Reichsregiment*) which had existed for two brief years, 1500-1502, should be restored. But here, once more, the old controversies reappeared. The Electors wished that the Council should constitute the supreme administrative body in home and foreign affairs, even when Charles was present in Germany, and that its members should be elected by the States with the sole exception of the President, who was to be nominated by the Emperor. Charles, however, was fully determined to protect his imperial prerogatives. His views as to the imperial office were, if possible, more exalted than those of his grandfather. In his opening speech on the 28th of January, the day consecrated to the memory of Charles the Great, he declared that 'no monarchy was comparable to the Roman Empire. This the whole world had once obeyed, and Christ Himself had paid it honour and allegiance. Unfortunately it was now only a shadow of what it had been, but he hoped with the help of those powerful countries and alliances which God had granted him, to raise it to its ancient glory.' 'My will,' he said subsequently, 'is not that there should be many, but one master, as befits the traditions of the Roman Empire.' Yet the needs of Charles were great, and had the Diet been of one mind it might have forced its views upon him. The old jealousies, however, still existed, and Charles, by playing upon these, was able to make it abate something of its demands. It was accordingly agreed that the Emperor should nominate, not only the President, but two assessors. Of the other twenty members, the seven Electors were each to send one delegate ; the six Circles, with Austria and the Netherlands, one apiece. From the imperial towns two more were to come, while one Elector in rotation, one temporal and one spiritual Prince, were always to have a seat. The Council, thus constituted, was to have the initiative in the negotiation of foreign alliances, and in settling feudal questions, subject, however, to the confirmation of the Emperor. Its powers, for the present at least, were only to continue during Charles' absence. At the same time, the Imperial Chamber (*Reichskammergericht*) was slightly altered. The Emperor was to nominate the President and two assessors. The others were to be elected by the Electors and the Circles, while two were to represent the hereditary dominions of the House of Hapsburg. The most difficult question yet remained. How were the members of these bodies to be paid? If no permanent revenue were established, continuity would be impossible, and if the Emperor were to pay them, the real control would lie with him. Accordingly, the old controversies began again. The plan of the Common Penny having failed (p. 111), the novel idea of establishing a system of custom-duties on all imports coming into the Empire was suggested. Had this been carried, a kind of customs-union (*Zollverein*) would have been set on foot which might in time have led the way to a closer political union. It was, however, violently opposed by the towns' and merchants, who declared that the burden would fall on them and ruin trade ; and, accordingly, the Diet fell back on the system of the 'matricula' of 1507 (cf. p. 114).

2 Difficulties also arose on the question of the army. The war with France had already been commenced by the invasion of Spanish Navarre by the French, and by the attack of Robert de la Marck, the Lord of Bouillon, on Luxembourg. Charles also was eager to enter Italy that he might put it to the arbitrament of war, 'whether he should become a very poor Emperor, or Francis a sorry King.' Yet all the Diet would provide was a levy of some 4000 cavalry and 20,000 infantry, levied on the separate states according to the system of the 'matricula.' It was further decreed that each contingent should be under its own officers, and that the commander-in-chief, though appointed by the Emperor, must be a German. This 'matricula' or imperial roll was the last ever drawn up, and thus became the model for future imperial levies. From 1535 onwards, the system was gradually adopted of substituting for the men themselves the money necessary to pay the contingent—the money being

assessed on the separate States, according to their liability on the roll of 1521. The grants were termed 'Roman Months,' because they originated with the vote for the Roman expedition of 1521.

In these constitutional struggles, Charles had obtained something. He had at least succeeded in retaining more control over the Council of Regency and the Imperial Chamber than his grandfather had enjoyed. Yet the Diet had gained much. It had now a real share in the executive and judicial administration of the Empire, and Charles would be more often absent than present. For the rest, as before, the reforms were mainly in the interest of the Electors and more powerful Princes. The towns, though represented in the Council, could easily be outvoted, and had failed, in spite of urgent protests, to secure any delegates in the Imperial Chamber. Devoid of popular support, the Imperial Chamber failed to enforce its judicial authority, while the next few years were to prove conclusively that the Council was powerless to maintain order.

3. The last question—that of the attitude of the Diet towards Luther—was to prove a far more serious question than any one at that time dreamt of—a question which was to affect deeply the future history not only of the Empire, but of Europe.

The Reformation was the outcome of two forces, independent in origin, and never wholly in agreement : the Renaissance, and the desire for reform in dogma and practice. Of these, the first owes its birth to Italy. The Italians, despairing of political unity or stability, yet excelling other people in material prosperity and comfort, betook themselves to the study of the past for which their unbroken connection with the language and memories of Rome well fitted them. The movement, beginning in the earlier decades of the fifteenth century, had made rapid strides before it closed, and was many-sided. In art, it was marked by a return to the study of the antique ; in literature,

The Renaissance and the Reformation.

by a fresh taste for prose and poetry, founded on classic models; in scholarship, it was accompanied by the discovery of ancient manuscripts, and the revival of criticism; in philosophy, it led to a revival of the knowledge of Plato; in natural science, to a more critical inquiry into the nature of the earth and its relation to the system of the universe.

But the principles which underlay and actuated these different energies were the same. Mediæval thought had striven to sacrifice the individual. It had taught men to crucify the body with its fleshly lusts, to check the rebellious passion for independence and individuality. It had bidden men accept without question the authority of the Church, and of the temporal power. The new spirit revolted from all these doctrines. It preached the dignity of man, and of this life. It questioned the virtue of asceticism, and lusted after the world in thought and deed. It proclaimed the right of the individual to think, and feel, and shape his creed according to the dictates of reason. It inculcated the lessons of inquiry, of criticism, of naturalism. Thus a new paradise was opened to the imagination, and men rushed headlong into it with a pleasing sense of freedom. There was much that was valuable, and indeed necessary to progress, in this movement of emancipation. It led to more accurate observation, to more careful criticism, to greater regard for literature, and to the triumph of individualism. Nevertheless, it had its darker side. It was accompanied by much riot and licence. The sensuous delight in form and colour betrayed some into sensuality ; the undue devotion to things of this world led to a mundane pagan spirit ; criticism, to scepticism and infidelity. The atmosphere of the Renaissance was indeed inimical to that of the Christian life, yet, with a few exceptions, the Italians made no direct attack upon the Church. The literary men were well content to leave an institution alone, which was so closely wrapped up with their past traditions and with the general culture of the day, and which so conveniently patronised them, and even tolerated their satires, so long as they left her government and her dogmas alone. With the philosophers it was different. Yet even they assailed Christianity rather than the Church ; and if Ficino tried to reconcile Christianity and Platonism, or Pomponazzi questioned the immortality of the soul, these scholars affected to distinguish between science and religion, and while they speculated as philosophers, professed to believe as Christians. Thus there is hardly any humanist of Italy, if we except Laurentius Valla, who attacked the claims of the Pope to interfere in temporal affairs, or the tradition that the Apostles' Creed was the work of the apostles ; and even he, for the sake of papal protection, easily retracted his errors.

For the rest, the Italian humanists were scarcely serious enough to undertake a reformation of the Church. Their temper, if not anti-religious, was irreligious, and their lives, with few exceptions, as loose as those of the churchmen whom they lampooned. Reformers there were indeed in Italy, but these had no connection with the humanists. They were men of the type of Savonarola, whose sole idea of reform was one of morals and of life, and who had no quarrel with the dogmas, or the organisation of the Church.

No sooner did the Renaissance cross the Alps than, in the hands of the more earnest-minded Germans, it became more serious and more theological, less philosophical and more dogmatic. Criticism they now applied to the Church, and in another sense to the Bible, with the intention not of destroying Christianity but of restoring it to its primitive purity.

Among numerous scholars who rose in Germany at the close of the fifteenth century, the two most characteristic Reuchlin and representatives of the age were John Reuchlin Erasmus. (1455-1522) and Desiderius Erasmus (1467-1536). Reuchlin is chiefly noticeable for his revival of the study of Hebrew, a study which he applied to the criticism of the Vulgate, and for his attempt to save the Jewish writings from indiscriminate destruction at the hands of the bigoted Dominican Hochstraten. Although a philologist, rather than a theologian, he may yet be called the father of Old Testament criticism, and during the struggle over the Jewish literature, the conflict between the old and new ideas is strongly emphasised.

But the most famous child of the German revival is Erasmus. Educated at the school of Deventer, a school which owed its origin to the Brethren of the Common Life, he was, at the date of the Diet of Worms, looked upon as the greatest scholar of his age, and enjoyed a reputation such as probably has never been equalled since. If Reuchlin may be called the father of Old Testament criticism, Erasmus may be termed the father of New Testament criticism, and of scientific theology. In 1505, he republished Valla's notes on the New Testament, the solitary piece of biblical criticism which had come from Italy. This was followed, in 1516, by his Greek edition of the New Testament, with a Latin translation and notes. The aim of these works was to revive the knowledge of the original, and by the collation of such MSS. as were procurable, to furnish as correct a version as possible of the text. In the notes, Erasmus applied the canons of ordinary criticism to the New Testament, and thereby laid the foundations of modern biblical scholarship. The aim of his third work, the *Enchiridion Militis Christi*, may be gathered from a letter to his friend Colet, Dean of St. Paul's : ' I write,' he says, 'to remedy the error which makes religion depend on ceremonies and on observance of bodily acts, while neglecting true piety.' With these views Erasmus was naturally a severe critic of the existing state of things. He lamented the ignorance of many churchmen who dreaded the new learning without understanding it ; who went so far as to denounce Hebrew and Greek as heretical because they were not the language of the Vulgate, and whose bigotry had just been so conspicuously displayed in the Reuchlin controversy. He despised the idleness of the monks, and the intolerable narrowness of the scholastic pedants, with their barren disputations and endless hair-splittings. He denounced the folly of that Church which insisted on every tittle of outward ceremony and dogma, and yet neglected practical piety. These were the objects of his satirical pen in his *Praise of Folly*, which was written in England in 1509. In this wonderful satire, Folly, declaring herself the real source of happiness, represents herself as the authoress of all the superstition, the pedantry, the idleness, the hypocrisy, which were so prosperous in the world.

Nor was the satire of Erasmus the only one which appeared at this time. The *Ship of Fools* by Sebastian Brandt in 1494, and the more famous *Epistolæ Obscurorum Virorum*, which arose out of the Reuchlin controversy, deal with much the same evils, though without the literary refinement of the northern scholar; while the *Ship of Fools* is specially noticeable as having been originally written in German, and therefore written for the people, not to the scholars. But although these and other writings indicate how deeply Germany was stirred by the corruptions of the Church, and although they had done much to prepare the way, there was as yet no idea of breaking away from her. Men still looked to internal reform by Council, or if not, by some other method.

It has been usual to accuse Erasmus of half-heartedness in the cause of religion, of carelessness in his private life, and of time-serving in his public conduct. There is certainly some truth in this attack, and assuredly he was not the man to raise the standard of avowed rebellion. As he himself confessed, he was not of the stuff of which martyrs were made. He was a scholar who loved peace, and had nothing of the religious enthusiast about him. But quite apart from his character, his whole intellectual position was incompatible with that of the Reformation, as the Protestants understand the meaning of the word. Erasmus belongs to that school of broad churchmen, who did not believe that the cure for the evils afoot was to be found in the assertion of new dogmas. In their view, too much dogma was insisted upon already. Much was at least not comprehensible to the multitude, and, if to be altered, should be altered by the slow dissolvent of learned criticism. Reform with them meant a gradual autumnal change, which might take place without violently breaking with the past, while the moral principles acknowledged by all should be enforced, and made more real. In short, Erasmus is the father of modern latitudinarianism, as well as of biblical criticism. His whole nature shrank from more violent methods, and he feared their results. He foresaw the extravagances, the controversies, and the schisms which would inevitably follow, and delay the triumph of rational theology. The Reformation of the sixteenth century could not be guided by him ; but, as it has been well said, perhaps the Reformation that is to come will trace itself back to Erasmus.

The final breach with Rome was not to come from scholars of world-wide reputation, but from the son of a Thuringian peasant who, although of robust mind, was an indifferent Greek scholar, and knew no Hebrew. In dealing with Martin Luther it is of importance to remember the various steps in his career. Martin Luther, 1483-1546.

Driven by the consciousness of sin and the desire of spiritual peace he had, at the age of twenty-two, entered the Order of the Augustinian Friars at Erfurt, much against the wish of his father (1505). Here he subjected himself to the severest discipline, but without avail. 'If ever a monk had got to heaven by monkery, I should have been he,' he said subsequently ; 'for all that a monk could do, I did.' Repeated acts of penance did not save him from new temptations, and God remained in his eyes an inexorable judge, demanding obedience to an impossible law. From this condition of despair, Luther was delivered by Staupitz, the Vicar-General of his Order, who counselled a closer study of the Bible, especially of the writings of St. Paul, and of the Latin father, St. Augustine. Here, in the Augustinian doctrine of justification by faith, he at last found peace; in the text, 'The just shall live by faith,' appeared the solution of his difficulties. The sinner was not to be saved by his own efforts or work, but by throwing himself unreservedly on the mercies of a loving God ; thus received into a state of grace, the faithful believer found penitence no longer painful, but a spontaneous act of love, while work and life for God alone became easy. In this view he was strengthened at a later date by discovering that the Greek word for *penitentia* was μετάνοια—in other words, that the efficacy of penance did not consist in the external ecclesiastical penalty, but in the inward change of heart. In thus asserting the Augustinian doctrine of justification by faith, Luther was only reviving what had been held by many Fathers of the early Church—a doctrine which had indeed of late been overclouded by the contrary one of the justification by works, but which had never been wholly discarded. It is no doubt true that these opposing and contradictory dogmas are incapable of entire reconciliation, nor must either of them be forced to their logical conclusion, for if we are justified by God's grace alone, where is the necessity for works ; and if by works alone we are saved, where is the need for a Redeemer? No doubt, once more, the doctrine of the justification by faith is, if it be carried to an extreme, apt to lead, and has in fact led, to fanatical fatalism and antinomianism. To Luther, however, it seemed that the evils which followed on the adoption of the contrary doctrine were worse ; as if frail men could by their unaided efforts extort salvation from the Almighty. To hold this view was to nurse that very spiritual pride which was the cause of the existing corruption. The only hope for moral reformation lay in bringing man to believe in his utter unworthiness in the sight of God ; thus alone could he attain that spirit of humility which was the essential preliminary to a godly life.

In 1508, Luther was summoned by Staupitz to teach at the university of Wittenberg, just founded by Frederick the Wise of Saxony. In 1510, he visited Rome, a visit which only served to strengthen him in his conviction that spiritual pride, the characteristic fault of the Renaissance, was the enemy to be withstood, and to deepen his dislike of those ceremonial observances of the Church which consecrated the belief in the efficacy of works. Luther had returned to Wittenberg to carry on his teaching, when the visit of Tetzel, a Dominican, to Germany, offering papal indulgences to those who would contribute money to the building of St. Peter's at Rome, aroused him to immediate action. The doctrine of indulgences originated in the not unnatural view, that while penitence reconciled the sinner to God, the wrong done to man had yet to be punished, and that the punishment, like that for worldly offences, could be commuted by a fine. But the system had been shamefully abused. The Church declared that she held, in the works of supererogation of the faithful, a treasure from which she could draw for the remission of penalties, and, in her eager desire to gain money, granted indulgences carelessly and without insisting on the previous penitence of the offender. She even claimed the power of remitting the punishment of those in purgatory. Whatever may be said in defence of the primitive system of indulgences, it cannot be denied that in their exaggerated form they led to grievous abuse, and involved a flat denial of the necessity of grace. Accordingly Luther, in pursuance of academic custom, nailed on the door of the church at Wittenberg his famous ninety-five theses, in which he controverted the theory of indulgences, and challenged all comers to disprove the correctness of his statements (October 17, 1517).

The views of Luther were not original. Several theologians before him, even Cardinal Ximenes himself, had protested against the scandalous abuse of indulgences. Nor did Luther dream of rebelling against Mother Church. He did not deny the value of indulgences altogether, but declared that, in his opinion, the Pope could not thereby remit the guilt of sin nor abate the penalties of those who had already passed to their account. Further, he declared that the extravagant views he was combating were the invention of the schoolmen, not of the Church, which had never formally accepted them. He therefore demanded an expression of the mind of the Pope and Church thereon. Luther asked for discussion and for argument ; he was met with assertion and denunciation. Tetzel in his answer disdained to discuss the question of indulgences at all, and he asserted the claim of the Pope to determine matters of opinion and to interpret Scripture. The Dominican Prierias declared that neither a Council presided over by the Pope, nor the Pope himself, could err when he gave an official decision, and branded all those as heretics who did not accept the doctrines of the Church and Popes, as the rule of faith. Cardinal Cajetan, who was sent as papal legate to the Diet of Augsburg in 1518, although he secretly agreed with Luther as to the abuse of indulgences, refused all disputation, and demanded a recantation and silence for the future. Luther's subsequent promise to keep silence on his part, if it were adhered to on the other, could not possibly be kept, and the discussion soon broke out afresh.

Meanwhile, the ground of controversy had shifted. It was no longer a question of indulgences, but of papal power and the authority of tradition. The extravagant assertions of the papal advocates were met by more outspoken, more violent, and sometimes by unseemly language on the part of Luther. Wider reading now convinced him that his views were not novel, but had been anticipated by others, such as John Huss, John Wessel, and even by the humanist Laurentius Valla ; while he was strengthened by the increasing support he met with in Germany. Ulrich von Hutten, a man whose love of satire outran his better taste, embittered the controversy by the biting epigrams of his *Vadiscus* (1519): 'Three things maintain the dignity of Rome—the authority of the Pope, the relics of the saints, the sale of indulgences. Three things are feared at Rome — a General Council, a reform of the Church, the opening of the eyes of the Germans. Three things are excommunicated at Rome— indigence, the primitive Church, the preaching of truth.' Finally, Luther, in his *Address to the Christian Nobility of the German Nation* (July, 1520), still more in his tractate on the *Babylonish Captivity* (October, 1520), was led on not only to deny the authority of the Pope, but to question the divine institution of the priesthood, and the authority of tradition, and to attack the mediæval doctrine of Transubstantiation. That Luther had now definitely put himself outside the Church, cannot be gainsaid. Yet at least it should be remembered that he was driven to his final position by the knowledge that he was already condemned, and that the Bull of excommunication had been issued as early as June 1520, although not published in Germany till later. Luther, therefore, throwing all hopes of conciliation to the winds, declared the Bull a forgery and the author of it Antichrist, and on December 10, 1520, burnt it publicly at Wittenberg.

Whether, considering the character of Luther, his earnestness, his bluntness, his fearlessness, his want of scholarly refinement, and his violence, he might have been checked by a more conciliatory attitude on the part of his opponents ; or whether, again, had he been conciliated, another leader in the existing ferment of German feeling would not have arisen, may well be questioned. But at least the conduct of the papal court could not have been more indiscreet or less statesmanlike. Leo X. himself, with his cynical indifference to such matters, might very possibly have acted otherwise ; but the attack on indulgences threatened the whole machinery of papal finance and administration, and the officials of the Curia drove him on. We cannot but deplore that a Church, which could treat with leniency unorthodoxy on such fundamental questions as the immortality of the soul, should have refused to listen to the criticism of her system of indulgences, especially as we know that the system, in its abuse at any rate, pricked the consciences of so many of her most loyal sons. That the conduct of Luther is open to blame must be allowed. That he too lightly cast away the traditions of the Church, and too confidently believed in the possibility of

finding all that was necessary to salvation, and for the organisation of the Church in the Bible alone; that many of his
doctrines have been exaggerated and have led to much evil;
that the immediate results of the Reformation were neither
to promote learning, nor to advance the spirit of toleration—
all this cannot be denied.   That the revolt which was thus
inaugurated was to break the unity of the Church, to lead to
endless schism, and verily to bring a sword on earth, we must
all regret.   But Rome, at least, determined that it should
be so; and we may fairly doubt whether the reform of that
corruption, which had eaten so deeply into her system, could
have been effected at a less costly price.

Such was the position of affairs when the Diet of Worms
met.   The question was whether the Diet would enforce the
Luther and   Bull and place Luther under the ban of the
the Diet.   Empire — a question fraught with momentous
issues.   Leo x., without allowing Luther to be heard in
self-defence, urged Charles to execute the Bull.   But though
the Emperor himself was in favour of such a course,
and was supported by his confessor Glapion, many of his
advisers, notably Chièvres, and Gattinara, his chancellor, were
of a contrary opinion.   They knew the support which Luther
had already received in Germany from the poorer nobles,
the poets, the lawyers, and the men of letters, and what that
support was we may learn from the papal agent, Aleander:
'Nine-tenths of Germany shouts for Luther; and the other
one-tenth, if it does not care for Luther, at least cries, Down
with the Roman court, and demands a Council to be held
in Germany.'   It was not to be expected that the Diet would
dare to disregard this popular feeling.   Moreover, although
the majority were wholly opposed to the doctrinal views held by
Luther, many of its members sympathised with his desire for
reform in matters of Church government and discipline.   The
Diet, therefore, demanded that Luther should be heard, declaring at the same time that, if he persisted in his heretical views,
contrary to the doctrine and faith 'which they, their fathers,

and fathers' fathers had held,' they were ready to condemn him. Besides all this, the advisers of Charles were not blind to the political advantages which might be gained from the situation. Maximilian had once said: 'Let the Wittenberg monk be taken good care of; we may want him some day,' —and the day had come. Leo was still hesitating between the alliance of Charles and Francis, and the threat of referring the whole question to a General Council might be used to force his hand.

Luther was accordingly summoned to Worms under promise of a safe-conduct. If now he had consented to retract his doctrines on matters of faith, and had confined himself to the question of internal reform, he would probably have received the hearty support of the Diet. But this was far from his intention, and his uncompromising conduct played for the moment into the hands of Rome. He had expected that he would be asked for a defence of his opinions; he was ordered to retract his heresies on points of doctrine. This he declined to do. To the demand that he would acknowledge the Emperor and the Diet as judges of his doctrines, he answered that he would not allow men to judge of God's word. He even refused to submit to the decisions of a General Council 'unless his views were refuted by Scripture or by cogent reason.' Thus he became in the eyes of Charles not only a heretic, but, what was worse, a rebel; and the alliance of the Pope having now been secretly secured, Luther was no longer wanted for political purposes. Charles, therefore, was eager for the publication of the ban and for an order that the books of the heretic should be burnt. So great, however, was the repugnance of the Diet to face the unpopularity of this act that Charles only succeeded in gaining its assent at its last session (May 25), after Frederick of Saxony and the Elector Palatine had left. Luther meanwhile had fled to the Castle of the Wartburg in Saxony, where he lay hid under the protection of Frederick the Wise. He had now been excommunicated, and the excommunication had been ratified by the

Diet. The future was to see whether the Emperor could enforce the decision of the Diet in Germany.

§ 4. *The War*, 1521-1523.

At this moment the attention of Charles was directed to the war against Francis. The humiliation of his rival, and the conquest of Italy, were the first essentials; till these were attained, the affair of Luther might wait. The French had been the first to assume the offensive. Already, in May, they had invaded Navarre, while in the previous March, Robert de la Marck, the Lord of Bouillon, had attacked Luxembourg. These expeditions, however, had both failed, and Charles now secured the alliance, not only of the vacillating Pope, but Leo X. and also of Henry VIII. Leo X. had been gratified at Henry VIII. the publication of the ban against Luther. He ally themselves with convinced himself that the victory of the French Charles V. in Italy would be more disastrous than that of Charles, and on May 25 definitely joined the Emperor. Ferrara and Parma were to be restored to the Pope. Milan was to be held as a fief of the Empire by Francesco Sforza, son of Ludovico il Moro; the French were to be driven from Genoa, and Antonio Adorno set up as Doge; the Emperor promised to protect the Medici in Florence, and to join the Pope in extirpating the heresy of Luther.

In November, Wolsey, after in vain attempting to continue his policy of mediation at the Conference of Calais, was forced at last to declare himself. He joined the league of Emperor and Pope, and promised to aid Charles in a joint invasion of France : the Emperor, on his part, engaged to marry the Princess Mary.

The English did not move ; but in Italy the imperial and papal troops were successful. Lautrec, the Success of French commander, deserted by the Swiss, imperial and papal troops who had been forbidden by the authorities at in Italy. home to fight against their countrymen, was forced to evacuate Milan, with the exception of the citadel (November 19), and Parma and Piacenza soon surrendered.

At this moment, when fortune seemed to smile on Leo X., he was struck down by fever (December 1). The character of his pontificate is such as we should expect from the son of Lorenzo the Magnificent. His name will always be associated with the artistic triumphs of Raphael, and remembered for his patronage of literature ; but this is his only claim to honour. His character is well illustrated by his saying at his election, ' Let us enjoy the Papacy now we have got it.' Though not profligate himself, he condoned profligacy in others, and at no time was luxury more profuse, or life in Rome more careless. He lived for pleasure ; in the spiritual duties of his office he took but little interest. The serious problems of the time he showed himself incapable of realising. If his careless generosity brought him popularity, it seriously encumbered the papal finances ; and if, when he died, the sky seemed fair, this was but the clearness which oft precedes the storm—a storm which was largely due to his want of seriousness, of insight, and of statesmanship.

Death of Leo X. Dec. 1, 1521.

To the surprise of all, the man chosen to succeed him was Adrian of Utrecht, once the tutor of Charles, and subsequently his Viceroy in Spain. His election was due to the impossibility of finding any one else who could obtain sufficient suffrages in the electoral college. Wolsey, who was a serious candidate, only secured seven. Giulio de' Medici and Alexander Farnese, both eventually destined to wear the tiara, as Clement VII. and Paul III., were equally unsuccessful. A long vacancy was considered dangerous ; and Cardinal de' Medici, who, in spite of the warm support of the Emperor, despaired of his own success, transferred his votes to Adrian. Thus two Flemings, hitherto closely associated, now held the two highest dignities in Christendom, and much might have been expected from such a remarkable event. These expectations, however, were not to be realised. The new Pope, indeed, presented a striking contrast to his predecessor ; but this very contrast served but

Election of Adrian VI. Jan. 1522.

to increase his difficulties. The Romans were annoyed at the election of 'a barbarian.' Their fears that Adrian might transfer the seat of the Papacy to Spain, expressed itself in the satirical advertisement, 'Roma est locanda,' posted on the walls of the Vatican. The Cardinals, who at first went in fear of their lives from the Roman populace, soon regretted their decision, and hated this austere reforming Pope, who tried to cut down their salaries and pensions, while he showed favour to his Flemish followers. The literary men were disgusted at his lack of sympathy with the new learning. Even his uprightness and holiness of life failed to make him friends among those who desired reform. His economies were attributed to parsimony; his retiring habits and his want of real initiative and of character lost him that support which otherwise might have been accorded to him. Nor was his attitude towards Luther, or to the political issues of the day, more fortunate. Fully convinced of the necessity of internal reform of abuses, he was none the less devoid of sympathy with the new theology. As inquisitor in Spain, he had adopted Spanish views, and thought that repression must precede reform; when the heretic had been disposed of, the Pope could begin to set his house in order.

On this point the Emperor agreed with him, but here agreement ceased. Adrian had served him well as tutor, and then as his viceroy in Spain; and now that his servant sat on the papal throne, he looked for a continuance of that service. He forgot that there was all the difference between Adrian, the viceroy of the King of Spain, and Adrian the Pope. Nor were their views the same. Charles was determined to be master in Italy; for that, not only the Lutheran question, but even the war against the Turk must wait, threatening though the attitude of Solyman was at this moment. Adrian, on the contrary, was not anxious to see the Emperor too powerful in Italy, and yearned to free the Papacy from the political trammels in which late Popes had involved it. To bring about a reconciliation between the two rivals, and then rally all Christendom in a crusade against the Turk, this was Adrian's dream.   For this purpose he assumed a position of neutrality and attempted the work of mediation.   The results of this policy were most unfortunate. The French party in Italy raised their heads; the Duke of Ferrara began to move (February, 1522); the opponents of the Medici in Florence and Siena renewed their intrigues with Francis; the Swiss again took service under France, and sent a contingent into Italy, which was supplemented by Venice.   So serious did things look, that Don Manuel, writing from Rome, advised a truce with Francis.

At this moment, however, the victory of Bicocca retrieved the fortunes of Charles.   In March, Lautrec had advanced against Milan, then held by Colonna for the   Battle of
Emperor.   Sforza at once marched from Pavia   Bicocca.
to relieve Colonna, and, after some manœuvring,   April 27, 1522.
entrenched himself in the Villa Bicocca, some few miles from the city.   The position was a strong one.   But the Swiss showed insubordination, and insisted on an attack, which Lautrec dared not refuse.   The Swiss had miscalculated their powers, and were repulsed.   Lautrec, who had made a detour with his French soldiers, with the object of taking the position in the rear, from whence alone an entrance seemed practicable, was delayed, and had to face the united force of the enemy, flushed as they were with victory over the Swiss.   He was beaten back with serious loss, and the imperial forces remained masters of the first important battle of the war.   The defeat ruined the French cause.   They still held the citadel of Milan, and the town of Novara, but had to evacuate the rest of the Milanese, and shortly after (May 30), they were   French
driven from Genoa.   The Doge, Ottavio Fregoso,   evacuate the
the leader of the French party, was taken prisoner, as   Milanese.
well as Pedro Navarra, the great Spanish general, who had been driven into the service of France by the niggardliness of Ferdinand.   Antonio Adorno was set up as Doge, as a vassal of Charles—and France thus lost the important harbour which

hitherto had given her an easy entrance into Italy. The victory of Charles only served to increase Adrian's desire for peace, but neither of the rivals would listen. In

Treaty of Windsor. June, 1522.

June, 1522, Charles, then on his way to Spain, signed the treaty of Windsor. Henry and the Emperor agreed that the humiliation of Francis was the necessary preliminary to a war against the Turk. They accordingly promised to engage in a joint attack on France, and to solicit the alliance of the Pope and Venice. Even the fall of Rhodes, the important outpost against the Moslem, held by the knights of St. John in the Mediterranean (December 20), although it caused great dismay in Europe and bitter grief to Adrian, did not cause the two great powers to forego their quarrels ; and finally in August, Adrian, warned by the intrigues of the French partisans in Italy that any idea

The League of August 1523. Death of Adrian, Sept. 14, 1523.

of mediation was vain, and that if the French were victorious the Papal States would be in danger, joined in a defensive league with the Emperor, a league which included England, Milan, Genoa, Florence, and Venice. Six weeks afterwards, Adrian died (September 14, 1523).

In spite of his narrowness and want of statesmanship, Adrian was a good man, and earnestly desired reform. Yet the desire only earned him the inveterate hatred of the Cardinals, and of the mob of Rome, who decorated the door of his physician with a wreath, dedicated ' to the liberator of his country.' The pathetic failure of Pope Adrian is perhaps the best vindication of Luther's revolt.

§ 5. *Luther and the Council of Regency.*

The absence of Charles in Spain, where he remained for seven momentous years (July 1522 to August 1529), indicates most forcibly where his real interests lay. Cruelly as he treated all those who had taken part in the revolt of the Communeros, he had, since the death of Chièvres in 1521, become a thorough Spaniard in sympathy. In that year, he finally ceded to

Ferdinand the Austrian lands of his House, and henceforth looked on Spain as the real centre of his Empire. The pride of the Spaniards, their determination to crush out heresy,—above all, their passion to dominate the world, he fully shared; and it was on Spanish troops and Spanish money that he mainly depended in his wars. He passed the largest part of his life in Spain. He retired thither, and there he died.

Charles in Spain for seven years, 1522-1529.

In this fact then, and in his imperial position, lies the best answer to Napoleon's taunt that Charles was a fool not to have adopted Protestantism and founded a strong monarchy on that basis. Whether such a policy on Charles' part would have succeeded, may well be doubted. He would have found arrayed against him the majority of the Electors and Princes, who, whatever their religious views, dreaded above all things a strong monarchical rule; and our doubt will be intensified if we remember the future policy of the Catholic League during the Thirty Years' War. But, however that may be, Napoleon did not appreciate Charles' character. As well might a leopard be bidden change its spots, as Charles be asked to lead a national German movement against all that Emperors, and Kings of Spain held dear.

Answer to the taunt of Napoleon.

To grasp the possible alternatives we have only to recall the political condition of Germany, already described at pages 106 ff. We there noticed four forces struggling for the mastery :—

The possible alternatives for Germany.

1. The dynastic aims of the Hapsburgs, bent on establishing a centralised monarchy.
2. The constitutional ideas of the Electors, aiming at an aristocratic confederation.
3. The anarchical elements, represented by the constant private warfare, and the social disturbances of the 'Bundschuhe,' or peasants' associations.
4. The desire for territorial independence, shared by most of the Princes.

On the question which of these should finally gain the
mastery, to a great extent depended the fate of the Reformation in Germany. The triumph of the first would, there can
be little doubt, have led to the extirpation of heresy, and the
establishment of autocratical rule, both ecclesiastical and
civil. Could the second succeed, there was some hope of a
Protestant reformed Church, based upon a reformed Empire,
and a revived spirit of German nationality against Pope as
well as Emperor. The third, if not suppressed, or guided,
would surely lead to an outburst of religious fanaticism, and
to religious as well as political chaos. The last, which as we
shall see was eventually to prevail, established Protestantism
on the principle of 'cujus regio ejus religio,'—that is, of
territorial independence in Church as well as State.[1]

[1] To understand the future course of the Reformation in Germany, it is
necessary to study the map, and note—

a. The extraordinary number of principalities into which Germany was
divided.

b. The division of the dominions of the greater princes among branches
of the same family, many of whom took opposite sides. This will be best
seen from the following table :—

PROTESTANT.	CATHOLIC.
HOUSE OF WETTIN, IN SAXONY.	
Ernestine, Electoral Branch at Wittenberg.	Albertine, at Meissen.
Ernest, 1464-1468.	Albert, 1485-1500.
Frederick the Wise, 1486-1525. John, his brother, 1525-1532.	Duke George, 1500-1535. Henry, his brother, 1535-1541, becomes Protestant.
John Frederick, 1532-1554.	Maurice, 1541-1553, secures the Electorate.
HOHENZOLLERN.	
Younger Branches.	Electoral Branch.
(1) Albert of Prussia, Grand Master of Teutonic Order, 1512-1568. Secularises his Duchy, 1525. (2) Albert Alcibiades, Margrave of Culmbach, 1536-1557. (3) John of Küstrin, Margrave of Neumark, brother of Joachim II., 1571.	Albert Achilles, 1470-1486. John Cicero, 1485-1499. Joachim I., 1499-1535. Joachim II., 1535-1571. Becomes Protestant in 1539, though he never breaks with the Emperor.

The departure of Charles for Spain gave some hope that a reform of the Church might go hand in hand with a reform of the Empire. In his absence, power fell into the hands of the Council of Regency under the presidency of Ferdinand, whom Charles had nominated his Stadtholder. The Council in cluded among its numbers some, who desired to extend the political reforms already begun, and who were also not unfavourable to Luther ; while the orthodox party, although still in the majority, were too much alarmed at the growing popularity of Lutheran opinion to assume a decided attitude. In spite, therefore, of the exhortation of Adrian that they would enforce the Edict of Worms, the Council decided, after a stormy debate, to refer the matter

The Council of Regency during Charles' absence.

Diet of Nuremberg, Nov. 1522.

PROTESTANT.	CATHOLIC.

WITTELSBACH.

(1) Bavaria. Munich.	Philip, his nephew, 1476-1508.
Albert II., 1460-1508.	
	Lewis V., 1508-1544.
William I., 1508-1550.	Frederick II., his brother,
(2) Palatinate.	1544-1556, becomes Pro-
Frederick the Victorious,1451-1476.	testant. *

WELF.

Duke Ernest I., of Luneburg, 1532-1541.	Duke Henry IV., of Wolfenbüttel, 1514-1568.

WURTEMBURG.

Ulrich I., 1503-1550, became Protestant 1534.

c. The number of ecclesiastical states. The three great electoral archbishoprics of Trèves, Mayence, Cologne—with the bishoprics of Metz on the Moselle, and Strasburg and Worms—so dominated the upper Rhine and its tributaries as to give it the name of Priest Street. The dioceses of Utrecht, Bremen, Münster, and Paderborn stretched in an almost continuous line along the north-west. To these we must add Hildesheim, Halberstadt, Magdeburg, Würzburg, Bamberg in central Germany ; and in the south, the archbishopric of Salzburg, and the bishopric of Trent. The existence of these numerous ecclesiastical principalities had a twofold effect. It caused a strong feeling in Germany against papal exactions, of which the bishoprics were the victims, or the agents ; while the desire on the part of the Princes to extend their dominions by secularising these ecclesiastical states, had a potent influence on many an Elector and Prince, both Catholic and Protestant. In many cases, too, the bishops were the relations of the Princes, and their policy was guided by family interests or rivalries.

* See also Appendix iv,

to the Diet, which met for its second session at Nuremberg on November 17. In the Diet, the struggle began again with like results. The orthodox party still found themselves in the majority, but, with the exception of Joachim, Elector of Brandenburg, the Archbishop of Trèves, and George, Duke of Saxony, were unwilling to proceed to active measures. The delegates from the imperial cities all supported Luther. Nuremberg, where the Diet sat, was hotly in his favour, and many of the lay Princes feared to oppose the sentiments of their subjects. Accordingly, after much debate and reference to committees, the Diet answered the Pope as follows : They regretted the confusion caused by the Lutheran movement, but had refrained from enforcing the edict for fear of civil war. The Pope himself had admitted the existence of evils in the Church, and these must be amended. They therefore asked that a free Christian Council —in which laymen as well as ecclesiastics should be represented—should be summoned in Germany to discuss grievances. Meanwhile, no further Lutheran books should be printed, or sermons allowed, which might stir the people to revolt.

At the same time the lay estates presented their hundred 'Gravamina,' enumerating the chief papal abuses from which The hundred Germany had suffered. It is not correct to say, Gravamina. as has been said, that the Diet had declared for Luther, for he had been condemned to silence, and the Diet had no intention of breaking from Rome ; but the enforcement of the Edict was delayed, and delay was all that his cause needed. His adherents were increasing apace : as Ferdinand said, 'There is not one man in a thousand who is not more or less infected by Lutheran heresy,' and this explains the unwillingness of the Diet to proceed against him. Indeed, had the Diet, and more especially the Council of Regency, truly represented public opinion, the Reformation might have been established on national lines. This was prevented by the constitution of the Diet. Moreover, the respect of

Germany for the Council had been lost by its failure to put down the ' Knights' War.'

Franz von Sickingen, the famous Imperial Knight who had taken so prominent a part in the election of Charles, had adopted the opinions of Luther under the guid- The Council ance of Ulrich von Hutten, that strange literary of Regency free-lance on the Reformer's side. True to and the
' Knights' the traditions of his order, Sickingen hated the War.' Electors, the Princes, and the cities. He accord- Sept. 1522. ingly had organised a League of the Knights of the Upper Rhine and neighbouring districts. The League demanded the restoration of the old liberties of the Empire, the abolition of trade monopolies, the abrogation of foreign law, the diminution of the number of clergy and of monks, the cessation of the drain of money through indulgences and other papal exactions. Seeing his opportunity in the weakness of the Council, Sickingen determined to attack the dominions of the Elector of Trèves, relying for support upon a Lutheran party which had been formed there. If he could win the country, he would at once establish the Reformed opinions, and gain for himself a splendid territory. In September, 1522, he accordingly laid siege to the city of Trèves. In vain the Council ordered him to desist. The city, however, held out. Meanwhile the Princes became alarmed, they feared that their turn might come next, and took the matter into their own hands. Despite the commands of the Council to keep the peace, they rose, and, led by Philip, Landgrave of Hesse, defeated Sickingen, who shortly after died in the defence of his Castle of Ebernburg, April 1523. Hutten fled to Switzerland, to perish miserably shortly after. The Council also attempted, though in vain, to prevent the Suabian League from taking upon itself the duty of suppressing those Knights within its jurisdiction who had joined Sickingen.

Failing thus to secure obedience or maintain order, the Council forfeited all support. Some opposed it for what it

failed to do, others for fear of what it might become.   It
had never represented popular opinion, and now became
Failure of   disliked by the Diet itself.   The cities had
the Council   always objected to it on account of the taxa-
of Regency.   tion it necessitated.   Most of the Princes were
behindhand with their dues, and feared that the Council
might proceed against them.   Even the Electors despaired
of their projected reforms.   It was accordingly soon deserted
by its most prominent members.   The Elector Palatine, who
had been appointed vice-president, left it ; and the Elector
of Trèves, George of Saxony, and Philip of Hesse, declared
against it.   Finally, the Diet of Nuremberg, at its third session
(March-April, 1524), decided that its members should be re-
elected, and that none of the present members should be
re-eligible.   The new Council was no more successful, and
though it lasted till 1531, it enjoyed little authority.   The
spirit of independence and territorialism was too strong, and
all hope that the Reformation might go hand-in-hand with a
national movement based on a constitutional reform of the
Empire was at an end.

But this was not the only question that came before this Diet.
Adrian VI. had died on September 14, 1523.   The new Pope,
the Cardinal Guilio de' Medici, who took the name of Clement
Clement VII. VII. (elected November 1523), had sent Cam-
and the Diet peggio, his legate, to demand prompt execution
of Nuremberg.
March-April   of the Edict of Worms.   The adherents of
1524.   Rome, although still in a majority, did not feel
strong enough to comply fully with the Pope's command.
They promised indeed that the Edict should be enforced as
far as possible, and that heretical books should be suppressed;
but, ' lest the good should be rooted up with the bad,' they
again insisted on the summoning of a General Council in
Germany, and meanwhile suggested that another Diet should
be summoned at Spires to settle religious matters.   Clement
was not unnaturally displeased, and was in the main supported by Charles, who, in July, issued a decree enjoining strict

obedience to the Edict of Worms. The Emperor denounced Luther in the strongest terms, forbade the meeting of the Diet at Spires, and declared that, although he was not entirely opposed to the summoning of a General Council, this was a matter for him and the Pope to decide, since it would be presumptuous for Germany to undertake the alteration of Christian ordinances by herself. At the same time he wrote to Clement, saying that only two alternatives were before them : either that he (Charles) should go to Germany and suppress the heretics by force, a course which would be not only dangerous but impossible ; or that a General Council should be called. The Council he suggested might be summoned to Trent, and then removed to Rome. This course, however, Clement was unwilling to adopt, and Campeggio, by his orders, had already begun to treat with the Princes least favourable to Luther, who met in Congress at Ratisbon in June, 1524. After deciding to inaugurate a reform of some of the worst abuses of Christian discipline, and of the system of indulgences, they prohibited the reading of Luther's books, and forbade students to attend the heretical university of Wittenberg.

The Catholic Congress of Ratisbon. June, 1524.

This Congress at Ratisbon marks a further stage in the controversy. Hitherto the question of Luther had been treated as one of national interest. Here we meet with the first attempt to organise a party of opposition ; the Lutherans were forced to follow suit ; and Germany began to fall into two hostile camps, so that all hope of settling the religious question, without destroying the unity of the Empire, was wrecked. It was however something that the reform of abuses had been definitely mooted, and had Pope and Emperor been at one, something might have come of it ; but this was prevented by the political issues which once more drove them apart, and so monopolised Charles' attention that, as he said, 'This was no time to speak of Luther.'

§ 6. *The Victory of Pavia.*

Charles had hoped much from the election of Clement VII. But he forgot that he had to deal with a Medici. The aim
Charles disappointed in his hopes of support from Clement VII.
of Clement was to further the interests of the Papal States, and of his House in Florence, whither he had sent as governor Alessandro, the young son of his cousin Lorenzo, Duke of Urbino, under the tutelage of the Cardinal of Cortona. To attain these ends he, like Leo. X., hoped to balance the powers of Francis and Charles. Although he pretended that he was anxious for peace, he really feared the outcome of a common under-
Yet is at first successful in Italy, 1524.
standing between the rivals. Meanwhile he played a waiting game; and anxious to find himself on the winning side, pursued a timid faithless policy of intrigue which deceived no one, and was to bring the Papacy to the depths of humiliation.

Fortune at first favoured Charles. In 1523, the Duke of Bourbon, the most powerful vassal of the French Crown,[1] High Chamberlain and Constable of France, had quarrelled with his King and joined the cause of the Emperor. He was now made generalissimo of the Italian army. In May, the French, beaten in several battles, in one of which the Chevalier Bayard found the death which alone he thought worthy of a knight, had been forced to evacuate Lombardy.

The success of Charles led Henry to renew his alliance,

---

[1] He was Lord of 2 principalities, 2 duchies, 4 counties, 2 viscounties, and 7 lordships. *See* Map of France.

Cause of the quarrel between Francis and Bourbon.—Charles, Count of Montpensier had been allowed by Louis XII. to marry Susanna, the heiress of Duke Peter of Bourbon. After the death of his wife without children, the Queen-mother, Louise of Savoy, claimed some of his possessions as niece of Duke Peter. Francis, with better right, demanded the restoration of others in fulfilment of Duke Peter's original promise, that in default of male issue he would leave all the alienable possessions of his House to the Crown.

much to the dismay of Wolsey, who wished to keep the hand of England free, and to prevent either rival from gaining too great preponderance. The King of England promised once more to invade France, and to supply Charles with the money he so sorely needed; while Bourbon was to do homage to the English King, as King of France.

Henry VIII. renews his alliance with Charles.

In July, Bourbon crossed the Alps, invaded Provence and attacked Marseilles—an important harbour, the basis of the operations of the French fleet in the Mediterranean —whence he threatened the communications of the Emperor between Spain and Italy. Contrary to expectation, Marseilles held out. The Marquis of Pescara, who was next in command, advised Bourbon not to attempt to storm it; while his soldiers, short of pay and food, refused.

Bourbon's unsuccessful attack on Marseilles. July, 1524.

Meanwhile, Wolsey was averse to an English attack on Picardy; Charles was unable to co-operate from Spain; and on the approach of Francis with his army, Bourbon was forced to beat a hasty retreat across the Alps with the loss of most of his artillery. Francis pressed close at his heels, and, crossing the Alps by the valley of the Durance, reached Pignerol on October 17, 1524. Milan at the moment was ravaged by the plague, and could scarcely be held. The Imperialists, therefore, after despatching a force of some 6000 men, under Antonio de Leyva, to hold Pavia, threw some troops into its citadel, and retreated under Lannoy and Pescara to Lodi, while Bourbon hastened to Germany to collect fresh forces.

Francis crosses the Alps and enters Milan. Oct. 29, 1524.

On the 29th of October, the French entered Milan by one gate, as the last of the Imperialists left it by the other. Had Francis pursued his advantage, he might have annihilated his enemy; but in a fatal moment, Admiral Bonnivet, the French commander, persuaded him to attack Pavia, and Pescara had time to recruit his exhausted troops. 'We are beaten,' said Pescara, 'but we shall soon be victors.' Yet. as in

1521, so now, Charles seemed likely again to lose the Milanese.
Clement, fearing the vengeance of the French, first tried
mediation. He suggested that Charles should
cede Milan to Francis, and content himself with
Naples. When Lannoy, Charles' viceroy in Naples,
refused to entertain so humiliating a proposal, the Pope
offered his alliance to the French, and attempted to win over
Venice. This conduct he attempted to justify on the plea of
necessity. He declared to the Emperor that he earnestly
desired peace, and called God to witness to the honesty of
his motives. Charles, however, was not deceived, and vowed
'he would revenge himself on this poltroon of a Pope, and
that perhaps some day Martin Luther might become a man of
worth.'

Clement VII. breaks with Charles.

The position of the Emperor indeed seemed desperate.
The alliance with England he could not depend upon. In
Germany the peasants' revolt had already begun.
He himself was sick with fever in Spain : above
all, he knew not where to turn for money with
which to pay the troops he had on foot. Even
Lannoy warned him that he was likely to lose a
crown in the attempt to save a dukedom. Two months later,
the victory of Pavia reversed all this, and placed Charles in
a position of which he could scarcely have dreamed. In
January, 1525, Bourbon returned from Germany with so
many troops, that the army of the Imperialists nearly equalled
that of the French, except in artillery and men-at-arms. But
he had no money to pay his men. Here Pescara came to his
aid. He succeeded in persuading the soldiers to await their
pay till February 10, by which day Pavia was to be relieved ;
and the advance was at once commanded. The city was
still held by Antonio de Leyva ; but the position of the
French army, which beleaguered it, was so strong that Lannoy
hesitated to attack. All attempts, however, to force Francis
to raise the siege by a diversion failed, and the garrison were
in such distress that they must soon have capitulated.

The fortunes of Charles retrieved by the victory of Pavia. Feb. 24, 1525.

Accordingly, after three weeks' delay, it was determined to hazard the chance of an engagement. On the night of February 23, a breach was made in the walls of the park of Mirabello, which stretched to the north of the French entrenchments, and on the following morning the attack was ordered. Francis, misled by Bonnivet, now rashly left his strong entrenchments, and determined to accept the offer of battle. The open ground at first favoured his artillery, and the movements of the men-at-arms. The Imperialists wavered in the first assault, and the King, assured of victory, cried, 'To-day I will call myself Duke of Milan.' But Pescara re-formed his Spanish infantry; the German landsknechts under Frundsberg supported them, and the French men-at-arms were driven back. In the shock of infantry which followed, the Swiss in the pay of France were the first to give way, and the Italian troops gave but poor support. The landsknechts in the French army for a while stood firm, till a sortie of Leyva from the beleaguered city took them in the rear, and the French army broke. Francis, as he attempted to restore the battle, had his horse shot under him, and was taken prisoner. He would have fallen in the general slaughter, had he not been recognised by one of Bourbon's men. The losses of the French were heavy, for no quarter had been given. Bonnivet, the French commander, La Palice and La Trémouille, who had both grown old in the Italian wars, Francis of Lorraine, and many others of note were slain; and Henri d'Albret of Navarre was among the prisoners.

The battle, fought on Charles' five-and-twentieth birthday, seemed to realise the wildest dreams of Maximilian. Never since the days of Charles the Great had the idea of an Empire of the West been so nearly realised. Not only Italy, but France seemed to be at Charles' mercy, and, if France had fallen under his rule, Europe could scarce have escaped bondage. But the victory was too complete. Europe, alarmed for its safety, drew together in self-defence, and the

hopelessness of Maximilian's dream was soon to be demonstrated.

§ 7. *The Peasants' War.*

While these momentous issues were being decided in Italy,
Germany had been the scene of a serious outbreak which
threatened the whole structure of society. The
causes of the Peasants' Revolt were primarily
social. Even before the appearance of Luther,
we hear of the 'Bundschuhe' and other organisations of the
peasants, and of revolts against their lords. Their grievances
were those common to the villein class in all feudal societies;
heavy services and dues, oppressive sporting rights, and
enclosure of common lands by their lords. From the first,
indeed, the higher clergy were specially marked out for
attack. The bishop and the abbot united in their own
persons the position of spiritual superior and feudal lord.
As feudal lords, they levied dues, exacted services, and tried
offenders in their courts. As ecclesiastical superiors, they
claimed the tithes, punished ecclesiastical offences in their
ecclesiastical courts, and threatened excommunication on the
impenitent or recalcitrant. Moreover, the heavy contributions demanded of them by Rome, forced them to exact their
dues to the full. Yet, at first, there was no connection
between these social grievances and the religious discontent.
It was, however, inevitable that in time they should become
identified. The more fanatical teachers of the new doctrines,
such as Carlstadt, were attracted to the movement. They
appealed to Scripture as justifying the revolt, and taught the
peasants to interpret the spiritual injunctions of the Gospel
literally, and to fight for religious and political freedom and
for social equality under the same banner. Thus in Germany,
as elsewhere, the religious motive came to the front, gave
expression to misery as yet inarticulate, and furnished the
malcontents with a gospel.

*Causes of
the Peasants'
War.*

The eastern districts of the Black Forest, between the watersheds of the Rhine and Danube, were the first to rise in May 1524. Their views were comparatively moderate, and were subsequently formulated in 'The Twelve Articles.' In this document, after an appeal to Scripture in justification of their *The Revolt in the Black Forest. May, 1524* demands, they claimed the right of electing their own ministers, and asked for the abolition of the lesser tithe, for liberty of chase, fishing, and hewing wood, the commutation of personal serfdom, the reduction of villein services and dues, the restora·tion of communal rights. The revolt was even here accompanied by some violence, but if it had been met by a spirit of conciliation on the part of the lords, and of firmness on the part of the government, it probably could have been arrested. The nobles, however, clung to their privileges; the Council was incapable, and Ferdinand was concentrating his energies on supplying troops and money for the Italian campaign.

The disturbances accordingly increased rapidly during the autumn of 1524; and by February, 1525, they had spread to the whole of Germany, from the left bank of the *Spread of the Revolt.* Rhine to the Tyrol, and from the lake of Constance to Thuringia and Saxony. The claims of the peasants became more extreme, the more moderate lost control, and the fanatics or the designing assumed the lead.

In Franconia, amidst violent excesses, we find the demands for social reform connected with a scheme of political reconstitution of the Empire on a democratic basis— *The rebels of Franconia and Thuringia.* a scheme which betrays the hand of a more educated mind. But it was in Thuringia and the district round the Harz mountains that the extravagance reached its climax. The leader, Thomas Münzer, taught doctrines which were subversive of all authority in Church and State, and of the existing conditions of society. Received at Mülhausen in Thuringia as a prophet, he proposed to make that town the seat of his authority, whence he should rule his kingdom according to revelation.

PERIOD IV.   M

For a moment the social fabric of Germany was imperilled. On all sides the peasants triumphed. The nobles were either driven from their strongholds or forced to join the leagues as 'brothers.' The smaller towns, many of which suffered from the same oppressions as the peasants—even some of the lesser imperial cities —joined the movement. Ulrich of Würtemberg seized the opportunity to attempt a recovery of the dominions which he had forfeited by misrule (cf. p. 131), and called the rebels to his aid.

Social Anarchy threatened.

Germany was indeed threatened with anarchy; yet it is doubtful whether the peasants had any chance of permanent success. The leaders were for the most part visionary and ignorant fanatics. Münzer was neither a prophet, nor a general, and the rebels had no effective organisation. Moreover, the middle classes, led by Luther, declared against them. Luther at first had preached moderation and reconciliation. While condemning the revolts against authority as contrary to divine law, he had rebuked the Princes and the lords for their oppression, and urged them to redress the grievances of their villeins. The extravagance of the peasants, however, shortly disgusted and frightened him. He disliked their views, and feared lest his own position and work might be compromised. He pointed out that the spiritual principles of Christianity might not without peril be transferred to the sphere of society and politics; and that, if the gospel demands the freedom of the soul, it does not thereby emancipate the body from the control of law. He denounced the rebels with his usual violence of language, and bade the authorities cast away all scruple, and 'stab and kill and strangle' without mercy.

Causes of failure of the Revolt.

At this moment the news of the victory of Pavia strengthened the cause of order. The Suabian League took up arms against Duke Ulrich. The Swiss, who had at first shown some sympathy with the peasants, and had supported the Duke, now withdrew their contingent, partly on account of disturbances at home, partly from fear of Charles' vengeance, and Ulrich was forced to beat a hasty retreat. On April 4, the army of the League inflicted a decisive defeat on the peasants at Leipheim, near Ulm. On the 15th of May, the Princes, once more led by Philip of Hesse, crushed the army of Münzer near Frankenhausen. Münzer was taken prisoner and was executed at Mülhausen. The Duke of Lorraine took Zabern in Alsace, and restored order in the Vosges. The reduction of the city of Wurzburg by the united forces of the Suabian League, of the Elector of Trèves, and of the Elector Palatine on June 7, decided the fortunes of Franconia; and shortly after, the peasants of the Upper Rhine and the Black Forest either came to terms, or were crushed. The Princes and the nobles, once more masters, rivalled the cruelties of the rebels. Numbers of unfortunate peasants were cut down without mercy, and the grievances of the survivors remained, with a few exceptions, unredressed.

The defeat of Leipheim. April 4.

But although the peasants failed in their attempt, the effect of the revolt upon the course of the Reformation was profound. The utter incapacity of the Council had been once more displayed, while the defeat of the peasants had saved Germany from religious and social anarchy. Of the four possible results of the Lutheran movement which we have indicated above (p. 165), two alone now remained. The question was whether Charles would succeed in completely re-establishing his authority, or whether the spirit of territorialism would be too strong for him. The cause of the Princes had indeed been strengthened. Once more, as in the case of the Knights' War, they had asserted their power, and, with the Suabian League, had shown themselves the real masters of the country. Luther had lost to some extent the support of the lower classes, and was forced to lean still more upon the Princes. Yet the position of the Emperor was most threatening. The opponents of Luther, with scant justice, laid the

Effect of the Peasants' Revolt on the Reformation.

responsibility of the disturbances to his charge, and many of the more timid and refined were alienated from his cause. Charles himself became still more convinced that heresy and rebellion were synonymous. He was determined therefore to crush out heresy, and the victory of Pavia seemed to offer him a brilliant opportunity. All depended upon what the issue of that victory should be.

CHAPTER IV

FROM THE TREATY OF MADRID TO THE TREATY OF CRESPI

Treaty of Madrid—League of Cognac—Sack of Rome—Medici driven from Florence—Battle of Aversa—Treaty of Barcelona—Peace of Cambray—Charles crowned Emperor—Diets of Spires and Augsburg—League of Schmalkalde—Zwingle in Switzerland—Peace of Nuremberg—Barbarossa of Algiers—Renewed war between Charles and Francis—Truce of Nice—Revolt at Ghent suppressed—The Anabaptists at Münster—Diet of Ratisbon—Campaign of 1542—Treaties of Crespi and Ardres.

§ 1. *Treaty of Madrid and League of Cognac.*

CHARLES maintained the same imperturbable composure at the news of his good fortune as he had displayed in the days when defeat seemed to stare him in the face. He forbade all public rejoicing. He attributed all to God, and protested that his only desire was for a lasting peace, so that he might turn the arms of Christendom against the Turk. But he had *Behaviour and difficulties of Charles after the victory of Pavia.* before asserted that the only hope of peace lay in the submission of France, and he had not changed his mind. Yet how was that submission to be effected? War was at the moment out of the question. Charles had no money, and even the payment of the troops was in arrear. The Peasants' War still continued in Germany, and Ferdinand could not help. Henry VIII. might perhaps have been prevailed upon to invade France, if the Emperor would have recognised his claim to the French throne; but Charles did not wish to see England thus aggrandised, and refused all definite promises. Wolsey therefore had his way, and, in August, concluded a treaty of alliance with the Regent of France, in which Henry, in return for an annual pension, promised to demand the liberty of the King on honourable terms. Italy was forming a league of self-defence, and Clement, though still full of promises, was known to be playing double. France, although she had lost an army and her King, was still France, and was determined to resist invasion to the last penny in her purse, and the last drop of her blood. War then was not to be thought of ; nor did Charles' prospects of gaining his end by treaty seem much better. His demands that Burgundy and Artois should be ceded to him, and that Bourbon should hold Provence independently of France, were indignantly rejected. To the mutilation of their territory, the French would not submit, and the French King declared that he would sooner die in captivity than buy his freedom by such dishonour. Francis, however, had not the strength of character of his rival, and presently began to pine for freedom. Hearing that it was proposed to send him a prisoner to Naples, he prevailed upon Lannoy to send him to Spain instead (June), for he hoped much from a personal interview with Charles. He did not understand the man with whom he had to deal. Nothing is more remarkable than the tenacity, often amounting to obstinacy, with which Charles clung to a decision once made. He looked upon his claims to Artois and Burgundy as just ; Burgundy especially was the cradle of his race, and had been wrongly taken from his grandmother, Mary of Burgundy ; it should be restored to him. In vain Francis and the French envoys pleaded for some abatement of his demands. Charles remained unmoved : he even refused to see the King of France until a serious attack of fever threatened the prisoner's life. The news that Clement and the Italians were making a league with France, that Francesco Maria Sforza of Milan, his own creature, was turning against him ; the attempt of Morone, the Milanese chancellor, to corrupt the honour of his best general Pescara—an attempt which Pescara,[1] urged by feelings of loyalty or self-interest, betrayed to his master—all this had no effect on Charles. Morone

[1] On the question of Pescara's motives, cf. Baumgarten, *Geschichte Karl V.*, ii. 453.

was seized, Sforza was declared to have forfeited his dukedom, and was besieged, in his citadel, by the imperial troops.

Francis, having recovered from his serious illness, tried to escape; but the plan was betrayed. There was nothing for it but to abandon Burgundy; and to this course the queen-mother, Louise of Savoy, now urged him. Francis accordingly yielded; but, asserting that he alone could obtain the consent of his people to the cession, offered to leave his two eldest sons as hostages, and promised to return to captivity if that consent could not be obtained. Charles was most unwilling to grant even this, and was supported by his chancellor Gattinara, who predicted the result. The condition of Italy was, however, desperate. Pescara died on December 3, urging his master almost with his last breath to make peace with France, if he would save Italy; all his other counsellors were of the same opinion. Charles accordingly gave way, and consented to the Treaty of Madrid.

By this treaty Francis was to cede Tournay, to 'restore' Burgundy in full sovereignty, to surrender all claims on Italy, as well as the suzerainty over Flanders and Artois. He was to withdraw his protection from his allies, pay the debt incurred by Charles to England in the late war, and aid him against the Turk. The Duke of Bourbon was to regain his forfeited possessions, and to receive besides the Duchy of Milan. In ratification of the treaty, Francis promised to marry Eleonora, the widowed Queen of Portugal, sister of the Emperor, and left his sons as hostages for the fulfilment of the treaty. The treaty was not, however, worth the paper it was written on. Although Charles had made Francis swear on the honour of a knight, and on the gospel, to fulfil the compact or return to captivity, no sooner was the latter free again than he repudiated it. The day before he signed it, he had protested to his own ambassadors that he would not consider promises thus extorted from him as binding, and gave them notice that he did not mean to keep it. We are astonished to find that this conduct

The Treaty of Madrid. Jan. 14, 1526.

excited no surprise in Europe.   Wolsey actually urged Francis
to take this course, and Clement absolved him from his oath.

The release of the French King, therefore, served but to
encourage the enemies of Charles, and, on May 22, the Pope,

The League
of Cognac.
May 22, 1526.

Francis, Sforza, Venice, and Florence concluded
the Holy League of Cognac, under the 'protection of Henry of England.'   Sforza was to be
confirmed in his possession of Milan ; all Italian states were
to be restored to the position they held before the war ;
Charles was to release the young French princes for a sum
of money, and pay his debt to England within three months.
The Leaguers proclaimed their desire to secure a lasting peace.
Charles and all other princes were therefore offered the
opportunity of joining the League.   But if the Emperor
refused, he was to be driven not only from the Milanese, but
from Naples, which was then to be held by the Pope on
payment of a yearly revenue to France.

Charles was now threatened by a coalition more formidable
than any previous one.   Nor was this all.   His army was in
a mutinous condition from want of pay and food, and in
danger from the determined hostility of the Italians.   Colonna,
and Pescara, two of his best generals, were dead, while
Bourbon had quarrelled with Lannoy, the viceroy of Naples.
In Hungary, Solyman was on the point of winning the
battle of Mohacs (August 28, 1526)—a victory which was
to give him the larger part of that country ; Francis was
negotiating with this enemy of Christendom, and even Venice
declared she preferred to be the vassal of the Turk rather
than of the Emperor.

Fortunately for Charles, the members of the League were
not hearty in the common cause.   Francis seemed determined to make up for the dreary days of imprisonment, and
spent his time in hunting and other pleasures.   He expressed
the most admirable sentiments as to the necessity of immediate
action, and made use of the League to try and extort easier
terms from Charles, yet did nothing.   Wolsey had no

intention of openly breaking with Charles, and prevailed on Henry VIII. to decline the office of Protector of the League. The Divorce Question had already arisen, and if this influenced Wolsey to prevent a reconciliation between Pope and Emperor, it also gave him strong reasons for not needlessly irritating Charles. Finally, the Duke of Urbino, the commander of the Venetian army, either from incompetence, or from a disinclination unduly to extend the power of the Pope, failed to prosecute the war with vigour. The Imperialists, therefore, were able to concentrate their efforts on the citadel of Milan, and on July 24, Sforza was forced to capitulate. The Colonnesi, headed by the Cardinal Pompeio, now rose, and were supported by Don Hugo de Monçada, the successor of Pescara.

Milan capitulates to the Imperialists. July 24, 1526

On August 22, they pretended to come to terms; but no sooner had Clement dismissed his troops, than Moncada and the Cardinal, rivalling the perfidy of Francis, appeared before the walls of Rome with the army of the Colonnesi. The citizens, assured that the Colonnesi only came to deliver them from the tyranny of the Pope, and threatened with destruction if they stirred, offered no resistance ; the papal palace, the houses of the cardinals and ambassadors, were sacked ; the Church of St. Peter was rifled, and the Host profaned ; and Clement, utterly defenceless, was obliged to submit to the terms dictated by the victors (September 21). He promised to recall his troops from Lombardy, to make a four months' truce with the Emperor, and to pardon the Colonnesi. The news, however, of the taking of Cremona by the army of the League inspired him in an evil moment to break his promises. He sent his troops to ravage the territories of the Colonnesi, and deprived Cardinal Pompeio of his dignities.

Monçada had told the Emperor to disavow his attack on Rome. This Charles did, but at the same time warned the College of Cardinals that if anything befell Christendom, it would be the fault of the Pope who, in thus joining the League, 'had sought the satisfaction of his own desires rather than the honour of Christ and his people's good.' The Emperor also despatched six thousand Spanish troops to Italy, and bade Ferdinand send eight thousand Germans under Frundsberg. In November, this enemy of the Papacy crossed the Alps with an army, levied mostly from the robber fastnesses of Germany, in which there were many Lutherans. By the end of December, he had reached Piacenza, in spite of the feeble attempts of the forces of the League to check him. At the same time Lannoy landed at St. Stefano, in Tuscany, with the levies from Spain. Clement was now 'in such a condition that he did not know where he was,' says an eye-witness. At one moment he haggled over terms of peace with Lannoy, at another he threatened him and his troops with excommunication. Finally, however, on the 15th of March, he made an eight months' truce. This did not, however, save him. Frundsberg had in February been joined by Bourbon with the troops from Milan. Their first idea had been to attack Florence. Hearing, however, that the city was prepared to resist, and was protected by the army of the League under the Duke of Urbino, Bourbon turned on Rome, declaring that his troops were mutinous and were dragging him there. As he advanced, his army was swelled by Italians bent on plunder. On the 6th of May, after being twice repulsed, the fortifications of the Eternal City were carried, though Bourbon fell, and Rome was for eight days in the hands of the spoiler. She had suffered much from the barbarians of old, but probably never did she suffer such brutality as now at the hands of Christians. The death of Bourbon, and the absence of Frundsberg, who had been left mortally sick at Bologna, removed the only men who might have restrained the fury of the soldiery. The Spaniards excelled in cruelty, the Lutherans in blasphemy and sacrilege. They sacked and plundered without discrimination of friend or foe. 'There is not,' says a contemporary, 'a house in Rome, not a church or monastery, either of Romans or of foreigners, great or small, which has

The sack of Rome. May 6, 1527.

not been sacked.' 'Cardinals,' says another, 'bishops, friars, priests, old nuns, infants, dames, pages, servants, the very poorest, were tormented with unheard-of cruelties, often three times over: first by the Italians, then by the Spaniards, afterwards by the lance-knights. Lastly, the villainous Colonnesi came, dying of hunger, and ravaged what the other soldiers had not deigned to take.' The sack of Rome may well be said to close the period of the greatness of Italy. No longer was she to be the leader of the new learning and of art.

Meanwhile, the unfortunate Pope lay besieged in the Castle of St. Angelo. He might have escaped while the city was being sacked; yet he delayed, trusting that the army of the League would hurry to his support. It came, indeed, at last; but the Duke of Urbino, declaring that he was not strong enough to attack, retreated, and, on June 7, Clement was forced to capitulate. He promised to pay the sums of money demanded, surrendered six towns as securities, and consented to remain a prisoner, with his thirteen Cardinals, until the first instalment should be paid. Some now advised the Emperor to take the lands of the Papacy and reduce the Pope to his spiritual functions; or, at least, 'to keep the see apostolic so low that he might always dispose of it and command it.' But though Charles declared the sack of Rome to be the judgment of God, he was probably sincere in regretting it,[1] and even had he wished to proceed to extremities, he was in no position to do so. Indeed, the capture of the Pope promised to bring him as little advantage as that of the King of France had done. The news of the sack of Rome had at last aroused the pleasure-seeking Francis, and caused England to change her policy of masterly inactivity. To this, Wolsey was driven by his imperious master. Henry VIII. was now bent on divorcing Queen Catherine, the aunt of Charles; it was therefore of importance, not only to gain the support of Francis, but, if possible, to earn the gratitude of the Pope. Accordingly, by the treaties of April 30, and May 29, Henry abandoned his claim to the

Henry VIII. allies himself with Francis. April–May, 1527.

---

[1] On Charles' responsibility for the sack of Rome, cf. Armstrong's *Charles V.*, i. 172

French throne in return for a perpetual pension; the infant Princess Mary was betrothed to the second son of the French King; and England promised to furnish Francis with money for his Italian campaign. In the following August, Wolsey held a conference at Amiens with the French

Conference at Amiens. August, 1527.

King. It was agreed that, during the captivity of the Pope, no Bull derogatory to the interests of either King should be admitted into their territories, that the Churches of France and England should be administered by their bishops, and that the judgments pronounced by Wolsey in his legatine and archiepiscopal courts should be enforced, notwithstanding any papal prohibition. The contracting parties also decided that the Pope, being in captivity, should be asked to intrust his power to another, who should take steps to meet present necessities. Wolsey even suggested that he himself should be appointed papal Vicar. The pretext for these strange proposals was the fear that Charles might use the spiritual powers of his prisoner to their disadvantage, but there is little doubt that Wolsey also hoped in this way to obtain authority for an immediate settlement of the divorce question.

Meanwhile, a new French army under Lautrec had invaded Italy, and shortly secured the whole of Lombardy except Milan

The French again enter Italy. July 30.

itself, which was stoutly defended by Antonio de Leyva. Had Lautrec concentrated all his efforts on the city, as he was urged to do by Sforza and the Duke of Urbino, it must have fallen; for Leyva

had but a handful of men, and was short of money and supplies. Leyva, however, it was known, would fight to the last; and Lautrec, unwilling to weaken his force by so desperate an encounter, turned southward to the relief of Clement (October 1527). The position of the Pope was indeed a pitiable one. Money he had none, and, without the payment of his ransom, he could not regain his freedom. Rome, meanwhile, continued to be the victim of the merciless soldiers. The Duke of Ferrara had seized Reggio and Modena; and even the

Venetians, although the allies of the Pope, had occupied Ravenna and Cervia, under the pretext that they did it to save those cities from falling into Ferrarese hands.

Worse than this, the Florentines had in May risen once more against the Medici, driven the Pope's two cousins, Alessandro and Ippollito, from the city, and re-established a Republic under the veteran Nicolo Capponi. Clement had sacrificed the interests of the Church in his attempt to strengthen the *Medici again driven from Florence. May 17, 1527.* temporal power and to aggrandise his family, and this was the result. Before Lautrec reached Rome, however, the Pope had at least regained his freedom. Charles realised that he was gaining nothing by keeping Clement in captivity ; he earnestly wished to make peace with him, and to proceed to the extirpation of heresy. He had therefore ordered Monçada to try to come to terms, warning him at the same time to beware that he was not tricked, as he himself had been, by Francis.

Accordingly, on November 26, the following agreement was made. The Pope was to pay a certain sum of money at once, and to promise more. He under-took not to oppose the Emperor's designs on Italy ; he granted him a 'cruzada' from the ecclesiastical revenues of Spain, and half of the ecclesiastical tithes of Naples ; Ostia, Civita-Vecchia, and Civita Castellana were to be left in *Clement comes to terms with Charles, Nov. 26. But flies to Orvieto, Dec. 6.* Charles' hands as guarantees, as well as five of the cardinals ; the Pope was to be freed on the 7th of the following month. On the preceding night, afraid lest he might even yet be kept a prisoner, he fled in disguise to the papal stronghold of Orvieto.

Even so, the affairs of Charles were going ill. Florence, although she had expelled the Medici, did not abandon the League. Leyva still held Milan, but warned Charles that 'God did not work miracles every day,' and that, if not speedily relieved, his troops, though they would not surrender, would be *Critical condition of the Imperialists in Italy.* starved. Genoa had been once more won for the French by Andrea Doria. Lannoy, the viceroy of Naples, had just died of the plague, and the imperial army, which had marched, under the Prince of Orange, to the relief of Naples, was surrounded by the French army under Lautrec. Naples seemed doomed, and Francis was jubilant.

Yet, as had been the case at every important crisis of this long struggle, the French, when most confident, were nearest defeat. Although the troops of the Emperor were ill paid and ill fed, and, on that account, insubordinate and ready for plunder, they were decidedly superior to those of Francis, both in powers of endurance and on the battlefield. They had hitherto been outnumbered, but their endurance had been wearing out their enemies, and they were soon to be in a position to meet them in the field. The fate of Naples depended on the command of the sea, and this was now in the hands of Andrea Doria and his nephew Filippino.

Francis quarrels with Doria. Andrea Doria had taken the lead in the revolution which had recently restored Genoa to the French. He soon repented of his deed. Not only did Francis personally affront him by refusing to pay him properly for the use of his galleys, and by denying him the ransom of the prisoners he had taken, but he also touched his patriotism by neglecting Genoa, and attempting to set up Savona, which the French had lately gained, as her commercial rival. On Doria's remonstrance, Francis sent a Breton to take command of the French fleet in the Mediterranean, and even thought of having the Doge arrested. Doria accordingly listened to the tempting offers of the Prince of Orange, and, on the 4th of July, ordered his nephew to sail from Naples. His departure at once enabled the city to provision itself from Sicily, and the danger of famine was removed. At this critical moment, the French army, which had also suffered from want of supplies, was attacked by a severe outbreak of the plague. To this Lautrec, with several of his officers, fell a victim, and the army was so decimated that the Marquis of Saluzzo, who succeeded him in command, determined to retreat to Aversa (August 28).

As the French attempted to execute this movement, the rear-guard, under Pedro Navarra, was overtaken by the enemy, and forced to surrender. The Prince of Orange, following up his success, pursued the retreating foe, and forced them to capitulate at discretion. The Marquis of Saluzzo remained a prisoner in his hands with Pedro Navarra, both to die shortly afterwards. The rest of the army were allowed to return to their homes under promise not to serve for the present against the Emperor. Doria now sailed to Genoa, and raised the city against the French. On the 28th of October, the governor Trivulzio was forced to capitulate, and Doria was successful in establishing a government which, if somewhat oligarchical, at least protected the city from those violent party factions which had torn it for years, and secured its independence until the year 1796. Doria then reduced Savona, and the French were driven from the Ligurian coast. In Lombardy the struggle continued for a while. Here Leyva, who still held Milan, was opposed by the troops of the League, commanded by Sforza, the Duke of Urbino with the Venetian troops, and the Count de St. Pol with the new levies from France. The armies of the League, after retaking Pavia, had surrounded Milan, but hesitated to attack the formidable Leyva. In the following June, the Count de St. Pol, as he rashly attempted to make a diversion on Genoa, was surprised by Leyva, who had received information of his movements, and was completely routed at Landriano (June 20). The besieging armies retreated, and Milan was saved.

Charles was not yet complete master in Italy. Asti and Alessandria were still in the hands of the French. Lodi, Cremona, and Pavia were held by Sforza ; the Republic at Florence still kept out the Medici, and Venice yet clung to

Marginal notes:

Battle of Aversa, Aug. 28. The French evacuate Naples.

The French finally driven from Genoa. Oct. 28.

Battle of Landriano. June 20.

the eastern coast of Apulia.   Further resistance on the part
of the League was, however, hopeless, unless supported by its
more important members, and these were soon to abandon it.
England had never intended to act as a principal in the war,
and was certainly unable to do so at present : she was weakened
by a serious outbreak of the sweating sickness, and the attention of her King was absorbed in the matter of the divorce.

Still more fatal to the cause of the League was the final
reconciliation of Clement with the Emperor.   The real desire
of Clement, since his escape from Rome, had been to
maintain his neutrality until peace was declared.   This, however, was difficult, besieged as he was by the importunate
agents of the League, and of Charles.   Moreover, Clement
cared chiefly for the temporal interests of the Papacy and the
aggrandisement of his family.   To regain the possessions of
which he had been robbed, to re-establish the Medici in

Clement and
the Emperor
reconciled
at the Treaty
of Barcelona.

Florence—these, rather than the freedom of Italy,
or the overthrow of heresy, were his aims.   As
these were not to be gained from the League,
the Pope decided after much hesitation to come
to terms with the Emperor, the more so, because the ultimate
success of Charles seemed certain.   Nor can it be denied
that, for once, Clement's private interests coincided with
those of the Church, for reconciliation with Charles offered
the only hope of making head against the formidable Luther.
His only apprehension was that Charles would put into effect
his threat of summoning a General Council, a threat which
he had enforced by his promises to the Diet of Spires in June
1526.   On this point, the Emperor's agents succeeded in
allaying the fears of the Pope, and no mention of a Council was
made in the treaty which was concluded at Barcelona on the
29th June, 1529.   By that treaty the Pope promised to invest
Charles with the kingdom of Naples, and to crown him
Emperor.   Charles undertook that the places seized from the
Papal States by the Duke of Ferrara, and by Venice, should
be restored ; he also promised to re-establish the Medici in

Florence. Finally, they both agreed to turn their united forces against the infidel and the heretic. Yet the treaty was to lead to another schism. On the 16th of July, Clement, yielding to the wishes of Charles, revoked the powers he had given to Wolsey and Campeggio to try the question of Henry's divorce in England, and cited the cause to Rome. Wolsey's dream of gaining papal sanction was broken, and soon Henry was to take the matter into his own hands and cast off the papal supremacy.

Meanwhile, negotiations for peace between the Emperor and Francis had been going on. The rivals had, however, challenged each other to single combat the year before, and their honour did not suffer them personally to correspond. The negotiations, therefore, had been conducted by two women—Margaret, Governess of the Netherlands, the aunt of Charles, and Louise of Savoy, the mother of the French King, both of whom were anxious for peace. Francis had been most unwilling to grant the terms demanded, yet he was in no condition to continue the war, and the reconciliation of Pope and Emperor forced him to abandon his scruples, and sign the Peace of Cambray, or Women's Peace, August 3, 1529.

Peace of Cambray. August 3, 1529.

The French King was indeed freed from the necessity of ceding Burgundy, and regained his sons, who had been left hostages in the hands of Charles, in return for a sum of money. The other terms were, however, sufficiently humiliating. Not only did Francis surrender all claims to Italy, and to the overlordship of Artois and Flanders ; but he had also to abandon his allies ; he even undertook, if necessary, to force the Venetians to disgorge the conquests they had lately made on the Neapolitan coast, and this in the face of his solemn engagement on the honour of a King to include them in any treaty which he might make. Francis, it must be confessed, rated a King's word rather low. The marriage, first arranged at the Treaty of Madrid, was ratified ; it was hoped that if Eleonora, the widowed sister of Charles, were wedded to Francis, the family tie might serve to heal the personal enmity of these two sovereigns, whose rivalry had plunged Europe into an eight years' war.

Before the negotiations had been brought to a successful issue, Charles had left Spain. It was his earnest desire to
Charles leaves
Spain for Italy.
August, 1529.
finish the war himself, and to receive the imperial crown from the hands of the Pope. It was at Piacenza therefore that he finally ratified the treaty. Italy was now at the mercy of Charles. He was, however, wise enough to adopt a conciliatory policy towards all her States, except the Republic of Florence. Venice was indeed forced to surrender to Charles her conquests on the east coast of Naples, and to restore Ravenna and Cervia
Settlement of
Italian affairs.
to the Pope, but was not further punished. To Francesco Maria Sforza was left the duchy of Milan, with the exception of Monza, which was granted to Antonio de Leyva, Charles' brave general, and of the citadels of Milan and Como, which Charles kept in his own hands.[1]

This policy had its reward. By a treaty of December 23, 1529, Venice and Sforza joined the Pope in contracting a defensive alliance with Charles ; while Savoy was strengthened as an outpost against France by the acquisition of the county of Asti. The affairs of Florence had yet to be settled. Charles would gladly have found some middle course. But the Florentines refused to readmit the Medici even as private citizens, and Clement insisted that they should be restored to power. The city, strengthened by the fortifications designed by Michael Angelo, and defended by the militia formed after the advice of Machiavelli, stood an eight months' siege, during which the Prince of Orange, Charles' general, was killed. No one, however, came to the aid of the unfortunate Republic, which was forced to accept as Duke, Alessandro, the cousin of the Pope, who had married Margaret, the illegitimate daughter of the Emperor.[2]

[1] On Francesco's death in 1535, the duchy was annexed by the Emperor.
[2] On the assassination of Alessandro, 1537, Cosimo of the younger branch of the Medici became Duke.

Meanwhile, on February 23, Charles had been crowned Emperor at Bologna by the Pope, and on the following day, the anniversary of his birth, and of the victory of Pavia, had received the iron crown of Italy.

Charles crowned Emperor at Bologna. Feb. 23, 1530.

During this long war, which had lasted eight years, we find the same story repeated again and again. Thrice the French seemed on the point of success, only to experience a crushing reverse which snatched from them all they had gained. The imperialist armies, whether composed of Germans or of Spaniards, ill paid and ill fed, often broke out in mutiny, and disgraced their feats of arms by plunder and atrocities of all kinds ; yet no sooner were they called upon to meet the enemy than they proved themselves superior whether in defensive or offensive operations ; while they were also, as a rule, better led.

Francis, after his capture at Pavia, never appeared in the field again, and although infinitely better supplied with money from his subservient people than was Charles, he was too careless and too fond of pleasure to make full use of his advantage. As for Charles, he had taken no active part in the campaigns at all. Absent in Spain, surrounded by difficulties which the vastness of his Empire entailed upon him, and ever in grievous need of money, it seemed sometimes as if he were forgetful of the war, and neglectful of his soldiers. Yet under this callous exterior there was a determination and fixedness of purpose which nothing could shake, and which, if it sometimes appeared to be sheer stupidity, yet succeeded in the end.

While the armies of Charles had thus been engaged in winning Italy from his Christian rival, Vienna seemed likely to fall into the hands of the infidel. In May, 1529, Solyman the Magnificent had allied himself with the Hospodar of Moldavia, and with John Zapolya, Waivode of Transylvania, the inveterate enemy of the Hapsburgs, and had invaded Hungary. His pretensions knew no bounds. 'As there is but one

Solyman invades Hungary. May, 1529.

God in Heaven, so must there be but one lord on earth, and Solyman is that lord,' he proudly asserted, a boast which he hoped to carry into effect by reducing the dominions of the Emperor in Germany. The Austrians, afraid to trust the fidelity of the Hungarian forces, had been unable to meet the Turk, and retreated from the country. Solyman, in possession of the sacred crown of Hungary, which was handed to him by an Hungarian bishop, passed on into Austria, and on the 20th of September laid siege to Vienna. But divided though Germany was, it was not so lost to shame as to allow the Crescent to be established on the walls of the Austrian city. The Reformers, although irritated by their treatment at the hands of the second Diet of Spires (cf. p. 198), answered to the appeal of Ferdinand and to the injunctions of Luther.

Siege of Vienna raised. Oct. 14, 1529.

Vienna was bravely held ; and Solyman, threatened by the levies which were coming to its aid, was forced to retreat after a fruitless siege of twenty-four days (October 14). Vienna indeed was saved, but Hungary was held by Zapolya, and Croatia and Bohemia threatened.

§ 2. *Progress of the Reformation in Germany.*

In the midst of the troubles of the Italian campaign, and in the face of the hostility of the Pope, any decisive action against the Reformers had been out of the question. It was at least necessary to procrastinate. Accordingly, at the Diet of Spires (Aug. 1526), the Emperor had promised, through his representatives, that a General Council should be summoned, but that, meanwhile, the penal clauses of the Edict of Worms should be enforced. At the same time, he had warned Clement VII. that if the Christian republic should suffer in consequence of a Council not being summoned, the blame must fall on him. At the Diet itself, the Catholics found

The Diet of Spires, Aug. 1526, and the Recess.

themselves in a majority in all the chambers, except that of the imperial cities, yet they were not prepared to advocate extreme measures. The *Recess*[1] declared that, until a Council should meet, each state should, in matters appertaining to the Edict of Worms, 'so live, rule, and conduct itself as it shall be ready to answer to God and his Imperial Majesty.' It is a mistake to hold that the Reformers were thereby authorised to set on foot their new ecclesiastical organisations. The concession was purely provisional, and they were to answer to the Emperor for what they did. None the less, the Elector of Saxony and Philip of Hesse proceeded to establish their Lutheran churches, and to appropriate monastic property for the purpose—a policy which was soon followed by others, especially by Albert of Prussia, who, in 1525, had already secularised the estates of the Teutonic knights, and converted his mastership into a dukedom.

Thus the Diet of Spires makes an important advance in the history of the Reformation. If, on the one hand, it was now clear that Germany was not to belong exclusively to the Lutherans, on the other, a great impulse was given to the principle of territorialism (*cujus regio ejus religio*), upon which eventually the ecclesiastical settlement of Germany was to be based. Three years later, the position of affairs had materially altered. The marked advance of the Reformed opinions had excited the apprehensions of the Catholics, while the successes of the Emperor in Italy, and his reconciliation with the Pope, had strengthened their cause. The rapid growth of the Zwinglian opinions in the south of Germany, opinions which were wholly distasteful to Luther, had weakened the Evangelical party, and the rash appeal to arms on the part of Philip of Hesse, to resist a supposed conspiracy against those who thought with him, had irritated the Princes.

This reaction of opinion expressed itself in the second Diet of Spires. The Recess of 1526 was revoked, all further

[1] The Recess (*Reichsabscheid*) was the collection of the Decrees of the Diet which had received the assent of the Emperor (*Reichsschlüsse*).

innovations were forbidden, and the 'sect' of the Zwin-glians was refused all toleration.   The minority, indeed,

here earned their name of '*Protestants*' by the protest they issued against these decrees—a protest which was signed by John, Elector of Saxony, Philip of Hesse, George, Margrave of Brandenburg, Ernest of Luneburg, Wolfgang of Anhalt, and fourteen imperial

cities.   But the protest was rejected by both Diet and Emperor ; and so evident was it that Charles only waited for an opportunity to take decisive action, that a meeting was held at Schmalkalde, at which the lawfulness of resistance was discussed, to be abandoned, however, for the present in deference to the scruples of Luther.

When on June 30, 1530, Charles, after eight years' absence, met the Diet of Augsburg in person, the moment seemed to

have arrived for a final settlement of his difficulties.   Italy was at his feet ; Francis had at last accepted his terms ; the Pope had promised to join with him in suppressing heresy, and had crowned him Emperor ; and, if Hungary was in the hands of Solyman, Germany at least was free from his attack.   The Protestants, conscious of their weakness, desired reconciliation.   This was strongly advocated by Melanchthon, and breathed in every line of the 'Confession of Augsburg' which was presented to the Diet, at the request of Charles that the Protestants would express their thoughts in writing.   In this famous Confession, the doctrine of Justification was stated in qualified terms ; the paying of honour to the Saints was not entirely forbidden ; although reasons were given why the Lutherans had permitted the Cup to the laity, the marriage of the clergy, and the secularisation of Church lands, and had rejected vows and private masses, no definite assertion was made as to the number of the Sacraments, or on the question of the papal power ; while the decision of other contested questions was to be left to the verdict of a General Council.

The tone of the document was avowedly defensive, and its aim was rather to show that the Lutheran doctrines were not heretical than to attack those of the Church.

The original intention of Charles had been to act as a mediator, and to settle the religious dissensions by fair and gentle means. He had asked the Evangelical party for an expression of their views. He now wished that their opponents should bring forward a distinct charge against the Reformers which would allow him to assume the part of an umpire. But the Catholics in the Diet refused; they declared that they had nothing new to propose, and accordingly prepared a confutation in which, indeed, they made some approach towards the Lutheran view of the doctrine of Justification, but in other respects insisted on the old doctrines, and demanded that the Protestants should return to the unity of the faith. The Emperor now abandoned the *rôle* of a mediator, and attempted to overawe the recalcitrants with threats. Alarmed, however, by the determined though respectful attitude of the Protestant princes, the Diet made one more attempt at reconciliation, and a small committee was appointed. On the question of dogma there seemed some chance of agreement, and a General Council might possibly have broken down the opposition of the Protestants. But, though this was earnestly desired by the Emperor, the Pope had no idea of complying with his wish; while on questions relating to the constitution and the practice of the Church, reconciliation was probably hopeless. These the Catholics regarded as of Divine institution; the Protestants, on the other hand, looked upon them as the work of men, and therefore capable of modification. Erasmus in his letters bitterly complains of the want of moderation on both sides; yet this is not the only occasion where attempts at compromise on serious religious issues have failed. Eventually, Charles adopted the views of the majority, and The Recess of the Recess of Augsburg proclaimed his intention Augsburg. of enforcing the Edict of Worms. The Protestants were given

till the ensuing April to consider whether they would volun-
tarily return to the Catholic Church.   After that date, measures
were to be taken for the extirpation of their sect.   But although
the majority of the Diet had thus shown themselves hostile
to the Reformers, they hesitated to put arms into the hands
Reorganisa- of the Emperor with which he might enforce the
tion of the Edict; rather they proposed to make use of the
Imperial
Chamber. Imperial Chamber for the purpose.   This court
Nov. 19, 1530. was accordingly reorganised and increased in
number; assessors suspected of Lutheran tendencies were
admonished, and the Chamber was ordered to enforce the
Recess.

In answer to this, the Protestant princes and city deputies
met at Schmalkalde on December 22, 1530.   They appointed
Formation of procurators to watch their interests before the
the League of Imperial Chamber; they agreed to protect each
Schmalkalde. other from any attempt on its part to enforce the
Dec. 22, 1530. Recess of Augsburg, and after much debate
decided that resistance was lawful even to the Emperor
himself, should he appeal to arms.   Hitherto Luther and the
theologians had preached the doctrine of passive obedience.
But the civilians brought forward arguments to prove that
the power of the Emperor was limited by law.   His title
was not hereditary, but elective; he had granted capitulations at his election; if, therefore, he acted illegally, he
might be resisted.   Convinced by these arguments, Luther
gave way, and was followed by most of those present, with
the exception of the Margrave of Brandenburg and the city
of Nuremberg.   Thus originated the League of Schmalkalde,
which was definitely formed in March 1531 and finally
organised in the ensuing December.   Its members were to be
represented in a Diet.   They promised to furnish contributions to a common fund, and intrusted the supreme command
of their forces to John, Elector of Saxony, and the Landgrave
Philip of Hesse.   The formation of the League of Schmalkalde marks a new period in the struggle.   In spite of the

scruples of Luther, the movement had become a political one. Henceforth Germany was to be divided into two hostile camps, each with its centre of unity, and the Protestants had taken measures for their common defence, by arms if necessary.

The next crucial question was, whether this League should include all those both in Switzerland and in Upper Germany, who had embraced the views of Zwingle. Although it may be doubted whether this Reformer would ever have been heard of had it not been for the impulse given to the cry for Reform by the appearance of Luther, yet the two movements were to a great extent inde- Zwingle. pendent of each other, and, from the first, presented essential points of difference. The son of the 'Amtmann' of the village of Weldenhaus, near St. Gall, Zwingle was born in 1484, a few weeks after Luther. He had in early life been influenced by the literary movement of the Humanists, and was well versed in the classics. Chosen as curate of the congregation of Glarus in 1506, he had accompanied his countrymen on some of the Italian expeditions, notably on that which ended so disastrously at Marignano, and henceforth never ceased to warn his fellow-citizens against the demoralising influences of this mercenary system of warfare.

It is, however, with his call to be curate at Zurich (1519-1525) that his career as a Reformer began. Starting, like Luther, with a crusade against the abuse of indulgences, he soon began to take up different ground. Zwingle curate at While Luther did not deny the Real Presence, Zurich. Zwingle looked upon the Sacrament merely as 1519-1525. a festival of commemoration, and pressed the Lutheran view of Justification to its logical conclusion—the doctrine of election and the denial of man's free will. Luther was willing to accept anything which could not be proved contrary to his interpretation of Scripture ; Zwingle would accept nothing but what he found there. Luther had a deep reverence for the Universal Church, and only left it after a struggle ; Zwingle based the right of each congregation to independent

action in matters religious on the republican organisation of
the village.   Luther had attempted to keep religious questions
apart from politics, and, when finally driven from this position,
threw himself on the side of authority as represented by the
Princes.   The religious ideas of Zwingle were intimately
connected with a scheme of establishing a more thorough and
representative democracy in Switzerland, in which the Forest
Cantons should lose their privilege of holding as many
votes in the Federal Diet as the other and larger Cantons.
By the close of the year 1530, the opinions of Zwingle had
not only been accepted by the Cantons of Zurich, Basel, Bern,
and Schaffhausen, and by many of the country-folk of Appenzell, Glarus, and the Grisons, but had spread among many of
the towns of southern Germany, notably those of Constance,
Ulm, Augsburg, and Strasburg.

Common danger had for a moment drawn the adherents
of these two Reformers together, to protect themselves
against the Recess of the second Diet of Spires.
But permanent union between such widely divergent views was scarcely possible.   Philip of
Hesse, who was himself inclined towards the
opinions of Zwingle, had attempted to effect a
reconciliation at his castle of Marburg in 1529.
The attempt failed—Luther showing the most uncompromising
hostility to the Zwinglian doctrine concerning the Sacraments
—and shortly after, Zwingle had to face a reaction in his own
country.   Like so many reformers, he was wrecked on the
shoal of politics.   The Forest Cantons had from the first been
the resolute opponents of the new teaching,
not only because they were strongly Catholic, but
because Zwingle's political reforms, if carried out,
would destroy the position they had hitherto enjoyed in the Federal Diet.   His political views also lost him
adherents in those Cantons that were in favour of his doctrinal
position.   The Hapsburgs cleverly fostered these divisions; war
ensued, and finally at the battle of Cappel, the army of Zurich,

Margin notes:

Temporary union between the followers of Luther and Zwingle soon comes to an end.

Reaction against Zwingle in Switzerland.

which alone stood by him to the last, was defeated, and Zwingle himself was slain (October, 1531). By the second Treaty of Cappel it was agreed that each Canton was free to retain its own creed. In the 'Common Bailiwicks,' the religion was to be decided by the majority. But no force was to be used, and the city Cantons were to abandon their foreign alliances.

The battle and the second Treaty of Cappel. Oct. 1531.

Switzerland was now definitely divided into Catholic and Protestant Cantons. The Catholics regained lost ground, and secured seventeen out of twenty-nine votes in the Diet. The Evangelical party held Zurich, Bern, Basel, and Schaffhausen; while Thurgau, Glarus, and Appenzell were divided. All hope that Switzerland would support the Protestants of Germany was now over; nevertheless the cities of southern Germany, deprived of their Swiss allies, were forced to join the Lutherans and to swell the numbers of the League of Schmalkalde. Thus, by the commencement of the year 1532, the position of the Protestants in Germany had improved.

Had Charles' hands been now free, doubtless he would have appealed to the arbitrament of the sword. But here again his political necessities stood in his way. The peace with France was by no means secure; nay, Francis was even intriguing with the League of Schmalkalde. Solyman was again threatening to invade his dominions. Spain, as usual, complained of his absence. In Africa the piracies of Barbarossa demanded his attention. Nor could Charles depend on the unqualified support of the Catholic princes. In June, 1531, he had with difficulty secured the election of his brother Ferdinand as King of the Romans by five of the Electors. But the election had been protested against by John of Saxony, and he was joined by the two Dukes of Bavaria and others, who, despite their Catholic sympathies, dreaded to see the power of the Hapsburgs increased. Disappointed in his hopes of settling the religious difficulty,

Charles prevented by European difficulties from taking action against the Protestants.

the Emperor was forced to procrastinate.　At the Peace of Nuremberg (July 1, 1532), he promised to suspend the proceed-ings of the Imperial Chamber until the convocation of a General Council; while at the Diet of Ratis-bon, which followed, he undertook, in the event of such a Council not being convoked by the Pope within six months, to summon a general assembly of the Empire for the settlement of the religious difficulties.

The Peace of Nuremberg. July, 1532.

Charles was at least rewarded by the loyal support of the Protestants against the Turk.　His army, recruited by Spaniards, Italians, and Netherlanders, was the largest force he had ever led, and Solyman, repulsed by the brave de-fenders of Güns, retreated without having dared to fight a pitched battle.　Yet the Emperor was in no position to make use of his victory.　The affairs of Italy and of Spain impera-tively demanded his presence.　Accordingly, in the autumn of 1532, he crossed the Alps, to be involved again in European complications, and for seven other years Protestantism was left unmolested.

Shortly after the Peace of Nuremberg, John the Steadfast of Saxony died.　He had gone much further in the direction of Protestantism than his brother, Frederick the Wise, whom he had succeeded in 1525. Frederick had never wholly broken from Rome; John had been one of the leaders in the League of Schmal-kalde, and had organised an Evangelical Church within his territories.　Yet, to the last, he tried to maintain a moderate line of policy, and hoped to find a place for the protestant churches without breaking up the Empire, or departing from the obedience of the Emperor.　With no remarkable intel-lectual gifts — corpulent and somewhat slow-witted, — the simplicity and honesty of his character, and the courage with which he clung to his convictions, make him something of a hero; and there is, perhaps, no one to whom Luther and the Protestants of Germany owe more than to this plain and single-hearted man.

Death of John, Elector of Saxony, 1532.

§ 3. *European complications and the fortunes of the Protestants, from* 1532 *to the Treaty of Crespi.*

At no time during the career of Charles v. are the contra-dictions and difficulties which surrounded him better illus-trated than during the period from 1532 to the Treaty of Crespi. Had his claims been less extensive he might have been more successful; but the very magnificence of his pretensions prevented the complete realisation of any one of them. As head of the Holy Roman Empire, it was his duty to defend the unity of the Church, to put down heresy, and to support the papal authority. Yet his position as King of Germany forced him to postpone the suppression of heresy to the imperative necessity of gaining the support of the Protestants against the Turk; while his claims on Italy brought him into constant conflict with the Pope. As King of Germany, it was his aim to increase the royal authority and suppress the tendencies towards disruption, and, as ruler of the Austrian territories, to further the family interests of the Hapsburgs; but both these aims incurred the hostility of many even of the Catholic princes. As King of Spain and master of Italy, it was incumbent on him to secure his dominions and the Mediterranean from the piratical incursions of the Moors. Yet here and everywhere, he was constantly being thwarted by his persistent rival, Francis I., who not only intrigued with the Pope against him, but, while persecuting the Reformers at home, entered into alliances with the Protestants of Germany, the schismatic King of England, and even the Infidel himself.

With the actual events of this period we must deal very briefly. They are not in themselves of great importance. Scarcely any new question is involved, with the exception of that of Africa, and the position of European affairs is not very materially altered. Charles had for the moment checked the attack of the Moslems from the East. He was now forced to turn his attention to their movement in the south-west.   By the conquests of Ferdinand the Catholic, the Spaniards had acquired possessions on the north African coast from Melilla to Tripoli, and reduced the rulers of Algiers and Tunis to the position of vassals.   Since 1510, however, the Spaniards had met with many reverses, especially since the rise of the two Barbarossas.   These two men, sons of a Greek or Albanian renegade, had made themselves masters of Algiers. Huroc, the elder, was slain in 1518, but Hayraddin, his younger brother, interfered in the dynastic disputes of Tunis, and, in 1534, added that country to his kingdom.   To gain the support of Solyman, he had consented to hold his conquests of him, and, in 1533, received the command of the Turkish fleet.   Meanwhile his own ships had been threatening the Mediterranean, harrying the coasts of Spain and Italy, and carrying off Christians to the slave-markets of Africa and the East.   This rise of a new Mahometan power in Africa, a power with which Francis was not ashamed to coquet, demanded instant attention.   Charles, therefore, having renewed his alliance with the new Pope, Paul III. (Farnese), and settled as far as was possible the affairs of Italy, passed on to Spain. Thence, with a fleet under the command of Andrea Doria, and an army which was not only recruited from various parts of his dominions, but was joined by the Knights of Malta, he sailed for Africa (June, 1535), nominally in support of Muley-Hassan, one of the claimants to the kingdom of Tunis.   The expedition proved a brilliant success.   Solyman could send no help, and Francis was either afraid or ashamed to aid. The harbour of Goletta was taken by storm, and the army of Barbarossa defeated on the field.   The Christian prisoners in Tunis rose against their captors, and Barbarossa was forced to evacuate the country, which was granted to Muley-Hassan under the suzerainty of Spain (August, 1535).   But though the expedition caused a great stir and increased the reputation of the Emperor, it did not materially improve his prospects in Europe.

The struggle with Barbarossa. June-August, 1535.

Francis had never intended to keep the Treaty of Cambray, and was determined to attempt the recovery of the duchy of Milan at least. He had accordingly been long The intrigues intriguing, both in Germany and Italy. To gain of Francis. the support of Clement VII. he had consented to marry his second son, Henry of Orleans, to Catherine de' Medici, on condition of a principality being granted to the Duke in Italy, a principality which might possibly include Milan ; but the death of the Pope (25th September 1534) had disappointed him of his hopes in this direction. Francis had also opened negotiations with the members of the League of Schmalkalde— who, however, refused to support one who persecuted the Protestants in his own kingdom—and had made a commercial treaty with Solyman, in which the plan of a joint attack on the Milanese was mooted. Francis had then begun an unsuc- cessful intrigue with Francesco Sforza, and, on the execution of his secret agent Maraviglia, had declared war against that Prince. To reach the Milanese it was necessary to pass through the dominions of the Duke of Savoy. Since the days of Charles VIII. of France, Savoy had been friendly to France, and had given free passage to her troops. But the present Duke, Charles III., had married Beatrix of Portugal, sister of the Emperor's wife, and now refused such passage. Francis therefore determined to occupy Savoy and Piedmont. At the same time he supported the Calvinists of Geneva, who were in rebellion against the Duke of Savoy and their bishop, and stirred up the Swiss of Bern to invade the district of Vaud.

At this moment, the death of Sforza of Milan (24th October 1535), altered the position of affairs. He was the last direct descendant of the House, and Milan accordingly Death of fell to Charles as suzerain. The Emperor, who Sforza. had only just concluded the expedition against Oct. 24, 1535. Barbarossa, was anxious to gain time, and amused the King with negotiations. Francis demanded Milan for Henry, Duke of Orleans, his second son. Charles offered to grant it to the

Duke of Angoulême, the third son of the French King, on condition of his marrying an Austrian princess.

Meanwhile the French had crossed the Alps by the Pass of Susa, and occupied Turin (April, 1536). Charles now threw

The French cross the Alps and occupy Turin. April, 1536. off the mask. He denounced the King as a faithless man, the ally of heretic and infidel, and challenged him to personal combat, suggesting that Burgundy and Milan should be the prize of victory. On this being refused, Antonio de Leyva crossed the Sesia at the head of the imperial troops (May, 1536). The Marquis of Saluzzo, who commanded the French army in Piedmont, deserted to the Emperor, and Charles, neglecting

Charles makes an unsuccessful attack on Provence. July-Sep. 1536. to secure Turin, pressed on into Provence in the hopes of bringing Francis to a decisive engagement. The French, contrary to their usual practice, adopted a Fabian policy. They devastated the country as they retired, and threw themselves into strong positions at Avignon and Valence. Unable to storm these places, the imperial army began to suffer from want and disease, to which de Leyva himself succumbed (September 10, 1536). Charles, despairing of success, was forced to evacuate the country (September 23), and retired to Spain 'to bury there his honour which he had lost in Provence.'

The attack of the Imperialists on Picardy and Languedoc

Campaigns in Picardy, Languedoc, Artois, and Piedmont. had been equally unsuccessful, although, during the campaign in Picardy, Francis lost Robert de la Marck, 'Le Jeune Aventureux,' the military companion of his youth, and the author of the Memoirs which bear his name. In 1537, the French invaded Artois. The war in Piedmont still continued, and Solyman,

Solyman defeats Ferdinand at Essek. Oct. 1537. in pursuance of his recent treaty, sent Barbarossa to attack the coasts of Naples, while, shortly after, he invaded Hungary in person, and defeated Ferdinand at Essek (October 8). This alliance of the French with Solyman excited the indignation of Europe.

---

[1] Ferdinand had been recognised as King of Hungary after the death of Lewis at Mohacs (cf. p. 184). But his claim was opposed by Zapolya, Woivode of Transylvania, who was supported by Solyman.

Paul III., who had hitherto adopted a neutral attitude, now intervened as mediator. Francis was not unwilling to treat, and Charles had nothing to hope from a continu- Revolt of ance of the war. The Lutherans were daily gain- Ghent, 1537. ing strength; the attack of the Moslem was threatening the imperial hold on Naples; while in the north, the people of Ghent had risen against the taxes imposed by the Regent of the Netherlands (1537).

Accordingly, a truce for ten years was made at Nice (June 18, 1538). By that truce the Peace of Cambray was confirmed. The rivals abandoned their allies, and each was The Truce to retain the conquests they had made. Thus the of Nice. Duke of Savoy was made the scapegoat. Savoy June 18, 1538. and two-thirds of Piedmont were retained by Francis, the Swiss henceforth occupied the district of Vaud, and the Emperor held the rest, with the exception of Nice, which alone was left to the unfortunate Duke. A conference at Aigues Mortes followed (July 1538), at which Francis, hoping to gain by conciliation what he had failed to attain by arms, adopted a most friendly attitude towards Charles. The Marshal de Montmorency, who had gained a great reputation in the campaign of Provence, urged the King to ally himself with Charles, and even suggested a joint invasion of England, where the anti-papal measures of Henry VIII. and the execution of Bishop Fisher and Sir Thomas More had excited much discontent. Although Francis stopped short of this, he turned a deaf ear to the petition for aid which the citizens of Ghent sent him, and shortly after gave the Emperor a free passage thither through France.

On the approach of Charles, the city, disappointed in its expectation of French assistance, submitted (February 6, 1540), to pay dearly for its rashness. Fourteen of the Charles sup- leading citizens were executed, the civic privileges presses the were forfeited, a heavy fine was levied, and a Ghent. garrison admitted within the walls. This com- Feb. 6, 1540. pleted the ruin of the ancient city, whose commercial supremacy, with that of Bruges, had already passed to Antwerp in consequence of the revolution in the routes of commerce caused by the discovery of the way round the Cape.

Now for a moment it appeared as if King and Emperor would lay aside their long rivalry and unite to resist both heretic and Turk. That Charles entertained such an idea is not to be wondered at. Solyman, encouraged by the French alliance, was menacing Hungary once more, and Barbarossa was still threatening the Mediterranean from Algiers.

Advance of Protestantism in Germany.

Nor was the danger less at home. Protestantism had made notable advances since the Peace of Nuremberg, 1532. In 1534, Duke Ulrich of Wurtemberg was restored to his duchy, from which he had been driven by the Suabian League in 1519, and which had been granted to Ferdinand, Charles' brother. The restoration was effected by Philip of Hesse, who defeated the troops of Ferdinand at the battle of Laufen (May 1534), but it was also approved of by John Elector of Trèves, who, although Catholic, was glad to see the House of Hapsburg humbled. Duke Ulrich forthwith established Protestantism in his duchy; the University of Tübingen became the stronghold of the Reformers, and a wedge was driven into the phalanx of Catholic states in South Germany.

In the north, indeed, the outbreak of the Anabaptist revolution at Münster, under John of Leyden, in the spring of 1534, had threatened to compromise the Lutheran party.

The Anabaptists at Münster, 1534.

This fanatic, who united unbridled licentiousness with strange religious views, attempted to establish a kind of socialistic state of which he proclaimed himself prophet and king. But only the most heated partisanship could find any connection between the views of Luther and of this wild fanatic. As had been the case with the Peasants' Revolt, Philip of Hesse, one of the most prominent of the leaguers of Schmalkalde, rallied to the cause of order. John of Leyden was executed, his followers dispersed, and Münster restored to its bishop, 1535. Purged from any complicity with the Anabaptists by the suppression of the revolt, the Lutherans continued to make fresh converts in the north of Germany. In the year 1535 Joachim I., Elector of Brandenburg, and in 1539 George, Duke of Saxony, of the Albertine branch of the house, both staunch Catholics, died. Of their successors, Henry of Saxony actually embraced the Lutheran creed, and Joachim II. adopted a conciliatory policy; while his younger brother John, Margrave of the Neumark, became a devoted adherent of the new opinions. Many other smaller princes followed, and, by the close of the year 1539, the only important Catholic states were those of Austria, Bavaria, the Palatinate, the Duchy of Bruns-wick-Wolfenbüttel, and the three ecclesiastical Electorates; moreover, the Elector of Cologne, Herman von der Wied, was known to be wavering Shortly after, both he and the Elector-Palatine embraced the Protestant cause.

George, Duke of Saxony, and Joachim I., Elector of Brandenburg, die and are succeeded by Henry and Joachim II. 1535-1539.

The crisis demanded instant action. But this was impossible unless the neutrality of France could be secured. Charles accordingly offered the hand of his eldest daughter to the third son of Francis, who, by the death of the dauphin during the campaign in Provence, had now become the Duke of Orleans. He promised to cede to the Duke Franche-Comté and the Netherlands, if Francis, on his part, would grant to him the duchy of Burgundy, abandon all claim to Milan and to the suzerainty of Flanders, and restore the conquests in Savoy and Piedmont to the Duke of Savoy. This would have meant the revival of the old dukedom of Burgundy, but as a fief of the Empire, and it is doubtful whether in any case Francis would have acquiesced in the final loss, not only of his conquests in Piedmont, but also of Milan. In short, the claims on Italy prevented any agreement. After tedious haggling as to whether the Duke of Orleans should have instant possession, and whether the territories should revert to Charles in the event of the Duke's death without issue, Charles invested Philip, his son, with the duchy of Milan

Charles anxious for a free hand, makes unsuccessful advances to Francis.

(October 1540), and Francis determined to appeal to arms once more.

With the prospect of war before him, the Emperor recognised the impossibility of using force against the Protestants.

Attempted reconciliation with Protestants at Diet of Ratisbon, 1541.

Reconciliation, if possible on the basis of comprehension, was the only alternative; and for that purpose he summoned the Diet of Ratisbon, in the spring of 1541. For a moment the chances of reconciliation seemed bright. There had risen of late in Italy a party of reform, led by Reginald Pole, then a fugitive from England, the Venetian Contarini, at this moment the papal legate in Germany, and Morone, Bishop of Modena. This group of literary men, who represented the reaction against the sceptical spirit which had dominated Italy during the days of Leo X., approached very closely to Luther's views on the doctrine of Justification, and were as eager as he to reform the abuses which disfigured the Church of Rome. Even Paul III. declared himself desirous of doing something. At Ratisbon, a conference of theologians was held, under the presidency of Granvelle, at which Melanchthon, Bucer, and Dr. Eck,[1] Luther's old opponent, appeared, and an agreement was come to on three of the articles of controversy—Original Sin, Redemption, and Justification. In the Diet itself, the majority of the Electors and of the deputies of the cities declared themselves in favour of this agreement, and Pole rejoiced at the approach of peace and concord. But these hopes were not to be realised. In the Chamber of Princes the opposition was very formidable. The Pope insisted that his supremacy and the Romish view of the Sacraments should be accepted, and Luther could not bring himself to believe in the sincerity of the Catholics. Even if the question had been untrammelled by political considerations, it is very doubtful whether any satisfactory conclusion could have been arrived at, and politics could not be excluded. Reconciliation with the Protestants would make Charles too

[1] Eck, however, had opposed it throughout. Granvelle the chancellor, Gropper and Pflug, two Catholic divines, were in favour of it.

powerful, as master of a reunited Germany, not to meet with strenuous opposition, both within and without the Empire. Francis and the Pope brought their intrigues to bear on the Princes, many of whom were jealous of Hapsburg influence and dreaded the loss of their political privileges. In vain did the Emperor suggest that the articles on which the theologians had agreed should be accepted for the present, and that, with regard to others, differences of opinion should be tolerated on either side. The agreement was rejected by the Chamber of Princes, much to Charles' indignation. Thus failed the last chance of a reconciliation between the two religious parties—wrecked on political rivalries—a reconciliation which might have altered the history of Germany and even of Europe. Yet, even so, the Protestants gained much. Charles, anxious for their support during the coming struggle, issued a declaration by which the enforcement of the Recess of Augsburg was still further delayed. Those who had secularised ecclesiastical property were permitted to retain it until the final settlement; Lutherans were to be admitted as assessors to the Imperial Chamber; and, until the meeting of a General Council, no one was to be prevented from adopting Lutheranism. So confident were the Protestants in the strength of their cause, that when Henry Duke of Brunswick attempted, contrary to this Recess, to force the decisions of the Imperial Chamber on Goslar, he was driven from his duchy by the League of Schmalkalde (summer of 1542), and the Catholics thus lost the only important lay principality which they held in Northern Germany.

While Francis had been doing his utmost to perpetuate the religious divisions in Germany, he had been diligently preparing for war. The Marshal Montmorency, who had advocated friendship with Charles, was disgraced; alliances were eagerly sought for; and finally, the assassination of the French agent as he was passing through the Milanese on his way to Constantinople (July 3, 1541), gave the French King a decent pretext for breaking the

Francis again declares war. July 1541.

truce of Nice.   War, however, was not actually declared till
1542.   During the interval Charles suffered two disasters at the
hands of the Mahometans.   In Hungary, Solyman, marching
to the support of the son of Zapolya (who had died in 1540),
inflicted a crushing defeat on Ferdinand at Buda (July 30,
1541), and in October, an expedition which the Emperor led
in person against Barbarossa in Algiers failed, chiefly owing
to wild weather on the African coasts.

The attempts of Francis to procure allies were not very
successful.   Henry VIII., at this moment engaged in the war

*Attempts of
Francis to
obtain allies.*
with James V. which ended in the defeat of the
Scots at Solway Moss (December), was in no
humour to support the French, their allies.[1]   Moreover, the old cause of quarrel between the English King and the
Emperor, arising out of the divorce of Catherine of Aragon,
had been in part removed by her death, and all idea of an
English alliance with the Protestants had been abandoned
with the divorce of Anne of Cleves and the fall of Cromwell
in 1540.   Henry therefore declined the offers of Francis, and
renewed his alliance with Charles.   The Protestants of Germany, satisfied with the concessions of the Emperor, remained
quiet.   The Pope, Paul III., adhered to his policy of neutrality.
Solyman, the Kings of Denmark and of Sweden, and the
Duke of Cleves, were therefore the only allies of France.
Of these, Christian III. of Denmark was irritated by the support which Charles had given to the claims of the Palatinate
branch of the Wittelsbach family on his throne ; Gustavus
Vasa, of Sweden, by the favour Charles had shown to a
revolt of his peasants ; while the Duke of Cleves disputed the
claim of the Emperor to the reversion of Gueldres, in virtue
of the will of Charles of Gueldres, who died without children
in 1538.

Francis, contrary to his usual strategy, refrained from

---

[1] James had married (1) Magdalen, daughter of Francis I. ; (2) Mary
of Guise.

directly attacking the Milanese, and, while he acted on the defensive in Piedmont, devoted his chief attention to the Netherlands and Rousillon. The results of the first campaign, 1542, were not important. Luxembourg was gained, only to be lost, and the invasion of Rousillon was foiled by the resistance of Perpignan. Never theless, at the beginning of the year 1543, the position of Charles was serious enough. Solyman was master of most of Hungary and was preparing for a decisive stroke ; Barbarossa was on the point of joining the French in an attack on Piedmont ; the Pope, angry at the refusal of Charles to invest his grandson, Ottavio Farnese, with Milan, at his concessions to the Protestants, and at the demand for a General Council, was leaning towards France ; Denmark had closed the Sound to German ships ; moreover, it was very doubtful whether Philip of Hesse, and John Frederick of Saxony would allow the Duke of Cleves to be overthrown, more especially as the Duke was the brother-in-law of John Frederick, and was known to have strong Protestant sympathies.

Campaign of 1542.

The Emperor, however, succeeded in his negotiations with England. On the death of James v. of Scotland, in 1542, the regent, Mary of Guise, had rejected all the advances of the English King, and continued the French alliance. Henry accordingly turned again to Charles. By the treaty of February 11, 1543, Emperor and King agreed to demand that Francis should give up his alliance with the Turk, indemnify the Empire for the sums it had incurred in the Turkish war, and, as security for the debts he owed the King of England, hand over Boulogne and other towns. If Francis refused these terms, the allies engaged themselves to pursue the war till Burgundy should be restored to Charles, and England had made good her ancient claim to Normandy and Guienne, and to the crown of France.

Henry allies himself with Charles. Feb., 1543.

In May, Charles hastily left Spain, and arrived in Germany. He secured the neutrality of John Frederick of Saxony, entered the territories of the Duke of Cleves, and forced

him to resign his pretensions to Gueldres (August). In September the joint attack of Barbarossa and the
Count of Enghien, at the head of the French
troops, on Nice, was foiled by the approach of Doria with
the Spanish fleet and the army of Milan. Francis had not
even the consolation of success to requite him for the odium
he incurred by his alliance with the infidel. In Hungary,
indeed, the advance of Solyman was unchecked, and by
the end of August nearly the whole of that country had
been conquered. But even this success cost
Francis dear. At the Diet of Spires, held
in February 1544, Charles denounced the
King of France as an enemy to Christendom.
He informed the Protestants of the offers
which Francis had made in 1539 to assist
him against them if he would cede Milan, and therewith made further concessions with regard to the religious
question. He promised that a general *free* and Christian
Council should be summoned, and that, if the Pope delayed,
he would next year call a Diet for the final settlement
of the religious question. The Protestants expressed their
horror at the unholy alliance with the Turk, and once more
the Emperor secured the aid of the Empire in his struggle
with the French. At the same time, Denmark abandoned the
French alliance. Francis was now threatened by a serious combination. In Piedmont, indeed, the Count of Enghien won a
decisive victory over the Marquis de Guasto and the army of
Milan at Cerisoles (April 11). But in June, the Imperialists, after
reducing Luxembourg, invaded Champagne and
advanced as far as the Marne, while the English
landed on the coast. Had Henry kept his engagement and
co-operated with Charles in a combined attack on Paris, the
capital might have fallen. Intent, however, on his own
schemes, he delayed to lay siege to Boulogne, which did not
surrender till September. Indignant at this breach of faith,
anxious to break the dangerous alliance between Francis and

The military events of 1543.

Diet of Spires, Feb. 1544.
Charles gains assistance of the Empire against France.

Success of the Imperialists.

the Turk, and to have a free hand to deal with the Protestants in Germany, Charles, who was, moreover, in serious want of money, now offered peace.

Francis, largely owing to his intemperate mode of life, was seriously ill. His mistress, Madame d'Estampes, feared that on his death all influence would pass to her hated rival, Diana of Poictiers, once the mistress of the King, now all powerful with the Dauphin. She was therefore anxious to secure for Orleans, the second son, an independent sovereignty. He was at enmity with his brother, and might be of service to her in the future. She therefore urged the King to accept the Emperor's terms. Francis listened; and on September 18, 1544, the Treaty of Crespi ended the last war between the two rivals. All conquests made since the truce of Nice were to be abandoned. The Emperor renounced his claims on Burgundy, and Francis gave up his own upon Naples, as well as the suzerainty of Flanders and Artois. The Emperor further promised to the Duke of Orleans, either the hand of his daughter, with the Netherlands and Franche-Comté, or that of his niece, the daughter of Ferdinand, with the duchy of Milan. Charles retained the right of deciding which of these two marriages should be carried out; and, on the completion of the compact, Savoy and Piedmont were to be restored to the Duke Charles III. Finally, the rivals engaged themselves to unite in defending Christendom against the Turk, and in restoring peace and unity to the Church. *Treaty of Crespi. Sept. 18, 1544.*

Henry, complaining bitterly of the Emperor's desertion, continued his war with Francis till the summer of 1546. He then promised to restore Boulogne to Francis within eight years on the payment of a sum of money, and of the perpetual pension already promised in 1525 and 1527. *Treaty of Ardres, June 7, 1546.*

The marriage of Orleans, from which the French King hoped so much, was prevented by the death of the Duke (September 1545). Francis was, indeed, no longer bound to surrender his conquests in Piedmont and Savoy, but these were poor compensation for four exhausting wars, which cost France, it is said, 200,000 men.

Francis survived the Peace of Crespi two years and a half, but these years are only noticeable for the persecution of the Huguenots in France, which will be treated of hereafter. On March 31, 1547, he succumbed to a disease which was the result of his careless life, just when he was preparing to intervene once more in the affairs of Germany. Few kings of France were so popular during their lives, or have retained such a place in history; yet it may be doubted whether Francis deserved his reputation. His character, though not wanting in some superficial attractiveness, was shallow and utterly wanting in high principle. His generosity led him into gross extravagance. His gallantry was spoilt by an entire absence of refinement and morality. His chivalry and his love of manly sports and of the chase, even his literary and artistic tastes, though praiseworthy in themselves, he shares with many a worthless character. Nor is it easy to see how he benefited his country, except by his patronage of art and literature, and by founding the College of France for the study of languages and science. No doubt his reign is marked by a great outburst of Renaissance architecture, of which the Louvre and some of the 'châteaux' on the Loire are the best examples. In literature, Rabelais; in painting, the two Clouets; in sculpture, Jean Goujon, have earned a European reputation; while of foreigners, the painters, Leonardo da Vinci and Andrea del Sarto, and Benvenuto Cellini, the metal-worker and sculptor, were welcomed at the court. It may, however, be questioned whether this artistic revival was due to royal patronage, and at least in the more serious business of government and administration, the name of Francis is associated with no important measure of reform. During his reign, the sale of offices became the custom, the corruption of royal officers increased, and the taxes grew. The independence of the Gallican Church was destroyed by the

Death of Francis I. March 31, 1547.

Concordat. The Estates-general were only twice summoned, and gained no further privileges. The nobles, it is true, were kept in check and amused in the foreign wars, or at the court; they lost much of their power, which was transferred to the bureaucracy; but in losing this they lost also their usefulness; they retained their privileges, they swelled the factions of the court, and formed a turbulent class which was to disturb France for many a year. The lower classes rose, indeed, to some prominence in the service of the State; but they were only powerful as servants of the King, and as members of a bureaucracy which strangled all local life and constitutional liberty. In short, during the reign of Francis the absolutism of the crown increased, without that beneficial administration which alone can justify it. Nor is his foreign policy any more worthy of praise. It may be true that he foiled the attempt of Charles to establish the universal supremacy of the Spanish Hapsburg monarchy in Europe, yet we can scarce forgive him for his alliance with the Porte. When we recall his cruel persecutions of the Huguenots at home, it is difficult to justify his support of the Lutherans in Germany. Jealous of the ascendency of Charles, he plunged his country into war as carelessly as a knight of old entered the lists, and, in spite of the lessons of the past, he grasped after the bauble of a kingdom beyond the Alps, and neglected to strengthen or extend the true frontiers of his country. A good captain of a division, rather than a general: a pleasant, clever, but wicked man, and a bad King, 'Le roi galant homme' left behind him an absolute monarchy, unchecked and unsupported by any constitutional system, an encumbered revenue, a heavy debt, a corrupt government, an immoral court, a factious nobility, and a nation flushed with the lust of war, and disturbed by religious discord. The troubles which came on France after the King's death are in part at least attributable to his policy, and yet it is these very troubles which, by contrast, have led historians to judge more favourably of his reign than it deserves.

CHAPTER V

FROM THE WAR OF SCHMALKALDE
TO THE TREATY OF CATEAU CAMBRESIS

Charles and the Protestants—Council of Trent, second session—Maurice won over—Death of Luther—Outbreak of war of Schmalkalde—Charles successful in Southern Germany—Council removed to Bologna—Battle of Mühlberg—Diet of Augsburg—Charles and Paul III.—The Interim—Charles and Julius III.—End of second session of Council of Trent—Maurice joins the Protestants—Treaty of Friedwald—Policy of Ferdinand—Charles flies from Innsbruck—Treaty of Passau—Death of Maurice—Diet and Peace of Augsburg—Truce of Vaucelles—Abdication and death of Charles—Last war between France and Spain—Battles of Gravelines and St. Quentin—Treaty of Cateau Cambresis.

§ 1. *The Schmalkaldic War and the battle of Mühlberg.*

On the signature of the Peace of Crespi, the hands of the Emperor were at last free to deal with the Protestants in

Charles at last free to deal with the Protestants.

Germany. To understand the conduct of Charles at this juncture, it is necessary to remind ourselves of the main aim of his life. He had inherited from Maximilian the idea of establishing an universal supremacy in Western Europe ; from his grandmother Isabella, that severe spirit of orthodoxy so characteristic of the Spanish nation. To a man with such views as these, the Lutheran movement was equally distasteful, both from a political and a religious point of view ; and, had he been able to follow his own convictions, he would have taken immediate steps to crush out the new opinions in the year 1521. But Charles was no fanatic, and the political exigencies of the moment had caused him to listen to the advice of his ministers, more especially of Gattinara, who bade him temporise, and try to win back the Lutherans by measures of conciliation. From that day to this, it had been necessary to pursue the same path, while of late he had entertained the idea of comprehension and possibly of settling the religious difficulty by a National Diet [pp. 204, 212, 216].

But although this policy had served the political ends of the Emperor, and prevented the Lutherans from joining his enemies in the field, it had not succeeded in bringing them back to the fold. In his determination to put an end to schism, by force if necessary, the Emperor had never swerved. Of late, more especially since the death of Gattinara (1530), he had learnt to depend more upon himself, and now at last the moment had arrived for action. Meanwhile, the Spanish leanings of Charles had been intensified. Since the resignation of the Austrian lands to Ferdinand in 1521, he had looked on Spain as the centre of his rule, and had identified himself with Spanish interests in Church and State. It was Spain that had chiefly supported him in his European struggles, and he now came, rather as King of Spain and Emperor of the West, than as a German prince, to re-establish the unity of the Empire and of the ancient Church. Charles, however, was too good a statesman to ruin his cause by over haste. He appreciated the strength of the Protestant position, and saw that he must proceed with caution. The Germans had often petitioned for a General Council, and if a Council could now be summoned, it might institute certain reforms, which might conciliate the more moderate, and strengthen his hand. For this, the consent of the Pope was necessary. Accordingly, Charles promised Parma and Piacenza to Ottavio Farnese, the grandson of Paul, and the Pope consented to re-summon the Council to Trent,[1] in March, 1545. Meanwhile, the Emperor met his Diet at Worms. The hopes of the Emperor with regard to the Council were not fulfilled. It did not open its session till December. It was not well attended; only some forty bishops came, and among them the Spaniards and Italians were in a decided majority. The Protestants therefore refused to acknowledge it as a free and general Council, more especially as it was decided

Agreement with the Pope.

Second Session of the Council of Trent. Dec. 1545.

[1] It had already been summoned in 1542, but had been postponed.

that its members should vote as individuals and not by
nations, a course of procedure which would ensure the
victory of the papal party. Moreover, the wish of Charles
that the Council should postpone the consideration of dogma,
and first proceed to the reform of abuses, was rejected. It
was agreed that both subjects should be taken together; and
on the question as to the authority of tradition, and the
doctrine of Justification, the views of Rome prevailed.

Charles, meanwhile, had met with more success in Germany
in his attempts to gain the German Princes to his side.

Charles
succeeds in
gaining over
many of the
princes of
Germany,
especially
Maurice of
Saxony.

William, Duke of Bavaria, who, by the death of
his brother (1545), had become sole ruler in the
duchy, had hitherto, although a Roman Catholic,
coqueted with the League of Schmalkalde. He
was now brought over by the promise of the hand
of Ferdinand's daughter for his son, with the
reversion of Bohemia should Ferdinand die with-
out male heirs, and by the hopes held out to him, that, if the
Elector-Palatine remained obdurately Protestant, the electoral
dignity should be transferred from the Palatine to the Bavarian
branch of the Wittelsbach family.   John of Brandenburg-
Küstrin, Margrave of the Neumark, and Albert Alcibiades of
Brandenburg-Culmbach, two of the younger members of the
House of Hohenzollern, annoyed at the reinstatement of the
Duke of Würtemberg (cf. p. 210), also joined the Emperor.
Charles was further successful in securing the neutrality of
Joachim, Elector of Brandenburg, Frederick, the Elector-
Palatine, and of some of the cities who had been members of
the League.

Of his allies, however, by far the most important was
Maurice of Saxony.   The history of the House of Wettin in
Saxony illustrates most forcibly the evil results of that custom,
so prevalent among the German princes, of dividing their
territories among their sons.   In 1464, Frederick II. of Saxony
had died, leaving his territories to his two sons, Ernest and
Albert, and from that day the jealousy between these two
lines had been extreme.   In the early days of the Lutheran

movement, while the Electors, Frederick the Wise, John, and John Frederick, the representatives of the elder or Ernestine branch, had, in their capital of Wittenberg, been the earnest supporters of reform, George, the representative of the Albertine line at Meissen, had been one of the most devoted advocates of the ancient faith. This cause of difference was but in part removed when Henry, the brother of Duke George, who succeeded him in 1539, accepted Lutheranism. Maurice, who succeeded his father Henry in 1541, had also declared himself a Protestant, and had married the daughter of the Landgrave, Philip of Hesse. Nevertheless, he had recalled some of the ministers of his Catholic uncle, George, and among them Carlowitz. He had also refused to join the League of Schmalkalde, weak and divided by jealousies as it was, and had always taken an independent position, which was disliked by his cousins at Wittenberg. The estrangement thus caused between him and John Frederick, the Elector, was aggravated by more personal grounds of quarrel. None of the princes of Germany had made greater use of the cry for secular-isation of ecclesiastical property than these Saxon princes, and this had led to fresh disagreements between the two cousins. The bishopric of Naumburg had been secularised by John Frederick; Maurice was anxious to do the same with the bishopric of Merseburg. They also quarrelled over their claims within the limits of the see of Meissen, which was under the common jurisdiction of both branches; while both were anxious to obtain possession of the two bishoprics of Magdeburg and Halberstadt, which had accepted Protestant-ism, and lay close at hand.

The Emperor, by cleverly playing upon these jealousies and by magnificent promises, succeeded in buying the alliance of Maurice. He consented to appoint him guardian of the bishoprics of Halberstadt and Magdeburg, entertained the proposal of assigning the bishoprics of Merseburg and Meissen to him as hereditary duchies, and finally promised to transfer to him the electoral dignity now held by John Frederick. On the question of religion it was not difficult to calm the apprehensions of the Saxon duke. He had been subjected to various influences during his youth; his mother, Catherine of Mecklenburg, was an earnest Protestant; his uncle, the Catholic George, had made a favourite of him and tried to influence his religious views. It is not, therefore, astonishing that Maurice, although by no means an irreligious man, had no strong convictions on points of dogma, nor that he viewed matters from the standpoint of the statesman rather than of the theologian. He had accepted Lutheranism because his people wished for it, and the promises of the Emperor seemed to give all that was needed. In religious matters, Maurice was to allow no further innovations until the final settlement, which was to be referred to a Council, 'and, if some points remained unsettled for the present, Maurice was to be under no apprehension.' The terms indeed were vague; but when people wish to be satisfied, they are not very exacting. On these conditions, therefore, Maurice engaged to join the Emperor in his attack on the Elector, John Frederick. He did not, however, thereby break his alliance with the Landgrave, nor declare war on the League of Schmalkalde.

While these negotiations had been going on, Charles had been holding diets and entertaining schemes of compromise.

Charles takes action against the Protestants.

June 1546.

His attempts, however, to gain comprehension either through a Council or a Diet had failed, and at last the moment for action had arrived. A truce had been effected with Solyman; France and the Pope were friendly, and Charles' concessions had brought over several of his opponents. Against the wish of Granvelle he therefore threw off the mask, and at Ratisbon published the imperial ban against those who refused to acknowledge the jurisdiction of the Imperial Chamber. Even now he did not speak of the war as a religious one; he proceeded, he declared, not against those who were dutiful subjects, but against those who would not submit to imperial laws; he was about to check insubordination, not to punish heresy. It is not necessary to accuse Charles of deliberate falsehood; indeed, as long as Maurice was on his side, it could scarcely be called a war against the Protestants. Nor, on the other hand, is it just to accuse the Protestants of having taken up the question of reform solely from political motives, in pursuance of their old struggle against the Emperor. Nevertheless, the cause of religious independence was now so closely identified with that of territorial independence, and the unity of the Church so intimately connected in Charles' mind with that of the Empire, that the religious and political issues could no longer be distinguished. The question at stake was this : should Germany be forced to accept the mediæval system of one Empire and one Church, or should the princes vindicate their rights to political and religious autonomy?

By a strange coincidence, Luther, who had been the prime author of the discord, and yet had striven so long to keep the religious question apart from politics, and had so reluctantly sanctioned the appeal to arms, passed away before the actual outbreak of hostilities. On February 18, 1546, he died in his native town of Eisleben, in his sixty-fourth year. Whatever may be our view as to the doctrinal position of the Reformer, it is as idle to deny his greatness, as to belittle the importance of the movement he originated. Of his faults, and he had many, some were those of his class and of his age, some were all his own. Luther was the son of a Saxon peasant, and never freed himself from the homely coarseness of his early surroundings. Scurrility in controversy was the custom of the day, and Luther did not rise above the common standard ; while nature had given him an uncompromising and dictatorial, and a somewhat violent character. Yet he was not deficient in more amiable qualities. His hospitality, his generosity, his geniality and affection, made him beloved at home and among his friends ; while his sterner virtues—his honesty, his piety, his earnest conviction, his unflagging industry, and, above all, his unflinching courage—even his adversaries have not been able to gainsay. It would also be a mistake to imagine

Death of Luther. Feb. 18, 1546.

that he had no refinement. Of this his hymns, many of which
are familiar to us, and, above all, his German translation of the
Bible, are sufficient proof. This magnificent work, which did
much to elevate and fix the literary style of Germany, is enough,
of itself, to give to Luther a high place among men of letters.

The position of the League of Schmalkalde on the pro-
clamation of the imperial ban was a serious one. They had
trusted too easily to the Emperor's promises,
and now found themselves unprepared for war.
The concessions of Charles had reduced their
ranks, and the only members of the League who
actually took up arms were John Frederick, the Elector of
Saxony, Philip, Landgrave of Hesse, Duke Ulrich of Würtemberg, and the towns of Augsburg, Strasburg, Ulm, and Constance. None the less, had the Protestants boldly taken the
offensive, they might have secured the Upper Inn and the
outlet of the Brenner Pass, and thus prevented the march of
troops from Italy, without which the Emperor could do little ;
or, again, they might have surrounded him in Ratisbon, where
he had but few troops. But the organisation of the League was
very faulty, there were many jealousies and quarrels, and
John Frederick was no statesman, and no general. The army
of the League, therefore, adopted a weak defensive attitude,
and entrenched itself between the Danube and the Rhine.
Charles, taking advantage of the dilatoriness of his enemies,
had time to concentrate his troops from Spain, Italy, and
the Netherlands, and then by superior strategy, in which he
was assisted by Alva, was able to avoid a decisive battle until
events in the north forced his enemies to retire.

It was not until Maurice had received a definite promise
of the Electorate that, on October 27, he declared himself.
Armed with Charles' orders to occupy the forfeited estates of
John Frederick, he then approached his own subjects. He
warned them of the danger of refusal, and by undertaking
that their religion should not be interfered with, at last
gained their consent to act. Finally, when John Frederick

*Critical con-
dition of the
League of
Schmalkalde.*

contemptuously rejected his proposal to occupy the Electorate quietly, he united his forces with those of Ferdinand and rapidly overran the whole territory, with the exception of Wittenberg, Eisenach, and Gotha (November 1546). The receipt of this news filled the members of the League with alarm, and their overtures of peace having been spurned by Charles, the Landgrave Philip and John Frederick hurried north, while the rest of the confederates dispersed to protect, if possible, their own territories. This enabled the Emperor to deal with his opponents in detail, and to make himself master in the south. The cities of the League were quickly occupied. The Duke of Würtemberg, and the Elector-Palatine, who, though taking no active part himself, had assisted the League with troops, submitted. They undertook to obey the Diet, and the decisions of the Imperial Chamber, and to pay a fine ; and Charles, on his side, promised, as he had promised to Maurice, that with regard to religious matters they should be left in peace until the final settlement. At the same time, Herman von der Wied, the Archbishop of Cologne, resigned his see (January 1547), and a Catholic succeeded him.

Maurice declares himself, Oct. 27, 1546. And overruns the Electorate, November.

Success of Charles in the South.

Elsewhere, however, matters were not going so well for Charles. John Frederick, on his return, not only easily recovered his dominions, but invaded the territories of Maurice, where he was well received ; Ferdinand, recalled by a Protestant insurrection in Bohemia, could give no assistance ; and Maurice in a few weeks lost all his lands except Leipsic and Dresden, which were too strong to be suddenly reduced. Nor could Charles respond at once to Maurice's call for help. His alliance with the Pope seemed likely to break up. The interests of Paul III. as an Italian potentate demanded that neither France nor Spain should become too powerful ; as a Farnese, it was his aim to increase the power of his family

Successes of John Frederick in Saxony.

Quarrel of Charles with Paul III. prevents his assisting Maurice.

The refusal, therefore, of Charles to appoint Ottavio Farnese as Stadtholder of Milan on the death of the Marquis de Guasto in March 1546, and the appointment of Gonzaga, an old enemy of the Farnese and a strong supporter of the imperial claims in Italy, had irritated the Pope, while the imperial successes now alarmed him. Emperor and Pope differed, too, with regard to the Council of Trent. Charles was most anxious that the Council should proceed no further in the definition of dogma, lest thereby the apprehensions of the moderate Protestants should be too soon aroused; Paul, less careful of the position of Charles in Germany, wished to maintain the infallibility of the Pope and of the Church, and hesitated to touch the thorny question of internal reform; he also feared lest the Emperor, victorious in the north, might come to Trent and claim to preside. True, therefore, to the traditions of papal policy, Paul began to waver. The time having expired for which he had lent his troops (December 1546), he recalled them, and refused to send any more. He declined to sanction the grant of ecclesiastical revenues from Spain which Charles had demanded for the war; and since Trent was surrounded by Austrian lands, in March he removed the Council to Bologna. Nor did the Pope stop here. He even entered into intrigues with Francis, who, disappointed in his hopes with regard to Milan by the death of the Duke of Orleans (September 1545), was negotiating again with the League of Schmalkalde, and stirring up revolts in Genoa, Siena, and Naples.

Council of Trent removed to Bologna. March 1549.

Fortunately for Charles, the dilatoriness and want of generalship of John Frederick saved Maurice from ruin, until the death of Francis I. (March 1547), relieved the Emperor from the fear of a French attack; and he was able, although tortured with gout and pale as a ghost, to march north, in April 1547. Even then the imperial army only numbered some 16,000 men, mostly Italians, Spaniards, and Hungarians; while the Elector

Charles marches North. April 1547.

had a much larger force at his disposal. This deficiency in numbers was, however, fully compensated for by the superiority of Charles' veterans, and by the utter want of generalship displayed by his opponent. Not only had the Elector despatched a considerable detachment to aid the Bohemians against Ferdinand, but he further weakened his forces by attempting to hold open towns. When the success of Charles, who entered Saxony from the south and rapidly reduced these positions, forced him at last to concentrate on Mühlberg, a town to the east of the Elbe not far from Dresden, he did not even then use all his troops to dispute the passage of the river, where Charles might, perhaps, have been successfully resisted. When the Emperor had crossed the river, the Elector in vain attempted to retreat. He was forced to accept a battle, in which his personal courage and that of his troops was of no avail against the well-disciplined veterans of his foe. After a short Battle of Mühlberg. April 24, 1547. struggle, the Saxons gave way; the Elector, surrounded and wounded, had no alternative but to surrender; and Charles and his foreign army had won a decisive victory with the loss of some fifty men. It was earnestly debated whether John Frederick should not answer with his head for his rebellion. Such condign punishment, urged Pedro de Soto, Charles' confessor, would have an excellent effect. But Wittenberg was strong, and too severe a treatment might raise further opposition; accordingly, by the advice of Granvelle and of Alva, his life was spared. Even so, the terms were hard enough. The city of Wittenberg was to surrender at once; John Frederick was to resign the electoral dignity and most of his territories, of which those in Bohemia were to go to Ferdinand; he was to submit to the decision of the Imperial Chamber, and remain a prisoner for the rest of his life. On these conditions the city of Gotha and the district around it, with a pension to be paid out of the other territories, were secured to his heirs, and a provision was to be made for his own support.

The capture of John Frederick was shortly followed by the submission of the Landgrave. Hitherto he had rejected the offers made by Charles. Now that opposition seemed hopeless, he was persuaded by Ferdinand and Maurice to accept the Emperor's terms, severe though they were. Most of the Hessian strongholds were to be delivered, and their fortifications demolished; the Landgrave was to acknowledge the imperial authority, and submit to the decrees of the Imperial Chamber; he was to set the Duke of Brunswick free, to pay a fine, and to place himself in the Emperor's hands. Charles, it is said, once master of the person of the Landgrave, took advantage of some looseness in the agreement, and, contrary to the distinct undertaking of Ferdinand and Maurice, refused to grant him his liberty, declaring that he had only promised not to keep him in prison for ever.[1] It does not appear that Charles actually broke his word, and the chief blame of the mistake must apparently fall on Ferdinand and Maurice, who gave promises to Philip without full authority. None the less, Maurice had understood Charles otherwise. He considered that he had been duped, and Germany believed it. Maurice never forgave the Emperor, and Germany did not forget.

§ 2. *From the Diet of Augsburg to the Peace of Augsburg.*

When on September 1, 1547, Charles met his Diet at Augsburg, he seemed at last about to realise his dream of re-establishing the unity of the] Church. All his opponents were either defeated or had come to terms, and all had agreed to accept the decisions of a General Council. The Diet unanimously declared itself to the same effect, and demanded that the Council should be recalled to Trent. The Chamber of the Princes further insisted that the decisions already published by the Council should be reconsidered. The lay Electors held that Scripture should be the only authority on

Diet of Augsburg.
Sept. 1547 to June 1548.

[1] The question whether Charles had used the words, 'nicht einiges' (any), or 'nicht ewiges (perpetual) Gefängniss,' appears to be an afterthought. Cf. Armstrong, ii. 156.

matters of dogma, and wished for reform of the Church in 'Head, and members'; the deputies from the imperial cities requested that the Council should be composed of learned men of all orders. Some desired that the Council should be under the presidency of the Emperor, and although this was not demanded by the whole Diet, nothing was said of the necessity of papal approval.

The Emperor, armed with this support, requested Paul to recall the Council from Bologna to Trent. He expressly stated that he did not approve of all that had been said against the papal authority, but urged the Pope to take advantage of this unlooked-for submission on the part of Germany. It cannot be denied that a serious question of principle was involved in this request. Although the Emperor did not definitely claim the right of presidency, yet the demand that the Council should return to Trent, where still some of the Spanish and Neapolitan bishops remained, practically assumed that the Council at Bologna was no true Council. Compliance with the demand of Charles would have emphasised the control of the temporal over the spiritual power, and dealt a blow at the independence of the Church, which claimed to be guided by the Holy Spirit. And yet if the Pope had really been in complete harmony with the Emperor on other matters, one of the many compromises which were suggested could probably have been carried out by the clever diplomacy of Mendoza, the imperial ambassador at Rome. Unfortunately, the affairs of Italy once more stood in the way of that reconciliation between Pope and Emperor which was so desirable for the welfare of the Church. On September 10 Pierluigi Farnese, to whom his father Paul had granted Parma and Piacenza, fell a victim to a conspiracy. He had been the centre of anti-imperialist intrigues during the winter and spring of 1546-1547; and Gonzaga, the imperial governor at Milan, who, with the consent of the Emperor, had supported the conspiracy though not the assassination, forthwith occupied Piacenza, ostensibly to preserve the peace,

Renewed quarrel between Pope and Emperor.

but really in pursuit of ambitious views of extending the imperial authority in north Italy. The angry Pope at once entered into negotiations with Henry II. of France. He was even heard to say that he would call hell itself to avenge him of his enemy. At the same time the prelates at Bologna, influenced, it must be allowed, by more worthy motives, replied to the Emperor's demand by summoning those ecclesiastics who had remained at Trent to join them at Bologna, whereby they might show that Germany meant to obey the Council. Charles might now have attempted to form a Council of his own at Trent; but he was too good a Catholic to think of starting a schism. Declaring therefore that he must take measures for the protection of that Church which the Pope neglected, he determined to settle matters in his own way. His confessor, Pedro de Soto, suggested that he should forbid all Lutheran preaching, insist on the restoration of secularised property, and of the Catholic ritual, and then leave every one to think as he pleased. But this, said Ferdinand, would require another war. The Emperor therefore fell back on the suggestion of his brother, that he should try to find some ground of union in Germany independently of the Pope. The Interim followed, a document drawn up
The Interim. by theologians from both sides, and accepted
May 19, 1548. without debate by the Diet, May 19. It affirmed that 'There is but one Church, of which the Pope is chief Bishop; but the power lies in the Church under the guardianship of the Holy Spirit, rather than in the Pope.' While insisting on the seven Sacraments in the Catholic sense, it agreed to the doctrine of Justification by Faith in somewhat vague terms, and declared that the questions of the celibacy of the clergy and of the Communion in both kinds should be left undecided until the calling of the future free Christian Council. It must not be supposed that Charles intended this settlement to be permanent; he only looked on it as a temporary measure which might entice the Protestants back to obedience to the Church and to the Empire

Nevertheless, had the whole Empire, Catholic and Protestant, accepted the Interim, a decided step would have been taken towards the establishment of a national Church under the control of the Emperor rather than of the Pope. Any such result as this was, however, prevented by the refusal of the Catholics to acknowledge the Interim as binding on them in their dealings with their subjects, and the only question was, how far Charles would be successful with the Protestants.

The attempts of Charles to re-establish his authority were not confined to the ecclesiastical sphere. He had also approached the Diet with schemes for strengthening the imperial power. He did not succeed in obtaining all he wished. His desire to revive, and, if possible, extend the organisation of the Suabian League (which had died out of late), though approved of by the smaller Princes, was resolutely opposed by many of the larger, even Maurice himself, and had to be abandoned. Nevertheless Charles gained much. He was allowed to nominate, for this term, the assessors to the Imperial Chamber, so long as they were Catholics, and was granted 'a Roman month,' as a fund for future contingencies. He also obtained his aim with respect to the Netherlands, which were now definitely organised as one of the Circles of the Empire, were put under imperial protection, and were to contribute to imperial taxation. But while in this way Charles hoped to gain for these hereditary possessions the support of the Empire, yet they were to retain their own privileges; and though their ruler was to have a seat in the Diet, they were to be free from its control, and from the jurisdiction of the Imperial Chamber. In June, 1548, the Diet was dismissed, and Charles proceeded to enforce the Interim on the Protestants. In the south, where the events of the previous year had made him master, he was able, partly by expelling the Lutheran preachers, partly by revolutionising the town councils, partly by means of his Spanish soldiery, to secure obedience. In the north, he had more difficulty. But even there, except in the case of the Lutheran city Magdeburg and a few imperial towns, he eventually obtained a general assent to a modified form of the Interim, drawn up by Melanchthon, and termed the 'Leipsic Interim.'

In November 1549, the position of the Emperor was much strengthened by the death of Paul III. That Pope, in the

The death of Paul in Nov. 1549, and the election of Julius III., strengthen the position of Charles. vain hope of prevailing on the Emperor to free Parma and Piacenza from their dependence on Milan, had assumed for a moment a conciliatory attitude, and spoke of confirming the Interim, and recalling the Council to Trent.   Many at Rome thought these concessions dangerous and opposed such a policy, and on Charles' refusal to comply with his demands with respect to Parma and Piacenza, the Pope had declared them annexed to the papal see and turned to France for aid.   His death, therefore, was welcome news to Charles, more especially as Cardinal Monte, who succeeded as Julius III. in February 1550, contrary to all expectations, declared for the imperialists.   He promised to recall

Second Session of Diet of Augsburg. July 1550. the Council to Trent, to consider the question of internal reform, and to come to terms with regard to the Interim.   Fortified by this unwonted alliance Charles found little difficulty in influencing the Diet (which was re-summoned to Augsburg in July), to submit to the Council of Trent; the Protestants even undertaking to appear there and plead their cause.

The success of his ecclesiastical policy now enabled Charles to return to his darling idea of establishing the hereditary

Charles' dynastic ideas. rule of the Hapsburgs over the Empire of the West.   But of this Empire the centre was to be, not Germany, but Spain and Italy, and its representative after his death, not his brother Ferdinand, but nis son Philip.   The plan, long cherished, had been steadily pursued.   In 1540, Philip had been recognised as Duke of Milan.   When Charles left Spain in 1543, he had intrusted the government to his son, although then only sixteen years old. In 1548, he had sent for Philip that he might become known in Germany, and had, though with difficulty, obtained for him an oath of allegiance from the Netherlands. Meanwhile, an intimate correspondence between the two had completely imbued Philip with his father's ideas. The Emperor now hoped to complete his scheme by securing for his son the succession to the Empire. He had originally intended to bring the subject before the Diet; but it was necessary first to overcome the not unnatural opposition of Ferdinand. After much difficulty, a compromise was arrived at between the two brothers (March 9). It was agreed that on the death of Charles, Ferdinand was to be Emperor; he was, however, to make Philip imperial vicar, and support his election as King of the Romans. Philip, on his part, promised to do the same for Maximilian, the son of Ferdinand, when he himself should ascend the imperial throne. Charles, though he had not obtained all that he wanted—for the Empire was to be shared in turn between the two branches of the family—had to all appearance won over Ferdinand to his scheme of a future union of the Empire with the Spanish monarchy of Philip. But, as a fact, he had excited the jealousy of Ferdinand, who intrigued with the Electors to defeat the plan which he had promised to further, and henceforth ceased to support his brother as he had hitherto done. The family quarrel thus aroused was shortly to cost Charles dear.

When, in November 1551, Charles went to Innsbruck that he might watch over the Council which had reassembled at Trent in September, he might well think that he had won; the unity of the Church seemed about to be re-established, and the imperial power to be revived, based on the support of the Spanish monarchy. The next few months were, however, to see this hope dispelled. The failure of the Council was to prove the impracticability of his ecclesiastical policy; the European opposition, to ruin his scheme of political supremacy. From the friendship of the Pope and the recalling of the Council to

Renewed quarrels with the Pope concerning the Council of Trent. Sept. 1551 to April 1552.

Trent, Charles had anticipated great things. A statesman rather than a theologian, he did not appreciate the
difficulties which surrounded the question of dogma, nor
those which concerned the independence of the Church as an
organisation of divine institution.   Although severely orthodox
himself, he did not see the necessity for further definition of
doctrine, and, above all, wished nothing to be done that might
irritate the Protestants, until the Council had approached the
question of reform.   The abuses of the Church he knew
had been the primary cause of the Lutheran revolt, and a
genuine reform of these would, he believed, enable him
successfully to overcome all further opposition in Germany.
He accordingly supported the demand of the Protestants
that they should be heard, and that the decisions of the last
session should be reconsidered, while he urged Julius to deal
forthwith with the question of reform.   It was not to be
expected that this policy would find favour among the more
orthodox, still less with the Pope.   When at last, in January
1552, the Protestants, having extorted a promise of safe
conduct, appeared at the Council, it at once became clear
that an accommodation was impossible, either on the question
of dogma, or of the constitution of the Council, or even of the
form of procedure.   The demands of the Reformers that Scripture should be the only standard of truth, that laymen should
have a vote, and that the Pope should claim no right of
presidency nor of veto, 'since a Council was superior to a
Pope,' seemed to the orthodox both godless and insolent ;
and Julius was determined to resist this serious attack on the
papal position.   Nor were the demands of Charles and his
Spanish bishops any more palatable.   The Emperor's idea
of reform was based on the ecclesiastical organisation of Spain.
There the crown was served by a church, the discipline of
which had been reformed by Ximenes, and which could be
used as a weapon for extending royal authority, and even for
checking papal pretensions.   The request more especially that
bishops should be resident and that the Pope should resign the
right of collation to all benefices was stoutly resisted by Julius ;

'rather than suffer that, we will suffer all misfortune,' he said. The Papal court subsisted on foreign benefices since the Italian bishoprics were poor, and the independence of national churches would destroy the Papal power. The Pope, moreover, was disturbed at the refusal of Henry II. to acknowledge the Council or to allow French bishops to attend it, and by that King's preparations for renewing the war in Italy. Evidently nothing was to be expected of the Council. It had only served to illustrate the conflicting interests of the Pope and Emperor, and the hopelessness of all reconciliation with the Protestants. Under these circumstances it was soon abandoned by the German bishops, and dragged on until the course of events in Germany caused its second suspension (April 28, 1552).

While Charles' ecclesiastical policy was thus breaking down, the whole fabric of his political scheme, of which his ecclesiastical views were but a part, was tumbling into ruins. Although Henry II. of France had viewed with apprehension the growing pretensions of Charles, he had not yet felt strong enough for active opposition. In the summer of 1551, however, hostilities broke out in Italy over the interminable question of Parma and Piacenza, in which Henry II. supported the cause of Ottavio Farnese. But Charles had no money to send to Gonzaga ; Julius III. was most anxious to keep matters quiet ; and Henry, on the point of invading Germany, consented to a truce (April 1552), by which Ottavio was to be left in possession of Parma for two years.

Failure of Charles' political schemes.

Henry II. rightly judged that the issue must be fought out in the north. Here the indignation against the Spanish rule and policy of Charles had been growing fast. The Interim had never been popular even with the Catholic princes ; it had been passed without the consent of the Church, and the concessions to the Lutherans were considered a dangerous compromise with heresy. The Protestants looked upon many of its clauses as popish, and resented the tyrannical means by

Interference of Henry II. in Italy and in Germany. 1551-1552.

which they had been enforced. Above all, Charles' behaviour
to the Landgrave irritated all; not only did Charles keep him
a prisoner, he forced him to follow him in his progresses,
and treated him with open contempt. Indeed,
Charles' conduct had changed. The certainty of
success made him abandon all idea of conciliation, and, tortured by gout and other ailments,
he became more irritable, more dictatorial, and more overbearing than he had ever been before.

Discontent
against
Charles
in Germany.

Already in February 1550, John of Custrin and Albert
Alcibiades of Culmbach[1] had formed a defensive league to
protect their common interests, and had decided
to approach the French King. Meanwhile, the
relations between the Emperor and Maurice were
daily becoming more strained. The victory of
Mühlberg won, Charles was most unwilling to make Maurice
too strong, and accordingly had hesitated to fulfil his promises.
The right of protection over Magdeburg and Halberstadt was
not granted; the representatives of John Frederick were not
forced to acknowledge their new master; and the Emperor had
been heard to say that in John Frederick ' he had a bear which
he could let loose against Maurice.' On the other hand, the
young Elector found that his position among the Protestants
and in his own dominions was daily becoming more difficult.
The unpopularity of the Emperor was transferred to him; the
treatment of the Landgrave was laid at his door; he was
looked upon as the arch-traitor who had ruined the Protestant
cause; and schemes were on foot of driving him from his
ill-gotten possessions by the aid of France. Maurice began to
fear that his new-won Electorate might be torn from him either
by the Emperor, or by the Protestant Princes. Apart from
these personal motives, which were strong, it cannot be denied
that Maurice also thought of the cause of Protestantism,
which would be seriously endangered if Charles should become
completely master. The interests therefore of Maurice's co-
religionists, as well as his own, urged him to offer his alliance
to the Princes on condition that they would guarantee him

Maurice's
intrigues
with the
Protestants.

[1] See Appendix iv.

the peaceful possession of his newly-won territories. Accordingly, since the spring of 1550, he had been making advances. None the less, the Protestant Princes not unnaturally suspected him, more especially as Charles had intrusted him with the enforcement of the Interim on the city of Magdeburg. It was not therefore till February 20, 1551, that Maurice was able to allay the apprehensions of the Protestants. He then convinced them that the expedition against the city was only intended to lull the suspicions of Charles; he promised them that the religion of the inhabitants should be in no way interfered with, and that he would be true to the Protestant cause. By two treaties (February and May, 1551), the Princes agreed to unite in common defence of the Protestant religion and the liberties of Germany, and Maurice was secured in his Electorate against all claims of the Ernestine branch.

The siege of Magdeburg was now continued. In November, 1551, the city surrendered. The citizens promised to implore the pardon of the Emperor, to pay a fine, and to conform to the Interim. At the same time they received secret assurances from Maurice that they should not be deprived of their privileges, nor disturbed in the exercise of their religion. Further, they elected Maurice as their Burgrave, a title generally held by the electoral house of Saxony, which gave him considerable jurisdiction over the city and its dependencies.

Magdeburg surrenders to Maurice. Nov. 1551.

Meanwhile, the question had been debated whether the League should remain a defensive one, and be confined to Germany, or whether it should look for help from outside. Maurice held that if the Protestants were to win they must gain the aid of France. In spite of the opposition of John of Custrin, who refused to go so far, the advice of Maurice was followed, and negotiations were commenced in October, 1551, which led, in January, 1552, to the Treaty of Friedwald. Henry II. had the effrontery to request that the religious affairs of Germany should be placed under his protection; but this the Protestants refused to grant

Treaty of Friedwald. Jan. 1552.

to the persecutor of their co-religionists at home, and no mention of the religious questions was made in the treaty. Henry II. promised to assist in obtaining the release of the Landgrave from prison, and in defending the liberties of Germany. The price of the French King was high. He was empowered to occupy, as Vicar of the Empire, Cambray, Metz, Toul, and Verdun—with reservation, however, of the imperial sovereignty—and the Princes promised at the next vacancy of the Empire to support his candidature, or that of some one agreeable to him. The cession of the three bishoprics of Metz, Toul, and Verdun, which dominated Lorraine, has been often and severely blamed. But we should at least remember that French was the common language of these districts, that the sentiment of German nationality, never very strong, had been weakened by the struggles of the Reformation, and that the French alliance was necessary, if Charles was to be successfully resisted in his attempt to subjugate Germany to a foreign Spanish rule. Maurice, however, did not rest satisfied with the French alliance. Ferdinand had gained from him a pledge that he would resist the plan of Charles with regard to the succession to the Empire. The friendly terms which were thus established Maurice turned to good account, and, by assuring Ferdinand that no attack should be made on him, secured himself against active hostility on the part of the Austrian prince.

While Maurice had been raising this formidable coalition against the Emperor, the relations between the two had been strictly amicable. Yet it is a mistake to suppose that Charles remained in ignorance of what was going forward. At this moment, however, Charles was ill, and in one of his fits of irresolution and lassitude. Dazzled, moreover, by the success of his policy since the battle of Mühlberg, he thought too lightly of the conspiracy, and hoped to deal with his opponents as he had done in 1546. He believed that he could either win over Maurice by further concessions, or ruin him by freeing John Frederick, and restoring to him his electoral dominions. The Emperor did not understand how circumstances had changed since 1546; he did not realise how unpopular his Spanish rule, his highhandedness, and his succession scheme had become in Germany, even with his brother Ferdinand; he omitted the French alliance in his calculations; finally, he mistook the man with whom he had to deal. With all his ambition Maurice really cared for the cause of Protestantism, and was determined to protect his subjects in their religion. It was improbable that he would ever have sacrificed that to any personal gains. Charles also forgot that he had taught a lesson in diplomatic tactics, which his pupil had learnt too well; a master of diplomacy himself, he was fairly beaten by this young man of thirty. Maurice to the last kept up appearances; he even pretended compliance with the Emperor's request that he would come to Innsbruck to discuss the situation. Then suddenly gathering his army, which he had held together since the siege of Magdeburg, he marched southward (March 18), and was joined by the young William of Hesse at Bischofsheim. At the same moment Henry II. invaded Lorraine. The French King declared he came to protect German liberty, and the Princes issued a manifesto in which they denounced 'the infamy and unreasonableness of the imprisonment of the Landgrave,' and 'the foreign beastly (*viehische*) hereditary servitude,' religious and political, which Charles had attempted to force on Germany. At Rothenburg, Maurice was joined by Albert Alcibiades of Culmbach, and advanced to Augsburg, 'the watch-tower of the imperial power,' which was hastily evacuated by the imperial garrison.

Maurice declares himself, and marches south, March 18. Henry II invades Lorraine.

It was now that Ferdinand assumed that attitude which was the outcome of his jealousy of Charles, and of his earlier negotiations with Maurice, an attitude which he was to maintain until the final abdication of his brother. Anxious to protect his own interests and those of his House, Ferdinand proposed to intervene as mediator; to come to terms with the Protestants, and, with a united

Policy of Ferdinand.

Q

Germany at his back, defeat the succession scheme of Charles,
and turn upon the Turk.   Accordingly he induced Maurice
Conference   to hold a conference at Linz, April 18, at which
at Linz.   they agreed upon the general terms of the future
April 18.   peace, and Maurice consented to a suspension of
arms on May 26, when negotiations should be resumed at
Passau.   Charles had authorised his brother to negotiate,
hoping thereby to gain time, but the results of the conference
were not entirely to his mind, and Maurice had once more
gained a diplomatic victory.   The neutrality of Ferdinand was
practically secured ; while Maurice had time to act before the
26th.   Marching on the Ehrenberg, he secured the castle
which commanded the pass to Innsbruck, where the Em-
Flight of   peror was ; and Charles, too ill with gout to ride,
Charles to   after a vain attempt to escape northwards to the
Villach.   Netherlands, fled with difficulty in a litter across
the Brenner to Villach.   Maurice was urged to end the matter
by seizing the Emperor himself.   'I have no cage big enough
to hold such a bird,' he answered, and preferred to treat.

On the 1st of June, negotiations were again resumed at
Passau between Ferdinand and Maurice, where the Electors,
The Treaty   many of the city representatives, and most of the
of Passau.   princes were present.   It is sometimes said that
Aug. 2, 1552.   Charles, in despair, left the negotiations to Ferdinand, and let things go as they would.   Nothing is further
from the truth.   At no time of his life are the tenacity and
obstinacy of his character better illustrated than at this
moment, especially when we remember how ill he was.
Unwilling to abandon his darling scheme of restoring unity
to the Church, and supremacy to the imperial authority, he
fought each concession clause by clause ; ever dreaming of
revenge, he laboured to gain time while he intrigued and
tried to organise an opposition on every side.   But all in vain.
Germany had suffered too much from his rule to care to fight
for it again.   The political tendencies of the time leant too
strongly to autonomy in Church and State ; and the Treaty of
Passau is mainly due to the growth of a middle party, both

Catholic and Protestant, who were weary of war, disliked the political schemes of Charles, and saw the necessity of compromise—a party which expressed the sentiments of Germany at large. On one point, however, the Emperor stood firm. He refused to acknowledge the authority of the conference at Passau as final; to the decisions of a Diet alone would he bow, and the terms granted at Passau must be provisional only. Maurice who, in despair at the obstinacy of Charles, had again taken up arms and besieged the city of Frankfort-on-the-Main (July 17), did not feel his position secure enough to refuse compliance, and, on August 2, agreed to the terms offered by the Emperor. The confederates were to lay down their arms before the 12th of August, when the Landgrave was to be set at liberty; a Diet was to be held in six months, when the matters in dispute should be finally decided, and, if no decision were come to, the present arrangement should continue. Meanwhile, all those who adhered to the Confession of Augsburg were to be unmolested, and Protestants were to be admitted as assessors to the Imperial Chamber. Even at the last Charles thought of refusing his consent, and of appealing to arms. Overborne, however, by the solicitations of Ferdinand, who warned him that he would have to fight the great majority of the Princes, Catholic as well as Protestant, he at last ratified the treaty (August 15), and set the Elector, John Frederick, as well as the Landgrave, free.

The Treaty of Passau represented, there cannot be a doubt, the general wish of Germany, both Catholic and Protestant. It received the hearty assent of all except a few devoted Catholics, and those who, like John Frederick, hoped to regain what they had lost, or, like Albert Alcibiades of Culmbach, looked to benefit by a continuation of the war. Much as Charles disliked the peace, any attempt to join the disaffected would have been madness. Yet with that doggedness which seemed to grow upon him with years, he did not abandon hope. The French had not been included in the treaty. A

successful war waged against them might yet regain him popularity, and place him in a position to make one more struggle
for all that he held dear.

Fortunately for the cause of Protestantism and the interests
of Germany, Charles' military enterprises failed. He secured,

Ill success indeed, the assistance of Albert of Culmbach,
of Charles and in October, 1552, laid siege to Metz. But
prevents his the skill and energy of the Duke of Guise, who
breaking the
Treaty. here won his military name, baulked the efforts of
Charles. The winter came on, and sorely tried the Spanish
and Italian troops; and, in December, 1552, Charles abandoned
the attempt, bitterly declaring that 'Fortune, like women,
favoured a young King rather than an old Emperor.' Nor
were his arms more successful in Italy. The republic of
Siena, torn by internal dissensions, had put itself under the
Emperor's protection, and admitted a body of soldiers
under Mendoza, the imperial ambassador at Rome. But the
severity of Mendoza's rule soon caused the Sienese to repent;
they applied to France for aid, drove out the Spanish troops,
and transferred their allegiance to France; while Solyman,
again in alliance with the French, sent a fleet which threatened,
though unsuccessfully, the city of Naples. In 1553, the
Emperor, who had retired to the Netherlands, was somewhat
more fortunate, and took the town of Terouenne. But in
Italy, all the attempts of the Viceroy of Naples, and of
Cosimo, Duke of Florence, to oust the French from Siena were
vain (till April 1556). Naples was again threatened by a
Turkish fleet, and the French conquered a part of Corsica then
belonging to Genoa. In Hungary, Isabella the widow of
Zapolya, and her son, leaning on Turkish support, finally
secured Transylvania; and Vienna itself might have been
attacked once more if Solyman had not been called off by a
Persian war, and distracted by the domestic troubles which
led to the execution of his own favourite son Mustapha.

At this moment occurred the death of Maurice, an event
which, under more prosperous circumstances, might have

offered Charles an opportunity of final victory. In the midst of the foreign war, Charles had not ceased to intrigue with the disaffected, more especially with Albert of Culmbach. In return for the assistance that prince had given him before Metz, he had confirmed those grants of money and of land which Albert had extorted from the Bishops of Bamberg and Wurzburg. These claims Albert had proceeded to enforce with arms, in spite of the order of the Imperial Chamber;[1] whereupon, in February 1553, Ferdinand and Maurice, who, with other Princes of the south of Germany, formed the League of Heidelberg to enforce the Treaty of Passau, marched against him and defeated him at Sievershausen, in the Duchy of Luneburg (July 9). The victory, however, was dearly bought, for Maurice died two days afterwards of his wounds. Thus, at the age of thirty-two, a Prince passed away who had played the leading part in the history of Germany since 1546. To this day his aims and his character are matters of hot dispute. By some he is looked

Death of Maurice at Sievershausen. July 9, 1553.

upon as the apt pupil of Machiavelli, a man devoid of religious conviction, or of any principle beyond that of calculating self-interest. Others represent him as the greatest statesman of the day; as the man who first guessed the designs of Charles, and whose treachery in 1546 was really only the first and necessary move towards the final vindication of the cause of Protestantism, forced upon him by the necessity of gaining a strong position before he could hope to resist the Emperor. As is so often the case with violent partisanship, the truth lies midway between these two extreme views. Although Maurice had no very strong convictions on the points at issue between the adherents of the two hostile creeds, and was, no doubt, influenced by ambition, yet it is unjust to accuse him of sacrificing the religion of his subjects to personal ends. In any case, whatever we may think of his motives, the ability of his statesmanship is beyond dispute. Once deceived by Charles, he quickly

[1] See Appendix iv.

learnt of him, and finally succeeded in outmanœuvring that master of diplomacy. To Maurice, at least, Protestantism owed its final recognition, and Germany her escape from the Spanish tyranny of Charles. Nor did the electorate of Saxony suffer under his hands. The country was well ruled, and education advanced. Nay, had Maurice lived longer or been succeeded by men of like calibre with himself, Saxony would probably not have seen herself eclipsed in the seventeenth and eighteenth centuries by her neighbours, the Hohenzollern Electors of Brandenburg. Whether it be true that, at the moment of his death, he dreamt of even greater things, and that he, in conjunction with Ferdinand, was intriguing with France to secure the imperial dignity for himself, we cannot say. Maurice was too good a diplomatist to show his hand before the decisive moment. But at least we may believe that Germany would not have fared ill under him as Emperor.

Neither Albert nor Charles benefited from the death of Maurice. The former was shortly driven from Germany to end his days as a pensioner of the French King, while his dominions in Franconia fell to his cousin, George Frederick of Anspach ; and Charles, despairing of resisting the united will of Germany, at last bowed to the inevitable. He abandoned his scheme of succession, and ceased to oppose a permanent settlement of the religious difficulties. To this course he was the more inclined, because he now thought of marrying Philip to Mary, the Catholic Queen of England, and thus uniting England with the Spanish monarchy. With this change of policy, the rivalry between him and his brother was at an end, and Ferdinand was given a free hand in Germany.

The affairs of Saxony first demanded attention. John Frederick, in spite of his remonstrances, was forced to rest content with some territorial concessions ; while the rest of the dominions, with the electoral titles, went to Augustus, the brother of Maurice.

Having settled this question satisfactorily, Ferdinand prevailed on his brother to summon the Diet to Augsburg in February, 1555. Charles, however, refused to take any part in the negotiations, and left Ferdinand to preside and to settle matters as he would, with the warning that he should do nothing against his conscience.

Diet of Augsburg. Feb.- Sept. 1555.

With a few exceptions all in Germany, both Catholic and Protestant, earnestly desired a settlement of the religious question, and the establishment of a peace which might protect them from such turbulent spirits as Albert Alcibiades of Culmbach. And yet the attempt to reconcile the conflicting interests of the two religions—always a difficult matter— was rendered doubly so by the complicated character of the imperial constitution. No sooner, therefore, did discussion begin than dissensions appeared, and these were fostered by the papal party. Fortunately, the death of Julius III., in March, forced his legate, Cardinal Morone, to retire from Augsburg. The next Pope, Marcellus II., only lived twenty days; and although his successor, Paul IV. (Caraffa), attempted to put every obstacle in the way, he was only able to limit the concessions granted to the Protestants.

Death of Julius III., March 1555, facilitates matters.

On two points, agreement was comparatively easy. It was declared that hereafter all religious disputes should be settled by peaceful means, and to this end, in all causes between a Catholic and a Lutheran, the Imperial Chamber was to be composed of an equal number of assessors from either party. The remaining questions presented greater difficulties. The Lutherans had originally wished that every individual should be allowed to conform to the Confession of Augsburg, whether the subject of a Protestant state or no. But this was dreaded by those Catholic Princes in whose dominions Lutheranism had made great strides, and the Reformers were forced to rest content with the stipulation, that every secular Prince or imperial city should be allowed to decide which of the two religions should be adopted within their jurisdiction, and that those who could not conform should be allowed to depart with their goods. A compromise was also arrived at with regard to the secularisation of ecclesiastical property within the jurisdiction of secular Princes. All such property as had been secularised before the Treaty of Passau, 1552, was to remain so, but no further exercise of the right was to be allowed. The Protestants, while conceding this point, demanded that ecclesiastical Princes should, like the secular Princes, be allowed to establish what religion they liked within their jurisdictions, and that any ecclesiastical Prince or Bishop who adopted the Lutheran Confession should retain his dignities and his revenues. This would, however, have dealt a fatal blow at the whole fabric of the Empire, and was stoutly resisted by the Catholics, and by Ferdinand himself. As the Lutherans stood out, Ferdinand thought seriously of postponing the consideration of this question, lest the rest of the treaty might be lost. Finally, however, an unsatisfactory compromise was arrived at. It was enacted, that if any ecclesiastic should hereafter abandon the Catholic religion, he should relinquish his office, with the revenues and patronage appertaining thereto. This clause the Lutherans allowed to be inserted in the treaty, but only under protest that they did not consider the reservation binding on them ; and further obtained the concession that those subjects of ecclesiastical Princes, who had already embraced Lutheranism, should be unmolested, and that those who might subsequently become Lutherans should be allowed to emigrate.

By the Peace of Augsburg, the attempt of Charles to re-establish the unity of the Church on the basis of a revived Empire of the West, received its final death-blow ; and the principle of autonomy in ecclesiastical matters was definitely recognised. Had Charles been victorious over his foreign enemies, in all probability he would, for a time at least, have gained his end. Had he been less ambitious, and confined his attention to Germany, he might possibly have succeeded in crushing out Lutheranism. But the very magnificence of his aims prevented their realisation. Again and again, when he was about to strike, some exigency of politics intervened to thwart him ; and eventually the principle of territorialism, when supported by the foreigner, proved too strong. Yet it would not be fair to charge the Protestants with having used a religious cry to further their political ends. In Germany, as elsewhere in Europe, the religious element perforce connected itself with politics. The Reformation furnished a creed and a new enthusiasm to the political aspirations already existing, and eventually gave the victory to those political tendencies which were the strongest. Had Charles been a different man, he might have adopted Protestantism and thereon founded a united kingdom in Germany. But this his character and his Spanish sympathies prevented, and, short of complete victory on his part, there was no alternative but that of decentralisation. Henceforth, Germany abandoned all hope of reconciling the two religions by means of a general or even a national Council in Germany. The Lutheran Church obtained a legal recognition, and the Protestant states claimed to pursue their course without the intervention of any external ecclesiastical authority. In this way the mediæval conception of Church and State was completely revolutionised, and the temporal authority gained an independence it had not enjoyed before. Nevertheless, the settlement was by no means final, and bore in it the seeds of future discord. The principle of individual toleration was not conceded. If the Princes usually adopted the religion of the majority of their subjects, the rights of the minority were not respected. The ' ecclesiastical reservation ' was certain hereafter to lead to serious disputes. Above all, the Calvinists, who were shortly to become the most active of the Reformers, were not included in the peace. The religious quarrels which ensued between them and the Lutherans embittered the political jealousies already existing. The Catholics took advantage of this, and Germany had yet to undergo the horrors of the Thirty Years' War, before the religious question should receive its final settlement.

While Germany had been absorbed in these momentous issues, the war with France had been continued on the borders of the Netherlands, and in Italy, with varying results. In April 1555, Siena was regained for the Imperialists by Cosimo, Duke of Florence. Elsewhere the events were unimportant, and, in 1556, a truce concluded at Vaucelles, led to a brief cessation of arms. By that date, however, Charles had ceased to be King of Spain.

Truce of Vaucelles. Feb. 1556.

Disappointed at the frustration of all his schemes, a victim to gout, asthma, and other ailments, he determined to abandon the heretical Germany to Ferdinand, and to resign the government of his other territories to his son. Charles fondly hoped that Philip, united to the Queen of England, and in the full vigour of youth, might yet establish a great Catholic monarchy with its centre in Spain, and resist the dangerous advance of heresy; nay, might some day bring the King of France to his knees, and establish Spanish supremacy in Europe. Milan and Italy had been already ceded to Philip on his marriage with Mary of England, but the division of authority had led to difficulties, and to some quarrels between father and son. In October 1555, therefore, one month after the peace of Augsburg, Queen Mary of Hungary resigned her post as Regent of the Netherlands, and the government of those territories, which had just been once more separated from the Empire, was handed over to Philip.

Preparation of Charles for his abdication.

Even then, Charles had apparently intended to retain the government of Spain somewhat longer in his hands, but Italy and the Netherlands could scarcely be defended without Spanish arms and money; accordingly, in the following January (1556), Philip was acknowledged King of Spain. Finally, in the September of that year, Charles resigned the imperial crown, although, owing to certain technicalities, Ferdinand was not elected for two years. By this act, the ambitious idea, first entertained by Maximilian, of uniting

Jan. 1556. Philip acknowledged King of Spain. Sept.: Charles resigns the imperial throne.

under one rule Spain, Italy, and the Netherlands with the German dominions of the Hapsburgs, was abandoned, and a return was made to the more reasonable policy of Ferdinand the Catholic. Henceforth until the disappearance of the Spanish line in 1700, the House of Hapsburg was divided into two branches, of which the Austrian ruled over the family territories in South Germany, and secured the elective throne of the Empire ; while the Spanish ruled over Italy, Franche-Comté, the Netherlands, and the conquests in the New World. It would probably have been well for Spain if she had never had a German Emperor as her King ; while the Netherlands, all that now remained to her of the patrimony of the Archduke Philip, was yet to prove a source of weakness and humiliation.

Charles, having resigned the burden of government to younger shoulders, retired to the Jeronymite monastery of Yuste in the province of Estremadura, in September, 1556. The traditional story of his life there requires some correction. He did not dwell in the monastery, but in a house prepared for him close by. Although he lived a religious life, attended regularly the services of the Church, and even submitted himself to the penance of flagellation, his daily lot was not otherwise one of extreme hardship. In the matter of diet, especially, he not only excused himself from fasting, ostensibly on the score of health, but indulged, to his cost, his love for rich and unwholesome dishes. He by no means shut himself off from all worldly concerns, but kept up an active correspondence with his son, and with his daughter Joanna, who acted as Regent of Castile during Philip's absence. He was most energetic in collecting the necessary taxes for the campaigns of 1557 and 1558, and one of his last acts was to urge the Regent to crush out the Lutheran heresy, which had appeared in Spain. Retaining in his retreat the same dogged adherence to the principles which had guided his life, Charles at last, in his fifty-eighth year, succumbed to

Charles at Yuste. Sept. 1556 to Sept. 1558.

Death of Charles V. 21st Sept. 1558.

the ailments which had been growing upon him of late (21st September 1558).

The Emperor has been so often before us, that it is need-less to say much more of him here. His character was late in developing, and it was not until the Diet of Worms, 1521, that he began to show his powers. From that moment, how-ever, he bent himself to the bewildering difficulties of his position with a consistency of purpose which is all the more remarkable when we remember his constitutional indolence and irresolution. It is the conflict between these three qualities—his obstinacy, his lethargy, and his irresolution—which explains the contradictions of his conduct. Self-pos-sessed and self-contained, yet with a fiery nature which at times betrayed itself, few save his two chancellors, Gattinara and Granvelle, and his confessor Pedro de Soto, were admitted to his counsels. If we except his wife Isabella of Portugal, who died in 1539, his son and his sisters, he made but few close attachments, and his heart was rarely stirred by any sentiment. He never forgave an injury ; he rarely did a generous deed. He was a man to command fear and even admiration, but not to inspire affection. A Netherlander at first, but never a German, he soon became a thorough Spaniard, and looked upon Spain as the model he would fain impose on Europe.

§ 3. *Last War between France and Spain.*

The wish of Charles to secure a few years' peace for his successor was not fulfilled. It was thwarted by the Duke of Guise, the representative of the war party in France, and by his brother the Cardinal of Lor-raine, but more especially by Paul IV. That fiery prelate, who was now in his eightieth year, although a leader in the Catholic reaction, had throughout his life been a strenuous opponent of the Spaniard in Italy. A member of

Paul IV. allies himself with France against Philip.

July 1556.

a Neapolitan family (the Caraffa) which had always supported the Angevin party in that kingdom, he had early incurred the displeasure of Charles, who had caused his name to be struck off the Council of Government, and resisted his nomination to the archiepiscopal see of Naples. Under these circumstances it is not surprising that, as Pope, he should adopt that anti-Spanish policy which had now become almost traditional with the Papacy. He remembered the days of Italian freedom, and considered the Spaniard the most dangerous of its enemies. 'The French,' he said, 'may easily be dislodged hereafter; but the Spaniards are like dog-grass, sure to strike root wherever it is cast.' Prompted by these motives, he had, in December 1555, made a secret treaty with France, with the object of driving the Spaniards from Italy, and now he urged Henry II. to break his truce with Spain. The Guises threw their influence on the side of war; and in July, 1556, in pursuance of a fanciful scheme of reviving the French claim to Naples, a treaty was made by which that kingdom was to be torn from Philip and conferred on one of Henry's sons, with the exception of some portion of the northern frontier, which was to fall to the Pope as his share of the spoil.

Paul had not waited for this alliance to commence hostilities, or to punish the Colonnesi, who supported the imperial cause. In answer to this, the Duke of Alva, who had just been appointed Governor of Naples, entered the Papal States (September), and, in the absence of the French, occupied the chief places in the Campagna. Indeed, had it not been for the scruples of the Duke, or rather of his royal master, Rome itself might have been taken; but Philip's orders were that he should bring the Pope to terms rather than ruin him. Alva accordingly listened to the insincere offers of the Pope, and delayed further operations until the advance of the French army under the Duke of Guise, at the beginning of the new year, forced him to retreat southwards. Alva now played a waiting game, and,

Duke of Alva invades the Papal States. Sept. 1556.

refusing to meet the French in a pitched battle, gradually wore them out, as Gonzalvo had done in 1503. The Duke of Guise,

French in-
vade Naples,
but are re-
called by
defeat of
St. Quentin.
Jan.-Aug.
1557.

frustrated in his attempt to take the town of Civitella (May 15), and wearied by these tactics, was forced to evacuate the kingdom of Naples, and shortly afterwards was recalled to France (August 15), by the news of the defeat of St. Quentin, 'having done little for his King, still less for the Church, and nothing for his honour.' Paul, deserted by his allies, was forced to accept the terms offered him, which,

Paul comes
to terms with
Alva.

however, were so advantageous that, as Alva bitterly remarked, 'they seem to have been dictated by the vanquished instead of the victor.' The territories of the Church were to be restored intact ; the remaining French troops were to be allowed a free passage to France ; the affair of the Colonnesi was to be submitted to the arbitration of Philip and the Pope. The Duke of Alva was actually to ask pardon, and receive absolution from the Pope, for having dared to take up arms against him.

This, the last war for the possession of Italy for many a long day, is noticeable for the strange contradictions it presents. Not only does the most bigoted of the Popes oppose the most bigoted of Kings ; he even calls to his assistance the Infidel and the Protestant mercenaries of Germany ; while his opponent, at the command of his master Philip, wages war on the Pope with every expression of reverence, and, when

Sicily, Naples,
Milan, finally
secured by
Spain.

dictating peace, does so, as a suppliant, on his knees. Yet, in spite of his haughty demeanour, Paul had failed. The French henceforth ceased to struggle for Italy ; Sicily, Naples, and Milan remained in the hands of the Spanish Hapsburgs until the extinction of their line in the year 1700.

In the war which had meanwhile broken out on the eastern frontier of France, the exhaustion of that country was plainly visible. The feudal levies responded but feebly ; the provincial legions of infantry, which had been organised by

Francis I. in 1534, had never been successful; and of the French peasantry, the Gascons alone appeared in any numbers. France was thus forced to fall back on six thousand German mercenaries. Emanuel Philibert, the dispossessed Duke of Savoy, a man of twenty-nine years, who commanded the army of Philip, had a much larger force drawn from the various countries under Spanish rule, and was aided by a contingent of English, who with difficulty had been prevailed upon to aid the husband of their queen. The financial straits of the two combatants were much the same, but the energy of Charles in his retreat at St. Yuste succeeded in wringing from the Spaniards a considerable amount of money. On the approach of the Duke of Savoy, Coligny threw himself into the city of St. Quentin (August 2), a town of importance, as being the entrepot for trade between France and the Low Countries. But the rash attempt of the Marshal de Montmorenci, who was in supreme command, to relieve it with a far inferior force, led to his total defeat (August 10). The Marshal himself, many nobles, and thousands of the common soldiers, were taken prisoners; as many more were slain. France, in a word, had not suffered such a defeat since Pavia. ' Is not my son in Paris ? ' asked Charles, on receiving intelligence of the victory ; and had Charles himself been in command, Paris might have fallen. But Philip, ever more fond of negotiation than of war, delayed till he should be master of St. Quentin. The city, defended by the energy and ability of Coligny, was not stormed till the 27th of August—and the delay saved Paris. Quarrels subsequently broke out in the Spanish camp, which led to the retreat of the English. The Germans complained of want of pay ; many transferred their services to the French ; and, after taking a few more places, the army of Philip went into winter quarters. In January, the surprise of Calais by the Duke of Guise reversed, at least in the opinion of the French, the disaster of St. Quentin. The

Campaign on the eastern frontier of France. Spanish victory of St. Quentin, Aug. 10.

English, in overweening confidence, had of late neglected
the defences of that town, and in the winter were accustomed
to withdraw a portion of the troops, because the
marshes were then believed to be impassable.
The Duke, informed of this, suddenly appeared
before the walls, and took by assault the two forts
of Newman Bridge, and Risbank, which defended Calais
from the sea and from the shore respectively. Lord Went-
worth, despairing of holding the city now that his position
was commanded, capitulated on January 8. The recovery
of this city, which had been in the hands of the English since
the days of Edward III., very naturally caused boundless
exultation in France. The taking of Thionville by the
Duke of Guise followed in June; and in July, the Marshal
de Termes, in command of the Calais garrison, secured
Dunkirk and Mardyke. But the Marshal had imprudently
ventured too far into the enemies' country, and had left
Gravelines unmasked behind him. As he attempted to retreat, he was caught between the
garrison of Gravelines and a Flemish force raised
by the Count of Egmont, and was completely
routed, falling himself into the enemies' hands (July 13).

*Calais taken
by the Duke
of Guise.
Jan. 1-8, 1558.*

*The French
defeated at
Gravelines.
July 13, 1558.*

This was the last action in the war. The renewal of
hostilities had not been of Philip's seeking, and he was now
doubly anxious for peace. The difficulty of supplying money,
always a serious matter, was now so great that Philip confessed to his ministers that he was on the brink of ruin.
The death of his father, Charles, on the 21st of September,
demanded his presence in Spain; and England was not to be
trusted to continue the war, especially as Mary was very ill.
Nor had France much to hope for from a continuation of the
struggle, now that the Pope had made his peace with Philip.
Her finances were exhausted, her people weary of a struggle
which brought them no benefit. Besides all this, heresy had
appeared both in France and in Spain. Henry II. therefore
listened to the advice of Montmorenci and of the Cardinal of

Lorraine. The first, as a captive and a rival of the victorious Duke of Guise, had personal reasons for desiring peace; the latter urged Henry to devote his attention to the extirpation of heresy.

Negotiations were commenced in October, but were delayed by the death of Mary of England in November, and the refusal of Queen Elizabeth to acknowledge the surrender of Calais. Philip, hoping perhaps thereby Treaty of to gain her hand, offered to stand by the English Cateau Queen and break off the negotiations, but only on Cambrésis. April 3, 1559. condition that she would support him with all her power as long as the war should last. This did not suit the cautious and parsimonious Queen, and she finally consented to leave Calais for eight years in the hands of France. France was also allowed, by the Emperor Ferdinand, to retain the three Lotharingian Bishoprics, Metz, Toul, and Verdun, but had to surrender all her other conquests to Philip and his allies, except Turin, Saluzzo, Pignerol, and a few other places of importance in Piedmont. These she was to hold until Henry's claim to that principality through his grandmother, Louise of Savoy, should be decided—a claim which he could hardly believe to be serious. Thus Philip regained the towns which France had taken in Luxembourg; Montferrat was restored to the Duke of Mantua; Genoa regained Corsica. On his side, Philip surrendered the few places he held in Picardy. The two Kings further bound themselves to do their best to procure the meeting of a General Council, which was necessary both for reformation of abuses, and for the restoration of union and concord to the Church. The treaty was to be ratified by a double marriage; Philip was to marry Elizabeth, the eldest daughter of Henry II., then a girl of thirteen, who had at first been suggested as the bride of his son Don Carlos; Margaret, the sister of the French king, was to espouse Emanuel Philibert, Duke of Savoy. In the tournament which was held to celebrate the marriage of Philip with the French princess, Henry II. received a wound from which he died, and was succeeded by his son Francis II., a youth of sixteen, who in 1558 had married Mary Queen of Scots.

The peace of Cateau Cambrésis, by which France 'lost as many provinces as she regained cities,' was far more disadvantageous than the military position, in spite of the defeats of St. Quentin and Gravelines, justified. It is therefore not unnaturally looked upon as a dishonourable one by most French writers. It reminds us once more of the taunt of Machiavelli that the French are not masters of diplomacy, and is perhaps not an unfitting close to that long struggle between the Houses of Valois and of Hapsburg, which commenced with the foolish expedition of Charles VIII., and in which France had continually been the aggressor. Her only permanent gains were those of Calais, and the three Lotharingian bishoprics; and these, balanced as they were by the loss of Spanish Navarre, were won at the price of an exhausted treasury and an impoverished people. She had no doubt taken a leading part in resisting the dangerous supremacy of the Austro-Spanish House, and in foiling the attempt of Charles to establish a universal monarchy in Europe. Yet it may be questioned whether she could not have done this more effectively if she had kept her hands off Italy, and had strengthened and extended her frontiers by winning Rousillon and Franche-Comté, and by pressing towards the Rhine. While playing the rival to the House of Hapsburg, she had not only contributed to the success of the Reformers in Germany, and to the advance of the Turk in Hungary, but had allowed Protestantism to gain a firm hold at home, and had fostered a military spirit among the smaller nobility, which was to give to the religious struggle in France some of its worst characteristics.

Throughout the long struggle nothing had been done to strengthen the government of France, or to develop constitutional life. The monarchy came out of the war bankrupt, and the government the prey of rival factions—factions which, if they did not cause the religious wars, most certainly prolonged

them and France, torn by civil and religious strife, had to wait
till the reign of Henry IV. before she could take that part in
European affairs to which her central position, the ability of
her people, and her magnificent natural resources entitled her.

Nor was Spain in much better plight. To outward appearances, indeed, the power of Philip seemed overwhelming.
He was King of the whole Spanish Peninsula with the exception of Portugal;[1] King of Naples and of Sicily, and Duke of
Milan, a position which enabled him to control the politics
of the Peninsula;[2] Master of Franche-Comté and of the
Netherlands. In Africa, he held Tunis and Oran, with places
on the Barbary coast, and the islands of Cape de Verd, and the
Canaries; while in the Pacific Ocean, the Philippines were
under his sway. In America, Spain held a large part of the
eastern coast, except Brazil, which belonged to Portugal, all
the islands in the Gulf of Mexico and the Caribbean Sea, and
the kingdoms of Mexico and Peru, which had been conquered during the reign of Charles. The Spanish infantry
was considered the most formidable in Europe, and the
treasures of the Indies were believed to be inexhaustible.

[1] For the character of the Spanish rule in Italy, cf. Armstrong,
Charles V., II. p. 291 ff.

[2] As we shall have to speak but little hereafter of Italy, it may be well
to give concisely the names of the chief dependent or independent states :

1. Piedmont, except Saluzzo, in the hands of Emanuel Philibert of Savoy.
2. Genoa and Venice, independent republics.
3. Parma and Piacenza, under the rule of Ottavio Farnese ; of these
   Parma had been restored to him by Paul III., and Piacenza by
   Philip II. in 1556.
4. Mantua, in the hands of Frederick, first Duke of Mantua, who also
   gained Montferrat from Charles V. in 1536, having married the
   heiress of William VII. (Paleologus), Marquis of Montferrat.
5. Florence, under Duke Cosimo dei Medici, who had just secured
   Siena, and assumed the title of Grand Duke of Tuscany in 1569.
6. The Duchy of Urbino, a papal fief, in the hands of Guidobaldo
   della Rovere.
7. The duchies of Ferrara, Modena, and Reggio, in the hands of
   Ercole II. of Este. On the extinction of the direct line in 1597,
   Ferrara was seized by the Pope, Clement VIII. Modena and
   Reggio went to Charles of Este, a collateral.

Yet Spain had suffered seriously from the long-protracted struggle. Her resources were nearly as much crippled as those of France; her government, if better organised, was fully as despotic, and all religious liberty had been crushed out; and she was shortly to give evidence of her weakness in the failure to put down the revolt of the United Provinces, and in the defeat of the Armada by the puny ships of England.

The peace of Cateau Cambrésis, therefore, closes one epoch and begins another. New actors came upon the scene.[1] The struggle for supremacy is stayed a while. Germany and Spain are for ever divided; the Turkish Empire soon ceases to be aggressive, and begins to suffer from internal decay. The remaining thirty-nine years we have to cover is chiefly taken up with the Counter-Reformation and the struggles to which that movement gave birth, with the religious wars in France, and with the revolt of the Netherlands against the religious and political tyranny of Spain.

[1] Charles, and Mary Queen of England died in 1558, Paul IV. and Henry II. in 1559.

CHAPTER VI

THE COUNTER-REFORMATION AND CALVINISM

The Counter-Reformation in Spain and Italy—The Theatines—The Jesuits—
Last Session of Council of Trent—The Inquisition—John Calvin and
Geneva—Characteristics of Calvinism.

§ 1. *The Counter-Reformation.*

WITH the abdication and the death of Charles v., the history
of Europe loses that unity which it received from the com-
prehensiveness of his policy, and from his striking personality.
None the less, a central point of interest is afforded us by
the movement of the Counter-Reformation, which affects all
Europe and focuses the political movements for
the next thirty years, or more. The Counter-
Reformation found its impulse in that profound
sense of dissatisfaction with the condition of the
Church to which Protestantism itself owed its origin. Like
the two orders of the Dominicans and Franciscans of the
thirteenth century, this movement took its rise in Spain
and in Italy. In the days of Alexander vi., when the
Papacy was immersed in secular interests, and was rapidly
forfeiting the respect of Europe, a thorough reform of the
Church in Spain had been inaugurated by Ferdinand and
Isabella and carried through by the energy and devotion of
Cardinal Ximenes. Under these influences a school of
theologians had been formed, who revived the doctrine of the
great Dominican of the thirteenth century, Thomas Aquinas,
and united learning with a life of purity and zeal. The
movement had at first met with little support from the
Papacy. The kings of Spain were determined to maintain
their independence in matters ecclesiastical, and had acted

Spain the home of the Counter-Reformation.

independently and often even against the papal will. Yet the spirit of reform soon spread to Italy. Adrian VI. had, while Regent in Spain, been influenced by the movement, and, as Pope (1522-1523), had vainly attempted to extend the reform to the Church at large. Under the leadership of Caraffa (1555-1559), who had before he became Pope spent some years in Spain, and still more of Loyola, Lainez, and Xavier, the Spanish founders of the Jesuits, the Counter-Reformation was to become the great support of papal authority.

Italy had never been much attracted by the speculative difficulties of Luther. No doubt The Oratory of Divine Love, It spreads a small band of literary men, with Contarini at to Italy. their head, had embraced the Doctrine of the Justification by Faith, but their party had been a small one, and did not represent any important section of opinion in Italy. Those of her children who approached the question of theology at all went further and deeper ; they questioned the truth of Christianity, or discussed the immortality of the soul. Meanwhile, the majority of the more earnest-minded, satisfied with the tenets of the Church and influenced by the spirit of reform which had spread from Spain, aimed, like Savonarola, at bringing doctrine to bear on life and conduct.

With this object many societies were formed in Italy at the beginning of the sixteenth century, of which the Theatines are The the most interesting. The members of this frater-Theatines. nity, of which Caraffa, the future Pope Paul IV., was one of the founders (1524), were not monks but clerks regular. They devoted themselves to preaching, to the administration of the sacraments, and to the care of the sick ; and took no other vow but that of poverty. Even from the Franciscans, the most corrupt of the older orders, the reformed order of the Capuchins arose.

The society, however, which was to play by far the greatest part in the coming movement, and in future history, was to be founded by a Spaniard. Ignatius Loyola (Don Inigo Lopes Ricalde y Loyola), cadet of a house of high nobility, who was born in 1491, had in early days devoted himself to the profession of arms, with all the fervour of a chivalrous spirit. A serious wound received at the siege of Pampeluna (1521) crippled him for life, and The Jesuits. Loyola, denied all hopes of a military career, turned, with the enthusiasm of his romantic and high-strung nature, to the service of the Virgin and the infant Christ, after experiencing much the same moral crisis as Luther had undergone. Returning to Spain after a pilgrimage to Jerusalem (1523), his first attempt at preaching brought him under suspicion of heresy, and he was ordered to undertake a course of theology before he resumed his teaching. In 1528, he came to Paris to pursue his studies. Here he made the acquaintance of three men whom he profoundly influenced—Peter Faber, son of a Savoyard shepherd, Francesco Xavier, and Iago Lainez, both countrymen of his own. In August, 1534, the four friends, of whom Faber at first was the only one in orders, formed a society. They took the vow of chastity, and bound themselves, after the conclusion of their studies, to pass their lives in poverty at Jerusalem, devoted to the care of the Christians or to the conversion of the infidel; or, if that were impossible, to offer their labour in any place whither the Pope might send them. Three years after (1537), the society, now increased to ten, set out on their pilgrimage to the Holy Land, and were ordained to that end. The war between Venice and the Turk, however, prevented their departure; and Loyola and his brethren becoming acquainted with Caraffa and the Theatines, changed their purpose, and determined to devote their energies to Christendom. Even then their difficulties were not over. They were charged with heresy, and, though acquitted, it was not till 1540 that they obtained with difficulty a confirmation of their 'company of Jesus' from Pope Paul III., and that Ignatius was elected as the first General. The society was organised in six classes: the novices, the scholastics, the lay coadjutors who administered the revenues of the colleges so that the rest of the

society should be free from such cares, the spiritual coadjutors, and the professed of the three, and of the four vows. Of
these, the spiritual coadjutors were the ordinary active members of the society, and from their number the rectors of
the colleges were chosen. The professed of three vows were
formed of men who, for exceptional reasons, were admitted
into the order without having passed through the inferior
grades, and held a position similar to that of the spiritual
coadjutors. The professed of four vows alone enjoyed all
the privileges of the order. They alone elected the General ;
from their number the provincials over each province into
which Christendom was divided were chosen by the General ;
and they alone, beyond the three vows of poverty, chastity,
and obedience, took a fourth of especial obedience to the Pope,
although his authority was limited by the power, exclusively
reserved to the General, of sending out, or recalling, missionaries. To reach this highest grade a man must, unless he had
been admitted to the number of the professed of three vows,
pass through all the others except that of the lay coadjutors—
a probation of thirty-one years—and was not ordained till he
became a spiritual coadjutor. The supreme official of the
order was the General, elected from the professed of four
vows by the provincial and two members from each province.
The rules of this remarkable society were so framed as to
reconcile the principle of absolute obedience with the utmost
freedom of action. In imitation of the Theatines, whose views,
however, the Jesuits carried much further, they rejected the
monastic habit, and were relieved from the more onerous and
ascetic practices of religion ; they were forbidden to weaken
their bodies with fasts and vigils, and were exempted from
the routine of devotional exercise and daily service. Nor
did the professed confine themselves to any special duties.
But if in this way they enjoyed a freedom denied to the
members of other religious orders, that freedom was controlled by the absolute authority of the society itself. They
were not permitted to hold any ecclesiastical dignity without

special leave of the General; they were to hold no property of their own; they had to cut themselves off from kith and kin, and to obey implicitly the orders of the superiors, the provincials, and the General, even against their reason and their conscience. 'It is your duty to obey the call of your superior at once, even if in so doing you have to leave a letter of the alphabet unfinished.' 'If,' said Ignatius, 'my conscience forbids me obey, I should at least submit my judgment to one or more superiors. Otherwise I am far from perfection.' Even their most secret thoughts were not their own. None could write or read a letter except under the eye of a superior, and it was the duty of their confessor and of each member to reveal to the General anything he might wish to know of their acts or thoughts. The General himself, although absolute within the rules of the society, and with right of nominating and recalling the provincials and the superiors, could not alter the constitution of the society without consulting a General Council. He was under the constant supervision of assistants elected for that purpose, and of a monitor, and could be deposed by a general congregation of the professed. Thus all individuality was merged in the company, and obedience usurped the place of reason, affection, and impulse. Bound by this iron chain of obedience, which was riveted by a system of espionage, this marvellous society went forth to guide and rule mankind. The young they influenced by education, the old by preaching and by the confessional. Believing that he who gains the young possesses the future, they founded schools and colleges where the education, like their other work, was gratuitous; they crept into the universities and sat in the professors' chairs. To make the confessional an efficient instrument for guiding the consciences of men, they soon developed a system of casuistry, in which the sins of men were nicely weighed and the principles of moral conduct sapped by the suggestion, at least, that the end justified the means. The Jesuits, however, did not confine themselves to educational or spiritual functions,

Not only did they become the confessors of Kings, they mixed themselves up in society and politics; they were found in every court of Europe supporting the orthodox, and conspiring to overthrow those who pleased them not. The growth of the company was as marvellous as its principles. When Loyola died in 1556, sixteen years after its foundation, the society numbered two thousand ordinary and forty-five professed members; there were twelve provinces, and more than one hundred colleges and houses. Under Lainez, who succeeded Loyola as General, the organisation was completed, and its growth was still more rapid, especially in Italy and Spain. Soon not only Europe, but India and America, received their missionaries. The society, as one might expect, was met by much hostility at first, on the part more especially of the older monastic orders and the friars; in later times, owing to the independent attitude it assumed, it was often at serious variance with the Papacy. Yet for the time at least the Papacy had gained an army of devoted soldiers. It now remained for the Church to define its articles of war, and to provide more efficient weapons. The Council of Trent was to do the first; the Inquisition to furnish the last.

The second session of the Council of Trent had been dispersed in 1552, in the confusion caused by the advance of Maurice of Saxony on Innsbruck (p. 242). In January, 1562, Pius IV. opened its third and last session. There was no longer any question of the admission of representatives of the Protestants; yet its work, if limited to Catholic nations, was neither unimportant nor easy. It had to determine the relation between the Pope and the Church; to settle the articles of faith which still remained in dispute, and to undertake those internal reforms the necessity of which all admitted. As might have been anticipated, these questions led to grave dispute. The Emperor Ferdinand, and the French king Charles IX. desired such a reform of the Church as might possibly lead to a reconciliation, or at least to a compromise

Third session of Council of Trent. Jan. 1562 to Dec. 1563.

with the Protestants. They demanded, therefore, that the marriage of the clergy should be allowed; that communion in both kinds should be granted to the laity; that the services of their Churches should be in the vernacular. The French, led by the Cardinal of Lorraine, went further, and raised the claim advanced at the Councils of Constance (1414-1418), and of Basle (1431-1443), of the superiority of a General Council over a Pope. The Spaniards, while they opposed many of the demands of the Germans and of the French, and were anxious to prevent any change in doctrine, objected to the extreme pretensions of the Papacy, and wished that the bishops should be recognised as holding their spiritual authority by divine institution and not as the mere delegates of the Pope. The papal party, on the contrary, were eager to affirm the supremacy of the Pope, and then dismiss the Council as soon as might be. Had their opponents been united, and had the German and French representatives been more numerous, something might have been done, for all were determined to assert the independence of the Council from papal control; they also wished to limit the authority of the Pope and to reform many of the abuses, more especially the financial extortions, of the Roman Curia. Unfortunately, their divisions gave the Pope an opportunity which he eagerly seized, and which was turned to good account by Cardinal Morone, who was appointed president in 1563. Quarrels for precedence between the representatives of France and Spain were studiously fostered. Separate negotiations were opened with Ferdinand and Charles; they were warned of the danger which might arise from too powerful an episcopate, and reminded that these continued quarrels among the Catholics would only favour heresy; they were urged to look to the Pope rather than to the Council for the reforms they needed. Since the Council had declared that the question of granting the Cup to the laity was to be left to the decision of the Pope, Ferdinand was promised that it should be conceded as soon as the Council closed; the election of Maximilian, his son, as

King of the Romans, should also be confirmed. The Cardinal of Lorraine, the chief representative of the French Church at the Council, was promised the legation in France, and even the reversion of the pontifical throne ; and in accordance with the policy of his family, the Guises, he joined the papal party, and influenced the attitude of the French court. To conciliate further the sovereigns of Europe, some articles which had been passed, and which touched unduly on the temporal power, were rescinded. The opposition of France and of the Emperor having been thus in part removed, the triumph of the papal policy was secured. The Italians, who outnumbered the rest, were almost unanimously on the papal side, which was also supported by the powerful advocacy of the Jesuit Lainez, and of Carlo Borromeo, the saintly Archbishop of Milan. Aided by the Spanish representatives, who were in agreement with them so far, the Italians succeeded in defining some of the more important doctrines in accordance with their own views, and in resisting all except some minor internal reforms.

Having now gained all that could be hoped for, the Pope was eager to close the Council. To this the Spaniards alone objected. Philip was anxious that it should continue its sessions until every disputed doctrine had been settled, and a thorough reform of the Church and the papal Curia had been effected. Here again the papal party triumphed. A report of the serious illness of the Pope finally overcame the opposition of Philip ; for a vacancy while the Council was still sitting would lead to serious difficulties. Accordingly, on December 3, 1563, the Council was finally closed. Although some points of doctrine were left undecided, those with respect to indulgences, purgatory, the sacraments, and the invocation of saints, were reaffirmed with new precision. Controverted questions were replaced by dogmas, doubtful traditions by definite doctrines, and an uniformity established in matters of faith hitherto unknown. If, in the matter of reform, a stricter

The Council closed. Its results.

discipline was enforced upon the inferior clergy, and the abuse of pluralities was checked, nothing was done to touch the prerogatives of the Pope, or of the cardinals. The Council of Trent may be said therefore to have defined the articles of the Counter-Reformation. The Catholic Church of the West was henceforth to be divided, and the Church of Rome may be said to have begun.

The decisions of the Council of Trent were accepted without reserve by the chief states of Italy, by Portugal, and by Poland. In Germany they were ratified by the Catholic princes at the Diet of Augsburg, 1566. Philip also confirmed them, 'saving the prerogatives of the crown.' In France a distinction was made; the decrees which referred to dogma were acknowledged, and, indeed, subsequently declared to need no confirmation by the temporal power; those, however, which referred to discipline, and which interfered with the Gallican Church, were opposed by the 'Parlements,' and by some of the lower clergy. Although gradually accepted in practice, and even acknowledged by the clergy at the States-General of 1615, they were never formally ratified by the crown.

To enforce the principles of this newly organised Church an instrument already existed. On July 21, 1542, Pope Paul III. had, on the advice of Cardinal Caraffa, authorised by Bull the erection of a 'Supreme Tribunal of the Inquisition.' Its organisation was based on the court instituted in Spain by Ferdinand and Isabella in 1483. Six cardinals were appointed universal Inquisitors on either side the Alps, with powers of delegating their authority to other ecclesiastics. All from highest to lowest were declared subject to their jurisdiction; no book could be printed without their leave; they could punish with imprisonment, confiscation of goods, and death; and from their judgment there was no appeal save to the Pope. How far these tremendous powers could be exercised in the various countries of Europe depended, no doubt, on the attitude of the temporal sovereigns, but in Italy there was little difficulty. The Spanish Inquisition willingly co-operated, and the tenets of the Council were enforced with merciless rigour.

The influence of the Counter-Reformation is seen in the revival of apostolic piety and missionary zeal by such men as Carlo Borromeo, nephew of Pius IV., Archbishop of Milan (1538-1584), and also in the altered character of the Popes. Of these Paul IV. (1555-1559), Pius V. (1566-1572), Sixtus V. (1585-1590), are true representatives of the time ; while the others, Pius IV. (1559-1565) and Gregory XIII. (1572-1585), although not men of remarkable zeal, could not resist the tendency of the age. The policy of all these Popes was much the same. They abandoned the pernicious system of nepotism—Pius V. finally forbidding all alienation of Church property ; they reformed the Court of Rome ; they enforced better discipline in the Church, and improved its services; they kept the cardinals in order, insisted on bishops residing in their dioceses, and, for the rest, gave to the Papal States an organised system of government and finance in which they had been hitherto wanting. Abandoning the idea of aggrandising themselves in Italy, they no longer struggled against the Spanish rule. Although they had their difficulties with the temporal sovereigns of Europe, they none the less supported the cause of authority and orthodoxy. They allied themselves with the orthodox Kings and Princes, whose younger sons they invested with episcopal sees, and granted them taxes from ecclesiastical revenues. Thus the Church of Rome had defined its faith, reformed some of its most flagrant abuses, organised within itself a force of devoted servants, and armed itself with the terrors of the Inquisition. Strengthened in this way, and by the revived associations and enthusiasms of the past, the Church, allied with the monarchs of Europe, went forth to stay the advance of heresy, and to win back, if possible, the ground she had lost by her *lâches*.

Of the Counter-Reformation, the two great exponents in the

field of temporal politics are Philip of Spain, and the family of the Guises in France. It was ever the aim of Philip to carry out his father's schemes with such modifications as the altered circumstances demanded. The loss of the Empire and of Germany forced him to lean more exclusively on Spain; the triumph of the Protestants in Germany and England destroyed all hopes of bringing them again within the fold, except by force, and this was not at first possible. But Philip never relinquished the hope of re-establishing the authority of the Catholic Church, backed up by a strong and wide-embracing monarchy under his own control. The political ambition of the Guises, and their attempt to place Mary Queen of Scots upon the throne of England excited the apprehensions of Philip, who hoped to secure that country for himself, and at first prevented his cordial co-operation with their attempt to master France. But in time these apprehensions were removed, and finally these two representatives of the Catholic reaction formed the 'League,' and united to enforce their rule on Europe. It is this which forms the connecting link between the revolt of the Netherlands and the civil wars in France, and gives a unity to the history until the end of our period.

§ 2. *Calvin and Geneva.*

While the Church of Rome was thus marshalling her forces, that form of Protestantism which was henceforth to be her most deadly foe was receiving its organisation at the hands of John Calvin.

It is a remarkable fact that Lutheranism has never made any permanent conquests outside Germany and the Scandinavian kingdoms, and that even in Germany the numbers of its adherents decreased after the middle of the sixteenth century. For this, three reasons may be suggested :— *Causes of failure of Lutheranism.*

(1) Many of the doctrines of Luther, notably those on

Justification, and on the Eucharist, were compromises of too subtle a nature to appeal to ordinary minds, even among the Germans themselves, and led to arid controversies and ignoble divisions.

(2) Moreover, by force of circumstances arising out of the political conditions of Germany, the movement had allied itself with the interests of the Princes, and with authority too closely to appeal to democratic impulses. The failure of Lutheranism to command the adhesion of the lower classes was illustrated even in Germany itself by the revolt of the peasants, the rise of the Anabaptists, and by the temporary success of the reform of Zwingle. From their extravagances Luther had drawn back with horror, and, becoming daily more conservative, had to a great extent lost the support of the more enthusiastic and thorough-going.

(3) Lastly, Luther had serious scruples on the question of employing force, and although he had finally sanctioned the appeal to arms, the war was to be a defensive one, waged by those in authority, and not in alliance with rebels. Luther had no idea of leading a religious and political crusade, or of promoting missionary enterprise outside Germany. For this the world had to look elsewhere.

The French have always been the most successful interpreters of new ideas to Europe. Their logical acuteness, their mastery of method, their gifts of organisation, as well as their language, with its matchless clearness and elasticity, have well fitted them for this office ; and these gifts were now to be illustrated in a pre-eminent degree by their great countryman John Calvin.

This son of the notary in the episcopal court of Noyon in Picardy, was born in the year 1509. At the age of twelve he had been appointed to a chaplaincy in the cathe-
John Calvin. dral, and received the tonsure. But, though he subsequently became a curé, he never proceeded any further in clerical orders ; for his father, thinking that the legal profession offered more promise, sent him to Orleans, and then to

Bourges to study law, 1529-1531. It was during these years that Calvin fell under the influence of Lutheran teachers, notably of Jacques Lefèvre, a man of Picardy like himself, and one of the fathers of French Protestantism In the year 1534, Calvin was driven from his country by the persecutions instituted by Francis I., and retired to Basle. Here at the age of twenty-five he published the first edition of his great work, *The Institutes*, a manual of Christian religion, which, although subsequently enlarged, contains a complete outline of his theological system, and which probably has exercised a more profound influence than any other book written by so young a man. In the year 1536, as he passed through Geneva, he was induced by the solemn adjurations of William Farel of Dauphiné, a French exile himself, to abandon the studies he so dearly loved, and devote himself to missionary effort. The imperial city of Geneva was of importance because it commanded the valley of the Rhone, and the commercial routes which united there; it enjoyed municipal self-government, but was under the ecclesiastical jurisdiction of its bishop and was threatened by the Duke of Savoy, who held the surrounding country and possessed certain judicial powers within the town itself. To emancipate themselves more completely from this double yoke of ecclesiastical and temporal authority was the constant aim of the patriots of Geneva, and with that view they had made an alliance with the canton of Freibourg in 1519, and that of Bern in 1526. An intermittent struggle had ensued, which was embittered by the adoption of the Lutheran Doctrine by the city in 1535, at the instigation of Farel. In 1536, war had broken out between the Duke and the canton of Bern, when the Swiss succeeded in conquering the whole of the country of Vaud, and thus relieved Geneva of all immediate danger from the Duke.

Calvin, induced to stay in Geneva at this moment, commenced forthwith to found a Christian church after the model of the *Institutes*; but the severity of his system led to a reaction, and caused his exile, and that of Farel, in 1538.

PERIOD IV.   S

Condition of Geneva.

Three years afterwards (September 1541), the city, torn by internal discord, and afraid of being conquered either by the

Duke, who was supported by the Catholics within the walls, or by Bern, which courted the Protestants, recalled the Reformer, and accepted his system of church-government. Leaving the municipal government of the city intact, he set up by its side an ecclesiastical consistory, consisting of the pastors, and twelve elders elected from the two councils of the town on the nomination of the clergy. The jurisdiction of this consistory was nominally confined to morals, and the regulation of Church matters. It could only punish by penance, and by exclusion from the Sacrament, but as it was the duty of the secular authority to enforce its decisions, every sin became a crime, punished with the utmost severity. All were forced by law to attend public worship, and partake of the Lord's Supper. To wear clothes of a forbidden stuff, to dance at a wedding, to laugh at Calvin's sermons, became an offence punishable at law. Banishment, imprisonment, sometimes death, were the penalties inflicted on unchastity, and a child was beheaded for having struck his parents. When offences such as these were so severely visited, we cannot wonder that heresy did not escape. In 1547, Gruet was executed, and in 1553, Servetus was burnt. This remorseless tyranny, which reminds one forcibly of the rule of Savonarola, was not established without opposition. A party termed the Libertines was formed, who endeavoured to relax the severity of the discipline, and to vindicate the independence of the secular authority. Nevertheless Calvin, aided by the French exiles who crowded into Geneva and obtained the freedom of the city and a share in the government, successfully maintained his supremacy until his death in 1564, when he was succeeded by his pupil, Théodore Beza.

Geneva had been relieved from fear of attack from the Duke of Savoy by the French conquest of his country in 1543, and although, in the October of the year in which Calvin died, the Duke obtained from Bern a restoration of all the country south of the Lake of Geneva which it had seized in 1536, he did not make any attempt on the city itself. Geneva continued to be an independent republic, forming from time to time alliances with some of the Swiss cantons, till 1815, when she finally became a member of the Swiss Confederation.

The predominant characteristic of the teaching of Calvin lies in its eclecticism. In his doctrinal views: in his tenets as to Predestination, the Eucharist, and the un- *Character-* questioned authority of Scripture to the exclusion *istics of* of tradition, he approached the views of Zwingle *Calvinism.* rather than those of Luther. But if in so doing he represents the most uncompromising and pronounced antagonism to the teaching of Rome, yet in his conviction that outside the Church there is no salvation, and in the overwhelming authority he ascribes to her, he reasserts the most extravagant tenets of Catholicism, and revives the spirit of Hebraism. That the religion he established, if not exactly ascetic, was gloomy beyond measure; that it has inspired no art except, perhaps, certain forms of literature; that his principles of church-government, though founded on a democratic basis, in practice destroyed all individual liberty; that, so far from advancing the spirit of toleration, they necessarily involved persecution—all this must be admitted. His strong predestinarian views, if logically acted up to, ought to have led to a fatalistic spirit most dangerous to morals, and paralysed action, as perhaps they have in a few cases. But few sane men have ever believed themselves to be eternally reprobate, or acted as if they disbelieved in free-will. The practical results of Calvinism have therefore been to produce a type of men like the founder himself, John Knox, and Théodore Beza, men of remarkable strength of will, extraordinary devotion, and indomitable energy, and to furnish a creed for the most uncompromising opponents of Rome.

Henceforth Geneva was to become the citadel of the Reformers; the refuge of those who had to fly from other lands; the home of the printing-press whence innumerable pamphlets were despatched; the school whence missionaries went forth to preach; the representative of the most militant form of Protestantism on a republican basis; the natural and inevitable enemy of the Counter-Reformation which was the ally of the Jesuits, and of the monarchical forces of Catholic Europe, headed by Spain.

CHAPTER VII

PHILIP AND SPAIN

Persecution of the Protestants—The mystery of Don Carlos—Wars against the Moors and Turks—Relief of Malta—Persecution and Rebellion of the Moriscoes—Battle of Lepanto—Conquest of Portugal—Internal Government of Spain and its dependencies under Philip II.

§ 1. *Persecution of the Protestants—The Inquisition.*

AT the date of the Treaty of Cateau Cambrésis (April 5, 1559), Philip was in his thirty-second year. He had already wedded and lost two wives. His first, Maria of Portugal, had died, in giving birth to Don Carlos, on July 8, 1545; his second, Mary of England, on 17th November 1558. After having settled the government of the Netherlands (cf. p. 319 ff.), Philip proceeded to Spain. A furious tempest greeted his arrival; nine vessels of his fleet were lost; and the King himself landed on the shores of his kingdom—which he was never to leave again—in a small boat.

Philip lands in Spain. Aug. 29, 1559.

Philip had not hitherto displayed those bigoted views of which he henceforth became the exponent. During his brief residence in England he had, in the vain attempt to conciliate the English, opposed or pretended to oppose the policy of persecution adopted by his unhappy wife. He had intervened to protect the Princess Elizabeth, and after her accession had first proposed to marry her, and, when that was refused, had continued on friendly terms. He even gave the Calvinists of Scotland his tacit support against Mary of Guise and her daughter. No sooner, however, did he finally settle in Spain than all was changed. Spain was the representative of all that was most fanatical in Europe, and Philip eagerly adopted the views

He devotes himself to the extirpation of Protestantism.

of that country. Henceforth the increase of his own authority, and the advance of Catholicism, became identified; the reformed opinions were in his eyes a gospel of rebellion and of opposition to authority, and to crush out this pernicious heresy under his absolute rule became the principle of his life.

During the early years of Charles v., a few Spaniards abroad had adopted reformed opinions, such as Francis de Enzinas, the translator of the New Testament into Spanish, and subsequently Professor of Greek at Oxford (1520-1522); while in 1553 Servetus the anti-Trinitarian suffered at Geneva. But it was not until the year 1558 that Protestantism seems to have made much head in Spain itself. By that time, however, not only had Spanish translations of the New Testament and various Protestant books been disseminated in Spain, but a considerable congregation of Reformers had been secretly formed, more especially in the towns of Seville, Valladolid, and Zamora, and in the kingdom of Aragon. On receiving intelligence of this new nest of heretics, Pope Paul iv. issued a brief, February 1558, in which he urged the Inquisitor-General to spare no efforts in exterminating this evil; and the dying Emperor, forgetting his dislike of papal interference, besought the Regent Joanna, and Philip himself, to listen to the Pope's exhortations. Philip required no urging. He published an edict, borrowed from the Netherlands, which condemned all to the stake who bought, sold, or read prohibited books, and revived a law by which the accuser was to receive one-fourth of the property of the condemned. Paul enforced the law by his Bull of 1559, commanding all confessors to urge on their penitents the duty of informing against suspected persons. He also authorised the Inquisition to deliver to the secular arm even those who abjured their errors, 'not from conviction, but from fear of punishment,' and made a grant from the ecclesiastical revenues of Spain to defray the expenses of the Inquisition.

This terrible tribunal, which had been established in its

final form by Ferdinand and Isabella in 1478, and freed from
appeal to Rome in 1497, consisted of a Supreme Council
formed of lawyers and theologians, mostly Dominicans, an
order to which Philip showed especial favour. The
Inquisition.
At the head of this Council stood the Grand
Inquisitor, appointed by the king himself, with numerous
subordinate tribunals, protected by armed 'familiars.'
Their trials were conducted in secret. Persons were
tempted or forced by threats to denounce their enemies,
their friends, and even their relatives ; a system of espionage was resorted to ; torture was freely used to extort confessions from the accused ; and the most harmless words were
often twisted into heterodoxy by the subtle refinements of the
Dominican theologians. They punished by forfeiture of goods,
by penance, by imprisonment, and in the last resort handed
over the condemned to the secular arm, to be burnt at an *Auto
da fè*. Supported by this unwonted harmony between Pope
and King, the Grand Inquisitor, Don Fernando Valdès, Archbishop of Seville, set vigorously to work. In Seville alone,
800 were arrested on the first day, and on May 21, 1559, the
first of the *Autos da fè* took place in the streets of Valladolid ; another was solemnised on the arrival of Philip in Spain,
and a third amid the *fêtes* attending his marriage with his
third wife, Elizabeth of France, in 1560. Indeed, no great
ceremonial was for some years considered complete unless
sanctified by an *Auto da fè*, and the Spaniards preferred one
to a bull-fight. It may be true that the cruelties of the
Inquisition have been exaggerated ; yet, at least, opinions,
which in other countries would have been tolerated, were
ruthlessly suppressed. Not only was all scientific speculation
tabooed, and Spanish scholars forbidden to visit other countries,
but the slightest deviation from the strictest orthodoxy was
severely visited. The Inquisition was even used against the
Church. Although the number of the clergy and the monks
was very large, and their wealth, especially in Castile, enormous, no Church in Europe was more completely under
royal control. The nomination to ecclesiastical offices was

exclusively in the hands of the king ; papal interference, unless
by his leave, was stoutly resisted ; and, if the Church was

The Inquisi-
tion and the
Spanish
Church.

rich, at least one-third of its revenues fell into the
royal coffers.   The power of the crown was also
enhanced by the devotion of the Jesuits to the
royal cause.   It was, however, on the Dominicans
that Philip mostly relied.   The ignorance and bigotry of the
members of this order of friars in Spain is only equalled by
their subservience to the royal will.   They dominated the
Holy Office of the Inquisition, and subjected to its discipline
not only Theresa, one of the most devoted of Spanish
saints, but the members of the powerful Society of Jesus,
and even the episcopal bench itself.   No less than nine
bishops were condemned to various acts of penance ; even
Carranza, Archbishop of Toledo, was attacked.   This learned
and zealous prelate, who had taken an important part in some
of the sessions of the Council of Trent, and in whose arms
Charles v. had died, was charged in August, 1559, with
heterodox opinions.   After his trial had dragged on for more
than seven years, Pius v. insisted on the cause being transferred to Rome.   But the death of the Pope again delayed
the matter, and it was not until April 1576 that the papal
decision was finally given.   The Archbishop was convicted
of holding doctrines akin to those of Luther, and was to
abjure sixteen propositions found in his writings ; he was to
do certain acts of penance ; to be suspended from his
episcopal functions for five years more, and meanwhile to
be confined in a convent of the Dominicans, his own order,
at Orvieto.

The efforts of the Inquisition succeeded in crushing out
Protestantism in Spain ; and its success unfortunately refutes
the comforting doctrine that persecution is powerless against
strong convictions.   But the success involved the destruction
of all intellectual independence ; Spain soon became one of the
most backward countries in Europe, and, if we except Cervantes
the author of *Don Quixote*, and Calderon the poet, she gave

birth to no writer of eminence. Nor did the Holy Office confine itself to the extirpation of heresy, or to the vigorous control of the clergy. Formed exclusively of nominees of the crown,[1] it became an instrument in the royal hands for financial extortion and for the pursuit of political offenders. Thus, custom-house officers were dragged before the Inquisition for having allowed horses to cross the frontier, on the pretext that they were for the service of the Huguenots; Antonio Perez, the notorious secretary of Philip, was arraigned before the Inquisition of Aragon; and foreign ambassadors were enjoined to obey its orders. At times the Pope remonstrated against these abuses of the Holy Office, which trenched upon the papal claims. But Philip answered 'that with his scruples his Holiness would destroy religion'; and long after the reign of Philip the Inquisition, as well as the Church, continued the humble servant of royal prerogative.

The Inquisition used to punish political offences.

§ 2. *The Mystery of Don Carlos.*[2]

According to some authorities the zeal of Philip did not spare his own son and heir, Don Carlos. The history of this unfortunate Prince was so distorted by the enemies of his father Philip during his own lifetime, and since then has become such a favourite subject of romance, that on some points it is difficult to arrive at the truth. Some declare that the estrangement between father and son was caused by the suspicion of a guilty passion between the Prince

Don Carlos. 1545-1568.

---

[1] The Grand Inquisitors during the reign of Philip were—

    1. Don Fernando Valdès, Archbishop of Seville, 1547-1566.
    2. Espinosa, the King's Secretary, Bishop of Siguença, and Cardinal, 1566-1573.
    3. Quiroga, Archbishop of Toledo, 1573-1594.

[2] For the mystery of Don Carlos cf. Prescott, *Philip II.*, c. vi.; Forneron, *Philippe II.*, c. xi.; Gachard, *Don Carlos et Philippe II.*

and his stepmother, Elizabeth of France, and this is the view
which has been adopted by those, like Schiller, who have
made Don Carlos the hero of a romantic tragedy.

We find that in the negotiations for the Treaty of Cateau
Cambrésis it had been suggested that Don Carlos should wed
the French Princess. The idea was dropped, and
the hand of Elizabeth was subsequently bestowed
on Philip, the father of the Prince. Nevertheless,
it is asserted that Elizabeth had learnt to love the
son ; that Don Carlos never forgave his father for having
robbed him of his bride ; and that the jealous husband threw
his son into prison out of revenge, and finally procured the
death by poison not only of his son, but of his unfaithful
wife. This tragic tale must, however, be rejected. Don
Carlos was only twelve years old at the date of the Treaty of
Cateau Cambrésis, and the story is not supported by any
contemporary authority. Even William of Orange, who in
his 'Apology' accuses Philip of poisoning both, is silent as
to the motive.

Less improbable is the story that Don Carlos had secret
sympathy with the Flemish malcontents, or at least some
leaning towards the Protestant heresy. This, it is said,
explains the wish of Don Carlos to be intrusted with the
administration of the Netherlands, the unwillingness of Philip
to publish the reason of his treatment of his son, and his
letter to his aunt the Queen of Portugal, in which he spoke
of 'sacrificing to God his own flesh and blood, preferring
God's service and the welfare of his people to all human considerations.' These expressions are, however, quite compatible with the third, and far more probable, hypothesis that
Don Carlos was mad. Two of his brothers had died of
epilepsy. Don Carlos, who was born in July, 1545, was a sickly
child, subject to serious feverish and bilious attacks ; that as
he grew in years he became, in spite of a certain reckless
generosity and an extravagant attachment to a few, arrogant,
violent, and unmanageable. A fall down a staircase on his

Reasons for his imprison-ment. Jan. 1568.

head, in April, 1562, which necessitated an operation of trepan-
ning, increased his violence, and from this moment his actions
were those of a crazy man. He insulted women of position
with opprobrious epithets. Twice he swallowed costly jewels.
He forced a shoemaker to eat stewed strips of a pair of
boots because they did not fit. He violently assaulted
the Duke of Alva, because the Duke was sent to the
Netherlands instead of himself, and even Don John, to
whom he was much attached. He declared that he
meditated killing a man whom he hated, and sought for
absolution beforehand. He attempted to fly from Spain, and
probably to rebel against his father. Of his insanity the
Venetian ambassador was convinced, and that this is the
explanation of the mystery gains confirmation from a secret
letter of Philip to the Pope, of which, although the original
has disappeared, a translation has been preserved, and in
which insanity is pleaded as the justification for the treatment of the Prince; while surely we cannot wonder that
Philip should be anxious to keep secret the fact that the
insanity of Joanna was reappearing in her great-grandson?
Nor, as far as we can see, does the actual treatment of Don
Carlos, while in prison, appear to have been exactly cruel. No
doubt, he was most carefully watched. He was not to be
allowed to talk on politics, or to have any news of the outer
world; he was only allowed books of a devotional character;
but his guardians were men of good birth, they were enjoined
to lighten his captivity by conversation, and he was not
tortured or starved.

We have yet to deal with the accusation that the unfortunate Prince was poisoned by the order of his father.
This was plainly asserted by William of Orange, Was he
and by Antonio Perez, who was at the time of poisoned?
the death of Don Carlos in the service of King Philip, and the
story was believed by many contemporaries. Yet both William
the Silent and Perez were, when they wrote, the mortal enemies
of the King, and although Philip was unfortunately not above

resorting to murder to attain his ends, we may at least allow that the charge in this case is not proven.

Don Carlos died on the 24th of July, 1568, and in less than three months he was followed to the grave by

Death of
Don Carlos,
24th July 1568;
and of
Isabella,
Oct. 3, 1568.

Elizabeth, his stepmother, who died in childbed, October 3, 1568. Two years later Philip married his fourth wife, Anne of Austria, his niece, and daughter of the Emperor Maximilian. She died on the 26th of October 1580. Of her children, all died young except Philip, who succeeded his father.

§ 3. *Wars against the Moors and Turks.*
The Rebellion of the Moriscoes.

By the ordinance of 1502, published by Ferdinand after the suppression of the Moorish rebellion in Granada (cf. p. 96),

Condition
of the
Moriscoes.

the alternative of baptism or exile had been offered to the Moors, and this had been extended to Aragon, and its subordinate kingdoms Valencia and Catalonia, in the early part of the reign of the Emperor Charles. To further the work of conversion churches had been built in the districts most occupied by the Moors, and missionaries despatched thither. The attempt, however, met with scant success. The bitter memories of the past, the deep racial hatreds, the imperfect acquaintance of the preachers with the language of the Moors, the differences of usage and of customs, presented insurmountable difficulties. Accordingly, in 1526, coercion was attempted. An edict was issued ordering the Moors to renounce their national usages, dress, and language, and the Inquisition was intrusted with the enforcement of the edict. Wiser counsels, however, for the time prevailed. The edict was not enforced; and the government was fain to rest content with an outward conformity, which was all that could, under the circumstances, be looked

for. The 'New Christians,' or Moriscoes, as the Moors
were called, at least did not disturb the peace. Taking
advantage of a strange clause in the Treaty of Granada,
which exempted them from certain duties paid by the
Christians in their trade with the Barbary coast, they
devoted themselves to commerce with that country. But
it was as artisans and in agriculture that they especially
excelled. As artisans their skill was displayed in many a
handicraft; while by their irrigation and by their husbandry
they turned the slopes and uplands of the Sierras in
Granada into one of the most fertile parts of Spain. The
fig, the pomegranate, the orange, and the grape grew side by
side with corn and hemp; their flocks of merino sheep were
famous; the mulberry tree formed the basis of an extensive
manufacture of silk. We may well deplore the fact that
this policy was abandoned; and yet amid the fanaticism
aroused by the crusade against the Protestants, the wonder
perhaps is that it continued so long. Moreover, at this
moment, a renewal of the struggle with the Moors of Africa
and with the Turk in the Mediterranean naturally revived the
national antipathy to the Moriscoes.

The unceasing raids of the corsairs of the Barbary coast
had not only rendered the sea unsafe, but devastated the
shores of Italy and Spain. Accordingly, two
expeditions were despatched against them from
Naples, which did not meet with much success.
The first, under the Duke of Medina Sidonia,
Viceroy of Naples, was directed against Tripoli, then held by
a Greek named Dragut, who had been taken prisoner by the
corsairs in early life, and had turned Mahometan. The Duke
was forced to put back by stress of weather; his ships were
subsequently put to flight by a Turkish fleet under Piali,
another renegade, who sailed to the assistance of Dragut,
and the island of Jerbah (Gelves), which had been occupied,
was retaken by the Turks (June 29, 1560). The second
expedition, which started in 1562, was almost annihilated

Expeditions
against the
Barbary
Corsairs.
1560-1564.

by a storm.   In the following year (April 1563), the Dey of
Algiers, encouraged by these disasters of the Spaniards,
attempted to drive them from Oran and the neighbouring
fortress of Mazarquivir (Mers-el-Kébir), two of the conquests
of Cardinal Ximenes, which, with Goletta near Tunis and
Melilla in Morocco, were the only remaining Spanish possessions on the African coast.   Mazarquivir was nearly lost,
when, at the last moment, it was relieved by a Spanish fleet on
June 8, and in the two succeeding years (1564 and 1565), the
efforts of the Spaniards were somewhat more successful.   In
September 1564, the island fortress of Peñon de Velez,
which lay to the west of the Spanish possessions, was taken
by Don Garcia de Toledo, who had succeeded Medina
Sidonia as Viceroy of Naples ; and in the following year the
estuary of the Tetuan, another stronghold of the corsairs,
was blocked up and rendered useless.   Further enterprise on
the coast of Africa was now stopped by the news that Malta
was hard beset by the Turks.   On the loss of Rhodes, in
1522, the Knights of St. John had received the grant of the

The relief   island of Malta from Charles v. (1530) ; from
of Malta.   that time forward they had formed a bulwark
Sept. 1565.   against the Turk from the east, and had joined
in most of the late expeditions against the Barbary coast.
Solyman I., often urged to reduce this important place, at
last despatched a powerful fleet against it in May, 1565.
Piali, the renegade, who had already distinguished himself in
1560, shared the command with Mustapha, a tried veteran
of seventy, while Dragut of Tripoli also added his contingent.
In vain did the Grand Master, Jean de la Valette, appeal
for aid to repel the attack.   Catherine de Medici was
at this moment intriguing with the Turks, and Venice was
afraid to arouse the anger of the Sultan.   Even Philip did
not seem inclined to listen ; the affairs in the Netherlands
and in France demanded his attention ; perhaps he did
not care to help an Order which, as it happened at that
time, was largely composed of Frenchmen.   Finally, however,

he listened to the warning of Don Garcia de Toledo that
Malta, if once in Turkish hands, could never be recovered,
and would give the Sultan the command of that part of
the Mediterranean; and on September 8, 1565, Malta was
relieved by Don Garcia when reduced to the last gasp.
That these events should have awakened the dislike of the
Spaniards for the Moriscoes at home, and that suspicions
were aroused of some correspondence between them and the
Moors of Africa, is not surprising. Nor under these circumstances can any serious objection be brought The Edicts of
against the first two ordinances; that of 1560, 1560-1567.
forbade the Moriscoes to acquire negro slaves, on the reasonable ground that thereby the number of the infidels was
constantly increased; that of 1563, prohibited the Moriscoes
from possessing arms without the licence of the captain-general.
These measures, however, did not satisfy Don Pedro Guerrero,
the Archbishop of Granada, nor the clergy of his diocese, and
in pursuance of a memorial which they presented, the government issued the following astounding edict. The provisions of
the ill-advised edict of 1526 were revived; the national songs
and dances of the Moriscoes were proscribed; their weddings
were to be conducted in public according to the Christian
ritual, and their houses were to be kept open during the day
of the ceremony, so that all could enter and see that no
unhallowed rites were solemnised; their women were to appear
in public with their faces uncovered; and lastly, the baths in
which the Moriscoes delighted were ordered to be destroyed
on the ground that they were turned to licentious purposes.
Still further, as if to outrage the feelings of the Moriscoes, the
edict was published on January 1, the anniversary of the
capture of the capital of Granada. It appears that many of
the local nobility protested against the execution of this
atrocious edict, and that the Marquis de Mondejar, the
captain-general of Granada, and even Alva himself, were
opposed to it. To expect that the Moriscoes would submit
to such interference with their most cherished customs—an

interference which did not even respect the domestic privacy
of their homes—was absurd, and if it was intended to seize
upon disobedience as a pretext for expelling them, the army
should at least have been increased.   The Grand Inquisitor
Espinosa was, however, above such considerations, and the
execution of the order was intrusted to Diego Deza, auditor of
the Holy Office, who was appointed President of the Chancery
of Granada.   Finding all remonstrance vain, the Moriscoes

Revolt of the
Moriscoes.
Dec. 1568.

made preparations to revolt in June, 1569.   Unfortunately some of the more hot-headed, led by a
dyer of the name of Aben-Farax, could not brook
delay, and in December, 1568, attempted a premature rising
in the Moorish quarter (the Albaicin) of Granada.   'You are
too few, and you come too soon,' said the Moriscoes of
Granada, and refused to move.   Disappointed in seizing the
city, the rebels retreated to the country, where they met with
more response, and signalised their success by horrible
ferocity.   Neither sex nor age were spared; and Christians,
we are told, were sold as slaves to the Algerian corsairs for a
carbine a piece.

The Moriscoes now elected as their King Aben-Humeya,
a young man of twenty-two, a descendant of the ancient

Aben-
Humeya
elected King.

house that once had ruled in Spain.   The
young King indeed dismissed Aben-Farax, and
did something to check the cruelties of his
followers.   The revolt was confined to a somewhat limited
area.   Its chief stronghold was in the Alpujarras, a low

Limits of
the rebellion.

range of hills which lies between the higher
peaks of the Sierra Nevada and the sea; thence
it spread to the neighbourhood of Almeria on the east,
and that of Velez-Malaga on the west.   The Moriscoes
held no large towns, and only ventured on occasional raids
upon the rich plain of La Vega, in which the town of Granada
lay, and upon the towns on the sea-coast.   Had the Sultan,
Selim II., listened to the appeals of Aben-Humeya, and
thrown himself with energy into the struggle, the rule of the

Mahometans might have been re-established in Granada. The Turks, however, were at this time too much engaged in the war of Cyprus, and the Moriscoes only obtained some Turkish mercenaries and some insufficient help from the Barbary corsairs; they were but poorly armed, and their cause was ever weakened by internal feuds and personal rivalries.

Under these circumstances, if the advice of the Marquis de Mondejar had been followed, the rebellion might in all probability have soon been quelled. Unwilling to drive the Moors to despair, he advocated a policy of conciliation, and attempted, though not always with success, to restrain the fanaticism and cruelty of his soldiers. *The counsels of the Marquis de Mondejar rejected.* Unfortunately, he was violently opposed by Diego Deza, who urged a war of extermination. The wish of Diego prevailed, and the Marquis of Los Veles, a nobleman of the district who held the office of Adelantado of the neighbouring province of Murcia, was appointed to the command of an army which was to operate from the east. The stern old veteran proceeded to conduct the war with such ferocity that he earned the name of the ‘Iron-headed Devil.’ The Spanish soldiery, formed chiefly of local levies, retainers of the nobles, and volunteers, were allowed to satisfy their unquenchable hatred of the Moriscoes, and proceeded to rival, if not surpass, the atrocities of the rebels. Even peaceful villages were sacked: the men were cut down without remorse; the women, when they escaped a worse fate, were sold into slavery. Meanwhile, in the town of Granada itself, some hundred and fifty Moors, who had been arrested on suspicion, were massacred in cold blood by the order of Deza (March 1569). Death in open war was better than such a fate. *Massacre of the prisoners at Granada.* The Moors, driven to despair, had no alternative but to fight to the last. The war was not marked by any great battles; the rebels, holding but few towns, and unable to meet the enemy in the open field, betook themselves to the hilly districts, where a confused though hard-fought struggle of

races and creeds was carried on.   The government, however,
was scarcely likely to succeed as long as the bickerings
between Mondejar and his rivals continued.   In the spring
of 1569, Philip, anxious to check these cabals, appointed

Don John
appointed to
supreme com-
mand.
Spring 1569.

Don John, his half-brother, the illegitimate son
of Charles v., to the supreme command.   At
the same time he was forbidden to take the field,
and as he was only twenty-two years old he was
to be guided by a council of war, of which Deza

and Mondejar both were members.   The only result, therefore, of the change was that the quarrel was transferred from
the camp to the council, where finally the views of Deza

The Moorish
population of
Granada re-
moved into
the interior.

triumphed.   In June, 1569, the whole of the
Moorish inhabitants of the town of Granada,
amounting to some three thousand five hundred
souls, were ordered to leave the city for the
interior, where they were to find new homes.

Mondejar, remonstrating at this act, was removed from his
post ; and on the 19th of October, Philip, who had come to
Cordova to be nearer the scene of operations, issued an edict
in which he proclaimed that the war henceforth would be
carried on with 'fire and blood.'

Philip had now definitely committed himself to the views
of Deza ; yet, owing to the incapacity of Los Veles, the royal

On assassina-
tion of Aben-
Humeya,
Aben-Aboo
succeeds.

army met with scant success.   At the close of the
year, Aben-Humeya fell a victim to the vengeance
of one of the women of his seraglio.   His death
was no loss to the cause of the Moriscoes, for although a man of much energy, and of some ability,

he had become intoxicated by success, and by his jealousy,
his selfishness, his licence, and his cruelty, had forfeited the
popularity he once enjoyed.   Aben-Aboo, who succeeded him
as King, was a man of higher integrity and patriotism, and of
greater constancy and courage.   He succeeded in obtaining
the sanction of his election from the Pasha of Algiers, in the
name of the Sultan, and under his rule the revolt spread

eastwards to the very borders of Murcia, and assumed a more formidable aspect than ever.

At last Philip, convinced of the inefficiency of Los Veles, removed him from his command, and allowed Don John to take the field, assisted by the Duke of Sesa, the grandson of Gonsalvo de Cordova. At the same time, fresh levies were raised from the towns of Andalusia, and many nobles, with their re- tainers, flocked to the standard of the young and popular Don John, who at once marched to the district on the east of the Alpujarras, and, in spite of several reverses, gradually wore down the rebels. On January 28, the strong town of Galera was invested, to fall on February 7, after a desperate struggle; the reduction of Seron followed, and soon the whole country to the east of the Alpujarras was re-won. Meanwhile, the Duke of Sesa had been equally successful in the north. Gradually working his way across the Alpujarras, he secured his conquests by a line of forts, and, in May, united his forces with those of Don John at Padules. At the same time an amnesty was offered to those who would lay down their arms. The cause of the Moris- coes was now hopeless. On May 19, El Habaquin, a leading Moorish chieftain, agreed, in the name of Aben-Aboo, to the severe terms imposed by the conqueror. The 'Little King,' as the Moorish prince was called, was to make public submission to Don John; the lives of the Moriscoes should be spared, but, like their fellow-countrymen of Granada, they were to be removed from their native district and distributed elsewhere in Spain. At the last moment Aben-Aboo refused these humiliating terms, and attempted to raise once more the standard of revolt, only to fall by the hand of one of his subjects who had been bribed by the government.

The rebellion was now at an end. By the edict of Octo- ber 28, every Morisco from within the disturbed districts,[1]

Don John takes the field. Jan. 1570.

Submission of Moriscoes. May 1570.

---

[1] There were Moriscoes in other parts of Spain, especially in Murcia, Valencia and even in the Vega of Granada, who were not disturbed.

including those who had remained loyal, was to be removed into the interior.   Their houses and lands were declared forfeited to the Crown; but their flocks, their herds and their grain were, if they so wished, to be taken at a valuation.   It was, however, ordered that families should not be divided, and the removal appears to have been effected in as humane a way as possible.   The districts appointed for their settlements were in the territory of La Mancha, in the northern borders of Andalusia, in the Castiles, Estremadura, and Galicia. Flogging and forced labour on the galleys was threatened against any Moor who should leave his abode without leave, and death to any one who dared approach within ten leagues of Granada.   The edict of 1566 continued in force; and by a subsequent one, to keep an Arabic book was declared an offence punishable with stripes and four years in the galleys. Andalusia now became a desert.   Meanwhile, in spite of these cruel laws, the exiles enriched their new homes by their husbandry and industry until the year 1609, when the fanaticism and national hatred of the Spaniards led to the final expulsion of this unfortunate people from Spain itself.   The treatment of the Moriscoes by the Spaniards forms one of the saddest episodes in history; yet, in justice, an Englishman should remember that the treatment of the Irish by Cromwell, if it was preceded by greater provocation, was fully as cruel.

The Moriscoes settle in other parts of Spain. Edict of Oct. 28, 1570.

§ 4. *Renewed struggle against the Turks.*
The victory of Lepanto, 1571-1574.

If the intolerance of Philip is responsible for the cruel proscription of the Protestants and the Moriscoes, his political interests at least did not lead him into such inconsistencies as those of other European sovereigns.   Indeed, when we consider the attitude of the great Powers in Europe towards the Turks at this moment, we shall be led to the conclusion that their policy with regard to heretics, as well as to infidels, was guided rather by political, than by religious considerations. The French, while they persecuted the Huguenots in their own country, were ever allying themselves with the Turks to oppose the Spaniard. Elizabeth of England, no doubt, gave grudging aid to the Calvinists abroad, and established a form of Protestantism in England; yet she proscribed the extreme Calvinists at home, and at times sought the alliance of the Turk; whereas if Philip was the persecutor of Protestants and infidels alike, the necessity of protecting Italy and Spain at least made him the resolute opponent of the infidel in the Mediterranean.

The rebellion of the Moriscoes had not yet been crushed out, when on May 1, 1570, the messenger of Pius v. reached Spain, praying for the help of the most Christian King against the Turk. Solyman the Magnificent had ended his long and triumphant career in 1566. Although his successor, Selim II., possessed none of his father's qualities, the vigour of the late administration was still represented by the Grand Vizier Mahomet; and at the close of the year 1569, Piali, one of the commanders of the attack on Malta, and now brother-in-law of the Sultan, had started on an expedition against Cyprus. Philip gave a ready ear to the papal appeal, but meanwhile Nicosia, one of the most important Cypriot fortresses, fell (September 1570). Venice in despair attempted, though unsuccessfully, to make a separate treaty with the Sultan; and it was not until the 25th of May, 1571, that the difficulties and jealousies were surmounted, and that the League was finally concluded. Venice had wished that the League should confine itself to the protection of Cyprus; but Philip, not unnaturally, was anxious to extend its scope; and accordingly Spain, the Pope, and Venice agreed to form a perpetual alliance against the Moors of Tunis, Tripoli, and Algiers, as well as against the Turk. They agreed to defend each other's territories, and to make no separate peace; each Power

League of Spain—Pope and Venice against the Turk.
May 25, 1571.

was to appoint a captain-general, and they should together decide on the plan of operations, while the supreme command was to be given to Don John of Austria. Finally, to defray the expenses of Philip, Pius granted a *cruzada*, and an *excusado*.[1] The treaty came too late to save the island of Cyprus; for on July 30, Famagusta had fallen, when Bragadino, the chief in command, was flayed alive, his skin stuffed and sent as a trophy to Constantinople. It was not till the 16th of the following September, that the fleet of the League finally left Messina. On reaching Corfu, intelligence was received that the Turkish fleet was in the Gulf of Lepanto. Against the advice of John Andrew Doria, who commanded the Genoese contingent, Don John was eager to close with his antagonist. He was supported in his opinion by the Marquis of Santa Cruz, the Grand Commander Requesens, and the young Alexander of Parma, as well as by the other captains-general, and on the 7th of October, the two fleets came in sight of each other. That of the Christians was composed of 264 vessels of all sizes, with 26,000 soldiers and 50,000 rowers and sailors aboard. That of the Turks, of some 300 vessels, and not less than 120,000 men.

In the action which ensued it was the object of the Turkish admiral Piali to turn the wings of his adversary. This move-

The battle of Lepanto. Oct. 7, 1571.

ment was, however, foiled by Barbarigo, who commanded the Venetian galleys on the left, and by John Andrew Doria on the right. They hugged the shore, and a terrible struggle ensued, in which the allies suffered severely. At last, the Venetians drove back their enemies, and though Barbarigo was mortally wounded, his loss was compensated by the death of Mahomet Sirocco, the Turkish admiral opposed to him. Meanwhile the centre,

---

[1] A *cruzada* was a licence granted by papal dispensation, allowing the eating of eggs and milk on certain days. This licence was sold by the King, and to induce people to purchase it, every one was forced to buy these articles whether they ate them or no. An *excusado* was the tithe upon one holding in each parish in Spain, granted to the King.

led by Don John, after a desperate conflict at close quarters,
which resembled a fight on land rather than on the sea,
was equally successful. Piali fell, and most of the Moslem's
ships surrendered or were destroyed. Finally Uluch
Ali, the Dey of Algiers, who had been severely handling
the Genoese opposed to him, seeing that all was over, took
refuge in flight, and the Christians remained the victors of
one of the greatest naval combats of the century. The
importance of the battle of Lepanto, which lasted for more
than four hours, will be best appreciated when it is remembered that the Turks had never hitherto been beaten at sea.
Although an accurate computation of the losses is not possible,
it may with certainty be affirmed that those of the Turks were
more than twice as heavy as those of their antagonists, and
that not more than fifty of their vessels escaped. Among the
captives were found, we are told, 12,000 Christians who had
been condemned to the galleys.

Some now thought that this crushing defeat should be
followed by an immediate attack on Constantinople. The
season, however, was far advanced, and it was Delays and
decided to postpone further operations until the jealousies of
spring. The delay was fatal. An attempt was made the allies.
to buy over Uluch Ali, a Calabrian renegade, who had not
forgotten his Christian parents from whom he had been
separated in youth. The offer was declined, and Uluch
shortly took the command of the new fleet which the Turks
had put on the sea with remarkable rapidity. Far different
was the conduct of the allies. In Spain there was the
usual procrastination. Nor were the interests of Spain and
Venice the same ; Philip desired to turn against the Moors
of Africa, and extend his conquests there ; Venice only cared
to strengthen her position in the Levant. In vain did the
aged Pontiff attempt to reconcile these conflicting views. He
died in the following May, and although Philip's fears,
that a Pope in the French interest would succeed him,
were removed by the election of Cardinal Buoncampagno

(Gregory XIII.), the papal 'Briefs of Fire' were not of much avail. The allies, indeed, at last sent out another expedition under Don John, which found the Turkish fleet off Modon on October 7, 1572, the anniversary of the victory of Lepanto. But Uluch Ali declined the contest; he remained under the guns of the fortress, and at the end of the month the allies again

Venice makes a separate treaty with the Turk. March 7, 1573.

dispersed. In the following March all hope of concerted action was destroyed by the news that Venice had come to terms with the Sultan; she surrendered Cyprus, and agreed to pay a three years' tribute to the Porte. The Turks could scarcely have hoped for better terms if they had won the battle of Lepanto.

Deserted by his allies, Don John, in the following October, sailed to the African coast and easily reduced the

Don John reduces Tunis, Oct. 1573; but it and Goletta are retaken by Uluch Ali, Sept. 1574.

town of Tunis. He now dreamt of obtaining the investiture of the African kingdom from his half-brother. The jealousy of Philip was instantly aroused; he urged that the fortresses of Tunis and Goletta should be dismantled, and, although this was not done, they were left with such an

insufficient force that Uluch Ali had little difficulty not only in retaking Tunis, but in reducing the fortress of Goletta (Sept. 1574). Such were the miserable results of the victory

The victory of Lepanto a barren victory.

of Lepanto. It did not save the island of Cyprus, which henceforth belonged to the Porte; it was followed by the loss of Goletta, one of the few remaining conquests of Charles v. on the coast

of Africa; it only served to display once more the jealousies of the European nations; and if for seventy years the Turks made no further advance, and never again seriously threatened the south-western shores of Europe, this was due far more to the internal decay of the Ottoman Empire, than to the victory of Lepanto itself.

§ 5. *The Conquest of Portugal.*

On August 4, 1578, Sebastian, the young King of Portugal, was killed at the battle of Alcazar-Kébir as he was conducting a crazy campaign against Abd-el-Melek, the Sultan of Morocco. The death of the young King, who appears to have been half-mad, at once aroused the determination of Philip to secure the crown of Portugal, and thus finally unite the Iberian Peninsula under one hand. The successor of Sebastian was his great-uncle, Henry. He was a Cardinal, and over sixty-six years of age. Nevertheless, it was hoped that he might yet have children, and the Pope was asked to authorise his marriage. Philip declared his indignation at this interference of the Papacy with what were 'so clearly temporal affairs,' but was relieved from further apprehension by the death of the Cardinal-King on January 31, 1580. The only claimant whom Philip had now to dread was Antonio, prior of Crato.[1] He was the illegitimate son, by a converted Jewess, of Lewis, Duke of Beja, the great-uncle of Sebastian, but he had been secretly legitimised by his father, had entered the order of St. John of Malta, and was prior of the rich commandery of Crato. If his legitimacy could be established, no doubt he was the next male heir. Philip, however, refused to allow his claim, and asserted his own right to the throne through his mother, the daughter of King Emanuel. To enforce this claim an army had been collected on the frontier under the Duke of Alva, which marched as soon as the intelligence of the Cardinal's death arrived. Those who did not submit were treated as rebels, and when the town of Setubal offered some

Death of Sebastian, King of Portugal. Aug. 4, 1578.

The Cardinal Henry succeeds; but dies. Jan. 31, 1580.

Philip claims the crown, and sends an army under the Duke of Alva.

---

[1] There were other possible claimants—Emanuel Philibert, Duke of Savoy, and the sons of Alexander Farnese, who could claim through the female line, but did not do so. Even Catherine de' Medici affected to base

slight resistance it was given over to pillage, 'because to deny the soldiers would have been a great injustice' (July 16, 1580).

Meanwhile, Antonio had been proclaimed King by a motley assembly of peasants at Santarem, and proceeded to Lisbon.

Antonio proclaimed King.

In vain Pope Gregory XIII. attempted to mediate. To propitiate Philip, who had a passion for relics, he sent a most precious gift, part of the body of one of the Holy Innocents; Philip accepted the gift, but declined his mediation, and for once did not procrastinate. The Marquis of Santa Cruz was despatched with the fleet to Setuval. There he took the Duke of Alva and his troops on board, and

Lisbon capitulates to Alva.

sailed for Lisbon. Antonio in vain attempted to resist. The citizens of Lisbon would not fight; they asked for terms, but had to capitulate at discretion; and Antonio, escaping with difficulty, reached Calais after many wanderings. The city of Lisbon was partly saved from pillage by Alva, but the neighbouring villages were sacked with such relentless cruelty that it even surpassed all that Alva could have imagined; and such was the insubordination of the soldiery that the Duke declared rope would fail

her title on descent from a distant King of Portugal, but did not at this time urge it. The question of the succession, and the close relationship between the royal families of Spain and Portugal will be best understood from the following table:—

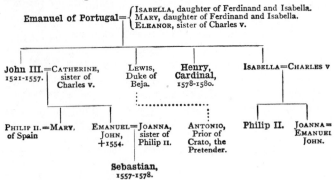

Emanuel of Portugal = { ISABELLA, daughter of Ferdinand and Isabella. / MARY, daughter of Ferdinand and Isabella. / ELEANOR, sister of Charles V.

John III. = CATHERINE, sister of Charles V.
1521-1557.

Lewis, Duke of Beja.

Henry, Cardinal, 1578-1580.

ISABELLA = CHARLES V

PHILIP II. = MARY. of Spain

EMANUEL JOHN, +1554. = JOANNA, sister of Philip II.

ANTONIO, Prior of Crato, the Pretender.

Philip II.

JOANNA = EMANUEL JOHN.

Sebastian, 1557-1578.

him wherewith to hang his mutinous soldiers. At Oporto, the same scenes were repeated by the troops under Sancho d'Avila, an officer who had already earned an evil reputation for mutiny in the Netherlands. On the 29th of June, 1581, Philip made his entry into Lisbon. Those few nobles who had dared to oppose him were treated with relentless cruelty; the majority attempted no resistance, and the people sullenly submitted. Antonio, with a price set on his head, wandered from court to court begging for assistance to regain his crown. In June, 1582, he succeeded in obtaining the help of a French fleet, which sailed to the Azores. The fleet, however, was dispersed by the Marquis of Santa Cruz; and for the rest of his life the unfortunate pretender found an asylum for the most part in England. Philip had gained his end, and Portugal was for a time united with Spain. The Spaniards, however, had never been liked in Portugal; the atrocities which accompanied the accession of Philip turned the dislike to hatred; and it was not many years before Portugal again threw off the hated yoke, and once for all declared her independence.

Philip enters Lisbon. June 29, 1581.

§ 6. *Internal Government of Philip II.*

Although the government of Philip II. was practically a despotism, it would be a mistake to suppose that no constitutional checks existed, or that they were entirely futile. The Cortes of Castile and Aragon still survived, and even in the subject provinces the old assemblies were not done away with. In Castile, the Cortes nominally enjoyed deliberative powers; no edict could constitutionally be issued except on their petition, and no tax levied except by their consent. Yet if Philip often summoned them, if he did not interfere with their debates, if he listened to their petitions, these were constantly disregarded on the plea that it was not expedient that they

The Government despotic; yet constitutional forms survive in Spain and its dependencies.

should be granted; and, when occasion demanded it, royal ordinances were issued, and fresh taxes imposed, without waiting for their assent.

The constitutional rights of Aragon and its dependencies, Valencia and Catalonia, were even more extensive. Any member of the Cortes could present a memorial of grievances; until these grievances were redressed the session could not be closed; and no law could be passed or tax imposed except by the unanimous vote of the assembly. The royal tribunals were subject to that of the Justiza, and any one who set foot in Aragon could escape from the jurisdiction of the royal courts by 'manifesting'—that is, by appealing to his aid. No foreigners could hold office in Aragon; the Inquisition, though established, met with constant opposition. With these privileges Philip came into open conflict when, in April, 1590, Antonio Perez, his secretary, fled to Aragon and claimed the protection of the Justiza (cf. pp. 307-9). On the pretext that Perez had, in the justification which he had just published, been guilty of blasphemy, he was, at the demand of the Inquisitors of Aragon, transferred to their own prison. The citizens of Saragossa at once rose against this violation The revolt of their 'fueros.' The Justiza was mobbed for of Saragossa, having surrendered the prisoner; the royal repre-1591. sentative, the Marquis of Almanara, was killed; and the Inquisitors, in fear of their lives, restored Perez to the 'Aljaferia,' or Justiza's prison. Four months later, another attempt on the part of the Inquisitors (September 1591) led to a renewed revolt, which was supported by the new Justiza, who had been just appointed. Philip forthwith ordered an army to march (October 24). The rebels had no army or organisation, and found little support, except from some of the more violent of the peasants, who betook themselves to brigandage. Accordingly, the royal army met with no resistance; and when it reached Saragossa on November 12, 1591, the city submitted without striking a blow. Although Philip published an amnesty, all the leading men who had taken any part were excepted; and the Justiza himself was executed, in violation of the law that he could not even be arrested unless by the order of the Cortes. A meeting of that body followed. In spite of the rule that it should be presided over by the King himself, or a prince of the blood, the chair was taken by Chinchon, the Archbishop of Saragossa, and the Cortes consented to the following invasion of their privileges. The King was to be allowed to nominate aliens as his viceroys; a definite time was to be fixed for presenting grievances; except for the voting of taxes, the right of any member to veto any measure was done away with, and matters were to be decided by the vote of the majority of each estate. This last concession practically made the King master of their decisions, since he had the power of adding to the number of deputies of each estate by summoning his nominees. Finally, for the appointment of the deputies of the Justiza, a complicated system was established which practically put the nomination in the King's hands, and made them the creatures of the royal will. Here, therefore, ended the real independence of the Cortes of Aragon, and of its Justiza. True, the country was not so severely taxed as Castile; yet, as in Castile itself, the shadow of constitutional liberty alone remained, while the reality had departed.

Interference with the privileges of Aragon.

An identical policy, although in a more exaggerated form, was pursued by Philip in Sicily, in Naples, and in Milan. Satisfied with getting the control of the central courts of justice, and of the supreme executive, into the hands of his nominees, Philip allowed the old assemblies, the feudal and municipal privileges, to continue. For the rest the royal authority was maintained by the Viceroy. He made use of class and local jealousies; he played off noble against burgher and peasant, laity against clergy; he resorted to wholesale corruption, and kept an army, mainly composed of Spaniards, to fall back upon in the last resort; and, if at any time

Government of Naples, Sicily, and Milan.

the Viceroy became too unpopular, he could always be made the scapegoat and removed. It was in Naples that the authority of the Viceroy was the least uncontrolled, that corruption was deepest, and the taxation heaviest; while Milan was protected by the privileges of the town and the pretensions of the archbishop, more especially under the well-known prelate, Carlo Borromeo; and in Sicily the feudal rights, and the municipal privileges of such towns as Messina and Palermo, were too powerful to be entirely overthrown.

Under such a system of government as this, it was inevitable that the real power should lie with the King and with those The Central central councils which controlled the adminis- Councils. trative and judicial system in the various parts of the empire. Of these there were as many as eleven,[1] of which the three following were the most important: the Council of State, the Council of Castile, and that of the Inquisition. The Council of the Inquisition has already been described (p. 279). The Council of State confined itself for the most part to foreign affairs. But since Philip looked upon Castile as the centre of his empire, it was but natural that the Council of Castile should become the most important.

[1] The others were:—

1. The Hazienda, for the administration of the revenue, and for the trial of cases concerning it.

2. The Council of The Orders, for the administration of the three Military Orders of St. Iago, Calatrava, Alcantara.

3. The Camera, originally a section of the Council of Castile, subsequently became practically a separate council.

4. The Council of War.

5, 6, 7, 8. The Councils of Aragon, Italy, Flanders, and Portugal. That of Portugal was created after the conquest of that country. That of Flanders soon ceased to be of much importance.

9. The Council of Indies, for the general administration of the Indies, and for the trial of cases, civil and ecclesiastical, arising thence.

Its functions were mainly judicial; it heard appeals from inferior courts, and under Philip II. was mainly composed of lawyers. It enjoyed, however, other powers; it kept the Church in control, it drafted laws, and was generally consulted on all matters of state interest. In fact, it became practically the Council of State for the interior. The nomination of the members of these Councils was exclusively in the hands of the King. With the exception of the Council of State they were composed of ecclesiastics as well as laymen, but the nobles rarely found a place there.

Excluded altogether from the Cortes of Castile, and with a very limited representation in that of Aragon,[1] the Spanish nobility took but little part in political affairs at home. They had enormous revenues; they were exempted from taxation; they filled most of the offices in the royal household; they often commanded the royal armies and fleets abroad; they acted as ambassadors, and as Viceroys in the dependent states and in the colonies; but at home they had little influence. They were no longer allowed to bear arms or levy their retainers, except in the royal service; and, except on special occasions, such as the rebellion of the Moriscoes, rarely appeared in the field unless on foreign service. The time which was not spent at court, was passed on their wide domains, where they copied on a small scale the magnificence and the etiquette of the court. Living thus in proud isolation, with much wealth but little power, they refused to mix, or to intermarry with the lower classes, and rapidly became a degenerate and useless class like the nobles of France in the eighteenth century.

[margin note: Exclusion of nobles from political power.]

The Councils, then, depending as they did on the royal will, were filled for the most part with the obsequious servants of a suspicious master who could ruin them at his pleasure,

[1] Only eight titled houses of the Grandees could claim a seat. Of the hidalgos, or lesser nobility, only those came whom the king chose to summon.

unless, indeed, as was sometimes the case, they were able to spread a net of intrigue round the King which he was, for a time at least, unable to break. If Philip usually asked the advice of his Councillors, he kept to his father's injunction, 'to depend on no one but himself.' He did not often appear at their sessions; sometimes he altered despatches before submitting them to his Councils; he generally received their opinions through a committee, or more often demanded a written report, which he took to his private cabinet and annotated with marginal comments. True to his boast, that 'with a bit of paper he ruled over both hemispheres,' he sat at his desk for hours together, sometimes assisted by a secretary, sometimes by his favourite daughter Isabella, often quite alone, and covered the state papers with notes in his crabbed hand with the assiduity of a clerk, and not uncommonly with trivialities, of which a schoolboy might be ashamed. Under these circumstances the actual authority exercised by any individual depended on his personal influence, and that of his clique, with the King. Although Philip would allow his ministers considerable latitude as long as he trusted them, his suspicions were easily aroused. He made use of one minister against another; he learnt from each severally the views and opinions of the others; he adopted the same system of espionage with regard to them as he did, through his secret emissaries, abroad, and his suspicion once aroused, the fall of the minister or viceroy was not far off.

Of the ministers who chiefly enjoyed his confidence the following may be mentioned. At the beginning of his reign

The chief ministers. three men were most influential: the Duke of Alva, Ruy Gomez de Silva, Prince of Eboli, and Espinosa. The Duke of Alva had been a trusted adviser of Charles, and had served him in his wars. Accordingly he

The Duke of Alva. recommended him to his son as the ablest statesman, and the best soldier in his dominions. Alva's love of carefully weighing all sides before arriving at a decision, coupled with his determination in carrying out the royal will, made him a congenial spirit. He was Grand Steward of the household, and a member of the Council of State, and for the first few years had much influence. From the very first however, he found a rival in Gomez. This noble- Ruy Gomez, man, descended from the younger branch of a Prince of Portuguese family which had settled in Castile, Eboli. had, as an imperial page, become the favourite of Philip when prince. The ascendency thus obtained he subsequently maintained by his knowledge of the humours of his master, his pliability, his obsequiousness, and his dexterity; while by his affability to others he succeeded in retaining popularity. After his marriage with Anna Mendoza, Princess of Eboli, a woman remarkable for her wit and for her beauty in spite of the loss of an eye, he was created Prince of Eboli, and made a member of the Council of State, and First Gentleman of the Bedchamber. Generally in favour of pacific measures, he was opposed to the policy of repression in the Netherlands, of which Alva approved. On this question Alva's advice prevailed; but with his departure to carry out the policy he advocated, the influence of the Duke declined. The King perhaps had learnt to resent his haughty demeanour; at all events Alva ceased to play an important part in affairs of state.[1] The influence of the Prince of Eboli was now supreme; and by his adroitness, and, if we may believe some, by the complaisance of his wife to the attentions of the King, he continued to retain his power till his death, in July, 1573 The third man of note during Philip's earlier years was Diego de Espinosa, who attracted the attention of the King by his extraordinary capacity for work, Cardinal and by his ability. He became President of the Espinosa. Council of Castile and of the Indies; he was also Inquisitor-

---

[1] After the return of Alva from the Netherlands, a quarrel broke out between him and the King about the marriage affairs of his son, and he was ordered to live in retirement at Uzada, 1579. There he remained till his services were required for the conquest of Portugal, 1580. He died in December 1582.

General, a member of the Council of State, and Bishop of Siguença, and, finally, was created Cardinal. This rapid rise, however, made him so arrogant that he shortly incurred the dislike of his master, and on being given the lie by the King in open council, Espinosa took to his bed and died of chagrin, in September, 1572.

After the death of Ruy Gomez in July, 1573, his policy was continued by the Marquis de Los Velez, the Queen's major-
Antonio Perez. domo, and by Antonio Perez. The history of the latter is so characteristic of the dealings of Philip with his ministers, that it requires more elaborate notice. Antonio Perez, the illegitimate son of Gonzalo Perez, Arch-deacon of Sepulveda—one of the secretaries of state of Charles v., and afterwards of his son—had learnt his business in the service of the Prince of Eboli. On his father's death, in 1566, Perez had succeeded to some of his duties, and on the death of his patron, the Prince of Eboli, he stepped into his place and continued his policy, supported by the powerful advocacy of his widow. Blindly devoted to the service of the King, and an adept at that system of espionage which Philip loved, he sought for confidences that he might betray them to his master, and flinched at no baseness to do him service. Of these despicable acts, the dealings of Perez with Don John will furnish the most flagrant example. We shall find (p. 353) that it was Perez who fed the jealousy of Philip for his half-brother ; that he made use of Escovedo, Don John's secretary, to tempt Don John into rash statements, only that they might be communicated to the King, and finally that it was he who saw Philip's order to murder the unfortunate secretary carried out. From that moment, however, Perez knew no peace. His enemies in the council fostered the report that he was the murderer of Escovedo, and implored the justice of the King. Philip at first promised to support his instrument, or, rather, his accomplice, but suddenly changed his mind, and had him and the Princess of Eboli arrested (July 28, 1579). The explanation of this strange conduct is still one of the mysteries

of that reign of mystery. The popular opinion, that it was due to the wounded pique of the monarch, who was affronted because the widowed Princess of Eboli preferred the embraces of the secretary to those of his master, is not very probable. The report was based on vague surmises, and is not supported by any definite proof; the Princess was now in years, and the mother of ten children; the wife of Perez remained the constant defender of her husband; nor is it easy to believe that Philip's confessor, Fray Diego de Chaves, would have shown such activity in the matter had the reason for the persecution of Escovedo been of this shameful character. It would appear more likely that Philip became convinced that Perez and the Princess had deceived him in the matter of Escovedo, and that, possibly to free themselves from a rival, they had by their slanders compassed the death of the unfortunate man. The conduct of the King seems to support this view. Afraid apparently of compromising revelations with regard to his treatment of Don John, and the murder of Escovedo, he at first seemed inclined to pardon Perez, and even to recall him to his work; and it was not until November, 1581, that, urged on by his confessor, he determined on a more rigorous course. From that moment, the affair became almost a personal struggle between the King and Perez. For five years the ignoble matter dragged on, while Philip was collecting evidence against his secretary. Perez was then (January 23, 1585) condemned to a fine and to two years' imprisonment, followed by eight years' exile. Even then an attempt was made to get hold of all compromising papers and letters. These had been hidden by the wife of Perez at the commencement of the affair, but, though imprisoned, she refused to surrender them, even after receiving her husband's leave. Meanwhile, Perez himself succeeded in escaping from his house, where he had been confined, and took sanctuary. This was, however, violated, and Perez was seized and put to torture. Nevertheless, on April 20, 1590, he managed to escape from his tormentors, dressed in his wife's clothes, and

fled to Aragon, where we have already met him (p. 300)
On the suppression of the revolt in that kingdom he once
more succeeded in escaping, this time to France.   Philip still
pursued him with fury ; he suborned agents to murder him ;
he tried to entrap him by means of a woman of Pau, but all in
vain.   Perez subsequently went to England, where he stirred
up Elizabeth to send the expedition to Cadiz (cf. p. 374).
He finally survived his persecutor, and tried to make his
peace with Philip III. by offering to betray the state secrets
of the countries which had given him refuge.   Philip, meanwhile, baulked of his prey, took vengeance on the Princess of
Eboli, and the heroic wife of the secretary.   The first was
treated with increased harshness, and died eighteen months
afterwards (February 1592) ; the second was imprisoned with
her children, during the rest of Philip's life.

With the fall of Perez in 1579, the party originally led by
Ruy Gomez lost influence in the royal councils.   Their places
were taken by Granvella, Don Juan de Idiaquez,
and Christoval de Moura.   Of these, Cardinal
Granvelle, son of the Chancellor of Charles v.,
and a native of Franche-Comté, had already
served Philip as a member of the Consulta in
Flanders, 1559-1563 (cf. p. 321).   Since then
he had filled the post of Viceroy of Naples, where
he had distinguished himself by forming the league which led
to the battle of Lepanto (cf. p. 293).   He was now appointed
President of the Council of Castile.   Idiaquez, son of a secretary
of state under Charles v., succeeded to Perez'
place as secretary, while Moura, a Portuguese, was
appointed member of the Council of Finance, and
took an active part in the conquest of his native country
(cf. p. 297).   This change of ministry was marked by a complete
revolution in the policy of the King.   Philip had hitherto pursued a pacific policy in Europe ; but from this moment he
began to embark on those attempts to make himself master of
France and England which finally ended in complete collapse.

Change of
Ministers and
of Policy, after
fall of Perez,
1579.
Cardinal
Granvelle,
1579-1586.

Idiaquez and
Christoval de
Moura.

Granvelle soon found himself supplanted by his colleagues; and on his death (September 22, 1586), Idiaquez and Moura, with the addition of the Count de Chinchon, an Aragonese, formed a triumvirate known as the Night Junta, to which all important affairs from every department were referred. Under the rule of this Junta, which lasted to the end of the reign, the administration became more corrupt, and the quarrels among the subordinates more frequent, while the irresolution and procrastination of the King increased as his health began to fail.

The Night Junta.

We should, however, fail to appreciate the influences which surrounded Philip if we omitted his confessors. These were two Dominican friars—Fray Bernardo de Fresneda up till 1577; from that date till 1595, Fray Diego de Chaves. Both these men added to their position as confessors a post in the civil administration. The former— 'the fat Bishop of Cuenca,'—whom Cecil's agent declared to be one of the 'chiefest' of the ministers, was appointed a member of the Council of War, and commissary-general of the revenue derived from the Cruzada. The second had even greater influence. Nominated a Councillor of State in 1584, we find De Chaves taking a principal part in the affair of Perez, in the suppression of the rebellion in Aragon, and in the conquest of Portugal. He did not scruple to betray to his master the secrets he learnt in the confessional, but in return for this devotion he at times demanded obedience. Thus, in 1591, we find him actually refusing the sacrament to Philip until the King should follow his wishes with regard to the appointment of the President of the Council of Castile.

The King's Confessors.

To this despotic rule, one thing alone was wanting—a standing army—and even there a beginning had been made. Although a large force had been kept on foot by Philip's father, it was only used on foreign service, and was stationed abroad. For service at home, Charles had depended on the militia levies from the towns, and the feudal service of the nobles and their

The beginnings of a standing army.

retainers.　To these Philip added the 'Guards of Castile, a considerable force of men-at-arms with their followers, together with some squadrons of light cavalry, who were put upon a permanent footing, and retained at home.　Henceforth the government had an army at hand wherewith to quell any domestic troubles.　But if Philip's rule may be justly called a despotism, here too, as ever, that despotism

The evils of the absolute rule of Philip.

involved the restraints and the intrigues of a bureaucracy—a bureaucracy which, though appointed by the King, sometimes became his master.　Nowhere perhaps can a more startling illustration be found of the evil results of absolute rule, especially when placed in the hands of a man of small intelligence, of narrow and bigoted views, and of suspicious temperament, yet with a tenacious love of power, and with indefatigable though misdirected industry.　Charles had, indeed, ruled despotically, and with some success.　But the son resembled his father in one point only, his self-control.　Neither good nor bad news made him display any emotion ; at most, when some untoward event was announced, he was seen to clutch his beard.　For the rest, Philip had not his father's gifts, and, with such a man, the consequences of the system were disastrous.　His determination to hold the reins of government, at least in appearance, necessarily caused delay ; and, coupled with his unfortunate delusion that 'time and he were a match for any other two,' led to that fatal habit of procrastination and irresolution which often ruined his most cherished schemes.　Dearly as he loved power, he was not strong enough always to take the lead himself ; and hence his eager desire for the opinions of his councillors.　No doubt he fancied that the ultimate decision lay with him ; yet often, in reality, he was guided by the individual who for the moment had his ear.　Under these circumstances it was inevitable that intrigue and corruption should gather round him, until they were often too strong to be withstood. Meanwhile, in the lower orders of the bureaucracy these evils grew apace, and were even acknowledged by Granvella himself.

Nevertheless, since it is not to be denied that Philip decided what influences should be near him, and thus gave the general tone to the character of the administration, he must be held primarily responsible for its harmful action. We have already shown how the isolation of the nobility was fostered ; how by the absolute authority which Philip exercised over the Church, combined with the powers of the Inquisition, all independence of thought was crushed ; how by a narrow bureaucratic system, the people were deprived of the substance of political power.

A few words remain to be said on the commercial and financial policy of the reign. The view prevalent at that time in Europe that gold and silver were the most desirable of all forms of wealth, and that a *Philip's Financial and* country benefited when the imports of those *Commercial* metals exceeded their exports, had a certain *Policy.* practical truth in it. It should be remembered that, in the absence of paper money, the amount of metallic currency required within a country would, relatively to the volume of trade, be greater then than now. Moreover, since national loans were only in their infancy, and a National Debt unknown, a well-filled treasury was necessary to meet great emergencies, such as a war. Above all, in those countries which did not themselves possess any mines, the only way of obtaining the precious metals was in exchange for home-made goods, or by trade. In such countries, therefore, the doctrine tended to stimulate, not to cramp industrial enterprise. The case of Spain, however, was different. The mines of the New World gave her the precious metals, and therefore she was tempted to discourage the imports of foreign countries, and even to forbid the exportation of gold and silver. Nor was this all. Trusting to the produce of the mines, the Spaniards both at home and in the colonies were encouraged in their national dislike for the more laborious, though more productive industries, and national indolence increased. The mines, moreover, were not nearly so productive as was hoped, and Philip soon learnt that the wealth turned out by the Flemish looms was infinitely greater than that produced by the far-famed mines of Mexico and Peru.

The absurd regulations with regard to trade, which were not however new, led also to disastrous results. In the vain hope of keeping prices down, the export of corn and cattle, and even dealing in corn within the country, was prohibited; importation of any kind from the Barbary coast was also forbidden. The effect of these and other absurd restrictions was that the cultivation of the restricted articles was checked, and that trade gradually fell into the hands of foreigners. Many of these, in return for loans, obtained licences from the King to export, while the demand for foreign goods gave the foreigner the command of the import trade. All articles of luxury came from abroad, and we know that the rebels of the Netherlands carried on a thriving trade in those very munitions of war which Spain used in her attempt to crush them. It has been computed that five-sixths of the home, and nine-tenths of the Indian trade were monopolised by foreigners. Thus Spain, by no means wealthy by nature, failed to enrich herself by trade and manufactures, and remained poverty-stricken. The evil was increased by the exorbitant taxation necessitated by Philip's wars, and by the expenses of the court. These taxes fell more especially on Castile and Naples, and were collected by such evil and corrupt methods that, while the people suffered much, the government often received but little.

The general effect of Philip's policy at home was to foster and exaggerate all the worst traits of the Spanish character—its intolerance, its ignorance, its indolence, and its pride; and if at the beginning of his reign Spain seemed to have touched her pinnacle of greatness, by the end of it she had made a long step towards her future decline. We must now pass on to

General results of Philip's Home Policy.

deal with Philip's policy in the Netherlands and abroad, to trace the failure of his attempt to reduce these provinces to the condition of his other dependencies, and the collapse of his wild idea of subjugating England and France to his despotic rule.

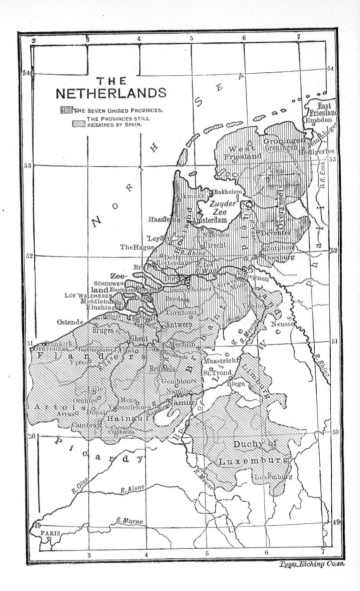

CHAPTER VIII

THE REVOLT OF THE NETHERLANDS

Policy of Charles v.— Regency of Margaret of Parma—The States-General of 1559 and their grievances—Granvella retires—Edict of Segovia—The Confederates at St. Trond—Alva—Execution of Egmont, Hoorne and Montigny—Jemmingen—The 'Beggars' seize Brille—Alliance with France —St. Bartholomew—Fall of Mons—Siege of Haarlem—Don Requesens— Military events—Conference at Breda—Exploits of Mondragon—Sack of Antwerp—Pacification of Ghent—Don John—The Perpetual Edict—The Archduke Mathias—Gemblours—Alexander of Parma—Union of Arras and Utrecht—Sovereignty offered to Duke of Anjou—The French Fury— Assassination of Orange—Successes of Parma—Henry III. and Elizabeth decline the Sovereignty—Leicester in the Netherlands—The Armada— Successes of Maurice—Death of Parma—The Archdukes Ernest and Albert—Truce of 1609—Condition of Netherlands.

THE revolt of the Netherlands has been generally looked upon as a notable instance of the resistance of a democracy to religious persecution. The statement, however, requires some modification. The religious element, no doubt, furnished a principle of enthusiasm to many, more especially in the northern provinces. Yet persecution was not the primary, nor indeed the chief cause of discontent, and many Catholics, at first, in any case, joined the party of resistance ;[1] while the oligarchical character of the government of many of the towns, and the influential position held by the nobles, more especially in the southern and western provinces, remind us that the

---

[1] Lord Buckhurst, the English envoy, declared that as late as 1587, the numbers of the Catholics in the disobedient provinces exceeded those of the Protestants.

movement was far more oligarchical in character than has often been allowed.

Of the seventeen provinces which formed the Netherlands at the accession of Philip II., the greater number had
Previous
history of the
Netherlands. been gradually collected together by the powerful
Dukes of Burgundy during the fifteenth century,
by successful marriages, by cession, and by
conquest. On the marriage of the Burgundian heiress Mary
to Maximilian they had passed to the house of Hapsburg,
and thence, by the marriage of the Archduke Philip and
Joanna, to their son Charles v. The tie which bound these
provinces together was purely a personal one. They were held
by various titles.[1] They were inhabited by peoples of different
race and language; the Dutchman in the north-east, the
Flamand in Brabant, the Walloon and the German in the
western and southern provinces. The social conditions also
varied. In Flanders and Brabant the country districts were
in the hands of a powerful nobility, the cities inhabited by an
industrial and turbulent people, controlled by opulent burghers.
In the north, the democratic element predominated, more
especially in the Frisian provinces, and the inhabitants spent
their life either in fishing and commerce on the sea, or in
saving their country from its inroads. These differences, social
and political, were reflected in the variety of their institutions.
Each province had its own peculiar government. Many had
especial privileges guaranteed them by charter, and no native
of one province could constitutionally hold office in another.

The attempt of the Dukes of Burgundy to establish a more
centralised system of government, and to fuse these hetero-
geneous elements into greater unity, had been strenuously

[1] Four were Duchies: Brabant, Guelderland, Limburg, Luxemburg.
Five were Lordships: West Friesland, Mechlin, Utrecht, Overyssel, Gronin-
gen. Six were Counties: Flanders, Artois, Hainault, Holland, Zealand,
Zutphen. Antwerp and Namur were Margravates. Of these Friesland,
Groningen, Utrecht, Guelderland, Zutphen were added by Charles v.

resisted, more especially by the burghers of Brabant and of Flanders, and the relations between the provinces and their rulers had often been severely strained. During the rule of the Archduke Philip (1494-1506) the struggle had abated, but with the accession of Charles v., the policy of consolidation and centralisation was again resumed. The Policy of boundaries were extended by the acquisition of Charles V. West Friesland in 1524, of the lordship of Gröningen in 1536, and of the duchy of Gueldres and of the county of Zutphen in 1543. By the treaty of Madrid (1526), Artois, Flanders, and Tournay were freed from their dependence on France, and in 1528, Charles acquired the temporalities of the bishopric of Utrecht, and the lordship of Overyssel. In 1548, the whole of the Netherlands were formed into the Burgundian Circle, while retaining their independence of the Diet and the Imperial Chamber, and Charles thought of erecting them into a middle kingdom under a separate government—a policy which was, unfortunately, reversed when, in 1555, Charles decided to leave these provinces to his son. Owing to his necessary absence from the country, the Emperor left the control of the government in the hands of Governesses—his aunt, Margaret of Savoy, ruling from 1506 to 1530; his sister, Mary of Hungary, the widow of Lewis, from 1530 to 1555—yet the policy of centralisation was steadily pursued. A States-General composed of clergy, nobles, and city representatives from each of the provinces, was summoned, although its meeting was not a success. A Central Court of Justice was again established at Mechlin, to which all provincial courts were declared subject. The control of the administration was placed in the hands of three Councils: a Privy Council, to act as a ministry of police and justice; a Court of Finance over the financial chambers of the provinces; and a Council of State, composed chiefly of the greater nobles, which, under the presidency of the Regent, was to administer foreign affairs and exercise a general super intendence over the other Councils. The provinces were placed in the hands of Stattholders, nominated from the ranks of the nobility by the Emperor himself. The other officials, both municipal and judicial, were usually appointed by him. The privileges of the towns were gradually circumscribed, and the attempt of Ghent to refuse a tax voted by the States-General, and generally to resist the centralising policy of the Emperor, was crushed out with merciless severity in 1540; the immunities and privileges of the city were declared forfeit, and the exclusive nomination of ten magistrates vested in the Emperor's hands (cf. p. 209).

It was on the question of heresy, however, that Charles proved himself most inexorable. Not only had the doctrines of Luther early spread among the Netherlanders, but the more extreme views of Calvin, which were even better suited to the genius and character of the people; while the extravagant and anarchical views of the Anabaptists of Munster had appeared at Amsterdam, and elsewhere. Untrammelled by the political difficulties which surrounded him in Germany, Charles was eager to crush out these opinions. A series of edicts, termed 'Placards,' culminating in that of 1550, threatened death by pit, fire, or sword to all convicted of heresy, or of harbouring heretics, of dealing in heretical books, of attending conventicles, of disputing on the Scriptures, or of image breaking. An attempt, indeed, to appoint one Inquisitor-General, with uncontrolled powers of enforcing these edicts, led to such discontent that the Inquisitor had to fly, and Charles was fain to content himself with dividing the office among four, who were not to proceed to sentence without the consent of the provincial council. If the number of victims under these 'Placards' has been grossly exaggerated, yet at least Charles had not refrained from persecution. Nevertheless, he was not unpopular in the Netherlands; the religious and political grievances had not as yet become identified. Charles was a Fleming born; in his earlier years he was entirely in the hands of his Flemish councillors, and if latterly the exigencies of his European position enforced his residence elsewhere, he often visited the home of his birth; and not only abstained from appointing foreigners to office in the Netherlands, but irritated his Spanish subjects by raising Flemings to the highest posts in Spain. His constant wars offered a profession to those who cared for the pursuit of arms, and the wide extent of his empire gave commercial opportunities of which the industrious Flemings were eager to take advantage. At no time was the prosperity of the Netherlands greater; the looms in the western towns were never busier; the lands of Flanders and of Artois were rich in corn; the north-east provinces furnished ample supplies of butter and of cheese, while the fishermen enriched themselves by the herring fishery. Antwerp, which of late had taken the place of Bruges as the entrepot of commerce, became one of the most populous and prosperous towns in Europe; its quays were crowded with the shipping, its banking houses with the business men, of every nation. The riches of the Netherlands may be estimated by remembering that in a few years they contributed no less than twenty-four millions of ducats to the finances of the Emperor. These contributions had, however, only been extorted with difficulty; the Netherlands complained that their revenues were expended on wars in which they were not concerned; the religious difficulties were increasing; and when Charles, in 1555, handed over the government to his son, it was pretty clear that this prosperous yet turbulent and independent people could only be kept loyal by clever and conciliatory statesmanship.

The succession of Philip II. at this critical moment was most unfortunate. His cold and arrogant behaviour was contrasted with the more genial manners of the great Emperor; he made no secret of his devotion to Spain and his contempt for his Fleming subjects, while his bigoted adherence to the Catholic faith was proved by his renewal of the edicts of 1550, in all their severity. Even the war with France was

Philip at once alienates the sympathies of the Netherlanders.

not popular in the Netherlands; they complained that their interests were sacrificed to those of Spain, and resisted the demands made upon their purses. The Peace of Cateau Cambrésis (1559) still further increased this discontent. By that treaty, the Duke of Savoy, who had been Regent in Brussels since 1555, was restored to his dominions in Italy. It therefore became necessary to choose another Regent. Here was an opportunity of conciliating the Netherlanders by appointing some Flemish noble, of whom there were at least two well qualified for the post. William of Nassau had, by the death of his cousin Réné in 1544, succeeded, not only to large possessions in Holland and in Brabant, but to the rich lands of Chalons in France, and the principality of Orange on the Rhone. Appointed Stattholder of Holland, Zealand, Utrecht, and West Friesland by Charles v., he had been intrusted by him with military command, and with the conduct of diplomatic missions, an employment for which he displayed a special gift. By character and position he would have been excellently well fitted for the position of Regent. Failing him, there was Lamoral, Count of Egmont, and Stattholder of Flanders and Artois, who although inferior to the Prince of Orange in ability and strength of character, had gained a great reputation in the battles of St. Quentin and Gravelines, and was, owing to his genial and impulsive nature, a general favourite.

Philip, however, had no intention of appointing any one who was likely to be too powerful or independent, and

Margaret of Parma appointed Regent. 1559-1567.
finally selected his half-sister Margaret, Duchess of Parma, the illegitimate daughter of Charles v., and wife of Ottavio Farnese, grandson of Pope Paul III. Margaret, who was at this time thirty-eight years of age, was the daughter of a Flemish lady. She had been brought up by two Regents of the Netherlands, Margaret of Savoy, and Mary of Hungary, and her appointment was not disliked. But although of masculine appearance and voice, she was a woman of no great political

ability, and was apt to adopt the policy of any one who for the moment was most influential, and unfortunately those in power were most unpopular. Philip had given instructions that she was to rule by the aid of the three Councils, that of Finance, the Privy Council, and the Council of State. The Council of State comprised amongst its members several of the higher nobility, the most notable of whom were the Prince of Orange and Egmont. It was nominally the supreme authority in the Netherlands ; but Philip gave orders that all the more delicate questions of State should be in the The Consulta. hands of an interior Council, termed the Consulta, which was composed of Count Berlaymont, Viglius, and Granvelle. Of this triumvirate, Count Berlaymont, the president of the Council of Finance, was a Fleming of good family, an honest man, but with narrow and despotic views. Viglius, the president of the Privy Council, was a jurist and a humanist of some reputation, and a friend of Erasmus ; yet he was so avaricious that he took orders in order to enjoy the revenues of several benefices ; he was wanting in initiative, and was the humble follower of Granvelle. This man, son of Charles' chancellor, was born in 1517, at Besançon, in Franche-Comté. Raised to the see of Arras at the age of twenty-five, he had, during the declining years of his father, and after his death in 1550, enjoyed the confidence of the Emperor, and was by him specially recommended to Philip, who appointed him president of the Council of State. Although a hard-working and able statesman of polished and insinuating manners, and with a real interest in the welfare of the Netherlands, he was ambitious, fond of power, corrupt, and greedy. He was disliked as a Burgundian by the Netherlanders, and detested as the representative of the views of Philip. Nor was the policy of the King calculated to smooth the susceptibilities of the Flemings. The Spanish troops, whose presence had been Unpopular measures of Philip. necessitated by the war, were not removed on the conclusion of peace, and made up for the arrears in their pay by extortion

and plunder; while the well-known intention of Philip to crush
out heresy caused widespread apprehension.   These, and
other grievances found expression at the meeting of the
Grievances   States-General, which had been summoned to
presented by   Ghent in August, 1559.   Philip indeed pro-
States-
General of   mised to withdraw the troops—a promise which,
1559.   owing to his procrastination, was not fulfilled till
October 1560—but the other grievances he did not deign to
notice.   Sooner than reign over heretics, he declared to his
ministers he would rather not reign at all; while the opposition shown to the foreigner caused him to remark: 'I, too, am
a foreigner; will they refuse to obey me as their Sovereign?'
Having thus disregarded the complaints of his people, Philip
left the Netherlands never to return again, after accusing
William of Orange, if we may credit a contemporary writer, of
being the real mover in the opposition which had shown itself
in the States-General.

    The departure of the King was followed by another measure
which seriously aggravated the discontent.   The ecclesiastical
Philip's   organisation of the Netherlands was very imperfect.
scheme of   There were only three sees—Arras, Tournay, and
ecclesi-
astical   Utrecht, and their dioceses were far too large to
reform.   be efficiently administered.   That of Utrecht
alone included three hundred walled towns and eleven hundred
churches.   The other parts of the Netherlands were either
under the jurisdiction of the Bishop of Cambray, a free
imperial city, or under that of foreign Bishops such as Liège,
while the duchy of Luxemburg formed part of four foreign
dioceses.   The confusion and conflicts with regard to appeals
were further increased by the fact that these bishoprics
were under the jurisdiction of foreign metropolitans: the
two first being subject to the archbishopric of Rheims,
Utrecht to that of Cologne.   Charles V. himself had
planned a reform; time, however, and opportunity failed
him, and it was left to Philip to carry it out on a more
extended basis.   The number of the bishoprics was to
be increased to fifteen; they were to be freed from all

foreign control, and to be organised under three archbishoprics—Mechlin, Cambray, and Utrecht, of which Mechlin, with Granvelle as its archbishop, was to enjoy the primacy; the requisite revenues were to be supplied from the abbey lands within each diocese, and the abbeys to be placed under priors dependent on the bishops : each bishop was to appoint nine additional prebendaries, two of whom were to be Inquisitors and to assist him in the work of rooting out heresy. The announcement of this scheme was met with a storm of opposition from Catholic and Protestant alike. The bishops, it was declared, would be the creatures of the crown; while the abbots, whose place they were to take, had been elected by the monks, and had represented the local interests in the provincial assemblies and in the States-General. The appropriation of the revenues of the abbeys was denounced as an act of spoliation, by the nobles especially, whose sons had often filled the place of abbot. The more careless and ignorant of the clergy feared the stricter supervision and discipline which would ensue. Above all, the measure was condemned as an attempt to introduce the Spanish Inquisition. It is true, no doubt, that some reform was needed, and that much of the opposition was due to interested motives; nevertheless it was unwise, if not unconstitutional, to introduce such a radical alteration in the ecclesiastical organisation of the country without the approval of the States-General, or even of the Council of State. The change would certainly have enhanced the despotic authority of the crown; while the inquisitorial powers given to the bishops at the very moment when Philip was crushing out Protestantism in Spain, were of dangerous import. In a word, the measure was inopportune unless it was avowedly intended to serve the interests of authority and of persecution, and if it was so intended, it demanded the most strenuous opposition. Accordingly, the scheme met with such resistance that it could not be fully carried out; Antwerp, which was specially protected against an increase of ecclesiastical power by 'La Joyeuse Entrée' (the charter of Brabant),

Gueldres, Utrecht, and five other places escaped. But even mutilated as it was, the measure served to unite the religious and political malcontents, and seriously increased the unpopularity of the government.

In April, 1562, the first attempt to rescue victims of the Inquisition was made at Valenciennes; at the same time the opposition of the nobles to Granvelle became more determined. As Archbishop of Mechlin, he was looked upon, though wrongly, as the prime mover in the matter; as president of the Council of State he was held responsible for all the hated measures of the King; while his acceptance of a cardinal's hat, in 1561, still further awakened the jealousy of his enemies. The malcontents found a leader in the Prince of Orange. In 1561, he had taken as his second

William of Orange heads the Opposition.

wife Anne, the daughter of Maurice of Saxony, the old opponent of Charles v. The marriage had been opposed by Granvelle as likely to strengthen the Protestant sympathies of the Prince, and from that time forward there was open war between them. Finally, in March 1563, Orange, Egmont, and Hoorne addressed a letter to Philip, in which they demanded the dismissal of the Cardinal, and declined to appear at the Council of State until their demand was granted. Even the Regent Margaret, who had hitherto been a strenuous supporter of Granvelle,

Granvelle retires. March 1564.

deserted him, and supported the request of the nobles. In March 1564, after long delay, Philip at last consented to dismiss his minister. This however, had but little effect; for Berlaymont and Viglius still remained, while Granvelle, from his place of retreat, continued to advise the King; the system of government was unaltered, the corruption continued, and the persecution did not cease. In the following August, Philip added to the discontent by ordering on his sole authority the publication of the Decrees of the Council of Trent. This act met with general disapproval, not only from the Protestants, but also from the Catholics, who looked upon it as an infringement of their liberties. William of Orange expressed the general opinion, when he declared in the Council of State that, in the existing condition of public opinion, the Tridentine Decrees and the edicts against heresy could not be enforced, and that it was time that the corrupt system of government, the perversion of justice, and the wranglings between the Councils should cease. To remedy this state of things the nobles, led by the Prince of Orange and Counts Egmont and Hoorne, urged on the Regent the necessity of summoning the States-General and of increasing its powers, of reforming the Council of State by the admission of more of the native nobility, and of more completely subordinating the other Councils to it. Margaret, who had now completely identified herself with the oligarchical party, adopted their views, and Egmont was sent to Spain to urge their acceptance on Philip (January 1565). Had Philip consented, the Netherlands might have remained loyal; but the reforms would have involved an overthrow of the bureaucratical system which had hitherto existed; the native nobility would have regained power in the States-General, and in the reformed Council of State, and a mitigation of the laws against heresy must have followed. Philip therefore was unwilling to comply. In June, 1565, he had sent Alva to the Conference of Bayonne, and had urged Catherine de Medici to proceed to stringent measures against the Huguenots, and he was not likely to stultify himself by tolerating heresy in his own dominions. He seemed indeed, at first, anxious to procrastinate. Granvelle's brother wrote in despair: 'Everything goes on from to-morrow to to-morrow: the only resolution is to remain irresolute.' Possibly Philip delayed in the hopes of winning over Egmont. At all events, in October the King threw off the mask, and in his famous despatches from the wood of Segovia forbade any change in the system of administration, and ordered the edict against heresy to be enforced with all severity.

Egmont sent to Spain, Jan. 1565. Philip refuses to listen.

The Edict of Segovia.

'Now we shall see the beginning of a fine tragedy,' said William of Orange. The Regent, and even Berlaymont and Viglius, were dismayed, and urged that Philip should be warned of the probable consequences. But William declared that, 'Since the word of his majesty was so unequivocally expressed, all that remained for them was to execute it.' It is generally believed that the Prince of Orange wished to precipitate matters ; in any case his prophecy was speedily to be fulfilled. In the agitation which ensued we find a new element appear-

General opposition.

ing. Hitherto the opposition for the most part had been confined to the higher nobility, men who held some office, and who had something to lose ; now the lesser nobility began to move. These, like the smaller nobility in France, had previously found occupation in the wars, where they furnished a famous force of cavalry. The peace had destroyed this occupation, and many had returned to their homes with a turbulent spirit, a love of extravagance and of licence engendered of the war, and ready for any opportunity of repairing their shattered fortunes. Others, however, were of a more serious turn of mind, who had, during their stay abroad, learnt and zealously adopted Protestant opinions, while all were inspired by a sturdy love of freedom. Of the less reputable, Henry, Viscount of Brederode, is a fair type. Philip van Marnix, Lord of Sainte Aldegonde, represented the fanatical party ; while Louis of Nassau, the impetuous brother of William of Orange, was the only states-

The Compromise.

man among them. Their views were expressed in 'The Compromise,' a document which was very numerously signed by Catholics as well as Protestants, and which declared that Philip had been induced by evil councillors to establish the Inquisition, in violation of his oath, and that they would resist it.

It does not appear that any of the greater nobles signed the Compromise. William of Orange himself openly condemned the violence of its tone ; yet his influence is probably to be traced in the more moderate petition which the Confederates,

led by Brederode, presented to the Regent on April 5, 1566.
In this petition, while protesting their loyalty, they expressed
their fears of a general revolt, and demanded Petition of the
that envoys should be sent to Philip to urge Confederates,
upon him the necessity of abolishing the In- April 5, 1566,
quisition, and of summoning the States-General by Bergen and
for the purpose of moderating the edicts. Montigny.
The Regent consented to despatch the Marquis de Bergen,
and the Baron de Montigny to Spain, and promised meanwhile some mitigation of the edicts. Montigny reached Spain
on June 17. But Philip, with his usual procrastination,
vouchsafed no answer until July 31. He then promised
that the Inquisition should be abolished, and that he would
content himself with the inquisitorial powers vested in the
bishops. Some hopes were held out that the severity of the
edicts would be moderated, and pardon was promised to any
whom Margaret might think deserving of it, on condition that
they would abandon the League of the Confederates and
engage to support the government. To the summoning of
the States-General he would in no case consent.

There is little reason to suppose that these terms would
have satisfied the Netherlanders even if the King had been
sincere. But we now know that he protested in the presence
of the Duke of Alva, a notary, and two jurists that, as these
concessions had not been granted of his own free will, he did
not feel himself bound to them. He wrote to the Pope
to the same effect, and forthwith began secret preparations for the despatch of Alva to punish those to whom a
pardon had just been offered. Meanwhile, events happened in
the Netherlands which, unfortunately, went some way to justify
Philip's conduct. The Confederates, in one of those drinking-
bouts with which they were too apt to inflame their patriotism,
had assumed the name of Les Gueux, possibly in allusion to a
remark of Berlaymont that they were nothing but a crowd of
beggars. In July, they held another meeting at St. Trond,
near Liège, where, in spite of the opposition of many Catholics,

notably Count Mansfeld, they determined to insist on complete toleration, and on some guarantee against the vengeance of

Meeting of Confederates at St. Trond. July 1566.

Philip. On the 28th, headed by Louis of Nassau, they presented their petition to the Regent, but were ill received; and so convinced were they that Philip would not long delay his vengeance, that Louis proceeded to subsidise a force of mercenaries in Germany.

At this moment an outburst of violent fanaticism ruined their cause. The activity and violence of the preachers,

Iconoclasm causes a reaction.

which had of late been increasing, led, in the early days of August, to a serious outbreak of iconoclasm. Commencing at St. Omer, the contagion rapidly spread, and in a fortnight four hundred churches were sacked in Flanders alone, while in Antwerp the cathedral was stripped of all its treasures. Images, relics, shrines, paintings, manuscripts and books shared a common fate. Only a few of the southern provinces were spared. The fanatics were joined by the criminal classes, and for a time anarchy reigned supreme. Margaret, bowing before the storm, followed the advice of William. She promised that the Reformers should be allowed to hold their meetings in the places where they had hitherto held them, until the King and the States-General should otherwise command. The Confederate nobles, on a promise of pardon, undertook to assist the government, and the Stattholders, despatched to their respective provinces, succeeded—some by concessions, some by more stringent measures—in partly restoring order. The violence had, however, done its work. The Catholics, shocked at the extravagance and profanity of the rioters, abandoned the movement in disgust. The Lutherans, anxious to throw blame on the Calvinists, with whom they had little sympathy, followed suit. Egmont and Hoorne made haste to rally round the government; even William was forced to execute some of the ringleaders in Antwerp before he could restore order. Margaret, taking advantage of this reaction, assumed a bolder line, and commanded that the towns which were least to be trusted should be occupied by royal garrisons, levied among the Walloon and Catholic provinces.

The Confederate nobles, who had not been directly concerned in these riotous proceedings, knowing that they would none the less be held responsible, now rose. Compromised, however, as they were by the extravagant conduct of the fanatics, and not quite prepared to make common cause with them, they failed to obtain adequate support. William forbade the citizens of Antwerp to march to the defence of the patriots, who had seized the village of Austruweel near by (March 13, 1567). They were defeated by the royal troops, and their leader, the brother of St. Aldegonde, was slain. On April 2, Valenciennes, which had refused to admit the royal troops, was taken ; and shortly the Regent was practically mistress of the country, with the exception of the province of Holland, and the city of Antwerp. Fortresses were built in the principal towns ; the meetings of the Calvinists were dispersed ; and many suffered death on the scaffold, or at the hands of a ruthless soldiery.

The Confederates rise, but are defeated.

Yet Philip was not satisfied. He had for some time determined to replace Margaret by a stronger hand, and, in spite of the opposition of his chief minister, the Prince of Eboli, to take summary vengeance, not only on the authors of the late excesses, but upon the greater nobles, whom he held responsible for the troubles. Of this intention William of Orange was fully informed through his secret and paid agents at Madrid, and, despairing of successful resistance for the present, he decided to retire. His conduct has been severely criticised. Had he stayed, it has been said, and raised the standard of civil war, the cruel rule of Alva might have been prevented, or the struggle would have been ended sooner and with more brilliant success.

Philip determines on stringent measures.

William of Orange retires to Nassau. April 30, 1567.

It must be admitted that there is something to be said for this view. Subsequent events proved that the political and religious issues must eventually become identified; and if so, the sooner that occurred the better. The government was as yet ill-provided with troops upon whom it could depend, and a victory at this moment would have rallied to the Prince's standard many who had not declared themselves, and yet have made him strong enough to suppress the most extravagant of his partisans. William might possibly have made the venture if Egmont could have been prevailed upon to move. But

Egmont declines to move. Egmont was a Catholic, and the movement had become decidedly anti-Catholic; he still remembered the conciliatory treatment he had received in Spain: he still trusted to Philip's clemency and shrank from open rebellion. Without Egmont, William was unwilling to take action. He was an aristocrat at heart: he looked for reform to a properly representative Estates-General, and was disgusted at the mob-rule which had of late prevailed. Although he had probably by this time embraced Lutheranism, he had no sympathy with the Calvinistic tenets, and scarcely realised their strength as the militant creed of those who fought for political liberty. Moreover, he had alienated the Calvinists by his conduct during the late troubles, and it was questionable whether they would heartily rally round him. Finally, the Lutheran princes of Germany could not be depended upon, and, of success without foreign aid, he despaired. With these views, he had no alternative but to fly; and, after vainly warning Egmont that he feared Philip was merely 'making a bridge of him whereby he might enter the Netherlands,' he took refuge, together with his brother and some of the other Confederates, in his county of Nassau (April 30, 1567).

William gone, all opposition was at an end. Antwerp opened its gates on the day he left for Germany. Brederode, who had held out at Viana in Holland, fled to Germany, to die in the summer of 1568, a victim to his intemperate mode of life; and shortly after all Holland submitted. The churches

were now taken from the Calvinists; the Regent issued a
new edict which threatened death to all Calvinistic preachers,
and all who had been a party to the late sacrilegious
attack on the churches.   The Prince of Orange had left none
too soon.   Three days before he crossed the frontier, Alva
had started from Spain (April 27).   The ques-   Alva des-
tion as to the despatch of Alva had been   patched to
debated in the royal council.   Ruy Gomez,   the Netherlands.
Prince of Eboli, the chief minister of Philip,   April 1567.
and others, urged that the Flemings were a people more
likely to be overcome by clemency than by arms.   This
was also the opinion of Margaret, who informed Philip that
order was now re-established, and that all that was needed
was 'not an army but a vigilant police.'   Philip, however,
was of another mind.   He had from the first chafed under
the restraints imposed on his despotic authority by the
privileges and independent spirit of the Netherlanders, especially in the matter of taxation.   He was determined to root
out heresy there, as he had done in Spain.   Above all he was
eager to inflict summary vengeance on the nobles, whom he
considered the real authors of the troubles, and the chief
obstacles to the triumph of arbitrary rule.   For this task no
more fit agent could have been found than the Duke of Alva.
With a father's blood to revenge, he had been nurtured in
the wars against the Moors.   At the age of thirty-nine he led
the army of Charles v. against the Lutherans at Mühlberg,
and since then had governed Italy with a rod of iron.   His
severity only increased with his age; and now at the age of
sixty, a good general, a severe disciplinarian, an enemy of all
political freedom, and a narrow bigot, he was a man after
Philip's own heart, and one to succeed if severity without
statesmanship could win success.   Appointed in the first instance
Captain-General, with supreme control over military affairs, he
was by a later commission, of March 1, 1567, invested with
supreme control in civil matters as well, and all authorities,
including the Regent herself, were ordered to obey his

commands. He was to inquire into the causes of the recent troubles, to bring the suspected to trial, with full authority of punishment or pardon, and to reduce the country to submission.

With these extensive powers, and with an army of about 10,000 men, chiefly composed of Spanish veterans, Alva reached Genoa on the 17th of May. Thence he marched to the Mont Cenis, and, passing the Alps, pressed northwards. His advance caused considerable apprehension at once to the city of Geneva and the French court. Condé, indeed, offered to raise a force and overwhelm him as he deployed from the mountain passes. But Catherine declined, and contented herself with levying a body of Swiss Catholics to watch his progress. Alva, however, was careful to give no

Alva reaches Brussels, Aug. 22, 1567. Margaret resigns, December. pretext for attack; enforcing the strictest discipline, he proceeded by way of Franche-Comté and Lorraine to Luxemburg. This he reached on August 8, and entered Brussels on the 22nd. Margaret, hurt at the way in which she had been treated, demanded her recall. Her request was not granted till December 1567, but her authority was at an end, and even her protests against the tyranny and cruelty of Alva's rule were disregarded. The horrors which followed have, perhaps, served to place her eight years' administration in too favourable a light. And yet, if she had at first acquiesced in the unpopular measures of Granvella, she had subsequently joined the greater nobles and backed their demands for some mitigation of the Inquisition, and for the summoning of the Estates-General. She had, indeed, put down the Iconoclasts with a severe hand, but in this she had been supported by the higher nobility, and probably would not have dissociated herself from their cause. With no great administrative ability, and with some want of initiative, she had a real interest in her charge, and a belief in the loyalty of the greater nobles and in their fitness to rule the country. She would probably not have altogether opposed their request for an extension of the authority of the Estates-General, for a reform of the Council of State, and for some toleration; and, had these been granted, the troubles might have ceased. There was, however, no prospect that Philip would grant such concessions, and under these circumstances a continuation of her rule was impossible.

No sooner had Alva reached Brussels than the scheme of Philip rapidly unrolled itself. In spite of the protests of Margaret, the Walloon soldiers in the chief towns were replaced by Spanish soldiery, who forthwith made up for the restraint imposed on them during their march, by a reckless cruelty and a licence which even Alva deplored. Egmont and Hoorne, enticed by fair promises, were arrested on the 9th of September, together with Egmont's secretary, Backerzell, and Van Stralen, the Burgomaster of Antwerp. To try such offenders the ordinary courts could not be trusted. Accordingly Alva created the 'Council of his Excellency' or of 'Tumults,' which became popularly known as the Council of Blood. This terrible tribunal was nominally composed of twelve judges. Two of these, Berlaymont and Noircarmes, were nobles, and six were lawyers of the country; but these eight only acted as assessors, or sub-commissioners, and the right of voting on the cases was reserved to three Spaniards, Juan de Vargas, Del Rio, and La Torre, the final ratification of their decisions being reserved to Alva, who was president. Of this trio, Juan de Vargas, who presided in the absence of Alva, was a miscreant who, after violating his ward, an orphan in Spain, had fled from justice, and earned immunity by subservience to the will of the King. He was in the habit of relieving the monotony of his work of blood by cruel jokes at the expense of the accused; while another judge, Hessels, who subsequently had much influence, is reported, when aroused from naps in court, to have cried out automatically: 'To the gallows, to the gallows.' To furnish victims for this

Egmont and Hoorne arrested, Sept. 9, 1567. Council of Blood erected.

court, commissioners, despatched to the provinces, arrested on the charge of treason all preachers, or harbourers of them, all members of Calvinistic consistories, all who had joined in destroying Catholic, or in building Protestant churches, and all who had signed the Compromise.   Except in more important cases, the commissioners or local authorities proceeded to judgment, the revision of their sentences being alone reserved for the Council itself; and rarely, if ever, was the revision exercised on the side of mercy.   The punishment was death and confiscation of goods, and Alva hoped from this source to replenish the exhausted treasury.   As to the precise number of the victims it is impossible to speak with certainty.   Alva is said to have boasted that he had executed 18,600 during the period of his rule.   This is probably an exaggerated statement, but that the victims are to be counted in thousands is not to be doubted, nor that the trials and executions were accompanied with all the refinements that cruelty could suggest.   It is indeed difficult to find a parallel in history for this irresponsible and tyrannical court, which was created by the mere word of Alva, without even the authority of his written instrument, much less of the royal warrant, and which violated every constitutional privilege of the Netherlanders.   Alva had indeed succeeded in his designs 'of making every man feel that any day his house might fall about his ears.'   Under the pressure of these cruel proscriptions, the tide of emigration, which had already begun under the rule of Margaret, assumed such proportions, even as early as October, 1567, that a decree was then issued threatening confiscation and death to all who left the country or abetted others in so doing.   This, however, only increased the panic; and by the end of Alva's administration, Granvella declared that there were 60,000 fugitives in England, and more in Germany.

The vengeance of Alva and his master could not, however, be sated until the heads of the most distinguished had fallen.   Since the arrest of Counts Egmont and Hoorne, the proceedings against them had been dragging slowly on, but in the early summer of 1568, events occurred to hasten the hand of Alva. William of Orange and his brother Louis had, by the end of April, succeeded in collecting a motley force of Germans, of Huguenots, and of exiles from the Netherlands, and now attempted a triple attack, in the hopes of exciting a rising against the Spanish rule. Two of the attempts (that of Hoogstraten on Brabant, and that of Coqueville, with his Huguenots, on Artois) failed, the latter being dispersed by a French corps which was despatched by Charles IX. But on May 23, Louis of Nassau succeeded in defeating a force of Spanish soldiers at Heiligerlee under the Count of Aremberg, the governor of Groningen, who himself fell in battle.

Louis of Nassau wins the battle of Heiligerlee. May 23, 1568.

The defeat of Heiligerlee hurried on the doom of the two Counts. Alva, anxious to retrieve the disaster in person, was determined not to leave them alive behind him. The counsel for the prisoners had hitherto delayed to produce their evidence, probably in the hope that the exertions made in favour of their clients by the Duke of Lorraine, by many of the German princes,[1] and even by the Emperor himself, might at least secure them a trial before the order of the Golden Fleece, of which they were members. This privilege was, however, refused them, on the ground that it did not extend to charges of treason. On the 1st of June, a decree was published, declaring that the time allowed for the production of witnesses had expired. On the following day, Vargas and del Rio pronounced the prisoners guilty of treason, and the sentence was confirmed by Alva. They were convicted of having given their support to the Confederate nobles, who signed the Compromise; of having shown favour to the sectaries in their respective governments of Flanders and Artois, of Gueldres and Zutphen; and of being parties to the conspiracy of the Prince of Orange. On June 5, they were led to execution

Egmont and Hoorne condemned and executed. June 5, 1568.

[1] The Duke of Bavaria was the brother-in-law of Egmont.

in the market-place of Brussels. A few days before, the secretary of Egmont, Backerzell, and the Burgomaster of Antwerp, had shared the same fate, after having been cruelly tortured in the vain hope of extorting evidence from them against Egmont and Hoorne. That the trial and condemnation of these two nobles was flagrantly illegal is not to be questioned. It violated the ancient privilege that no Fleming should be tried by a foreign judge, and the right, definitely acknowledged by a law of 1531, of the Knights of the Golden Fleece to be tried by their own order, a law which Philip himself had confirmed in 1550. Moreover, the court had been erected without a royal warrant; and the cause was decided before the defendants had produced their evidence. Nor does it appear that, apart from the technical aspects of the question, Egmont and Hoorne had been guilty of treason. As Catholics they certainly had no sympathy with the Sectaries; and this their conduct at the time of the Iconoclastic riots shows; and if they indirectly supported the movement of the Confederates who signed the 'Compromise,' there is no proof that they intended to appeal to arms, or to throw off the Spanish yoke— or that they did anything more than insist, perhaps with somewhat too great vehemence, on the constitutional privileges of their country.

There yet remained one more noble for whose blood Philip thirsted. Of the two envoys sent to Spain in 1566 (cf. p. 327)

Montigny condemned and secretly executed in Spain. March 1570. the Marquis of Bergen had died in May 1567. In the following September, as soon as the arrest of Egmont and Hoorne was known in Spain, Bergen's companion, the Baron de Montigny, brother of Count Hoorne, had been seized. But it was not till February, 1569, that proceedings against him were commenced. The results of the examination to which he was then subjected were sent to the Council of Blood, which after a year's delay condemned him to death (March 4, 1570), without giving him the opportunity of defending himself. The verdict was kept close, and finally Philip ordered that he should be secretly executed in Spain. This was represented to the unfortunate man as an act of mercy, whereby he would be saved from the humiliation of a public execution—while it was publicly announced that he had died a natural death. His property, as well as that of the Marquis of Bergen, was, however, confiscated. So successfully was the secret kept, that this act of perfidy and tyranny was never known till 1844, when access to the records at Simancas was granted by the Spanish government. Philip might now indulge the hope that he had rid himself of all his enemies; but Granvelle with truer insight remarked that 'as they had not caught William, they had caught nothing.'

From the tragedy in the market-place of Brussels, Alva marched against Louis of Nassau, and on July 21, defeated him at the battle of Jemmingen. In vain did William of Orange strive to retrieve this disaster. In spite of the express command of the Emperor Maximilian, who was attempting to mediate, he crossed the Meuse on October 5, 1568, and entered Brabant with a levy of German mercenaries, to which were subsequently added a body of Huguenots under the Comte de Genlis. In mere numbers Orange had the advantage over his adversary, but in nothing else. Alva avoided a pitched battle, and with his veterans completely outmanœuvred the ill-disciplined troops of William, who soon became insubordinate and began to desert. No city opened its gates; and the Prince, disheartened at the want of support which he received, was forced to retreat to Strasburg, whence, after disbanding most of his worthless troops, he and his brother joined Coligny, and took part in the campaign of 1569 in France.

Louis of Nassau defeated at Jemmingen. July 21, 1568.

Fruitless expedition of William of Orange. Oct. 1568.

The expeditions of William and of Louis had been premature. The Netherlands, cowed by the late reign of terror, and always slow to move, had not answered their appeal, and Alva felt so secure that he determined to furnish Philip with tangible evidence of his success. He had long talked of 'the stream fathoms deep' of wealth which he would cause to flow from the Netherlands. The confiscations of the disloyal

Financial tyranny of Alva.falling short of his expectations, he now proposed to tax the wealth of all. In March, 1569, summoning in haste the Estates of each province, he demanded a tax of one per cent. on all property, moveable and immoveable, a tax of five per cent. on every sale of landed property, and one of ten per cent. on every sale of moveables. The two first were heavy enough, but the third amounted to nothing less than a proscription of all trade.   Before a commodity reached the hands of the consumer it would have to pay the tax at least four times—first, as raw material ; then, when it passed from the manufacturer to the wholesale dealer ; again, when it was sold to the retail dealer ; and, finally, when it was bought by the consumer.   The absurdity of this tax was patent to all but Alva.   Viglius, and even Berlaymont and Noircarmes tried to dissuade him from his purpose ; and, although most of the provincial assemblies, inspired by fear, at first consented, the opposition of Utrecht, which was soon imitated, forced Alva to postpone its enforcement for two years, in return for a stated sum.   In July, 1570, an amnesty was proclaimed, although with so many exceptions as to render it nugatory ; and no sooner did Alva, on the expiration of the two years' respite, attempt to enforce the hated tax (July 31, 1571) than a storm of opposition arose.   In vain did Alva offer to remit the tax on raw materials, and on corn, meat, wine, and beer.   In spite of the threat of a fine on those who refused to sell, merchants declined to deal, shops were shut, trade was at a standstill, debtors were not able to meet their creditors, and many banks broke.   The distress caused by the lack of employment was also aggravated in the northern provinces by a fearful inundation, caused by a north-westerly gale which had destroyed the dykes in the winter of 1570.   The numbers of the 'wild beggars'—already considerable— seriously increased, while the Spanish troops, furious for their pay, which Alva was unable to provide, became daily more insubordinate. The words of Margaret were now fulfilled. 'This man,' she said, 'is so detested by the people that he will make the very name of Spaniard hateful.' Even Alva himself acknowledged that all had turned against him, and demanded his recall. Philip, informed of the universal disaffection, had, in September, 1571, appointed the Duke of Medina Celi as Alva's successor, but his love of procrastination caused delay, and the Duke had not left Spain when the news arrived that Brille had been seized by the 'Beggars of the Sea.'

Of those who fled from the tyranny of Alva, some had betaken themselves to the sea, and carried on an organised system of piracy against Spanish commerce. Although common fear of the Guises had led to friendly relations between Philip and Elizabeth in the early part of her reign, and still prevented open hostility between them, Elizabeth had, more especially since the overthrow of Mary Stuart at Carberry Hill (June, 1567), given a tacit approval to the attacks of the English seamen on the Spanish settlements and trade, had harboured the Dutch privateers, and even allowed them to sell their plunder in English markets. In 1568, she had actually seized a Genoese loan, which was on its way to the Netherlands. Philip had in retaliation supported the Ridolfi plot of 1571, in favour of Mary Queen of Scots and the Duke of Norfolk. The plot failed indeed, yet at this moment Elizabeth was not anxious openly to defy the Spaniard. She therefore ordered the Dutch privateers, then under the command of William de La Marck, a noted and unprincipled freebooter, to leave the shores of England. The fleet of twenty-four vessels accordingly put out to sea, and La Marck, after attacking a Spanish merchant fleet which he met in the channel, suddenly seized the town of Brille, at the mouth of the Meuse (April 1, 1572). The seizure of Brille had not been authorised by William of Orange, who was not yet prepared for

Brille seized by the 'Beggars.' April 1, 1572

active operations, nor was it intended at first to be more than a temporary raid. Nevertheless, it was the first act in the Revolt of the Netherlands. The news of the ' Beggars' ' exploit spread like fire. Flushing, which commands the opening of the Scheldt, was the first to rise; Enkhuizen, the Spanish arsenal on the Zuyder Zee, soon followed, and shortly after, the chief towns of Holland and Zealand—with the exception of Amsterdam and Middleburg—as well as those in Guelderland, Overyssel, Utrecht, and Friesland, declared for the Prince of Orange.

General revolt of the Northern Provinces.

From this time forward the revolt of the Netherlands becomes closely involved in the wider range of European politics, and with the diplomatic relations of the great powers of France, Spain, and England. As is more fully explained in the chapter on the religious wars in France (pp. 411, 429), the policy of the French court was at this moment in favour of supporting the Netherlands. Since the treaty of St. Germains (August, 1570) Coligny had been in power, and had prevailed on Catherine, and on her feeble son, Charles IX., to divert the attention of the French from their civil and religious troubles at home, by reviving the slumbering hostility against Spain. Even Elizabeth of England, angry at the support Philip had given the Ridolfi plot, and anxious to prevent either the dreaded union of France and Spain, or the incorporation of any part of the Netherlands into France, listened to these schemes, and entertained the idea of marrying Anjou or his brother Alençon, to whom the sovereignty of the Netherlands was to be offered. William of Orange had eagerly embraced the French Alliance; and the outcome of the negotiations was the taking of Mons, the capital of Hainault, on May 24, by Louis of Nassau, assisted by a Huguenot force under the Comte de Genlis. On the 15th of July, the nobles and deputies from six cities of the northern provinces met at Dort. While still acknowledging the

The French support the Rebels.

Louis of Nassau takes Mons. May 24, 1572.

sovereignty of Philip, they recognised William as their Stadt-holder, voted him a sum of money, and gave him authority to take measures for liberating the country from Spanish tyranny William, assured of support from the northern provinces, and trusting in the co-operation of the French, had already crossed the Rhine on the 7th July, with the intention of raising the southern provinces. A bitter disappoint-ment was, however, in store for him. On July 19, Genlis was defeated and taken prisoner in his attempt to relieve Mons, which had been invested by the son of Alva; and although the advance of William in the following August was well received by most of the southern towns, his hopes were suddenly dashed to the ground by the news of the massacre of St. Bartholomew (August 24, 1572).

Genlis de-feated before Mons. July 19.

The reasons for this astounding revolution in the policy of the French court are dealt with elsewhere (cf. p. 413 ff.). We are here concerned with its effects on the struggle in the Netherlands. The news of the massacre of St. Bartholomew fell 'like the blow of a sledge-hammer' on William of Orange. He continued, indeed, his march to relieve Mons, but Alva, who had assumed the command on the 27th of August, avoided, according to his wont, a pitched engage-ment; the troops of William, discouraged by the defection of the French, became insubordinate; the Prince himself was only saved from surprise in a night attack by the watchfulness of his spaniel, and was forced to fall back on the northern pro-vinces. Louis of Nassau, thus deserted by his brother, and no longer in hope of French assistance, capitulated on September 19. His troops were allowed to retire, in spite of the treacherous request of Charles IX. that they should be cut to pieces, but the city was cruelly treated in violation of the terms of capitulation. The fall of Mons decided the fate of the southern provinces. City after city returned to its allegiance and was admitted to pardon,

Change in the policy of the French court. Effects of the Massacre of St. Bar-tholomew.

Fall of Mons. Sept. 19.

with the exception of the city of Mechlin. This prosperous
city, that it might serve as an example, was given over to

Reduction of Southern Provinces.

pillage for three days by the commands of Alva ;
churches and monasteries were ruthlessly sacked,
and Catholics as well as Protestants suffered
at the hands of the brutal soldiery.

The struggle round Mons had at least given the northern
provinces time to strengthen themselves, and to Holland the
Prince of Orange retired, to organise resistance. It was now
the plan of Alva to try and isolate the revolt by reducing the
chief towns in the north, and so to place the disaffected pro-

Campaign of Don Frederick in the North.

vinces between two fires. The work was intrusted
to his son, Don Frederick. Zutphen was taken
and its garrison put to the sword. The provinces
of Guelderland, Overyssel, and Groningen submitted, and
Don Frederick passed on westwards to Holland, where
Amsterdam was the only city held by the Spaniards. After
razing the small town of Naarden to the ground, in violation
of the terms on which it had capitulated, Don Frederick laid
siege to the important town of Haarlem. The city lies on

Siege of Haarlem. Dec. 9- July 14.

the narrowest part of the neck of land which
separates the Zuyder Zee from the German
Ocean, and which at that point is barely five miles
broad. Its occupation by the Spaniards would
completely isolate the northern portion of Holland. Alva,
fully realising the strategical importance of the city, ordered
his son, who had a force of 30,000 men, to take it at all
hazards. The task, however, proved most serious. The city
was protected on the east by the large though shallow lake of
Haarlem, and by land was only approachable from the west.
The inhabitants, warned by the experience of Zutphen and of
Naarden that they could expect no mercy, resolved to resist to
the last ; and although the garrison was but some 4000, it took
the Spaniards more than seven months before they could
reduce the city (December 9—July 14). The siege was marked
by great cruelty on both sides ; and, after the surrender, the

city became a shambles, over 2000 being murdered in cold blood. The news of the fall of Haarlem is said to have raised Philip from a bed of sickness; but the city had been dearly won. Don Frederick had lost 12,000 men, and the cruelties of the victors only nerved the Netherlanders to greater efforts. 'Our cities,' said William, 'are pledged to each other to stand every siege, to dare the utmost, to endure every possible misery, yea rather, to set fire to all our homes and be consumed with them, than ever to submit to the decrees of this cruel tyrant.' The independence of Holland, indeed, may be said to have been won by the defence of Haarlem. Fifteen days after the fall of the town, the Spanish soldiers, furious at the arrears of their pay, mutinied. They were conciliated by the promise of the pillage of the town of Alkmaar if they could take it, but this they failed to do; and on the 11th of October, Alva suffered a still more serious check in the destruction of his fleet off Enkhuizen. Defeat of Spanish Fleet off Enkhuizen.

Philip, disheartened at the failure to crush out the revolt, and assailed on all sides with complaints of the fiendish cruelty and the incapacity of Alva, decided, after long hesitation, to supersede him. The Duke de Medina Celi had been in the Netherlands since June, 1572; but, as it was not thought wise to change masters at such a crisis, he had refrained from taking over the reins of power, and remained a very unfriendly critic of Alva's administration till August, 1573, when he returned to Spain to swell the number of those who condemned the policy of indiscriminate vengeance. Finally, on the 17th of November, the new Lieu-tenant-Governor, Don Louis de Requesens, Grand Commander of Santiago, arrived at Brussels. Alva left the country, as he bitterly complained, without having gained the approbation of the King, while he had incurred universal detestation 'of Catholics as well as Protestants, of the clergy as well as the laity.' The tyranny and ferocity of his rule almost surpass belief. Every form of Alva superseded by Requesens. Nov. 17, 1573.

torture which ingenuity could devise had been exercised on his unfortunate victims, and he will ever remain in history as the incarnation of fiendish cruelty. And yet, it must at least be confessed that the policy he adopted was one after Philip's own heart in all but its failure, and that he had at least succeeded in restoring the King's authority in the southern provinces.

It was the avowed intention of the new Governor-General to abandon the system of wholesale proscription pursued by

Alva, and to try and win back the Netherlands by conciliatory measures. Nevertheless, his attention was at first necessarily directed to military affairs. In the north the cause of the patriots prospered. On the 21st of February, 1574, Mondragon, who had held the important town of Middleburg, was forced to capitulate, and thus the whole of the island of Walcheren, which commands the two mouths of the Scheldt, was finally lost to Spain; while the town of Leyden, which had been invested since November, 1573, still held out for the Prince of Orange. These successes in the north were, however, neutralised by the terrible disaster of Mooker Heyde on the Meuse (April 14, 1574). Here Louis of Nassau, as he attempted to force his way to join his brother at the head of a motley body of French and German mercenaries, was completely routed by the Spanish general Sancho de Avila. Louis himself, with his brother, Count Henry, and Duke Christopher, son of the Elector-Palatine, were among the slain. The death of Louis, 'the Bayard of the Netherlands,' was a serious blow to William, who had now lost three brothers in the field;[1] and Requesens, having with difficulty quieted a serious mutiny of the victorious troops, ordered the reinvestment of Leyden (May 26, 1574), which had been suspended owing to the advance of Louis. In the opinion of Requesens, religion had but little to do with the rebellion. He accordingly offered a general amnesty to

Marginal notes:
Military events of the year 1574.
Taking of Middleburg, Feb. 24.
Defeat of Mooker Heyde, April 14.
Siege of Leyden, Nov. 1573-Oct. 3, 1574.

---

[1] Adolf fell at Heiligerlu 1568.

all, with a few exceptions, who would return to Mother Church. But although this view of the Grand Commander was correct enough with respect to the original causes of the revolt, matters had changed, at all events in the northern provinces. There religious and political discontent were fast becoming identified, and already in the summer of 1572, William had complained of the cruelties exercised by the patriots on priests and monks. The offers, therefore, of the Governor-General were rejected, and with the cry, 'Rather Turks than Papists, better be drowned than taken,' the citizens of Leyden prepared to hold out to the last gasp. All hopes of succour by land had been destroyed by the defeat of Mooker Heyde. Nevertheless, the sea remained. This was indeed fifteen miles away ; but the dykes were cut ; and, after a long and anxious delay, the wind shifted to the north-west ; two furious gales on the 18th September and the 1st and 2nd of October helped to heap the waters of the ocean on the land, and enabled the fleet of Admiral Boisot to approach. The Spaniards, with Valdés their commander, fled at the advance of this new enemy, and the city was saved (October 3).

The relief of Leyden, the most brilliant success of the war— a success commemorated by the foundation of the University— proved conclusively that although the Spaniards might conquer by land, they were no match for the 'Sea Beggars' wherever a ship could float. While this memorable siege had been proceeding, Requesens had been attempting to conciliate the southern provinces. On the 7th of June, an assembly of the Estates of Brabant had been held at Brussels. The King's pardon, above mentioned, was published, and the abolition of the Council of Blood and the tax of the tenth penny promised. The Estates, not satisfied with this, demanded the departure of the Spanish troops, the exclusion of foreigners from office, and the restoration of municipal privileges to the cities, while they were niggardly in their offers of money. Requesens had no authority to grant these demands, and the attempt

Meeting of Estates of Brabant. June 1574.

at complete restoration of the King's authority in the south
had to be postponed.   The alternative was to make peace
with William and the northern provinces.   To this end,
negotiations had begun as early as the previous autumn,

Conference
at Breda.
March-July
1575.

and finally in March, 1575, a conference was
held at Breda.   The commissioners who had
been appointed by the Estates of Holland and
Zealand demanded the dismissal of the foreigner,
the summoning of the Estates-General from all the provinces,
and the toleration of Calvinistic opinion.   The royal commissioners offered to dismiss the foreign soldiers, if the Prince
would disband the German and other foreign mercenaries in
his service, and they consented to the summoning of an Estates-
General.   They, however, asked that in return for the
guarantee of the King's sign-manual and the pledge of the
Emperor that the royal promises should be kept, the Prince
should give hostages and surrender some of the most important
towns he held.   William was not likely thus to deprive himself of effective means of resistance, and an agreement was
highly improbable on such terms, even if the religious difficulty
had not presented an insurmountable obstacle.   The utmost
that the royal commissioners would offer was that those, who
would not return to the Catholic Church, should be allowed
to sell their property and leave the country.   Requesens,
despairing himself of peace on such conditions, had made
the curious suggestion to Philip that he should surrender the
Netherlands to some other ruler, who would not have the
same scruples with regard to toleration.   'They might be
exchanged for Piedmont with the Duke of Savoy or be granted
to Philip's second son.'   'To my son—never,' wrote Philip on
the margin of the despatch.   'I would rather he were a pauper
than a heretic.'   And in his answer to Requesens he suggested
the advisability of adopting Alva's last advice to burn all the
cities which could not be held ; then after secretly tempting
the adherents of the Prince to win pardon by assassinating
their master, he relapsed into one of his long periods of

silence. Under these circumstances peace was clearly impossible. The negotiations were broken off in July, 1575, and Requesens with a heavy heart, a mutinous soldiery, an empty exchequer, and a ruined credit, prepared for further operations.

Meantime, steps had been taken by Holland and Zealand to form a union and to reorganise the government. There had been a tendency of late on the part of the burgher aristocrats to place restraints on the authority of the Prince. But he refused to accept the responsibilities of rule under such conditions; and accordingly, in June, 1575, he was intrusted with absolute power in all matters concerning the defence of the country, subject only to the power of the purse, which was reserved to the Estates. The magistrates and other officials were to be nominated by him out of a list supplied by the Estates. The Estates also demanded that he should suppress the open exercise of the 'Roman religion.' William, however, insisted on substituting for these words 'any religion at variance with the Gospel.' The clause, even as amended, showed very clearly that the religious question was coming more and more to the front, and the difficulty of any compromise on this question, not only with the King, but with those southern provinces where Catholicism was strong. In October of the same year, the Estates of Holland and of Zealand took a still more decisive step. Hitherto they had declared themselves the loyal subjects of King Philip; they now resolved to forsake the King and seek the sovereignty of some other prince. But their efforts were not successful. Elizabeth, to whom they first offered the sovereignty, played her usual game. She listened graciously to their offers; she allowed them to purchase arms and levy soldiers at their own expense in England; but on the question of the sovereignty she reserved her decision 'until she had done all in her power to bring about an arrangement between them and their King' (April, 1576). An offer made at the French court to the Duc

Increased authority given to the Prince of Orange.

d'Alençon was no more successful; and while these fruitless negotiations were being pursued the patriots suffered a serious reverse in the north of Zealand. Of the three islands, Tholen, Duiveland, and Schouwen, which lie between the northern outlet of the Scheldt and the Meuse, the last had remained

Mondragon secures the islands of Duiveland and Schouwen.

Oct. 1575-June, 1576.

in the hands of the Spaniards. In September, 1575, an attack, led by Mondragon and supported by the fleet, was made thence on Duiveland, which was taken in October. A landing was then effected on Schouwen, and the town of Zierickzee was besieged, to fall in the following June, 1576. By this brave exploit of Mondragon the island province of Zealand was cut in two, and the northern outlet of the Scheldt commanded.

In the midst of this transient success, Requesens died suddenly of a fever aggravated by the anxieties of his post

Death of Requesens, March 5, 1576, followed by an interregnum of eight months.

(March 5). Philip allowed several months to slip away before he finally decided on his successor. Meanwhile, the Council of State carried on the government. Of the old members there remained only the Duke of Aerschot, Count Berlaymont, and Viglius. To these, several Netherlanders and one Spaniard, Jerome de Roda, were added; while Count Mansfeld, a German, was intrusted with supreme military command. Although the Council of State was thus formed almost exclusively of natives, its administration was still very unpopular. Aerschot was secretly a partisan of William. The other two original members had been associated with Cardinal Granvella, and Berlaymont had besides been one of the judges of the Council of Blood. In spite of the desire of the majority for a thorough change in policy, the Council was divided, wanting in capacity, and absolutely devoid of funds. Above all, it failed in maintaining the discipline of the Spanish troops. No sooner had the town of Zierickzee fallen (June 21), than the soldiers, furious on account of the arrears of their pay, mutinied once more, deserted Mondragon, and left Zealand for Brabant (July 15).   The mutiny spread rapidly, and Alost in Flanders was seized.   The indignation and fear thus aroused led the Estates of Brabant, then sitting at Brussels, to take measures of self-protection.   On July 26, they forced the trembling Council of State to issue an edict against the mutineers.   They then threatened the Spaniards in the city, levied troops, and finally, on September 4, arrested the members of the Council themselves.   This only served to further irritate the soldiery. The officers, already jealous at the appointment of Mansfeld, now with few exceptions made common cause with their mutinous troops, more especially Sancho de Avila, who was in command of the citadel of Antwerp.   Many of the German and Walloon mercenaries joined, while De Roda, flying from Brussels to Antwerp, declared himself the only representative of the King and openly supported d'Avila.   The mutineers now held the citadels of almost every important town in the south, with the exception of Brussels, and in many cases obtained possession of the towns themselves, which they treated with great cruelty.   Meanwhile, Orange had seized the opportunity to try and win over the southern provinces. Although the religious divisions between the north and south had of late become accentuated, all were at least united in their desire to drive out the foreigner, more especially the foreign soldiery, and to reassert their political privileges. William, appealing to this common motive, urged them to sink all differences, and with one heart and will to work for the liberation of their country.   Inspired by his stirring words, delegates from the Estates of the southern provinces appeared at Ghent, in the middle of October, to confer with the representatives sent by the Estates of the north.   Hardly had their conference commenced when the violence of the mutineers reached its climax.   On the 4th November, the troops at Alost marched upon Antwerp, joined hands with the garrison under d'Avila, overcame the German and Walloon regiments which had been sent by the Estates of Brabant to hold the

Revolt of Spanish soldiery. July 1576.

town, and with the cries, 'St. Iago, Spain, fire, murder, and pillage,' wreaked their vengeance on the city. Catholics and

The mutineers sack Antwerp. Nov. 4, 1576.

Protestants, native and foreign merchants, women and children, the poor as well as the rich, were attacked without discrimination. Eight thousand persons were massacred; the finest buildings were burnt; property to the value of twelve millions was destroyed or seized; and Antwerp, the richest city of the Netherlands, and 'one of the ornaments of Europe,' became 'the most forlorn and desolate city of Christendom.'

The sack of Antwerp served, at least, the cause of William. On the 8th of November, the Pacification of Ghent was signed

Pacification of Ghent. Nov. 8, 1576.

by the delegates of the northern and southern provinces assembled at that city. By this famous treaty, it was agreed that the Spaniards should be at all hazards expelled from the Netherlands, and that an Estates-General from all the provinces should be summoned to take measures for the common safety and future government. The Prince of Orange was to continue lieutenant, admiral, and general for his Majesty in Holland and Zealand. There should be freedom of trade and communication between the provinces. All prisoners should be released, and all confiscated property restored. The placards and ordinances against heresy should be suspended until the Estates-General had decided on the matter. No attack, however, should be made on the Catholic religion outside the provinces of Holland and Zealand, and if the property of prelates and other ecclesiastics in the north were alienated, it should not be done without compensation. Lastly, no province was to have the benefit of this treaty until it had given its adhesion. The Pacification of Ghent was received with enthusiasm by the whole of the Netherlands; and, although the religious difficulty was postponed rather than solved, there seemed a reasonable prospect that both Catholics and Protestants would at last unite, on the basis of mutual toleration, to throw off the Spanish yoke. The Pacification was at first followed by encouraging results.   On November 11, the Spanish garrison surrendered the citadel of Ghent.   That of Valenciennes was bought from the German soldiery, and at Successes the same time the islands of Schouwen and of the Duiveland were abandoned by Mondragon.   All Patriots. Zealand, with the exception of Tholen, was again free from Spanish rule.   Shortly after, Friesland and Groningen were regained by the national party ; and in January, 1577, the Pacification of Ghent was confirmed by the Union of Brussels, an union which was numerously signed in every province except that of Luxemburg.

Meanwhile, the new governor had arrived.   One day before the Antwerp massacre, and four days before the publication of the Treaty of Ghent, Don John of Austria, Don John the illegitimate son of Charles v., rode into of Austria Luxemburg, having crossed France in the disguise arrives at Luxem- of a Moorish slave.   Philip had at last made up burg. his mind to bow before the storm.   He hoped Nov. 3, 1576. that by a show of conciliation, and by restoring the government to the condition in which it had been at the death of Charles v., he might secure the authority of the crown and the exclusive exercise of the Catholic religion, and yet recover the obedience of the Netherlands.   Don John appeared well fitted to carry out this policy.   The great, though somewhat undeserved, reputation he had gained by the suppression of the Moorish rebellion in Granada and by the victory of Lepanto, his imperial descent, his fascinating manners, had made him universally popular, and he started on his errand with all the enthusiasm of a darling of fortune and of a young man of twenty-nine.[1]   His ambition was not bounded by the Netherlands.   He dreamt, after a rapid settlement of the difficulties there, of either marrying Elizabeth of England, or of overthrowing that heretic Queen and ascending the throne as the husband of her rival Mary Queen of Scots.

[1] Some, however, fix the date of Don John's birth two years earlier, 1545.

He was soon, however, to be rudely awakened. He did not even dare to leave Luxemburg, and was forced to content himself with negotiating from thence with the States-General. This assembly, warned by the Prince of Orange not to trust to promises, demanded the following concessions as the price of their obedience (December 6, 1576) : the Spanish troops must be removed at once ; all prisoners must be released ; and the Treaty of Ghent must be confirmed. One at least of these demands, the dismissal of the Spanish soldiery, Don John was willing enough to grant. Yet in pursuance of his scheme of invading England, he wished that they should go by sea, and that ships should be provided for the purpose. The Estates, ignorant of this design, suspected some future attempt on the Netherlands, and insisted on their departure by land. Philip peremptorily ordered an accommodation, and Don John, forced to abandon the projected invasion of England, signed the Perpetual Edict on February 17, 1577. The Spanish soldiers were to depart by land ; all prisoners were to be released on both sides ; all privileges and charters were to be confirmed, and the Estates-General were to be convened as they had been in the time of Charles v. On these terms the insurgent provinces promised to recognise Don John as Governor-General, to surrender the citadels which they held, to disband their own troops, and to take an oath to maintain the Catholic religion.

The Perpetual Edict. Feb. 17, 1577.

The Spanish soldiery departed at the end of April, and Don John, entering Brussels on May 1, met at first with such success in his policy of conciliation, that he seemed likely to add the pacification of the Netherlands to his other laurels. But, apart from the intrinsic difficulty of the attempt, there were two fatal obstacles in his way—the wariness of his enemy, William the Silent, and the suspicions of his master. William had been disconcerted at the signature of the Perpetual Edict, which had been done without his approval, or that of

Don John enters Brussels. May 1, 1577.

his deputies.   He had not expected that Don John would be so compliant, or he would have raised his terms.   From letters which he had intercepted, he had good cause for distrusting the sincerity of the Spaniard, and he knew that peace on such terms would mean his own ruin.   He had accordingly refused to recognise the Edict, or to publish it in the provinces of Holland or Zealand, and he now proceeded to take measures against it.   He turned to the lower classes and excited their opposition ; he entered into negotiations with England and France, and even plotted to secure the person of Don John.   On the other hand, Don John listened to schemes for the assassination of the Prince, while he wrote to Philip abusing the Netherlanders as 'drunkards and wine skins,' and urging him to prepare for war.   Finally, on July 10, the Governor-General despatched his secretary Escovedo to Madrid to represent his views to the Spanish King.   Unfortunately, Philip had meanwhile conceived a profound jealousy of his half-brother.   He suspected him of some design on the government or crown of Spain, a suspicion which was studiously fostered by Antonio Perez, his minister and confidential adviser.   The representations of Escovedo were therefore disregarded, the urgent solicitations of Don John for counsel or assistance were left unanswered for more than three months, and in the following March, Escovedo himself was assassinated by the orders of Perez, and with the connivance of the King.

William rejects the Perpetual Edict.

Philip's suspicions of Don John.

The brilliant dreams of Don John had indeed been rudely dissipated ; and when, on September 23, William of Orange, after an absence of eighteen years, entered Brussels, the capital of Brabant, it seemed as if the whole of the Netherlands would soon be lost to Spain.   But the near prospect of success served only to revive those feelings of disunion and personal jealousy, which had been temporarily laid aside under the pressure of Spanish tyranny.   The northern provinces, it must be remembered,

Causes of disunion in the Netherlands.

had only lately been united to those of the south. Of the southern provinces, those which lay closest to Holland and Zealand were inhabited by a people of kindred race indeed, but who spoke a different dialect, the Flamand; while in the more southern and eastern provinces, the infusion of Romance blood was strong, and the common language French. These differences of race and past history were illustrated in the religious leanings of the people. In the north, the Protestant, in the south, the Catholic religion predominated, and now that the fear of Spain was declining, a narrow spirit of intolerance began to be displayed on either side. To these causes of disunion we must add the oligarchical jealousy of the southern nobles, mostly of the Catholic persuasion, at the growing importance and the democratic leanings of the Prince of Orange—a jealousy which led to the strange idea of offering the office of Governor-General to the Archduke Mathias, the brother of the Emperor Rudolf, subject to the fuller approval of King Philip. The adroitness of William, however, enabled him to turn this move of his opponents to his own advantage. He openly supported the candidature of the Archduke, who was elected Governor-General on the 18th of January. Meanwhile, the revolt of Ghent against the newly appointed governor, the Duke of Aerschot, one of those who had called in the Archduke Mathias—a revolt secretly approved of by William—showed that the latter had the support of the lower classes. And Mathias, afraid of opposing so popular a man, not only confirmed his election as 'Ruwart' of Brabant, an office generally held by the heir of the ruling prince, and as Stadtholder of Flanders, but acknowledged him as his lieutenant-general, and promised to rule with the consent of the States-General and of a Council of State. At the same time, by the New or Nearer Union of Brabant, the Catholics and Protestants engaged to respect and to protect each other against all enemies whatsoever.

Archduke Mathias elected Governor. Jan. 18, 1578.

Yet while William had been thus dealing with those factions which threatened to ruin his cause, the Spaniards had been again preparing for war. Philip, at last aroused from his strange apathy, had ordered the Spanish veterans to return from Italy. Reinforced by these troops, which were led by Alexander of Parma, and by others from France under Mansfeld, Don John marched against the ill-disciplined army of the States, and, aided by the skilful generalship of Alexander, inflicted a disastrous defeat on them at Gemblours, near Namur. The victory secured the valley of the Sambre, forced William and the Archduke to abandon Brussels, and went far to ruin the cause of liberty in the southern provinces. In the north, however, the reverse of Gemblours served rather to advance the interests of William. In March, his brother, Count John, was elected governor of the important province of Guelderland; and in May, the adherents of the Prince succeeded in overthrowing the Catholic magistrates of Amsterdam, and thus securing the capital of Holland, as well as Haarlem, for the Protestant cause.

The defeat of Gemblours. Jan. 31, 1578.

Meanwhile the Catholic nobles, disappointed in their expectations of Mathias, turned to Francis, Duke of Anjou, the brother of Henry III. of France. Never since the days of Coligny's brief supremacy, had Catherine altogether abandoned the idea of taking advantage of the disturbed condition of the Netherlands to extend French influence in the Walloon provinces of Hainault, Artois, and French Flanders. At this moment, she would probably have preferred to gain her end by friendly negotiations with Philip, and possibly by a marriage of one of her sons with a Spanish princess. But Anjou was little pleased with his position in France; he was attracted by the hope of carving out a new principality for himself; and, accepting the offer, arrived at Mons, in Hainault, in July 1578. William, although unwilling to see French influence predominant in these parts, did not

Duke of Anjou appointed defender of the liberties of the Netherlands. July 1578.

deem it politic to oppose Anjou, and hoped that the enterprise
might excite the jealousy of Elizabeth, who, while she
coqueted with the Duke as a suitor for her hand, was determined not to see the Low Countries under French control,
and had already promised some help to William. The
Duke of Anjou was accordingly recognised as 'the defender
of the liberty of the Netherlands against the tyranny of
the Spaniards.' He was assured of the offer of the
sovereignty should the Netherlands find it necessary to
throw off the supremacy of Spain. Meanwhile, he promised
to make no alteration in the government of the country,
and to hold all conquests he might make for the States
(August 20). Before these confused negotiations had led
to any definite result, Don John, worn out by disease, and

Death of
Don John.
Oct. 1, 1578.
Succeeded
by Alexander
of Parma.

sick at heart at the failure of his magnificent
schemes, at the neglect shown to him by King
Philip, and at the murder of Escovedo, had
passed away. He died in his camp at Bouges,
near Namur, on the 1st of October, 1578, at the
age of thirty-one, having appointed his nephew, Alexander of
Parma, as his successor. Although there is no probability
in the rumour that he was poisoned by the orders of Philip,
the suspicion and neglect with which he had been treated at
least contributed to his death.

Alexander of Parma, who succeeded Don John as governor,
was the son of Ottavio Farnese and Margaret of Parma, the first
Regent during the reign of Philip II. He had been brought up in
Spain with his cousin Don Carlos, and his uncle Don John of
Austria. His love of adventure and of military exercises had in
earlier days shown itself in an inordinate passion for duelling;
but the war against the Turks gave him a more honourable
field, and at the battle of Lepanto he had distinguished himself
by the most remarkable personal bravery. Now at the age of
thirty-three, he was more than the equal of his uncle, Don John,
as a soldier, and infinitely his superior as a diplomatist and a
statesman. Great, however, as were the abilities of the new

governor, it must be remembered that the position of affairs at this moment gave him opportunities which had been denied to his predecessors. The racial and religious differences between the northern and southern provinces were becoming daily more accentuated. In the southern and western provinces disunion was rapidly spreading. The decisions of the States-General, especially with regard to taxation, were little observed. The soldiery were ill-paid, ill-disciplined, and mutinous; the intolerance of the Catholics and Calvinists was becoming more pronounced; the social and political rivalries were daily forcing themselves more prominently to the front and threatening civil war or anarchy. William had of late been forced to lean on the lower classes, and he was not able to keep them in control. In Ghent, especially, the turbulence reached its climax under the demagogue Imbize, supported by John Casimir of the Palatinate, an ambitious and weak prince, who had just arrived with a motley force of German mercenaries and English soldiers, sent by Queen Elizabeth. The rise of this fanatical party not only excited the indignation of the Catholics, or 'Paternoster Jacks,' who still represented the majority in the southern provinces, but also alienated many of the 'Malcontent' nobles, who had hitherto supported the national cause. Of these divisions, Alexander was quick to take advantage. Partly by conciliation, more successfully by bribery in money, or in promises of advancement, he succeeded in reconciling many of the nobles. Among these, we may especially note Egmont, the degenerate son of his father, and Champagny, the brother of Granvella, while Parma even approached William himself with brilliant offers if he would but desert the cause.

The most signal result of Alexander's diplomacy was seen in the Union of Arras (January 6, 1579), between the Walloon provinces of Artois and Hainault, and the towns of Lille, Douay, and Orchies in French Flanders—a League which, in the following May, came to terms with Alexander, on condition that the foreign troops should be dismissed, and the provincial privileges respected. In answer to this, the northern provinces of Guelderland, Holland, Zealand, Utrecht,

Union of
Arras,
Jan. 6,
answered by
the Union
of Utrecht,
Jan. 29, 1579.

and Friesland formed the Union of Utrecht (January 29). The object of the union was declared to be the strengthening of the Pacification of Ghent. The allegiance to Spain was not thrown off, but the provinces bound themselves to protect each other against all force brought against them, either in the name of the King or of foreign Potentates. Each province was, while renouncing its right of making separate treaties, to retain its especial liberties and privileges, and to decide on the religion it should adopt, although individual freedom of conscience was to be allowed ; the Roman Catholic provinces were asked to join on the same terms. The Confederacy was to be ruled by a General Assembly formed of deputies from each provincial assembly. It was to have a common currency, a common system of taxation, and an executive Council, responsible to the General Assembly. This famous document was originally only signed by five of the northern provinces, but the other two—Groningen and Overyssel—subsequently joined, as well as the towns of Ghent, Bruges, Ypres, and Antwerp. Although the Union was originally intended to be temporary, it became the basis for the future federal constitution of the Seven United Provinces, as the Union of Arras formed the germ of the future reconstituted Spanish Netherlands.

While the inevitable cleavage between the north-eastern and south-western districts was thus appearing, Parma made

Success of
Parma in
south-western
provinces
and in the
north.

notable advances in the central provinces. In the summer of 1579, Maestricht, on the Meuse, fell after a four months' siege, and Mechlin was treacherously surrendered by De Bours. In May of the following year, the famous Huguenot, De la Noue, was taken prisoner near Ingelmunster. Even in the north, Count Renneburg had betrayed the town of Groningen, and John of Nassau, the brother of William, disgusted at the people's lack of patriotism, and at their want of discipline, abandoned his Stadtholderate of Guelderland and retired into Germany.

Encouraged by his success, in June, 1580, Philip took the decisive step of publishing a ban against the Prince of Orange. He was declared a traitor and a miscreant. All loyal subjects were forbidden to communicate with him, or to give him food or shelter, and a purse of twenty-five thousand crowns of gold and a patent of nobility were offered to any one who would deliver him into Philip's hands, dead or alive. Philip in this had acted by the advice of Granvella, who declared that William was a coward, and that the fear of assassination would either cause him to submit, or 'die of his own accord.'

Philip publishes the Ban against William of Orange. June 1580.

Nevertheless, though the ban may well be called the death-warrant of the Prince, he was not in the least dismayed. In the *Apologia* which shortly appeared, William boldly defied his enemy. He asserted that Philip had murdered his son Don Carlos, his wife Elizabeth, and the Emperor Maximilian. He declared that as Philip's claim to rule the Netherlands was forfeited by his tyranny, he was no longer their legitimate king, nor he himself a rebel. Finally, professing that he would gladly endure perpetual banishment or death if he could thereby deliver his people from their calamities, he placed himself in the hands of God, 'who would dispose of him and of his goods as seemed best for His own glory, and his salvation.' Nor did William content himself with words. He had long been convinced that, unless foreign help could be obtained, the southern provinces, at least, were lost. Duke Casimir had, by his incapacity, done the cause more harm than good, and had left the country without even paying 'his 30,000 devils' of German mercenaries. The Archduke Mathias was evidently not the man to strengthen any cause, and further help Germany would not give. France alone remained. Accordingly negotiations were again

William publishes his Apologia, and enters into negotiations with the Duke of Anjou.

reopened with the Duke of Anjou, who, in 1579, had left the Netherlands for England, enticed by the hope that Elizabeth, if she could only see him, might accept his hand. Certainly the personal appearance of the Duke was not likely to further his suit, for although he had the gracious manners of all the Valois princes, and was 'a good fellow and a lusty prince,' he was of puny stature, his face was pitted by smallpox, and he had an enormous nose. The virgin Queen was, moreover, playing with him. To marry Anjou and assist him in the Netherlands without a definite promise of French assistance, would be to incur too rashly the enmity of Philip II., and Henry III. would not promise; to allow him to conquer the Netherlands for France was not to be endured. She had raised her lover's hopes, only to draw him out of Flanders, and there was no alternative but to keep him dangling on as her suitor, and nothing more. Anjou was accordingly dismissed with fair promises, and, in the hope of securing his bride, eagerly accepted the offers of the States.

By the Treaty of Plessis-les-Tours (September, 1580), which was ratified in the following January, the Duke was granted the hereditary sovereignty over the Netherlands.

Sovereignty over the Netherlands conferred on the Duke of Anjou by Treaty of Plessis-les-Tours. Sept. 1580. He was always to reside in the country, to appoint no foreigner to office, not to attempt any alteration in the government, nor interfere with the privileges of the provinces; he was to procure the assistance of the King of France, but to permit no incorporation of territory with that country. Any violation of these conditions was to cause an immediate forfeiture of his sovereignty. On the 26th of the July following (1581), the Estates finally renounced their allegiance to Philip, and the Archduke Mathias left the Netherlands in October, though Anjou was not finally accepted till February, 1582. The northern provinces were most unwilling to receive this foreign ruler. In July, 1581, William had already, after many refusals, accepted the title of Count of Holland and Zealand, with the sovereignty during the war. These provinces, therefore, only consented to acknowledge the Duke of Anjou on the express terms that no alteration should be made in the practical supremacy of the Prince of Orange. Thus to all intents the Netherlands were now divided into three divisions: the western provinces, which had again submitted to Spanish rule; the north-eastern under William; and the central, which acknowledged the sovereignty of the French Prince. The policy of William in the matter has been severely criticised, and certainly the previous conduct of Anjou in France (cf. pp. 418 and 423) was not of very hopeful augury. Yet, although a desperate remedy, the French alliance was not altogether a bad idea. There was some hope that a Catholic sovereign who would consent to tolerate the Protestants, might unite once more all the elements of opposition to Spain. Catherine and King Henry III. were at this time half inclined definitely to adopt an anti-Spanish policy (cf. p. 426); while, if the English marriage had also come about, Coligny's idea of a great coalition against Spain might have been realised at last. Unfortunately, all turned out for the worst. Elizabeth, after sending for Anjou once more, and even exchanging betrothal rings with her lover, declined to take the decisive step, and Anjou finally left England for the Netherlands. There the Flemings and the French quarrelled; religious intolerance added to the discord; the successes of Parma continued; and Anjou, irritated by the restraints imposed upon him, rashly and foolishly attempted a *coup d'état*. He succeeded in some of the smaller towns, but failed at Bruges; while at Antwerp, the citizens rose and cut down nearly 2000 of his soldiers (January 16, 1583). Anjou, with shameless effrontery, attempted to throw the blame upon his subjects, while he intrigued with Parma, and offered to join him in return for the cession of certain towns on the French frontier. Even then, William did not think it wise to irritate the French. Negotiations were continued after the departure

Triple division of the Netherlands.

'The French Fury.' Jan. 16, 1583.

of the Duke for France (June 28), and were only ended by his death in the June of the ensuing year.　Before that

Anjou leaves the Nether-
lands.
June 28, 1583.

event, Parma, taking advantage of the confusion and distrust caused by 'the French Fury,' partly by arms, partly by bribery, recovered nearly all the central provinces except Flanders, and even there Bruges was surrendered through the treachery of Chimay, the son of the Duke of Aerschot.

One month after the death of Anjou, William of Orange was assassinated.　The ban had been his death-warrant.　No

Assassination of William of Orange.
July 10, 1584.

less than five attempts had been made, of which one had been nearly fatal to the Prince, and by the anxiety it caused, contributed at least to the death of his wife, Charlotte of Bourbon.　Finally, on the 10th of July, 1584, when fifty-one years of age, he was shot at Delft by Balthazar Gérard, a fanatic of Franche-Comté, who had long looked upon himself as predestinated to do the deed.

The great man, who thus passed away, is a good example of the chastening influence of a life of responsibility and danger. The troubles of his country, and the anxieties they brought upon him, had weaned him from the extravagance and dissipation of his youth and had deepened his character.　A Catholic by birth rather than conviction, his adoption of Lutheranism, 2nd subsequently of Calvinism, were probably in part due to political interest; and although there is no reason to doubt the sincerity of his ultimate beliefs, his past experience led him to realise, as few of his contemporaries did, the value of toleration—a belief which cost him the support of some of his more fanatical followers.　Few would deny that he was ambitious, but his repeated refusal to accept the sovereignty offered to him — a refusal which some think mistaken—proves at least that he knew how to keep his personal interest in control.　That he was no great general, and that he was deficient in military courage, may be true; yet, if it be remembered that he commanded mercenaries who were not to be trusted, or civil levies which could indeed defend a town, but were scarcely fitted to meet the veterans of Spain in the open field, we shall probably applaud his wisdom in avoiding pitched battles. It is, however, as a statesman and a diplomatist that he excelled. Absolute straightforwardness is difficult in diplomacy, but William was infinitely more straightforward than the shifty Elizabeth, the Machiavellian Catherine, or the treacherous Philip ; while his constancy under reverse, in spite of a constitutional tendency to depression, justly entitles him to his motto, ' Je maintiendrai.' The extravagant denunciations of the Prince by his enemies may be taken as a measure of his ability ; the number of his devoted followers, of his personal fascination ; the future glories of the 'United Netherlands,' as an incontestable proof of the greatness of the man who is justly called their 'Father.' Nevertheless it is improbable that William, had he lived, would have won back the south-western provinces. The cleavage, as we have seen, had already begun—a cleavage which future history has proved to be deep and permanent—and the success of Parma in the south-west seemed already pretty well assured. No doubt William hoped for an alliance with the Huguenots and with Henry of Navarre, who, by the death of Anjou, had become the heir to the French crown, an idea which explains his marriage with Coligny's daughter.[1] He seems even to have looked for a coalition of all Protestant powers. But Henry had enough to do at home, and Elizabeth

---

[1] William married four times :—

    1. Anne of Egmont.
    2. Anne, daughter of Maurice of Saxony.
    3. Charlotte of Bourbon, daughter of Louis, Duke of Montpensier.
    4. Louisa, daughter of Admiral Coligny.

Of his eleven children, the following are the most important :—

    1. Philip William, son of Anne of Egmont, a captive in Spain since 1567 ; *ob. s.p.* 1618.
    2. Maurice, son of Anne of Saxony, Stattholder from 1587 to 1625.
    3. Frederick Henry, son of Louisa de Coligny, Stattholder from 1625 to 1647.

was a broken reed; while the quarrels between the Lutherans and Calvinists, and the advance of the Catholic Reaction, would probably have prevented effective help from Germany. William had laid the foundation of the independence of the Seven United Provinces, and had he lived he would not in all probability have done more than antedate by a few years the recognition of that independence.

'Had William been murdered two years earlier,' said Philip, 'much trouble might have been spared me; but it is better late than never.' His second son, Maurice,

Maurice elected Captain-General of Holland and Zealand. who was elected Captain-General of Holland and Zealand, and head of the Council of State, which was appointed provisionally, was only seventeen; Hohenlo, the son-in-law of William, who was appointed commander-in-chief, was a drunkard; while Treslong, the admiral, quarrelled with the Estates, and was superseded by Justin, an illegitimate son of William, a man of no experience. Of the confusion which naturally ensued, Parma made good use. The most important towns in the South, which remained unsubdued, were Dendermonde, Ghent, Brussels, Mechlin,

Success of Parma. and Antwerp, all of them lying on the Scheldt or its tributary the Senne. Alexander offered good terms; he promised to respect their privileges, to make no inquiry into conscience, and to free them from foreign garrisons. Many of the old adherents of Orange deserted the cause in despair, and by the end of July, 1585, all these towns had surrendered or had been taken, with the exception of Antwerp. Against that important place, Parma now concentrated all his

The siege of Antwerp. Aug. 17, 1585. efforts. The enterprise was a difficult one; Parma had no fleet; Philip, at this moment occupied with the affairs of the League in France (cf. p. 428), gave him scant assistance; and, had the citizens of Antwerp followed the example of those of Leyden in the year 1574, and completely flooded the country, he could scarce have approached the city. For this sacrifice, however, they were not prepared, and the half-measures which they adopted did more harm than good. Parma accordingly was able to reach the Scheldt to the seaward of the town, and began a bridge which should cut off all communication with the sea. The besieged, when too late, made energetic attempts to defeat his purpose, and once, by means of the dread fire-ships, nearly succeeded in breaking through the barrier. But Parma was not to be baulked. In spite of all their efforts, the bridge was completed, and, after a six months' siege, St. Aldegonde the Burgomaster, surrendered (August 17). The victory was not tarnished by any outrages. An amnesty was proclaimed, though the city had to pay a fine ; all religions except the Catholic were proscribed, but those who would not conform were allowed two years' grace. But if the capitulation of Antwerp raised the military fame of Parma to the highest pitch, and practically secured Brabant to the Spaniards, the actual gain was not very great. Ostend and Sluys still held out, and although they were subsequently won (Sluys in August 1587), the Dutch succeeded in permanently holding Flushing and the entrance to the Scheldt. By so doing, they not only destroyed the commercial importance of Antwerp, which depended on her communication with the sea, but contributed to the decline of the industries of the other great Flemish cities. Amsterdam now took the place of Antwerp ; the Scheldt was closed to Flemish commerce, and never till our day, when that river was finally declared open, did Antwerp become again that entrepot for trade, for which her geographical position so well fits her.

While this memorable siege had been progressing, the sovereignty over the Netherlands was going a-begging. Two parties had now arisen there : those who based their hopes on French assistance, and those who looked to England. The French party were at first successful. Undismayed by the treachery of Anjou, and in spite of the opposition of the Province of Holland, they offered the sovereignty to Henry III., 'upon conditions which should hereafter be settled,'

Sovereignty refused by Henry III., Oct. 1584, is offered to Elizabeth.

October, 1584. So brilliant an offer was indeed tempting, and, had the hands of Henry been free, he probably would have accepted it. But the last of the Valois was in the toils of the Catholic League. After much hesitation he had, in July, 1585, submitted to its dictation (cf. p. 429), and accordingly he declined the profer.ed dignity.

Disappointed in their hopes of French assistance, the Netherlanders turned to England. Elizabeth had received with satisfaction the news of the refusal of the sovereignty by the French King. Well aware of the designs of Philip on England, she was anxious to save the United Provinces from reconquest by Parma, and was willing to aid them with men and money. Nevertheless, with her usual parsimony, she was determined to obtain good security for repayment, which should take the form of cautionary towns, while she feared to accept the sovereignty lest such a step might pledge her too deeply to a definite anti-Spanish policy. This was, however, just what the Netherlanders most desired. The negotiations therefore, which had begun before the fall of Antwerp, were long protracted, and it was not until November, 1585, that the Netherlanders finally consented to her terms. The Queen engaged herself to maintain a permanent force of 5000 foot and 1000 horse in the provinces at her own

charges; for the repayment of the expense thus incurred, Brille and Flushing were to be placed in her hands, to be garrisoned by an additional contingent; she was also to have the right of nominating two members of the Council of State of eighteen, to which the administration of affairs had been intrusted after the death of William the Silent. The Earl of Leicester, the favourite of the Queen, was appointed commander of the forces; the governorship of Flushing was intrusted to his nephew, Sir Philip Sidney, and that of Brille to Sir Thomas Cecil, son of Lord Burleigh.

Elizabeth declines the sovereignty, but despatches the Earl of Leicester. Dec. 9, 1585.

On the 9th of December, the expedition sailed. The

Netherlanders were not, however, yet satisfied. Anxious apparently to compromise the Queen still further in their cause, they offered the post of Governor-General of the United Provinces to Leicester, with supreme military command by land and sea, and supreme authority in matters civil and political.

Leicester accepts the office of Governor-General.

He was to swear to maintain the ancient laws and privileges of the country, and to govern with the assistance of the Council of State ; he might, however, summon the States-General at his will, and was to enjoy the right of appointing to all offices, civil and legal, out of a list presented to him by the states of the province where the vacancy should occur. The Earl not only accepted the brilliant offer, but, elated by the magnificent reception he received, was even heard to say that his family had been wrongly deprived of the crown of England.[1] By this conduct the susceptibilities of Elizabeth were aroused. As a Queen, she was angered at 'the great and strange contempt' of her subject who had dared accept the 'absolute' government without her leave ; as a woman, she was jealous of her favourite who looked for honours from other hands than hers ; as a diplomatist, she feared that this rash act of Leicester would destroy her game, and that Philip would strike at England. She therefore peremptorily commanded him to make 'public and open resignation' of his office. For two months the Queen was implacable. At last, however, a most secret letter from her 'sweet Robin' salved her woman's pride. Burleigh and Walsingham warned her of the fatal results of her capricious conduct ; and she consented that the Earl should, provisionally at least, retain the authority of 'absolute governor' (April 10). We even find her subsequently declaring 'that she misliked not so much the title, as the lack of performance' of their promises by the Dutch.

Indignation of Elizabeth.

The quarrel between the Queen and her favourite was at an end ; not so its consequences. The authority of the Earl

[1] The Earl of Leicester was the brother of Guildford Dudley, the husband of Lady Jane Grey, executed 1554.

had been discredited by the humiliating position in which
he had been placed by his own vanity and rashness, and by
the pique of his mistress. The suspicion and
disgust thus engendered among the Netherlanders
were increased by the reports of negotiations between Elizabeth and Parma—reports which were
but too well founded ; for as the projected invasion of England
became more certain, the efforts of the Queen to avert the
blow by peaceful negotiations increased. Nothing could have
been more unfortunate than the policy thus adopted.
Philip's object was simply to gain time until he should be
ready for his great stroke; and, although Elizabeth hoped to
include the Netherlands in any peace she might make, her
previous conduct certainly gave no security that she would
refuse to sacrifice their interests if necessary. These apprehensions were naturally most acutely felt by the 'States
Party,'—that is, by the governing classes, who were represented in the Provincial Estates, and in the States-
General—men like Paul Buys, the ex-advocate, and John
Van Olden Barneveld, the advocate of Holland. This party
had hitherto taken the lead in the struggle against Spain,
and, although still in favour of the English alliance, were
unwilling to see their country made the victim of a woman's
pique, or of a faithless Queen's diplomacy.
Leicester, stung by their reproaches, with that
vanity and love of flattery which were his chief
faults, accordingly turned to the people and
adopted a democratic policy which was still more distasteful
to the official classes, and to the patrician burgher families.
In violation of the law that no person should hold office
in any province of which he was not a native, he raised
three creatures of his own to power : Deventer, a native
of Brabant, was appointed burgomaster of Utrecht ; Daniel
de Burgrave, a Fleming, was made his private secretary ; and
Regnault, another Fleming, a renegade who had once taken
service under Granvella and Alva, was placed at the head of

Marginal notes:

Leicester loses the support of the 'States' Party.

Leicester leans on the democratic party.

the new Finance Chamber—a chamber which Leicester erected with the hope of putting a stop to frauds on the revenue, and of finding 'mountains of gold.' The merchants were further irritated by the refusal of Elizabeth to remove the staple for English cloth from Embden, in East Friesland, to Amsterdam or Delft, and by the prohibition of all exports to Spanish territories—a measure which did far more harm to Dutch trade than it did to that of Spain, and which was so unpopular that it had shortly to be rescinded. A Calvinist himself, the Earl gladly adopted the views of the democratic party in religious matters. Declaring that the Papists were favourers of Spain, he banished seventy from the town of Utrecht and maltreated them elsewhere ; while with the object of declaring Calvinism the state religion, he summoned a religious synod at the Hague. By this conduct he abandoned the principle of toleration which William the Silent had ever advocated ; he threatened the compromise laid down at the Union of Utrecht (cf. p. 358) whereby each province had been allowed to settle the religious question for itself, and he alienated the best statesmen of the day, men who objected to Church influence in secular affairs, who feared the in- temperate zeal of the Calvinist ministers, and wished to avoid the establishment of a theocracy after the fashion of Geneva. The adherents of the Earl did not stop there ; they denied the authority of the States-General and of the Provincial Estates, and declared that sovereignty resided in the people. In pursuance of these theories the government of Utrecht, where Leicester generally resided, was revolutionised, and Paul Buys, one of the most prominent of the burgher party —seized with the tacit acquiescence, at least, of Leicester— was kept six months in prison without trial. Thus the Earl, instead of uniting all parties in common opposition to the Spaniard, had become a partisan, had made enemies of those who had been the most strenuous advocates of the English alliance, and deepened those provincial, class, and religious differences which henceforth were to be the chief bane of Holland. Nor was Leicester more fortunate in his relations with his own subordinates; he quarrelled with

Leicester quarrels with his subordinates.

Sir John Norris, who had been in command of the English contingent before his arrival, with the knight's brother Edward, and his uncle the treasurer, and with Wilkes, one of the English members of the Council of State. Although Leicester was not altogether responsible for these dissensions, they did not improve the Dutch opinion of him, and, added to the niggardliness of Elizabeth's supplies, seriously crippled his efforts in the field. It was fortunate, under these circumstances, that Philip was too intent on securing the victory of the League in France, and on his preparations for the Armada, to send efficient help to Parma. As it was, the year 1586 was one of

Disasters of the year 1586.

disaster for the patriots. On June 7, Grave was treacherously surrendered to Alexander by its governor. On the 28th, Venloo capitulated, and Parma became master of the Meuse almost to its mouth. Finally, the attempt of Leicester to take the town of Zutphen on the Yssel, which was still held by Parma, led to the death of Sir Philip Sidney, the brilliant nephew of the Earl, who was mortally wounded as he took part in an heroic, though unsuccessful effort to intercept a convoy of provisions thrown into the town by Parma (October 2). The only successes on the English side were the surprise of Axel on July 17, the reduction of Doesburg, September 12, and the taking of some of the outlying forts of the town of Zutphen.

The only remedy for the ill that had been done was that Elizabeth should accept the sovereignty, and send a good army into the field. This Leicester earnestly pressed on the Queen, and the proposal met with the support of Burleigh. Elizabeth, however, objected to the one, 'because it bred a doubt of perpetual war'; to the other, 'because it required an increase of charges'; and the departure of Leicester on a visit to England at the end of November only added to the confusion and disagreements in the Netherlands. The government during his absence was nominally left to the Council of State. To Sir John Norris was given command of the English forces, to Hohenlo that over the Dutch and German troops. Leicester, however, knowing that the majority in the Council were against him, and that these two officers were his deadly enemies, had left a secret paper by which he forbade the Council to set aside any appoint- ments to the command of forts and towns without his consent. Unfortunately, two of his last nominees turned traitors. Sir William Stanley surrendered the town of Deventer, near Zutphen, and Rowland York betrayed Fort Zutphen to Tassis, the Spanish commander of the town (January 29). These acts of treachery on the part of Leicester's own nominees, added to the negotiations of Elizabeth with Parma, which were now well known, roused the indignation of the States Party in Holland to boiling pitch. Barneveld declared ' that the country had never been so cheated by the French as it was now by the English, and that the govern- ment had become insupportable.' Envoys bearing a bitter remonstrance were despatched to Elizabeth, and Maurice was again provisionally appointed Governor-general, with Hohenlo for his lieutenant-general. The visit of the envoys was most inopportune. At the moment of their arrival the question of the fate of Mary, Queen of Scots, who had been convicted of complicity in the Babington Plot, was agitating the English Queen. Four days after their arrival, Elizabeth at last consented to sign the death-warrant (February 1), and on the 8th, Mary's head fell on the scaffold. It was now thought imperatively necessary to conciliate Philip, or to husband all the resources of England for defence against the invasion which was otherwise inevitable. Under these circumstances, Elizabeth was in no mood to listen either to the remonstrances of the Dutch against the conduct of her favourite, or to their demands for increased help and money. ' No reason that breedeth charges,' said Walsingham,

Leicester temporarily leaves the Netherlands. Nov. 24, 1586. The dis- content increases.

'can in any sort be digested.' In March, indeed, Lord Buckhurst was despatched to Holland, and by his wise and conciliatory policy did much to heal the breach. But with the return of Leicester in July, the quarrels again broke out. His attempt to relieve the town of Sluys, which he found invested by the Duke of Parma[1] on his return, failed, and on August 4, that important basis for an attack on England was in Parma's hands. The fall of Sluys led to recriminations between Leicester, Maurice, and Hohenlo. Meanwhile, the altercations with the States Party continued, while the continued negotiations between Elizabeth and Parma deepened the suspicions against the English. The Dutch even declared that Elizabeth's aim was to secure possession of more towns, that she might thereby make a better bargain for herself, while she sacrificed her allies. That the Queen herself entertained so base an idea is not proved; yet we have Leicester's own words to show that he at least did not shrink from such a course 'if the worst came to the worst.' When, therefore, in the autumn of 1587, Leicester made a vain attempt to revolutionise the governments of Amsterdam and Leyden (October, 1587), as he had previously done in the case of Utrecht, a cry was raised that he was playing again the game of the false Anjou (cf. p. 361), and there was no alternative for him but to retire. He was accordingly recalled by his mistress in December to bask in her royal smile, although he did not actually resign his authority till the following March 31. Elizabeth would not hear a word against her favourite. In her letter of recall she threw the blame entirely on her allies; she upbraided them for their ingratitude, their breach of faith, their false and malicious slanders against the Earl, and concluded this marvellous epistle with a gracious promise that 'out of compassion for

Marginal notes:
Leicester returns. July, 1587. The discontent increases.

Leicester finally recalled. Dec. 1587.

---

[1] Alexander had become Duke of Parma on the death of his father Ottavio, September 1586.

their pitiful condition, she would continue her subsidies for the present, and that if she concluded a peace with Spain, she would take the same care for their country as for her own.'

It would be unfair to hold Leicester altogether responsible for the failure of this ill-starred expedition. Some of the leading men, like Hohenlo, were violent men, especially when in their cups; the parties and factions which divided the Netherlanders were not of Leicester's making; the complicated and loose character of the government, and the religious difficulties, were sure to lead to trouble; except in the provinces of Holland and Zealand, little zeal was at this time shown in the cause, and Stanley and York were not the only traitors. But if the task imposed on Leicester had been a delicate one, certainly no person was less fitted than he to carry it through. His arrogance, his imperiousness, and his implacable temper made him many personal enemies, and led him to chafe against any control or contradiction; his vanity caused him to listen to the flattery of his creatures, and to break with the leading statesmen of the time, because they dared criticise his conduct; his strong Calvinistic prejudices ill fitted him to hold the balance amid the religious parties of the Netherlands; and if he was courageous and open-handed, he was certainly neither a capable statesman nor a good general. Yet, after all, the chief fault lay in the policy of the Queen herself. Her refusal to accept the sovereignty and throw herself heartily into the cause of the Netherlands, the niggardliness of her supplies, and the harshness of her terms—above all, her suspicious negotiations with Parma—these were the chief causes of complaint. Nor was this conduct the result of mere caprice. Well aware of the preparations of Philip against England, she still vainly hoped that, if she refrained from the irretrievable step of assuming the sovereignty, she might make use of her position in the Netherlands to secure a lasting and honourable peace for herself and them. She accordingly allowed herself to be

Review of his administration.

deluded by the comedy of negotiation, which Alexander was playing, at his master's orders, with the sole intention of deceiving her till the time for action was ripe. With the same idle hope, she had disavowed the action of Sir Francis Drake, who, in the preceding April, had 'singed Philip's beard' by entering the ports of Cadiz and of Lisbon, and destroying some two hundred and fifty vessels. Her conduct was in keeping with her policy to the Protestants in Scotland and in France—a policy which has been generally praised, if not for its honesty, at least for its cleverness. It has been asserted that by this trimming attitude she prevented a coalition of the united forces of Catholicism, before which England must have succumbed; however true that may have been in the earlier years of her reign, it was certainly so no longer, for Philip was now determined on his invasion of England. Once,

indeed, he had feared the designs of the Guises; but the Duke of Guise was now in his pay. In January, 1584, Mendoza, Philip's ambassador, who had been summarily dismissed from England on account of his known connection with Throgmorton's plot, informed Elizabeth 'that as he had failed to please the Queen as a minister of peace, she would in future force him to try and satisfy her in war,' and he had been true to his word. Removing to France, he became thenceforth Philip's most active agent in making preparations. In May, 1586, the Queen of Scots had ceded to Philip all her claims on the crown of England, unless James accepted Catholicism before her death, and her execution finally removed all his scruples. Under these circumstances, Philip was determined to endure the ill-disguised acts of enmity on the part of the English Queen no longer. She had aided the rebels in the Netherlands; she had supported the Pretender to the crown of Portugal; above all, the piratical attacks of the English sea-dogs were bleeding Spain to death. England must be conquered. If that could be effected, the Netherlands would be soon subdued; and, since the victory of the League

Philip determines to invade England.

seemed assured in France, Philip might well hope soon to be master in London, Amsterdam, and Paris. Had Elizabeth at the time of Leicester's expedition cast all fears to the winds and thrown her energies once for all on the side of Henry of Navarre, and on that of the Netherlands, Philip would have had his hands too full to strike. Even as it was, Alexander was prevented from co-operating in the attack on England by those very Netherlanders whose sympathy Elizabeth had done her best to alienate.

Five months after the departure of the Earl, the Armada, under the Duke of Medina Sidonia, sailed. The scheme for invading England had been elaborately planned between Philip and Parma. The Armada was to proceed from Lisbon to the throat of the English Channel, off Calais. There it was to wait for Alexander, who was to come forth with his army, numbering some 17,000 men, shipped on the flat-bottomed boats he had prepared, and assume the command of the whole expedition. The Channel was then to be crossed. The Duke of Parma was to land and march on London, while Medina Sidonia was to guard the harbours from the Dutch and English fleets. The first experiences of the Spanish fleet were not encouraging. Many of the ships proved unseaworthy, Medina was forced to put into Corunna to refit, and it was not until the 28th of July, that the Armada sighted the Lizard. The delay had been of value. Elizabeth, although she had continued her negotiations with Parma to the very last, had made some preparations. On land, indeed, little had been done ; but when the Spaniards appeared off Plymouth a motley fleet of some one hundred and ninety-seven ships had been collected. Of these only thirty-four belonged to the government ; the rest had been provided by the merchants of London and other towns, or by private individuals.

The Armada sails. May 30, 1588.

The Armada sights the Lizard. July 28.

It appears, however, that the strength of the Armada has been exaggerated. Although it is impossible to speak with absolute accuracy, it would appear that the number of the Spanish vessels actually engaged was some one hundred and twenty, while that of the English was about one hundred and seventy. The tonnage of the individual Spanish ships was greater, but in everything else the advantage was on the English side. They had more guns—a weapon which the Spaniards, depending as they did on boarding their adversary, despised. The number of effective fighting men was probably greater than that of the Spaniards, if we omit the galley slaves; certainly the proportion of sailors to the soldiers was greater in the English fleet; the sailors were far better seamen than those on the Spanish ships, and they had amongst their captains such men as Drake, Hawkins, and Frobisher, who had spent their lives at sea. The Spanish ships, if higher and of greater size, and therefore dangerous at close quarters, were unwieldy and undermanned. In a word, as Drake well said, if the English could 'fight loose and at large,' their victory was assured; and this they succeeded

Running engagement up the Channel. July 30-Aug. 6.

in doing. In a running engagement up the Channel, which lasted eight days, the English hung round the Spanish fleet, generally to windward of them, poured their shot into the hulls of the Spanish ships, and were away again before they had suffered much punishment. The English fired low; the Spaniards, anxious to disable their enemies preparatory to boarding, fired at the masts and rigging, and often missed their aim. When, therefore, the Armada at last reached

Armada in Calais roads. Aug. 6-7. The fire- ships.

the Calais roads, the absurdity of the idea that they could drive the English fleet from the sea was already palpable; and unless that could be done, it would have been madness for the Duke of Parma to venture out to sea in his flat-bottomed boats, encumbered as they would be by troops. This he himself had foreseen; but in any case, the swarm of Dutch craft which lined the coast prevented him from the attempt. Nothing clearly could be done unless the Armada could command the sea, and this it completely failed to do. On the night of August 7, the English sent six fire-ships against their enemies as they lay at anchor. The fire-ships might easily have been towed aside by boats, for they had no explosives on board. But the Spaniards remembered the fire-ships of Antwerp; a shameful panic seized the men; the great hulks slipped their anchors; two were set on fire, others became entangled with each other, and the rest of the fleet were driven seaward by awkward squalls which sprang up from west-south-west. On the following morning, the English pursued; and in the engagement which ensued, while the English lost not a single vessel and scarce a hundred men, the Spaniards had sixteen of their ships disabled and lost four to five thousand men. Unfortunately the English were now short of powder and of shot and of provisions.[1] The Lord-Admiral, Lord Howard of Effingham, however, 'put on a brag countenance and gave them chase, as though they wanted nothing,' and the Spaniards, afraid to face the English ships again, were fain to drop before the wind which soon began to freshen into half a gale from the west, and threatened to drive the fleet upon the Zealand sands. A sudden shifting of the wind to the south-west saved them from this disaster; but the change was only the prelude to a violent gale, which, finally bursting upon the half-disabled ships on August 14, scattered them far and wide. Of the one hundred and thirty-four sail which left Corunna in July, some fifty-three alone, painfully and one by one, found their way back to Spain, and even these were so damaged as to be useless.

Final engagement. August 8.

The great enterprise of Philip had been ruined by the combined action of the English and the Dutch. Yet, unfortunately, the disagreements caused by the expedition of Leicester were long in disappearing. On the retirement of the Earl, Maurice of Nassau, who was already Stattholder of Holland and

---

[1] This is generally attributed to the parsimony of the Queen. But on this and other popular errors cf. *State Papers relating to Defeat of the Spanish Armada*, Navy Records Society, Introduction.

Zealand, had been appointed Captain-general of those provinces ; [1] but his authority was disputed by Leicester's party,

Troubles in Holland after departure of Leicester. more especially in the provinces of Utrecht, Friesland, and in North Holland. They declared that the Earl had only temporarily retired, and refused obedience to Maurice and the States-

General. The difficulties were further increased by quarrels
with Lord Willoughby, who had been left in command of the
English forces, and was himself an adherent of the Earl.
Under these circumstances, Alexander had easily reduced most
of the contumacious cities ; and, on April 10, a quarrel between
Maurice and the English officer, Sir Robert Wingfield, enabled
him to secure the important city of Gertruydenberg. In the

Dutch and English expedition to Portugal. April-July, 1589. same month, however, a joint Dutch and English expedition was made against Portugal, which, although it failed in its immediate object—the restoration of the pretender Don Antonio to the crown—did some damage to Spanish shipping,

and gave earnest of a better feeling between those two
countries, whose interests were so closely knit together. In

Breda secured by a stratagem. Feb. 28, 1590. the following February, a clever stratagem, heroi-cally carried out, won Breda for the patriots, and during the following summer, Maurice began to display his military powers by the reduction of

several places of importance. Nevertheless, the dissensions
still continued. The two English councillors, and the commander of the English auxiliary forces, who, according to the
original treaty, still retained a seat in the Council of State,
were ever quarrelling with the Hollanders. The province of
Holland, which contributed at least a half to the expenses of
the war, did not consider its representation on the State
Council an adequate one ; the States-General, in which the
influence of the delegates of Holland was predominant, began

[1] In 1590, Maurice was also appointed Stattholder and Captain-general
of Guelderland, Utrecht, Overyssel ; but he never was appointed Captain-
general of the whole Union.

to disregard the authority of the Council, while its authority in turn was often disputed by the other Provincial Councils. It was fortunate, under these circumstances, that the attention of Philip was at this time directed elsewhere. In France alone his fortunes seemed prospering. If the victory of the League in that country could be secured, England and the Netherlands might yet be conquered. Besides, Philip was becoming jealous of the Duke of Parma. No one could serve Philip long without arousing his suspicions; and Alexander had no lack of enemies who spread rumours of his intention to make himself independent in the Netherlands.[1] He was therefore neglected, and with troops mutinous for want of pay, operations on a large scale were impossible. Finally, in spite of his remonstrances, Farnese was ordered to 'talk no more of difficulties' but to march into France to the assistance of the Duke of Mayenne, August 3, 1590 (cf. p. 434),

Farnese marches into France. Aug. 3, 1590.

and although on December 3, Parma returned from his French expedition, it was with enfeebled health, exhausted funds, and an army seriously reduced in numbers.

Maurice at last had his opportunity. This second[2] son of William the Silent, and, through his mother, the grandson of Maurice of Saxony, whom he resembled in feature and in character, had not as yet attracted much attention. Some indeed thought him nothing more than a petulant and unmannerly schoolboy; shrewder observers, however, admitted that he was a man of 'deep if sullen' wit, and that as he grew up to manhood he did not indulge in the vice of deep drinking so prevalent among Dutchmen of that day. With politics he had hitherto concerned himself but little, and had been content to follow the lead of

Early life of Maurice.

---

[1] That Alexander had been approached on this subject is true; but that he ever entertained such a proposal there is not the slightest proof.

[2] The eldest son, Philip, had been kidnapped from school and sent to Spain in 1567. When he returned in 1596, he had become a Catholic and a supporter of Spanish rule.

Barneveld. Meanwhile he had devoted himself to mathe-
matics, the science of fortification, and to tactics, and subsequently, assisted by his cousin, Lewis William, Stattholder
of Friesland—an odd little man with bullet head, bright eyes,
His military   and shaggy brown beard—had turned to military
reforms.   reform. A more elaborate system of drill was
introduced, which might give greater elasticity to the army in
the field ; appreciating the value of fire-arms, he increased
the proportion of musketeers to pikemen in the infantry,
and armed the cavalry with carbines.   To this he added the
use of the spade, which had hitherto been despised as beneath
the dignity of the soldier, and formed a school of engineers.
In his anxiety to put an end to the system of pillage which
disgraced the armies of the day, and which had made the
Spaniards a terror, he severely punished such offences ; while,
to remove all pretext for such conduct, he was careful to
prevent the peculation which had been rife among the officers,
and insisted on the soldiers being punctually paid.   By these
means he had succeeded, in spite of much hostile criticism
and ridicule, in making the small army of the Hollanders a
thoroughly effective one ; while he himself at the age of
twenty-three had become a master of scientific fortification
and siege operations.   The moment had now come to use his
remodelled forces.   On May 24, 1591, he laid siege to
                 Zutphen on the Yssel, and in six days reduced
Exploits of   that town, which had hitherto proved impregnable.
Maurice.
May-July,   The reduction of Deventer, on the same river,
1591.   followed on June 10.   Sixteen days later, he
appeared before the walls of Groningen, and reduced several
places in the neighbourhood.   Farnese, aroused by the news
Continued   of his exploits, attempted in July, to make a
success of   diversion by attacking the fort of Knodsenburg
Maurice.
Sept.-Oct.,   on the Waal, but was outmanœuvred by his
1591.   young antagonist, and was forced to retreat, and
in August was compelled by illness to retire to Spa.
Maurice now took the town of Hulst on September 24,

and on October 21, Nymwegen, at the frontier of the Netherlands, on the Waal.

In January, 1592, the Duke of Parma was peremptorily ordered by Philip to advance once more into France. Maurice, thus free from all apprehension, again took the field. After a siege of forty-four days, the town of Steenwyck fell (July 3), on the 26th, the fortress of Coeworden capitulated, and thus the keys to the districts of Friesland, Groningen, and Drenthe were in his hands. Thus in two

Alexander's second expedition into France. Further conquests of Maurice.

summers, Maurice had not only secured once more the control of the Waal, but had driven the Spaniards from most of the strongholds they had hitherto held in the northern provinces of Guelderland, Overyssel, and Drenthe; Groningen alone remained, and this was to be reduced in the following year.

In the winter of 1592, Alexander, Duke of Parma, the only man whose military genius Maurice had need to fear, passed away. He had returned from his second French expedition at the end of May, a dying man, but even if he had been himself, the suspicions of Philip would have effectually paralysed his

Death of Alexander of Parma. Dec. 3, 1592.

efforts; for that jealous King, persuaded by enemies of the Duke that he had designs on the sovereignty of the Southern Netherlands, had already appointed his successor, and had intended to remove him by force if necessary. Never were suspicions more unjust; and Farnese, in obedience to his master's orders, was preparing a third expedition into France, when he was suddenly struck down at Arras (December 3). Thus, at the age of forty-seven, passed away the first soldier of his age, and one of the most devoted servants Philip ever had. The only blot on his political career is to be found in the unscrupulous character of his diplomacy. But even here, he was at least faithful in his baseness; if he deceived others, it was in obedience to his master's orders, and the suspicion with which Philip treated him in his later moments was as cruel as it was unjust. The fourteen years of Parma's governorship may be looked upon as the critical period in Philip's reign; they witnessed the final move in the political game which the King of Spain was playing for the mastery of Western Europe, and when Parma died the game was nearly lost. Yet such success as Philip had, was largely due to Alexander. Although the Duke had failed in the impossible task of subduing the northern provinces, he had at least secured the southern and western ones for Spain, and postponed the triumph of Henry of Navarre. Had Philip had more such servants, he might have succeeded better.

On the death of Parma, the government had been provisionally placed in the hands of Count Peter Ernest Mansfeld, a veteran now in his dotage. The real successor was to be the Archduke Ernest, brother of the Emperor Rudolf. The Archduke was Philip's nephew. He proposed to marry him to the Infanta and to gain for him the crown of France (cf. p. 435). Thus, Philip hoped that the Spanish Netherlands might be united to France, and ruled by a submissive relation. At least, Philip seemed determined that the new Governor-general should not be a man to excite his fears. The Archduke was thoroughly incapable, very indolent, very fat, fond of drinking and of gambling; withal a melancholy man, a victim to gout, and one who wept when complaints were made to him. It was not until January, 1594, that the Archduke arrived in Brussels. By that time his chances of the French throne seemed remote, and his arrival with no troops and no money, but 'with 670 gentlemen, pages, and cooks, and 534 horses to draw his coaches,' did not augur very well. A jealous scramble for places ensued; the proud Spanish and Flemish nobles were insulted by his want of courtesy, and the soldiery mutinied for want of pay. Under these circumstances Maurice was able to reduce the only two important places which were held by the Spaniards in the northern provinces. On

[margin notes:]
Archduke Ernest appointed Governor. Jan. 1594.

Maurice reduces Gertruydenberg, June 24, 1593; and Groningen, July 22, 1594.

June 24, 1593, the successful siege of Gertruydenberg gave him the command of the Meuse. On the 22nd July of the following year (1594), the taking of the town of Gröningen, after sixty-five days' siege, practically secured that province.

After the death of the Archduke Ernest, which occurred on February 20, 1595, the attention of Philip was once more concentrated on France. In January, Henry iv. had at last declared open war against Spain, and the army of the Netherlands was required for service against him Fuentes, therefore, who held the post of Governor provisionally, and the Cardinal Archduke Albert, brother of Ernest, who was appointed in January 1596, both took part in the campaigns in the east of France (cf. p. 440), and had but little time to give to the Netherlands. Death of Archduke Ernest, Feb. 20, 1595. Succeeded by the Archduke Cardinal Albert, Jan. 1596.

The Dutch, free from immediate apprehension, were therefore enabled to share in the brilliant English expedition to Cadiz, which ended in the destruction of a Spanish fleet and in the sack of the city (July 2, 1596). In August, indeed, the Archduke Albert succeeded Dutch and English expedition to Cadiz. July, 1596.

in wresting the town of Hulst from Maurice ; but in October, Holland joined the League which Henry iv. and Elizabeth had made against Spain in the previous August, and on the 24th of the following January (1597), Maurice decisively defeated the Archduke at Turnhout near Gertruydenberg. This important Triple league against Spain. Aug.-Oct., 1596.

victory was followed by a three months' campaign, from August to October 1597, on the frontiers of the duchy of Cleves—which was being used by the Spaniards as a basis of operations against the disobedient provinces—a campaign in which, by the reduction of nine cities and five castles, Maurice materially strengthened his eastern frontier on the Rhine. Successful campaign of Maurice. Jan.-Oct., 1597.

The Dutch had entered the League with France and England in the hope that they might by such help finally secure the recognition of their independence. But Henry was now weary of war, and had already opened those negotiations which, in spite of the remonstrances of the

Dutch, ended in the Peace of Vervins (May 2, 1598, cf. p. 444). As the recognition of their independence was denied them, the Dutch declined to take part in the treaty. Nevertheless, the Peace was accompanied by some change in the position of the obedient provinces; for as Henry would no longer brook the presence of the Spanish King on his eastern frontier, Philip consented to renounce his claim to them, as well as to Franche-Comté, on condition that the sovereignty should be conferred on the Archduke Albert, who was to marry the Infanta Clara Eugenia Isabella (May, 1598). It was, however, stipulated that these provinces should fall again to Spain in the event of there being no issue of the marriage; Philip had reason to believe that the Archduke could have no children, and by a secret treaty, his nephew acknowledged the suzerainty of Spain, and promised to allow Spanish garrisons to hold the cities of Antwerp, Ghent, and Cambray. A desultory war, which did not materially affect the issue, continued between the Spanish and disobedient provinces till 1609. A truce of twelve years then virtually recognised the independence of the United Netherlands—an independence which was not, however, formally acknowledged till the Peace of Westphalia in 1648.

The seven United Provinces which thus broke away from Spain were Guelderland, Utrecht, Friesland, Overyssel, Gröningen, Zealand, and Holland. These occupied a stretch of country on the shores of the German Ocean, running from the duchy of East Friesland to the estuary of the Scheldt, both sides of which they held. They thus completely commanded the various mouths of the Rhine, as well as those of the Meuse and the Scheldt. On the east and the south their boundaries were East Friesland, the territories of the bishopric of Münster, the duchy of Cleves, the bishopric of Liège, and South Brabant. Of the United Provinces, the sea was at once the enemy and the friend; a large proportion of their territory had been reclaimed from its embrace, and it was only kept back by expensive dykes. Some of the water of the Rhine had even to be conveyed to the sea in canals above the level of the fields (poulders), yet so much below the level of high tide that this had to be kept back by gates, which opened and shut as it ebbed and flowed. Yet it was this very sea which they had so often called to their assistance against their human foes, and which gave them the trade upon which their prosperity depended. The condition of these provinces, compared with that of the obedient provinces, had undergone a marvellous change since the accession of Philip. At the commencement of his reign, Flanders and Brabant were by far the most wealthy districts; Antwerp was one of the great entrepots for the trade of Europe, and their other great towns were the centres of busy industries; while their contributions to the royal exchequer equalled those of all the other provinces together. At the close of the struggle these provinces were a desert; the wolves, we are told, roamed over the vacant fields; the looms were silent, and whole streets in the towns were empty; trade had shifted to the north, and Amsterdam had usurped the place of Antwerp. Already the Dutch were becoming the carriers of Europe, and taking the lead in colonisation to the east. Yet the young State was threatened by many dangers. The jealousy of England for her trade was likely to prove formidable, and the internal dangers were many. The government was a loose federation of provinces of very unequal size and wealth, and each province a federation of municipal councils, which, with the exception of those in Overyssel and Groningen, were filled up by co-optation, or by election on a very narrow franchise. The authority of the

[marginal note: Contrast in condition of the United Netherlands and the Spanish Netherlands.]

[marginal note: The constitutional and other difficulties.]

States-General, therefore, which was the legislative assembly of the federation, and that of the States Council which formed the Executive, was continually being disputed by the Provincial Councils; while the burgher aristocracy which ruled the towns was disliked by the nobles in the country, and looked upon with jealousy by the unenfranchised. The predominant power of the province of Holland, which contributed more than half of the annual budget, and the existence of the Stattholder and Captain-general,[1] who held the supreme military and executive power, no doubt gave a practical unity to the government. But there was ever a tendency on the part of the Stadtholder to break away from the burgher aristocracy, and to base a more extended sovereignty and a more united kingdom on the support of the unprivileged classes. Religious differences embittered these dissensions; the burghers generally supported the new Arminian views, the Stadtholder those of the more extreme Calvinists; and thus there arose two parties whose quarrels were often in the future to shake the federation to its base.

[1] Maurice after 1590 was Stattholder and Captain-general of Holland, Zealand, Guelderland, Utrecht, and Overyssel, but never Captain-general or Stattholder of the Union.

CHAPTER IX

THE REFORMATION AND THE CIVIL WARS IN FRANCE

§ 1. *The Rise of the Huguenots during the Reign of Francis I.*

Francis and the Reformers—Massacre of the Vaudois—Henry II. and the Re-
formers—Parties at Accession of Francis II.—Tumult of Amboise—
Accession of Charles IX.—States-General and Colloquy of Poissy—
Massacre of Vassy—First Civil War—Dreux—Assassination of Francis of
Guise—Pacification of Amboise—Second Civil War—St. Denis—Edict of
Longjumeau—Third Civil War—Jarnac and Moncontour—Peace of St.
Germain—Massacre of St. Bartholomew—Fourth Civil War—Treaty of
La Rochelle—Change in Views of Huguenots—Fifth Civil War—Accession
of Henry III.—Peace of Monsieur—Guise and the Catholic Leagues—
Sixth and Seventh Civil Wars—Treaties of Bergerac and Fleix—France
and the Netherlands—The Catholic League—Treaty of Joinville—Eighth
Civil War—Courtras—The Barricades—Assassination of Henry of Guise
and Henry III.—Henry IV. and the League—Ninth Civil War—Arques
and Ivry—Henry 'receives instruction' and enters Paris—War with
Spain—Edict of Nantes—Peace of Vervins—Conclusion.

WHILE France, in pursuit of her policy of opposition to the
House of Hapsburg, had been allying herself with the Protestants of Germany, heresy had been growing   The first
apace within her own borders. Jacques Lefèvre   French
of Etaples may fairly claim the title of father of   Reformers.
French Protestantism. A lecturer on theology at Paris, he
had in a commentary on the Epistles of St. Paul (1512) taught
the Doctrine of Justification by Faith five years before Luther
had denounced indulgences. In 1521, he had, under the
patronage of Briçonnet, the Bishop, collected a small band
of men at Meaux in Champagne, of whom Farel of Dauphiné

was the most important, and had also influenced Louis de Berquin, the friend of Erasmus, who was a nobleman and a courtier.

The rise of these new opinions had at once excited the fears of the Sorbonne or theological faculty in the University of Paris, and of the 'Parlement' of Paris. But Francis had no love for either of these institutions. The 'Parlement' had opposed him in the matter of the Concordat (cf. p. 81), the Sorbonne had viewed with jealousy his new foundation, the 'Collège de France' (cf. p. 218). Moreover, he disliked the monks and friars, while his sympathy with literature and culture, the redeeming traits of his otherwise worthless character, as well as the influence of his sister, Margaret of Navarre, led him to tolerate the new opinions; indeed, he is said to have entertained the idea of founding a literary and philosophic institution in France with Erasmus at its head. Accordingly in 1523, he saved de Berquin from the 'Parlement,' and had he been victorious at Pavia he might have continued this policy of toleration. His defeat and imprisonment, however, altered the condition of the Protestants for the worse, for his mother, Louise of Savoy, took advantage of his absence to crush out heresy. Leclerc, a wool-carder of Meaux, was burnt, July, 1525; Briçonnet was ordered to disperse the brotherhood of Meaux (October 1525); and de Berquin was again arrested (January, 1526). He was, indeed, once more saved from his enemies by Francis, who, on his return to France, even appointed Lefèvre tutor to his children. But a change soon came over the policy of the fickle King. His political necessities demanded an alliance with the Pope, who was forming the Holy League against the Emperor (cf. p. 184), and with the clergy at home, who could supply him with money wherewith to continue the war. He had never sympathised with the religious views of the reformers, but only with the literary side of the movement; while the iconoclastic

Francis at first inclined to toleration.

Persecution begins in absence of Francis. 1525.

Francis adopts a policy of persecution. 1529.

and other extravagances of some of the more hot-headed reformers gave colour to the suggestion that the movement had a political significance. De Berquin, although in no way responsible for these extravagances, refused to listen to the timid caution of Erasmus 'not to disturb the hornets,' and in consequence was seized again and executed (April, 1529).

In 1534, an intemperate placard on the abuses of the Mass not unnaturally increased the indignation of the King; in 1535, the outbreak of the Anabaptists in Münster still further frightened him; and in January 1545, convinced by the misrepresentations of the 'Parlement' of Aix that the Vaudois of Provence were attempting to set up a republic, he gave the fatal order which, whether he intended it or no, *Massacre of* led to a massacre. More than twenty towns *the Vaudois.* and villages were destroyed, and some three *1545.* thousand Protestants in the valley of the Durance perished. The reign of Francis closed in the following year with the execution of the 'fourteen' poor artisans at Meaux, the cradle of French Protestantism.

§ 2. *The Reign of Henry II., 1547-1559.*

Meanwhile, the French Protestants had come under the influence of Calvin. In 1535, he had dedicated his *Institutes* to Francis I., in the hope, it is said, of *French Pro-* convincing the King that his doctrines were not *testantism* dangerous, and from that moment the French *becomes* *Calvinistic* rapidly assimilated the teaching of their great *and* countryman. French Protestantism now became *aggressive.* dissociated from the literary movement with which it had hitherto been connected, its churches were organised on the democratic system of Geneva, and the movement soon became for the first time political and aggressive. Under these circumstances it is no wonder that persecution increased after the death of Francis I., especially when we remember that the young King (he was twenty-nine) had not the literary sympathies of his father, and that the Constable de Montmorenci and the Guises, who had been out of favour during the later years of Francis, were again recalled. Accordingly,

Increased persecution under Henry II.

at the beginning of the reign of Henry II., a special chamber of the 'Parlement' was erected to try cases of heresy, which gained the name of 'La Chambre Ardente,' from the number of victims it sent to the flames. In 1551, the Edict of Châteaubriant gave to the ecclesiastical courts jurisdiction in matters of heresy without appeal to the 'Parlement,' and in 1557, an attempt was made to introduce the Inquisition into France; Paul IV. published a Bull appointing a commission consisting of the three cardinals of Lorraine, Bourbon, and Châtillon, with the power of delegating their authority.

In spite of these severe measures the number of converts grew apace, and this was the chief motive which induced Henry II. to conclude the treaty of Cateau Cambrésis in April, 1559. Although there appears to be no foundation for the assertion that the Kings of France and Spain bound themselves by a secret clause of that treaty to unite against the heretics, yet negotiations to that effect certainly followed.

In June, Philip proposed to aid the French King in exterminating the Protestants; and Henry, while declining the offer, suggested a joint expedition against Geneva. The political rivalry, however, of the two countries was too deep to permit of joint action at present, and Henry pursued his course

Opposition of the 'Parlement' of Paris.

alone. Here he met with unlooked-for opposition on the part of the 'Parlement.' Heresy in France had hitherto been within the cognisance of the civil courts, and the 'Parlement' had therefore protested as well against the Edict of Châteaubriant as against the Bull of Paul IV. On the latter point the King had given way, but the other cause of dispute remained, and was aggravated by the appearance of a moderate party in the 'Chambre de la Tournelle,' or criminal session of the

' Parlement,' who declared that persecution was ineffective, and that they would not punish heresy with death. The King was most indignant, and was on the point of proceeding against the leaders, Du Faur and Anne de Bourg, when, at the tournament held to commemorate the Peace, the lance of Montgomery laid him in the dust and transferred the crown to his son, Francis II., a youth of sixteen (July, 1559).

§ 3. *The Reign of Francis II., July,* 1559—*December,* 1560

The Protestants, or Huguenots,[1] as they began to be called, were now too powerful to be put down by such persecution as was possible. They numbered some 400,000, of whom the largest proportion were either burghers and tradesmen of some substance, or belonged to the smaller nobility, a military class who were only too ready to appeal to arms. Nor were they destitute of leaders from the higher nobility and from those of influence at court, notably Condé and Coligny. And yet, had a strong and popular King succeeded, or had there existed in France a well-knit and healthy constitution, some compromise might have been effected, or, failing that, the new opinions might have been at once suppressed by a vigorous use of force. But France was suffering from the evil results of the prolonged foreign war, and from the misguided policy of her Kings since Louis XI. The financial distress, the heavy and unequal taxation, which fell almost exclusively on the lower classes, caused widespread discontent against the government. The bureaucracy and the judicature, largely owing to the system of purchase, were hopelessly corrupt, and had lost respect. The Church, though exceedingly wealthy (its revenues amounted to two-fifths of the total revenue of the country), was suffering from the effects of the Concordat ; its benefices

Condition of Huguenots at accession of Francis II.

Disorganised condition of France.

---

[1] Probably a corruption of the German word ' Eidgenossen ' (confederates), first applied to the Protestant party in Geneva.

were monopolised by the nobility and the courtiers, and absorbed in a few hands; thus John, the Cardinal of Lorraine, held three archbishoprics, seven bishoprics, and four abbeys. Its leaders were for the most part men of secular interests, swayed by the factions of the court, and caring little for the spiritual needs of their dioceses. The States-General had been rarely called of late, and had lost all constitutional life. The towns, with no real share in the government of the country, were inclined to stand apart, and depend upon themselves. The greater nobility aimed either at controlling the crown, or, failing that, at establishing themselves as hereditary governors of their provinces. The smaller nobility, excluded from trade and from all professions except those of the army and the Church, now that the war was over, either crowded into the Church, to secularise it more completely, or formed a turbulent military class who welcomed the chance of renewed war. France, in short, nominally under the control of a closely centralised monarchy, was suffering from that worst form of anarchy which comes of a bureaucracy when it has become disorganised. To complete the misfortunes of France, the House of Valois was represented by four boys of no character, intellect, or physique, who were the victims of court intrigue and factions, which were to make the crown still more unpopular, and soon to hurry the country into civil war.

The three most influential parties among the nobles were led by the Bourbons, the Constable Anne de Montmorenci, and the Guises. Of these the Bourbons stood nearest the throne. The eldest, Antony of Bourbon, was King of Navarre, in right of his wife Jeanne of Navarre, the daughter of Margaret, the tolerant sister of Francis I. But, although he adopted the Calvinistic views of his wife, and was popular and a good soldier, his weaknesses and irresolution unfitted him for the leadership, which fell to his youngest brother Louis de Condé, who also leaned to the new opinions, and was a man of far more character.

The Bourbons.

The second brother Charles, Cardinal of Bourbon, remained a Catholic, dissociated himself from the policy of his family, and subsequently strove for a brief season to be called Charles x. of France. Closely connected with the Bourbons stood the two nephews of the Constable—Gaspard de Coligny, Admiral of France, and D'Andelot, Colonel-General of the infantry, both strenuous Huguenots. The eldest Odet, Cardinal of Châtillon, although sympathising with the reformers, was never of much weight.

The Constable Anne de Montmorenci, who headed the second party, was a devoted Catholic, and a stern soldier, whose severity and devotions in time of war had led men to say, 'Beware of the Constable's Pater Nosters.' His policy had ever been that of alliance with Spain and suppression of heresy— *The Constable Anne de Montmorenci.* a policy which had lately triumphed in the Peace of Cateau Cambrésis. Yet his jealousy of the Guises and of the queen-mother caused him for the present to join the party of the Bourbons.

Lastly came the Guises. This family, the cadet branch of the House of Lorraine, was founded by Claude, second son of Réné of Lorraine, the grandson of Réné le Bon, of Anjou, through his daughter Iolante. *The Guises.* Claude had earned a reputation by his defence of the eastern frontier after the defeat of Pavia, 1525, and had married his daughter Mary to James v. of Scotland. In reward for his services, Francis i. had erected Guise, Aumale, and Mayenne into duchies which Claude left on his death (1550) to two of his sons, Francis, Duke of Guise, and Claude, Duke of Aumale; while two others, Charles and Louis, entered the Church to become the Cardinals of Lorraine and Guise. Duke Francis had surpassed his father's fame by his defence of Metz (1552-1553), and by the taking of Calais (1558). Ostentatious and open-handed, he courted popularity, and what he lacked in statesmanship was supplied by his younger brother Charles, the Cardinal, who, in spite of his avarice and his arrogance, was scrupulous in the outward observance of his clerical duties, a master of diplomacy, and an accomplished scholar of persuasive speech. Although we must wait till the next generation for the full development of the schemes of this ambitious family—schemes which no doubt expanded as the opportunities presented themselves—yet the foundations were already laid by these two remarkable men. The key to the policy of the Guises is to be found in the fact that they were only half Frenchmen, and that they were only remotely connected with the royal family. Looked upon as upstarts by the older nobility, and afraid of being excluded from power by the Bourbons, they asserted their descent from the House of Anjou, and even from the Karolings. The family of Anjou, if still existing in the male line, would have been nearer to the throne than the Bourbons themselves. But the male line had died out with Charles of Maine (1481), and accordingly the Guises pressed the claims of the female line, through which they could trace their descent from Réné of Anjou. Their half-foreign extraction presented greater difficulties. These they had no doubt in part removed by their military exploits in defending France. Now that the war was over, they naturally adopted the cause of Catholicism, which gave them a certain popularity among the lower classes, more especially of Paris, which city remained intensely Catholic throughout. Their foreign policy, although Catholic, was not Spanish at this date, for they dreamt of supporting the claim of Mary, Queen of Scots, wife of Francis ii., to the throne of England, and of uniting the three countries into a strong monarchy which might balance the Austro-Spanish power.

Amid these conflicting factions, belonging to none of them, yet anxious to control them all, stood Catherine de Medici, Catherine the Queen-mother. 'What,' said Henry iv. of de Medici. her subsequently, 'could a poor woman have done, with her husband dead, five small children upon her hands, and two families who were scheming to seize the throne

—our own and the Guises? I am astonished that she did not do even worse.' The clew to the policy of this much-abused woman lies in her foreign extraction and her previous life. A Florentine and a Medici, she was unpopular in France, while she failed to secure the love of her husband, Henry II., and saw her influence eclipsed by Diana of Poictiers, his mistress. This exclusion from all influence working on a jealous nature, had bred an intense passion to rule. Had direct rule now been possible for her, Catherine might have done well enough; for though devoid of moral elevation, she was not vicious. She was very industrious and painstaking, and anxious to please. She wished to maintain the independence of the country against the designs of Spain, as well as the authority of the crown which was threatened by the internal factions; if a Catholic, she was certainly no bigot, and would probably have granted at least a contemptuous toleration to the Huguenots. But when power was denied her, and her position was threatened, like a true Medici she betook herself to intrigue—so often the resource of the weak—and pursued a policy of balance which was all the more fatal because it did not succeed.

As Francis was over thirteen, it was not necessary to have a regency. None the less, it would have been natural that Antony of Navarre, as the nearest male relation of The Guises full age, should be called to power. This was, in power. however, prevented by the Guises. Uncles of the Queen, they succeeded in obtaining complete control of the young King; and Catherine, seeing that they were too strong to be opposed, jealous of Navarre, and disliking Montmorenci on account of his insolent behaviour to her during her husband's life, threw herself on their support. Montmorenci was dismissed, and retired to his estates at Chantilly; Coligny was deprived of his governorship of Picardy, nearly all the governors on whom the Guises could not depend were removed, and while the Duke controlled the army, the Cardinal of Lorraine became the head of the civil administration. Having thus

monopolised the government of the kingdom, the Guises
resumed the procedure against the refractory members of the
'Parlement,' which had been stayed by the death of Henry II.
Anne de Bourg, condemned by a special commission, was
executed in spite of his appeal against the legality of the
court, and the others were suspended or imprisoned.

But the triumph of the Guises was not to go unchallenged,
and a formidable opposition was aroused in which their
political and religious opponents joined hands.   The nobility
were indignant at being deprived of their governorships, and
asserted the right of the princes of the blood against these
upstart foreigners.   The heavy taxation and the poor success
of the war in Scotland, where Mary of Guise, assisted by her
brothers, was carrying on an unequal struggle against the
'Lords of the Congregation,' added to the grievances.   Those
who wished to revive the authority of the States-General seized
the opportunity to attack the despotic government of the
Guises, and the religious discontent served as a rallying-point.
In the spring of 1560, De la Renaudie, a noble of Perigord,
formed a plot to remove the King, who was at Amboise, from

The Tumult of Amboise. March 17, 1560. the hands of the Guises, and to place the Prince
of Condé at the head of the government.   The
plot, however, was betrayed.   De la Renaudie
was killed in a skirmish, and the other conspirators cruelly
punished, some being hung from the balcony of the castle.

Although the 'Tumult of Amboise' was by no means
exclusively confined to the Protestants, it marks the moment
when they finally became a political and aggressive party, and
when they were joined by the smaller nobility of the provinces;
while it furnished the government with a pretext for declaring
that the interests of the monarchy and of the Catholic Church
were identical.   For the moment the Guises pretended somewhat to change their policy.   On first hearing of the plot,
they had issued an Edict in the King's name promising forgive-
ness for all past deeds ; and, although the Edict of Roromantin,
which followed in May, 1560, gave exclusive jurisdiction

over matters of conscience to the ecclesiastical courts, it urged the desirability of proceeding gently in the matter. The Guises even listened to demands of Coligny, which were supported by Catherine and Michel L'Hôpital, who had just been made chancellor, to summon a States-General, and a Council of the French prelates for the discussion of grievances, political and religious. To these proposals, however, they had consented in the belief that they could postpone the ecclesiastical Council under pretext that the Council of Trent was shortly to be reopened, and that they could secure a subservient majority in the Estates-General by influencing the elections, and by excluding and imprisoning those who would not subscribe to the articles of the Catholic faith.

The death of Mary, the Regent of Scotland (June 10, 1560), and the Treaty of Leith (July 6), by which the French were to evacuate Scotland, and King Francis and his wife, Mary Stuart, were to abandon their claims to the throne of England, had removed the apprehensions of Philip. He therefore offered to help the Guises in securing their power. The Pope and the Duke of Savoy were to send troops to exterminate the Vaudois and to attack Geneva, while Philip was to invade Navarre. Condé and the King of Navarre having rashly answered a summons to Orleans, where the court had assembled for the meeting of the States-General, were seized ; an unsuccessful attempt was made to assassinate Navarre ; and Condé, tried before a special commission for complicity in the late conspiracy, was condemned to die. The triumph of the Guises seemed secured, when it was snatched from them by the sudden death of the young King from a disease in the ear (December 5, 1560).

The triumph of the Guises prevented, by death of Francis II. Dec. 5, 1560.

§ 4. *Charles IX., December* 1560—*May* 1574.

The Guises, baulked of their prey, went at first in such fear of their lives that they shut themselves up in their palace,

and Catherine at last seemed to have her opportunity. As
Charles IX. was only ten, a regency was necessary, and, beyond
all dispute, the office should have been held by
Antony of Navarre. But he agreed to surrender
his right to the Queen-mother, reserving for
himself only the office of Lieutenant-general.

*Catherine
rules in the
name of
Charles IX.*

Catherine was delighted. 'He is so obedient,' she wrote to
her daughter the Queen of Spain, 'that I dispose of him as I
please.' She now hoped to act the part of mediator between
the two religious parties, and, by playing off the Guises
against the Bourbons, to rule. Her first difficulty was with
regard to the States-General. Summoned on December 15,
1560, to Orleans, they were prorogued till the following
August, when they met again at Pontoise.

This, the first meeting of the States-General for seventy-seven
years, is noticeable as illustrating the political ideas of the
Huguenots, who found themselves in a majority,
and for the remarkable reforms proposed, which,
if carried out, might have saved France from
civil war, and altered her future history. The nobles, while
insisting on their privileges, urged the reformation of the
judicial system, and the substitution of an elective magistracy
for one which, through the system of purchase, was rapidly
becoming hereditary; they denounced the chicanery of the
ecclesiastical courts and the abuses of pluralities and non-
residence; they petitioned that nobles who preferred the
Calvinistic worship should be allowed to use the churches for
their services.

*The States-
General.
August 1561.*

The demands of the Tiers État went further. They asked
that the Prerogative should be limited by triennial meetings of
the Estates, and by the appointment of a Council from which
the clergy should be excluded. They petitioned for the sale
of church lands. From the interest of the capital thus
obtained, the clergy were to be paid fixed stipends, and the
balance was to be spent on paying the debts of the crown,
and in loans to the principal cities for the furtherance of their

commerce. They demanded that persecution should cease, since 'it is unreasonable to compel men to do what in their hearts they consider wrong, and that a national Council, in which the laity as well as the clergy should have votes, and in which the Word of God should be the sole guide, should be summoned for the final settlement of religious questions. This would have meant the establishment of the Reformed opinions in France, and for this Catherine was certainly not prepared, for the Huguenots after all only represented some one-thirtieth of the nation.

Nor did the results of the 'Colloquy of Poissy,' which was held near by at the same time, offer better hopes that comprehension would be possible. At this conference eleven ministers—among whom were Theodore Beza, the disciple of Calvin, and Peter Martyr the Italian —and twenty-two laymen appeared. But as might be expected, the attempt served rather to accentuate the differences between the two creeds. The only practical result of the Colloquy was that the bishops, to meet the demands of the third estate with regard to Church property, pledged themselves to pay by instalments the sum needed for the redemption of those crown lands which had been alienated to satisfy the public creditors. *The Colloquy of Poissy.*

Comprehension was plainly impossible. It remained to be seen whether toleration was practicable. This was attempted by the Edict of January, 1562, which, while it insisted on the Huguenots surrendering the churches which they had occupied, allowed them, until the decision of a General Council, to assemble for worship in any place outside walled towns. Thus the policy of L'Hôpital seemed to have triumphed. The Huguenots were given a legal recognition, and ceased to be outlaws. But the appearances were delusive, and the Edict of January really only precipitated civil war. L'Hôpital himself had confessed, at the opening of the States-General, that 'It was folly to hope for peace between persons of different religions. A French- *The Edict of Jan. 1562.*

man and an Englishman,' he said, 'who are of the same religion have more affection for one another than citizens of the same city, or vassals of the same lord, who hold to different creeds.' Nor was this all. Religious differences were in many cases embittered by personal rivalry, by selfish interests, and by political prejudices, and all these had been intensified by the demands of the third estate. If granted, the demands would have revolutionised the constitution of the country, and they could only have been successful if backed up by the nation. But the third estate, nominated for the most part by the municipal oligarchies, represented neither the views of the peasants in the country districts nor those of the lower classes in the towns, who were mostly Catholics. Those whose interests and prejudices they assailed formed the great majority of the nation, and these henceforth learnt to look upon the Huguenots as their deadly enemies. The higher nobility were frightened at the demand for resumption of the crown lands, many of which were in their hands; the Church resented the cry for disendowment; the lawyers were indignant at the attack on their privileges, and were as jealous as ever of the claims of the States-General to rule the country. It is, in fact, from this time that we must date the uncompromising hostility to the Reformers of these three powerful bodies—the nobility, the clergy, and the lawyers— many of whom hitherto had not been unwilling to show some favour to the Huguenots. The only chance of the Huguenots now depended on the maintenance of peace. Although they had not gained all that they desired, and although the Edict was only to be provisional, their adherents were increasing so fast that in a short time they might hope to be able to command respect. One archbishop—that of Aix—and six bishops, besides the Cardinal of Châtillon, were said to favour the new opinions. Throgmorton informed the Queen of England that even Charles IX. himself was wavering. Catherine did not object to her ladies reading the New Testament and singing the psalms of the Huguenot Marot, and certainly she would not have hesitated to continue her policy of toleration if she could thereby have secured her authority. Unfortunately the administration was not powerful enough to enforce the law, and the religious and political animosities were too deep. The leaders of the Huguenots could not entirely control the more hot-headed spirits, and iconoclastic outrages occurred, more especially in the south ; while the Catholics were determined to overthrow the Edict as soon as possible.

Already in April, 1561, Montmorenci had been reconciled to the Guises. They now succeeded in gaining over the unstable King of Navarre by offering him the island of Sardinia and a kingdom in Africa, or possibly a divorce from his Protestant wife, Jeanne d'Albret, and the hand of Mary, Queen of Scots, with the crown of Scotland, and some day that of England. In the south, massacres and outrages occurred ; and finally, on Sunday, March 1, the Duke of Guise coming The massacre across some Huguenots who were worshipping of Vassy. in a barn at Vassy, in Champagne, ordered his March 1, 1562. followers to disperse the meeting as being contrary to the law. The Huguenots, though unarmed, probably made some resistance, and the affair ended in the massacre of some fifty or sixty men and women, while two hundred more were seriously wounded. As the town of Vassy was apparently not a 'walled' one, the Huguenots were probably within their rights. In any case, the Duke had no authority to take the execution of the law into his own hands. It may be true that he had not intended his followers to proceed to such extremities, but at least he never denounced or punished the perpetrators. For the rest, the massacre of Vassy was not the only one that had occurred since the Edict, and it is important only because it was committed with the acquiescence of one of the great party leaders, and because in thus transferring the quarrel from the country to the court, it rendered war inevitable. The question was, Who should secure the person of the King? The Duke advancing

rapidly, entered Paris (March 16) in spite of the order of
Catherine to the contrary.   On her retiring with the young
King to Fontainebleau he followed her; and the
Queen-mother, seeing no other alternative, consented to return to Paris (April 6), Charles IX.
crying 'as if they were taking him to prison.'
Catherine, after attempting to support the weaker
party, had ended, as was her wont, in siding with
the stronger.

*Duke of
Guise enters
Paris,
March 16;
and secures
the person
of the king.
April 6.*

Meanwhile, Condé had retreated from Paris (March 23)
to Orleans.   Being joined there by Coligny and d'Andelot
he published a manifesto in which he justified his
appeal to arms, and declared that he did so to
free the King from unlawful detention by the
'Triumvirate'—Guise, Montmorenci, and the Marshal St.
André.   Thus, if the Catholics were the first to break the
peace at Vassy, the Huguenots were the first to appeal to
arms.   Many have blamed them for want of patience, and
held that, if they had refrained from raising the standard of
rebellion, they would in time have gained toleration.   Calvin
had always been opposed to war, and Coligny only consented
after much hesitation, overborne, it is said, by the entreaties
of his wife.   But it is extremely doubtful whether they could
thus have disarmed persecution; the Catholic party were
determined to crush out heresy; and, as it was, the victims of
1562 exceeded those of the massacre of St. Bartholomew.
A more serious charge is that the Huguenots, under the
garb of religion, were pursuing political objects; but this
assertion may be brought with equal truth against all parties
in the religious struggles of the century.   In France, as elsewhere, the religious disaffection furnished a rallying-point for,
and a creed to, all the smouldering discontent in the country.
With some the religious, with others the political, and even the
personal element was strongest.   'The grandees,' says a Venetian
observer, ' adopted reform for ambition, the middle classes for
Church property, the lower classes for Paradise.'   Moreover,

*Condé's
Manifesto.
March.*

the accusation would be equally true of the Catholics. If Condé was fighting for the control of the government, he had a juster claim thereto than the half-foreign Guises. The political aims of the Huguenots, as represented at Orleans, were more worthy of support than the absolutist opinions of the Guises. If the Huguenots may be charged with reviving feudalism at one moment, and of being republicans at another, the Guises at first fought for political as well as religious tyranny, and latterly masqueraded as the champions of pure democracy. Finally, the cause of the Huguenots, although that of a minority—and, it must be confessed, an unpopular minority—was yet the cause of national independence, which was threatened by the ever-tightening alliance of the Guises with Philip of Spain. Nor must it be supposed that there was nothing deeper on either side; indeed, it was the presence of religious convictions which gave to the struggle at once its earnestness and its ferocity.

The geographical distribution of the two parties does not bear out the idea that there is a natural affinity between Protestantism and the Teutonic races, and between the Celtic and Romance nations and Catholicism. It is true that the lower classes in Celtic Brittany were strongly Catholic, but so was the north-east of France, in which the Teutonic element was strong, while the Huguenots found their chief support in the south-west, which was Romance. The main stronghold of the Huguenots may be described as a square enclosed between the Loire, the Saône, and the Rhone on the north and east; the Mediterranean, the Pyrenees, and the Bay of Biscay on the south and west; while Dauphiné and Normandy were their outposts. Yet even here it was only in Eastern Languedoc and in Dauphiné, and later, at La Rochelle, that they solidly held their own, or that they were supported by the majority of the population, both noble and non-noble. Elsewhere, in those provinces where the nobles inclined to Protestantism, the peasants generally remained Catholic. While the Huguenots

The geographical and social distribution of the two parties.

had, with the exception of Condé and his relations, few ad
herents among the grandees, they found their main support in
the smaller nobility and in the trading classes of the towns.
Of these, the nobility formed, at their own charges, a most
admirable light cavalry, and, in spite of the inferiority of
their arms, proved in many a battle that they were more than
a match for mail-clad men-at-arms. Unfortunately their
poverty, their dislike of discipline, and their local interests
rendered them unfit for a long campaign, and this accounts
for the fact that their victories often led to such poor results.

On the side of the Catholics were ranged the mass of
the greater nobles, the Church, and the official classes of
the magistracy and bureaucracy, the peasants of the rural
districts, except in the Cevennes and Dauphiné, and the lower
classes in the towns, more especially of Paris, and later, of
Orleans and Rouen. The intense Catholicism of these and
other towns is to be explained by the influence of the religious
houses, and in Paris of the University which, with its sixty-five
colleges, formed almost a town of itself, and, together with the
monasteries, owned a large part of the city and its suburbs.
The moral strength of Catholicism depended on the conservative instincts of the people and on their religious traditions,
which were so closely intertwined with the business and
pleasures of life, and which were shocked by the iconoclasm
of the Huguenots ; while the feudal, separatist, and republican
tendencies of the Huguenots at once prevented harmony
among themselves, and opened them to the charge of being
enemies to unity and centralisation—always dear to the French
mind. The Catholics had also the possession of the King's
person and of the financial resources of the government and
the Church, and were assisted by the subsidies of Philip II.
Finally, the Catholics were able to recruit their troops by
mercenaries not only from the Catholic states of Germany,
but also from the Lutherans, who gave but scant support to
their Calvinistic brethren. That under these circumstances,
coupled with the fact that they never numbered more than

one-tenth of the population, the Huguenots maintained the struggle so long as they did must be, in the main, attributed to the zeal and devotion of many—notably of the ministers—to the stubbornness of the *bourgeoisie*, the superiority of their cavalry, and the ability of their leaders, especially of Condé and of Coligny.

The war began in August by the taking of Poictiers by St. André, and the surrender of Bourges, which gave the centre of France, up to the gates of Orleans, to the Catholics. In September, the Huguenots secured the alliance of Elizabeth of England, who feared lest the triumph of the Guises might mean that the whole of the resources of France would be used to place Mary Queen of Scots on the English throne. Yet with her usual caution, Elizabeth demanded the cession of Dieppe and Havre as the price of her assistance. The indignation, however, caused by the cession of these towns was scarcely balanced by the niggardly help which the Queen vouchsafed to the Protestants ; and on the 28th of October, the Catholics gained a brilliant success by the capture of Rouen, the capital of Normandy, which henceforth became ' one of the eyes of the Catholics.' The loss of the town was, however, sufficiently compensated for by the death of the fickle Antony of Navarre of a wound received at the siege, for thereby the headship of his house devolved on Condé, and on his own son the future Henry IV., a boy of ten years old. In December, the attempt of Condé to neutralise the effect of the loss of Rouen by an attack on Normandy led to the battle of Dreux, on the Eure, which was really a victory for the Catholics. The losses on their side were indeed the heavier; the Marshal St. André was slain, and the Constable Montmorenci taken prisoner. Nevertheless, Condé himself fell into the enemy's hands, and Coligny was forced to retire on Orleans. In February of the following year, Coligny again returned and took several towns of importance in Normandy.

First Civil War.

Aug. 1562-March 1563.

Rouen taken by the Catholics. Oct. 26, 1562.

Battle of Dreux. Dec. 19, 1562.

But the Duke of Guise had taken advantage of his absence
to besiege Orleans (February 5), and the city seemed doomed,

Assassination
of Francis,
Duke of
Guise.
Feb. 18, 1563.

when the Duke was assassinated by a fanatic
named Poltrot, who believed that it was the
will of God that he should rid the world of
'the butcher of Vassy.'

The death of the leader of the Catholics revived the hopes
of Catherine that she might succeed in keeping the balance

Pacification
of Amboise.
March 12, 1563.

between the two parties. Accordingly, on March
12, the Pacification of Amboise was signed. By
that treaty, Condé and Montmorenci were exchanged; nobles were permitted to hold Protestant services in
their houses; in each *sénéchaussée*,[1] one city was to be granted,
in the suburbs of which the Huguenots might worship; and
in every town where the Protestant service had been held in
the preceding March one or two places were to be designated
by the King, where it might be continued *inside* the walls.
From these provisions, however, Paris was to be excepted.
The treaty was followed by a united attack on Havre, from
which the English were driven on the 25th of July,
and Elizabeth was forced to surrender her claim to the
restitution of Calais. Coligny was opposed to the treaty. It
did not, in his opinion, give sufficient security to the Protestants; but Condé, who was as rash in making peace as he
had been in declaring war, had fallen under the fatal influence
of Mdlle. de Limeuil, one of the ladies of Catherine's suite, and
was deluded with the promise that he would be appointed
Lieutenant-general, and could then watch over the interests
of his party. In this he was disappointed; for Catherine, to
escape from her promise, had Charles, who was now thirteen
declared of age; and although she herself was anxious to
prevent any further hostilities, such was not the wish of the
Pope, of the Guises, or of Philip.

At a conference held at Bayonne in June, 1565, Alva, in
his master's name, urged the Queen-mother to dismiss the

[1] Cf. Appendix I. for meaning of this.

chancellor L'Hôpital, to 'show herself a good Catholic,' and to proceed to stringent measures against the Huguenots. Very possibly she might have complied if Philip had consented to further her dynastic aims by giving the hand of Don Carlos to her second daughter, and that of his sister, the widowed Queen of Portugal, to her favourite son, Henry of Anjou; Philip, however, rejected the proposal, and Catherine refused to follow his advice. Nevertheless, the alarm of the Protestants was natural; it was rumoured that a League had been made and a massacre of the Protestants decided upon, and finally, the levying of some Swiss Catholic troops, osten- The Con-
sibly to watch the march of Alva from Piedmont spiracy of
to the Netherlands (cf. p. 332), led to the con- Meaux, and
the Second
spiracy of Meaux in September, 1567. The Civil War.
Protestant leaders proposed to seize the person Sept. 1567-
March 1568.
of the King, to insist on the removal of the
Cardinal of Lorraine, and to demand that unrestricted liberty of conscience should be conceded. The court, warned at the last moment of its danger, escaped with difficulty to Paris, escorted by the Swiss troops; and the Cardinal, after a hair-breadth escape, fled to Rheims. Condé then advanced on St. Denis, where he was attacked by the Constable The battle of
with an overwhelming force (November 10, 1567). St. Denis.
But the Huguenots fought so stubbornly, and the Nov. 10, 1567.
Parisian levies so badly, that the battle was indecisive. On the Huguenot side, more men of note fell, yet on the Catholic side, the Constable Montmorenci was mortally wounded. The death of Montmorenci for the moment strengthened the hands of Catherine and the influence of L'Hôpital. Accordingly, in March, 1568, the Edict of Longjumeau The Edict of
confirmed the Treaty of Amboise, which was to Longjumeau.
last 'till by God's grace all the king's subjects March 1568.
should be reunited in the profession of one religion.'

Catherine hoped that the Catholic party would be weakened by the death of Montmorenci. She kept the office of Constable vacant, and conferred on the Duke of Anjou, the brother of the King, the less ambitious title of Lieutenant-general. But her hopes of thus maintaining peace were not to be realised. The 'Parlements' throughout France had opposed the Edict of Longjumeau, and that of Toulouse went so far as to execute the King's messenger on the charge of heresy. The Huguenots, not unnaturally, refused to surrender all the cities, as they had promised in the treaty. The Cardinal of Lorraine returned, and, in August, 1568, a plot was formed to seize Condé and the Châtillons, who only succeeded in effecting their escape to La Rochelle owing to a sudden flood in the Loire. L'Hôpital, in despair, retired; and Catherine was once more forced to adopt the policy of the Guises. The Edicts of Toleration were revoked, and the 'Patched-up Peace,' as it was called, was at an end. In this, the third Civil War, Orleans, which had been surrendered at the last truce, became one of the Catholic outposts; while La Rochelle, which only declared for the Huguenots in February 1568, was the chief Protestant stronghold. No serious battle, however, occurred till the spring of the year 1569. Then the Duke of Anjou, a young man of eighteen years, won the battle of Jarnac on the Charente (March 13th), in which Condé was slain after he had surrendered. The death of Condé was looked upon as a serious blow to the Huguenot cause. But it is doubtful whether they lost much, for, although Condé was popular, and did not, like his brother, sacrifice his religious convictions to his personal interest, he was an ambitious man, and his aims had been chiefly political. His moral character was, moreover, weak; and, though a brave soldier, he was not a general of the first order, while as a statesman his conduct often verged on foolhardiness.

Third Civil War. Sept. 1568-Aug. 1570.

Battle of Jarnac. March 13, 1569.

The expectation of the Catholics that the victory of Jarnac would put an end to the war was not fulfilled. The battle was not much more than a cavalry skirmish. The death of Condé left Coligny in supreme command, and served, as a contemporary says, 'to reveal in all its splendour the merits of the admiral,' who was in every way, except as a diplomatist, the superior of his predecessor. Even the loss of d'Andelot, who at this juncture died of fever, did not prevent the Huguenots from meeting at first with considerable success.

In May, 1569, Wolfgang, Duke of Zweibrücken (Deux Ponts), entered France at the head of 'reiters' from lower, and of 'landsknechts' from upper Germany, and a force of French and Flemish troops under William of Orange and Louis of Nassau. Forcing their way to the Loire they seized La Charité, a place of considerable importance as commanding the passage of the river from Burgundy and Champagne, and, although Wolfgang himself died of fever during the campaign, his troops effected a union with Coligny near Limoges (June 12).   Unfortunately, instead of attacking Saumur, which commanded the road to Anjou and Brittany, they turned south against Poictiers. The city was bravely held by Henry, Duke of Guise, the young son of Francis, who here first displayed his military genius ; and, after seven weeks, Coligny was forced to abandon the siege by the advance of the Duke of Anjou.   Coligny was anxious to avoid a battle, for William of Orange had departed to raise fresh troops in Germany ; his losses before Poictiers had been considerable ; and, as usual, he had found it difficult to keep his forces long in the field.   But the Germans demanded pay, which he could not give, or to be led against the enemy ; and Coligny, forced to accept the challenge of Anjou with far inferior forces, suffered a serious defeat at Moncontour (October 3), where he was severely wounded.   Had Anjou at once pursued, the Huguenots might have been completely crushed ; fortunately, whether owing to the jealousy of the Guises at this success of Anjou or no, it was decided first to reduce Saint Jean d'Angély.   The city fell, indeed, after seven weeks' siege, but 'as the siege of Poictiers was the beginning of the mishaps of the Huguenots, so that of Saint

Expedition of the Duke of Zweibrücken and William of Orange. May 1569.

Battle of Moncontour. Oct. 3, 1569.

Jean d'Angély was the means of wasting the good fortune of the Catholics.' La Rochelle still held out; the winter came on; the Duke of Anjou resigned his command, while his successor, the Duke of Montpensier, retired to Angers.

Meanwhile in October, Coligny, now recovered of his wounds, had started on a brilliant expedition. He crossed

Expedition of Coligny. Oct. 1569- June 1570.

the south of France, his army growing like a snowball, and reached the Rhone; thence, hugging the right bank of the Saône, he marched north- wards to Arnay Le Duc, where an indecisive engagement with Marshal de Cossé (June 25), caused him to retreat to La Charité, and thence to his own castle at Châtillon-sur-Loire. Coligny had not, indeed, succeeded in carrying out his plan of uniting with William of Orange, who was collecting a force on the German frontier, and of forcing his way to Paris, but the campaign showed conclu-sively that the Huguenots were not yet crushed.

Philip II. would send to the Catholics nothing but promises; Queen Elizabeth, unwilling to see the Huguenots completely routed, was considering the question of aiding them; Charles was jealous of the military success of his brother Anjou; and Catherine was not sorry to listen to the advice of Francis of Montmorenci, eldest son of the old Constable, to come to terms once more.

By the Peace of St. Germain (August 8, 1570), which closed the third Civil War, the Huguenots not only regained all that

Peace of St. Germain. Aug. 8, 1570.

they had obtained by the Edict of Longjumeau, but were allowed to celebrate their services in two cities of each of the twelve provinces of France, and received as securities four cities which they were to hold for two years—La Rochelle, Montauban, Cognac, and La Charité. They were also to be restored to all their property, honours, and offices, and were given the right of challenging a certain number of the judges in the 'Parle-ments,' and a right of appeal from that of Toulouse, which had been the most violent. Thus the Huguenots had at last obtained liberty of conscience, and terms with regard to the holding of services, which, if not completely satisfactory, were perhaps as much as they could expect. Moreover, they might well hope that this time the terms would be kept, for the Treaty of St. Germain was followed by a complete change in the foreign policy of the court.

Catherine had hitherto followed two lines of conduct. At one time she had tried to act as a mediator between the two religious parties ; at another to support the weaker, and thus maintain a balance. But both had failed. The crown was not powerful enough for the first, and, instead of succeeding in the second, she had been obliged to join the stronger party. A third alternative remained. Might it not be possible to revive the national hostility to Spain ; sink religious differences in a foreign war ; form a great Protestant league against the Pope and Spain ; divide the Netherlands with England and William of Orange ; and at home secure the authority of the crown? Such were the views of Coligny, which were now to be adopted by the King and Catherine. Charles IX., feeble though he was, was not without some traces of better things ; he had always been averse to civil war, and saw that Spain had been the chief gainer from the discords of France, since, as Marshal Vielleville had said long ago, 'as many gallant gentlemen had fallen in one battle as would have sufficed to drive the Spaniards out of Flanders.' The Spanish victory of Lepanto over the Turks in October, 1571, only served to intensify Charles' dread of Philip. Moreover, as we have seen, he was jealous of the fame his brother, the Duke of Anjou (the favourite of his mother), had gained in the late campaign, and hoped that he might eclipse it by leading a national war against the Spaniard. But the support of the King would have been of little value had not Catherine also favoured the designs of Coligny. Philip had refused to further her dynastic interests at the Conference of Bayonne, in June 1565 (cf. p. 407). His third wife, Elizabeth of France, had died in

Marginal note: Change in the policy of the French Court.

1568. He now declined either to marry Margaret of Valois, Catherine's second daughter, or to urge the claims of that lady upon the young King of Portugal. Accordingly Catherine wished to marry her to the young King of Navarre, the first prince of the blood, whose possessions[1] stretched from the Pyrenees to the other side of the Garonne, and whose friendship, whether he was converted or not, might be of great assistance to her. His mother, however, Jeanne d'Albret, dreaded the influence of the depraved court of France on her son, and rightly suspected the character of the young princess; and Catherine, eager to gain the assistance of the Admiral, who alone was likely to overcome the scruples of the Queen of Navarre, listened to his suggestions, and negotiations were opened with William of Orange and with England. The Prince eagerly welcomed these overtures. He had long realised that the revolt of the Netherlands against Spain would not be successful if fought solely on religious lines. The Protestants were too scattered, and too much divided among themselves, for that; and the only chance lay in waging a political war against Spanish tyranny, in alliance with foreign powers. Accordingly Louis of Nassau was sent to negotiate, and there was talk of an alliance of France, England, and the Empire, and of a division of the Netherlands between them. In pursuance of this scheme, Elizabeth of England was approached; but though at this time quarrelling with Philip over the exploits of the 'Sea-dogs' on the Spanish Main, and angry at the support he had given to the Ridolfi plot in 1571, she had insuperable objections to see Antwerp and the Scheldt in French hands. It was therefore proposed that she should marry the Duke of Anjou, and that he should be declared sovereign of the Netherlands (cf. p. 338). To this proposal Elizabeth appeared more favourably inclined, and

---

[1] Henry held Lower Navarre and the Principality of Béarn in his own right, and, as fiefs, the Duchies of Vendôme, Beaumont, and Albret; the Counties of Bigorre, Armagnac, Rouergue, Perigord, and Marle; the Viscounties of Limoges, and other lordships. See Map of France.

Walsingham, her agent in France, was closely questioned as to the personal appearance of the Duke. The negotiations broke down, indeed, in January, 1572, owing to the preference of Anjou, who had been influenced by the Guises, for the hand of the Queen of Scots, 'the rightful Queen of England,' but even then Alençon, Anjou's younger brother, was suggested; and a correspondence on the subject, which, on the part of Elizabeth at least, was only entered into to gain time, continued until arrested by the massacre of St. Bartholomew.

While Elizabeth trimmed, events moved rapidly. On the 1st of April, 1572, the Comte de la Marck, a Flemish refugee, being expelled from Dover with his ships by the order of the English Queen, who was not yet prepared for an open breach with Philip, seized Brille and Flushing, and Holland and Zealand rose. In May, Louis of Nassau, having by the connivance of Charles raised a force, chiefly of Huguenots, in France, took Mons, the capital of Hainault, while Elizabeth, not to be outdone, allowed English volunteers to cross to Flushing. The dream of Coligny seemed likely to be fulfilled, and Charles appeared to be on the point of declaring war on Spain.

La Marck seizes Brille. April 1, 1572.

Unfortunately, the apprehensions of Catherine had been in the meantime aroused. She had consented to the Treaty of St. Germain because she feared the Guises; she was now threatened by the more distasteful ascendency of Coligny, who, if we may believe Tavannes, advised Charles that he would never be truly King until he had emancipated himself from his mother's control. She therefore returned to the idea, often entertained, and often pressed upon her, of getting rid of the leaders of the Huguenots, more especially of Coligny. At what date she finally decided on this course it is impossible to say with certainty, but there is evidence to show that the scheme had assumed practical shape as early as February, 1572. Even then had the movement in the Netherlands met with complete success, King Charles might have made up his mind to

Catherine becomes alarmed at the growing influence of Coligny.

declare war against Spain ; Elizabeth might have cast away her doubts, and some of the Protestant princes of Germany would have joined the alliance. The position of Coligny would then have been too strong for Catherine, who, as she had often done before, might have submitted to the inevitable, and the hopes of Burleigh and Walsingham of beating back Catholicism behind the Alps and the Pyrenees might have been realised. Unfortunately, de la Noue was driven from Valenciennes, a French detachment under the Count of Genlis was cut to pieces by the son of Alva in an attempt to relieve Mons (July 19), and Genlis himself was taken prisoner. The hands of Catherine were now free, and she planned the assassination of Coligny with the Duke of Anjou and Henry of Guise.

Genlis defeated and taken prisoner. July 19, 1572.

The attempt was made in the midst of the festivities which followed the marriage of Henry of Navarre and Margaret. Whether, if it had succeeded, Catherine would have been satisfied, or whether she hoped that the murder would cause the Protestants to rise, and thus give the Catholics an excuse for proceeding further, it is impossible to say. In any case, the assassin missed his aim ; Coligny escaped with a serious wound, and it was necessary to proceed to further extremities. Accompanied by the Duke of Anjou, by Birago a Milanese, the successor of L'Hôpital in the chancellorship, and by others, the Queen-mother visited the King, and, with threats and imputations that he was too timid to act, at last persuaded him. 'By God's death,' said he, 'since you insist that the admiral must be killed, I consent ; but with him every Huguenot in France must perish, that not one may remain to reproach me with his death, and what you do, see that it be done quickly.' The King's consent obtained, the plan was rapidly concerted between Catherine, Anjou, Henry of Guise, and Charron, the 'Prévot des Marchands' of Paris. Whether, even then, it was intended to dispose of more than some of the

Attempted assassination of Coligny. Aug. 22, 1572.

The Massacre of St. Bartholomew. Aug. 24, 1572.

leaders is doubtful, but, when once the order had gone out, the fanatical mob of Paris could not be restrained. On Sunday morning, August 24, the massacre began, and was subsequently taken up in the provinces.

Such appears to be the truth with regard to the causes of this pitiful tragedy, which some think had been premeditated as early as the Treaty of St. Germain itself. All direct evidence, however, has been destroyed, and the facts have been so distorted by partisanship, that certainty is no longer possible. The number of victims has been variously stated ; but at the lowest computation they were not less than 1000 in Paris, and 10,000 elsewhere. Among the victims, besides Coligny, were Teligny, his son-in-law, and La Rochefoucauld, an important noble of Poitou. Navarre and the young Condé were spared, but were forced to abjure Protestantism, and were practically prisoners in the hands of Catherine and the Guises. As to any future policy, the Court had not made up its mind. Catherine, it is said, had hoped that, if the responsibility could be thrown upon the Guises, the Huguenots would rush to arms and attack them, and that an obstinate struggle would then ensue, which would weaken the two factions, and justify the King in interfering to restore order ; thus both parties might be destroyed, and she and her favourite son Anjou might be left without dangerous rivals. Accordingly the King at first announced that the affair had been the result of the long-standing quarrel between the Guises and the Châtillons, which the Government had done its best to suppress. But as the Guises would not accept the responsibility, the King changed his tone, justified the crime by declaring that the Huguenots had been plotting against the crown, and, with singular baseness, urged Alva to put to death all the Huguenot prisoners he had taken before Mons. At *No change in* the same time, Catherine was eager not to *foreign policy* alienate the Protestants abroad. She looked *contemplated.* upon the massacre as a domestic incident, and was not unwilling to continue the policy of Coligny now that he was gone

This she was the more anxious to do, because she now entertained the idea of securing the crown of Poland, just vacant
by the death of the last of its hereditary Kings, the Jagellons,
for her favourite son Anjou.   It was therefore announced that
the Edict of Amboise would be kept, and negotiations were
continued with the Protestant powers.   This policy met with
some success.

The rulers of Europe expressed delight or disapprobation
according to their sentiments, but guided their policy as
their interest demanded.   Philip was at first beside
himself with joy ; it meant, he thought, the end of
the French alliance with the Netherlands ; Alva,
however, warned him that the overthrow of the Huguenots
would strengthen France too much.   Elizabeth declared her
disgust, but could not afford to quarrel with France ; while
William the Silent, especially after the fall of Mons on September 19, was not in a position to abandon all
hopes of French assistance.   The Protestant
Princes of Germany at first showed great indignation, but did nothing to interfere with the candidature of the Duke of Anjou, who was elected King of Poland
(May 9, 1573).

At home, Catherine was not so successful, and ' France,' says
Sully, ' atoned for the massacre by twenty-six years
of disaster, carnage, and horror.'   On the news of
the massacre, the survivors took up arms, but they
were not strong enough to meet their enemies in the field, and
the resistance was confined to a few cities, of which
Nîmes and Montauban in the south, Sancerre
and La Rochelle in the west, were the most important.   The Government in vain attempted their reduction.
The siege of La Rochelle cost the lives of some 20,000 men,
and of more than 300 officers of some distinction.   Sancerre
was reduced to such straits that cats, rats, mice, and even dogs,
were eaten ; the last, says Jean de Lery, whose narrative has
not been inaptly called a cookery book for the besieged, were

found to be rather sweet and insipid. At last, on June 24, 1573, the Government despairing of success, and unwilling that the Polish ambassadors should find their new King, the Duke of Anjou, who was in command of the army, besieging a Protestant town, concluded the Treaty of La Roch- Treaty of elle. By this treaty the Huguenots were promised La Rochelle. liberty of conscience throughout France, and the June 24, 1573. right of holding services in La Rochelle, Nîmes, and Montauban. These towns were also to be free from royal garrisons. In August, by the mediation of the Polish ambassador, Sancerre was admitted to the same terms. But the treaty could not last. It was doubtful whether the Government were sincere, and it was not likely that the Huguenots would consent to forego their rights of worship. Besides all this, their cause was being strengthened by the rise of the 'Politiques,' or Rise of the 'Peaceable Catholics' as they called themselves. Politiques. This party, born of the horror and weariness which the Civil War had caused, was anxious to establish peace on the basis of mutual toleration. Its leaders were the two sons of the old Constable, Francis, Marshal of France and Governor of Paris, and Henry Damville, Governor of Languedoc. Their jealousy of the Guises they had inherited from their father, yet their ideas as to toleration would have been most distasteful to him, and, still more so, the opinions of his two youngest sons, William (Thoré), and Charles (Méru), who adopted the Huguenot faith. The Politiques were strongest in the south, where the adherents of the two creeds had been more equally balanced, and where the struggle had been most severe. As a whole they were not actuated by high principle. If they adopted the views of L'Hôpital it was from cynical indifference to religion, rather than from conviction as to the merits of toleration, and the leaders at least were largely influenced by ambition or personal motives. Indeed, the massacre of St. Bartholomew was followed by a general lowering of tone and of morality throughout France.

Closely connected with the Politiques stood Navarre and

Henry of Condé, who had been forced to abjure their faith
and were practically prisoners in royal hands, and the King's
brother, the Duc d'Alençon, who selfishly sided with
Huguenots in the hope of securing the crown on the death of
Charles IX.   At this time, too, the results of the massacre
were seen in a complete transformation of the views of the
Change in the Huguenots.   Hitherto, the party had been domi-
character and nated by the nobility, great and small, who, in
views of the   spite of the feudal colour which they gave to
Huguenot
Party.   the movement, had asserted that they were not
fighting against the crown, but for the removal of foreign
and unpopular ministers, while the third estate had limited
its demands to an extension of the powers of the States-
General.   But now many of the greater nobility had fallen,
and many had abjured their faith.   The importance of the
bourgeoisie and of the ministers had consequently increased,
and under their influence republican ideas had become more
prominent; while the feudal element, which was still represented by the smaller local nobility, went to strengthen
separatist tendencies.   The change was accompanied by the
appearance of numerous political pamphlets, of which the
most striking were the *Franco-Gallia* of Hotman, and the
Vindiciæ contra Tyrannos from the pen of Languet, or possibly
of Duplessis-Mornay, the faithful adviser of Henry of Navarre.

The *Franco-Gallia*, adopting the historical method, asserts
that the Teutonic nations saved France from the tyranny of
The Franco-   Rome, revived the free institutions of the Gauls,
Gallia, and   and established an elective monarchy, which
Vindiciæ
contra Tyr-   governed through the people and for the people,
annos.   in whom eventually the sovereignty resides.   The
decadence of this free constitution began with the Capetian
Kings, who in time overthrew the privileges of the Estates,
and introduced the despotic rule of King and 'Parlement.'
The writer goes on to illustrate from the history of France
the evil results of the rule of women, and holds that this is
the reason for their exclusion from the throne, rather than

any fundamental law, like the Salic Law, which conflicts with the primeval right of free election.

The author of the second treatise, the *Vindiciæ*, adopts the opposite method, and seeks to prove his point by a deductive argument. Both King and people have made a contract with God : the King to rule his country well, the people to depose him when he fails to do so. Hence resistance to a tyrant is a duty. Nevertheless, the right of resistance does not belong to individuals, except, indeed, against an invader, an usurper, or a woman, if such, in defiance of law, seek to rule a country ; for they are outside the law. In other cases, not the individuals, but their representative, the magistracy, should be the judge of breach of contract. Thus, although the doctrine of resistance is clearly enunciated, the resistance must come from the properly constituted authorities, and the writer objects to anything which savours of anabaptism or other extreme views.

The Huguenots did not limit themselves to theory. On the 24th of August, 1573, the anniversary of St. Bartholomew, the Protestants of Languedoc and Upper Guienne formed two federative republics, each divided into dioceses with small deliberative assemblies, which were to send deputies to the central assemblies at Nîmes and Montauban. These, with an elective governor, were to have the power of levying troops and of imposing taxes on Protestant and Catholic alike. This republican form of government, in which we see the Presbyterian ideas of church-government applied to secular politics, was to be extended to all parts of France which the Protestants might subsequently win. After thus settling the government of the south, the Huguenots sent a petition to the King demanding complete liberty of conscience and of worship throughout the kingdom, and the cession of two fortresses in each province as a security. The Politiques at the same time published a manifesto demanding toleration. 'If Condé had been alive and in possession of Paris he would not have asked

Political organisation of the Huguenots.

so much,' said Catherine. And on February, 1574, the fifth
war broke out. An unsuccessful attempt on the part of
Navarre and Alençon to fly from St. Germain,
led to the imprisonment of the Marshal Montmorenci, and Marshal de Cossé, another Politique.
Henry of Condé effected his escape, and negoti-
ated with the German princes for help. Before, however,
any event of importance occurred, the unfortunate
King, Charles IX., passed away (March 30, 1574),
tortured to the last by remorse, and terrified by
visions of the massacre to which, in an evil hour, he had
consented.

Fifth Civil War.
Feb. 1574- May 1576.

Death of Charles IX. March 30, 1574.

§ 5. *The reign of Henry III., March* 1574—*July* 1589.

The death of Charles IX. gave Henry a pretext for hastily
leaving Poland, where he had already become unpopular. He
did not, however, appear to be in any hurry to
reach his new kingdom. Warned by his mother
to avoid North Germany, since 'the German princes
had too many causes of quarrel with France,' he
passed through Austria and Italy. At Venice, he wasted two
months in luxury and debauch, and is said to have been
corrupted by the licence of that town. On his arrival in France
(September, 1574), he seemed for a moment inclined to adopt
a conciliatory policy. But his mother, now that her favourite
son was King, hoped that if he were victorious over the
Huguenots her influence would be paramount, and expected
everything from the hero of Jarnac and Moncontour. The
King therefore announced that he would recognise liberty of
conscience, but would not tolerate religious practices which
deviated from Catholicism, and that he would speak of peace
when his castles and his cities had been restored.

Henry III. leaves Poland and reaches France.
Sept. 1574.

Thus the war dragged on, though without any decisive
events, and soon Henry III. began to crave for peace that he
might indulge in his pleasures. The definite alliance of the
Politiques with the Huguenots of the south, which took place

in December, enabled the rebels to hold their own. In September, 1575, Alençon, and in the following February, Navarre, effected their escape. Meanwhile Duke Casimir, son of the Elector Palatine, who dreamt of heading an aggressive Calvinistic party in Europe, had invaded France, ravaged Burgundy and the Bourbonnois, and, in March, joined Alençon at Sozé. Finally, by the exertions of Francis of Montmorenci, the Marshal, who had been released by the King, the Peace of Monsieur (May, 1576) gave to the Huguenots better terms than they had hitherto obtained. They were allowed to worship where they liked, except within two leagues of Paris, and within the domains of any lord who might withhold his sanction. Cases in which Protestants were concerned were to be tried by 'Chambres mi-parties' in each 'Parlement,'—that is, by courts composed of an equal number of judges of the two religions. The Estates were to be convened at Blois; and eight cities were to be held by the Huguenots in pledge of the fulfilment of the treaty. The Duke of Alençon, or Anjou, as he had now become in consequence of the accession of Henry of Anjou to the throne, was to receive the duchies of Berry, Touraine, and Anjou, with reservation of the rights of suzerainty to the crown. To Henry of Navarre was given the governorship of Guienne, and to Henry of Condé that of Picardy, with Péronne as his residence. The last concession was an important one, for Picardy hitherto had been very Catholic in its sympathies, and had divided the Huguenots from their Protestant allies in the Netherlands. The Peace of Monsieur was received with violent indignation by the Catholics of France, and led to an agitation which was directed almost as much against the crown as against the Huguenots.

Peace of Monsieur. May, 1576.

The idea of forming associations of 'Better Catholics' was no new one. Shortly after the Edict of Amboise, in 1563, we find mention of several, such as the Fraternity of the Holy Ghost in Burgundy, and the Christian and Royal League of Champagne. With the massacre of St. Bartholomew

these associations had fallen into neglect; they were now to be revived on a much more important scale. The first of
The Catholic Leagues. these new leagues was that of Péronne, organised by Humières, the old governor who refused to surrender the fortress to Condé (1576). The example was speedily followed elsewhere, and formed the counterpart to Huguenot federation in the south (cf. p. 419). The organisation of these leagues was a military one. Their objects were declared to be: the defence of the Roman Catholic and Apostolic Church; the preservation of Henry III. in the obedience of his subjects, and after him 'of all the posterity of the House of Valois'; the execution of the resolutions which should be presented by the Estates which were about to meet; and the restoration of the ancient liberties as they existed in the time of Clovis, the first Christian King. In this declaration
The Guises adopt democratic views. we are reminded of a new departure in the policy of the Guises. Hitherto they had attempted to secure their power as the first ministers of the crown, and supported the principles of despotic rule. But Henry III. threatened to shake himself free from their influence, and was already leaning upon his favourites 'the Mignons.' Accordingly, Henry of Guise, who, by the death of his uncle, the cardinal, in 1574, was the undoubted leader of his house, assumed a position of antagonism to the crown, and even began to dream of some day winning the throne itself. The unpopularity which Henry III. incurred by the Peace of Monsieur and by his foppish follies, caused the Duke to lean on popular support, while many of the Catholic nobles had joined the Politiques. Thus the party of the Guises, without completely breaking with the upper classes, began to seek its fulcrum in a lower stratum.

The change is represented not only in the articles of these Catholic Leagues but also in the Catholic pamphlets of the day, which began to borrow the popular doctrines of the *Franco-Gallia* and other Huguenot writings. Denying the application of the Salic Law to France, they asserted that the title of the House of Lorraine was superior to that of the Bourbon, and even to that of the House of Valois itself, since it could trace its descent through the female line from Charles the Great himself. In the face of these new developments, Henry III. followed for some time an oscillating policy. At first he forbade all Associations. Subsequently he abandoned that idea, and tried to utilise them for the purpose of influencing the elections to the States-General which were to meet at Blois according to the Treaty, in the hope, by the aid of the Catholic majority thus obtained, of putting down both the Guises and the Huguenots. In this he was only partially successful. The Huguenots, indeed, despairing of success owing to the terrorism and intrigues of the League, declined even to send deputies from those districts and towns which were in their power, and the Catholics finding themselves in a majority, demanded that there should be only one religion in France. Yet so great was the dislike to a continuance of the war that they refused the necessary supplies, and brought forward constitutional demands which made Henry III. only too glad to be quit of them (March 1577).

Henry III. tries to make use of the States-General.

In the war which had broken out in the meantime, the King was somewhat more successful. The Duke of Anjou (Alençon), who had now deserted the Huguenots, took command of the royal army ; the aristocratic prejudices and the religious indifference of the Politiques could ill agree with the earnestness of the republican and Calvinistic burghers ; and Damville, who by the death of his brother had now become Duke of Montmorenci and Marshal of France, soon abandoned the alliance and made his peace with the court (May, 1577). Under these circumstances the Huguenots lost ground. In May fell La Charité on the Loire ; in August, Brouage, a place next in importance to La Rochelle ; and it was only the want of union among the Catholics themselves, and the utter weariness of the country, which enabled the Huguenots to gain such favourable terms

Sixth Civil War, 1577.

as they did by the Treaty of Bergerac (September 17, 1577).
Their right of worship was indeed restricted to the domains
Treaty of
Bergerac.
Sept. 17, 1577. of nobles, to all cities where worship was held at
the date of the peace, and elsewhere to one city
or its suburbs in each sénéchaussée—Paris itself
being specially excluded. The 'Chambres mi-parties' were
also confined to the four southern 'Parlements' where the
Huguenots were strongest. But they still had eight cities
intrusted to them in pledge for six years, and Condé received
St. Jean d'Angély instead of Péronne. The King was probably sincere in desiring to maintain the Peace of Bergerac, for
he was anxious if possible to escape from the thraldom of the
Guises, and the violations of the treaty which occurred were
due to the insubordination of the governors of provinces, to the
popular fanaticism, and to the stubborn ill-will of the Law Courts.

In 1580, indeed, 'The Lovers' War' broke out. This was
caused, however, rather by quarrels between the King and
Seventh
Civil War,
April 1580, to
Peace of
Fleix, Nov.
1580. Henry of Navarre concerning the dower of
Margaret, and it is noticeable that the great
Protestant leader, de la Noue, disapproved of it,
and that neither La Rochelle nor the southern
towns took part in it. It was ended by the Peace
of Fleix, in Perigord (26th November, 1580), which confirmed
the Treaty of Bergerac, and closed the Seventh Civil War.

The Peace of Fleix was followed by five years of feverish
peace, which served only to illustrate the utter disorganisation of
Disorganisa-
tion of France. the country and the demoralisation of all classes.
Although there were not wanting earnest, if
fanatical, adherents of the two creeds, these formed an ever
lessening minority ; and for the most part, as a competent
observer tells us, 'Men were combating not for the faith, nor
for Christ, but for command.' Of the greater nobles, the
Guises were attempting to overawe the crown, if not to seize
it for themselves ; the rest, like Henry de Montmorenci the
Marshal, and the Duke of Mercœur, strove to make themselves
independent in the provinces of which they were governors

The smaller nobility played the same game on a less magnificent scale, and in some cases had degenerated into brigands; while many, both great and small, spent their leisure in duels and assassinations, often caused by some shameful intrigue. Even the women resorted to the dagger to free themselves from an inconvenient lover, or to avenge some act of infidelity. While the upper classes were thus disturbing the country with their ambitions and their vices, the lower classes were bemoaning their social grievances, and threatening social war. At the head of this seething mass of iniquity, and of political, social, and moral anarchy, stood a vacillating, effeminate King, and an intriguing Queen-mother.

Henry III. had in earlier life shown some character. He was far more able than his brothers, the unfortunate Charles IX., or the Duke of Anjou (Alençon); and had distinguished himself in the battles of Jarnac and Moncontour. His natural gifts, however, had been choked in a life of licence and of luxury, and ever since his accession he had gone from bad to worse. He dressed himself more like a woman than a man; he surrounded himself with favourites, and with lap-dogs; he relieved the monotony of his debaucheries by ridiculous acts of penance and superstition which deceived no one. No doubt, the idea of raising new men to power to balance the ambitions of the older nobility was not altogether a foolish one, and some of the favourites, like Épernon, Joyeuse, and the Marshal de Biron, were men of capacity. But others, like Villequier and D'O, would have disgraced any court; while all were influenced by sordid and unworthy motives. By the King's side stood the Queen-mother, still intriguing for power though life was fast ebbing, and descending to the arts of a procuress to win her opponents. Clearly there was no hope for France until the last of this degenerate race of the Valois had disappeared. The only chance for a continuance of internal peace, such as it was, lay in a vigorous foreign policy, which might have monopolised the attention of the turbulent spirits, and put the King at the head of a united people.

For this, the offer of the sovereignty of the Netherlands
to the Duke of Anjou, in September, 1580, furnished an

Sovereignty
of Nether-
lands accepted
by Anjou.
Sept. 1580-
Feb. 1582.

opportunity which Catherine, angry at the recent
occupation of Portugal by Philip (cf. p. 298),
eagerly embraced.   Even the King himself approved ; while Elizabeth received with favour
the advances of Anjou for her hand in marriage.
The sovereignty was finally conferred on the Duke in February,
1582.   In the June of that year, Catherine sent an expedition

Expedition
to the Azores.
June 1582.

to the Azores in support of Antonio, the Pretender of Portugal.   William of Orange might
well hope that France was about to return to
the policy of Coligny, and, in alliance with the Protestant
Queen of England, and the Netherlands, finally to join
issue with the representative of the Catholic reaction.   His
hope was not, however, to be realised.   Henry iii. was not
prepared for so bold a course, and was half-jealous of his
brother.   Elizabeth had been only scheming to prevent the
Netherlands from being incorporated into France, and, if
possible, to embroil France with Philip, and, for all her love-
making, had no intention of really marrying Anjou.   The

The French
Fury.
Jan. 16, 1583.
Anjou leaves
Netherlands,
June 1583,
and dies.
Assassina-
tion of
William of
Orange.
July 10, 1584.

expedition to the Azores, as well as another which
was despatched in June, 1583, was destroyed by a
Spanish fleet under the Marquis de Santa Cruz.
Anjou, ill satisfied with the restricted authority
granted to him, rashly attempted to establish himself in a more independent position by seizing
Bruges and Antwerp (January 16).   The attempt
failed, and in June, 1583, Anjou retired from the
Netherlands to die in the following June.   One
month after (July, 1584), William the Silent fell a victim to the
pistol of Balthazar Gérard.

The deaths of Anjou and of William the Silent both led
to most momentous consequences.   The first made the Protestant, Henry of Navarre, the heir-presumptive, and rendered
a renewal of civil war almost inevitable ; the second was

followed by the offer of the sovereignty of the Netherlands
to Henry III. It seemed by no means impossible that Henry III.
would reconcile himself with his heretic heir, and
accept the offer made him. At once the apprehensions of the French Catholics, of the Guises,
and of Philip were aroused, and the outcome was
the Catholic League. Following the model of the Catholic
Associations of 1576, the League was formed in
Paris. The city was divided into five districts:
the president of each of these, assisted by an elective Council of
Eleven, formed the famous *Sixteen*. This Council deliberated
on the measures to be adopted, and its decisions were communicated to the faithful through the agency of professional and
trade associations. The example of Paris was rapidly followed
in the provincial towns; and France was threatened with the
tyranny of a central club with its affiliated societies, whose
authority was maintained partly by terrorism, partly by the
fanaticism excited through the preaching of friars and Jesuits.

Sovereignty of Nether- lands offered to Henry III Oct. 1584.

The Catholic League.

Although Henry of Guise did not altogether approve of the
democratic principles adopted by the Catholic League, his interests demanded that he should put himself at the head of it.
But this was not the only important change in the policy of
the Guises. The reputation of the family had been originally
made in defending France against Spain, and Francis, Duke
of Guise, had always been anti-Spanish in his views; while
Philip, on his side, was most unwilling to see Mary, Queen of
Scots, their kinswoman, triumphant in England, and had even
sent secret help to the Scottish rebels. Of late, however, the
more imperative necessity of preventing the French from
assisting the Dutch, or from incorporating any part of the
Netherlands into France, had caused Philip to alter his views.
Negotiations had accordingly been entered into with Henry of
Guise as early as the end of the year 1581, and Philip pretended
to favour the family designs in favour of Mary Stuart, now a
captive in the hands of Elizabeth. The death of Anjou, and
the danger of reconciliation between Henry III. and the heretic

Henry of Navarre, still further aroused the apprehensions of Philip.   He therefore approved of the organisation of the

Treaty of Joinville. Jan. 1585.

League, and in January, 1585, concluded the Treaty of Joinville with Guise.   The allies bound them selves to eradicate heresy, and to proclaim the Cardinal of Bourbon, the Catholic uncle of Henry of Navarre, King in the event of the decease of Henry III. ; the viscounty of Béarn and French Navarre was to be ceded to Philip, as a price of his assistance.   In March, 1585, the Leaguers issued a manifesto, in which they declared their intention to restore the dignity and unity of the crown, to secure the nobility in their ancient privileges, to drive unworthy favourites from the court, to relieve the country from new taxes, and to prevent future troubles by settling the succession on a Catholic king, and by providing for regular sessions of the States-General.

Meanwhile, to enforce their views they had seized the three bishoprics, Metz, Toul, and Verdun, most of the towns of Picardy, all Champagne, and the larger part of Burgundy, Normandy, and Brittany ; while in June they presented an ultimatum to the King insisting on the withdrawal of the late Edict of Toleration.   The formidable movement which was thus inaugurated was the outcome of the union of three forces :—

1. The determination of the Catholic party to oppose the claims of a heretic heir.

2. The jealousy of the Guises for the King's 'Mignons.'

3. The European policy of Philip II., who not only dreaded the French alliance with the Netherlands, but also feared that it might lead to a definite alliance with the Protestant Queen of England, and thus shatter his hopes of re-establishing his authority and that of the Catholic Church.

It remained to be seen what line of conduct Henry III. would adopt in the face of this formidable conspiracy.   Sixtus V., who had just succeeded Pope Gregory XIII. (August 26, 1585), did not altogether approve of the League.   'I fear me,' he said, 'that matters will be pressed so far that the King, Catholic though he be, will be constrained to appeal to the

heretics for aid to rid himself of the tyranny of the Catholics,'
and this for a moment did not appear impossible.   Henry III.
went so far as to acknowledge Henry of Navarre as his lawful
successor, and laughed at the claims of the Cardinal as those
' of an old fool.'   He forbade all Leagues and Associations, and
even made an unsuccessful attempt to seize the Duke of
Guise at Metz.   But a continuation of such a bold policy
was scarcely to be looked for from such a King.   Elizabeth,
although she could scold Henry for submitting to rebels within
his kingdom, would not depart from her position of dubious
neutrality ; Henry of Navarre, although professing his willingness ' to be instructed,' refused to declare himself a Catholic ;
while Catherine, who was hoping to secure the succession for
her daughter Claude and her husband the Duke of Lorraine,
warned the King of the danger of opposing so powerful a
coalition.   Henry, to his ruin, listened to his   Henry III.
mother's advice, and allowed her to yield, in his · submits to
name, to the demands of the Leaguers at the   the League.
Conference of Nemours (July 5, 1585).   The   Sixtus excom-
Edicts of Toleration were revoked, and they of   municates
the Huguenot faith who would not conform were   Navarre.
to leave the country.   Sixtus, now partly relieved   Sept. 9, 1585.
from his apprehensions, issued a Bull of Excommunication
against Henry of Navarre.

The capitulation of Henry III. to the League brought
Henry of Navarre prominently to the front.   He had already
shown his military abilities during the Lovers' War, and,
in 1581, he had been appointed 'Protector of the Churches.'
He now became the representative of all those whose
bigotry or whose interest did not destroy their patriotism.
It is interesting to note how completely the posi-   Altered
tion of the two parties was reversed.   The charges   position of
of opposing the legitimate successor, of holding   the Hugue-
republican doctrines, and of alliance with the   Catholics.
foreigner, once brought against the Huguenots, could now be
laid at the door of the Catholics ; while the Huguenots could

claim to be fighting for the principle of legitimacy and of national independence. Navarre was, accordingly, supported by the Politiques and by the Constable Henry of Montmorenci, who was, however, chiefly influenced by personal jealousy of the Guises. Even the 'Parlement' of Paris remonstrated against the intolerance of the Edict, and against the Papal Bull. Although opposed as before to the concession of the right of worship to the Protestants, its members were in favour of liberty of conscience, and resented, as they had always done, the papal claim to interfere in the internal affairs of France. Thus the party of the Huguenots was by no means a contemptible one. The centre of their position lay in the territories belonging to Henry of Navarre, or under his control. These, spreading from the Spanish frontier to the Dordogne, and from the Bay of Biscay to Languedoc, comprised Lower Navarre and Béarn, which Henry held in his own right, and seven fiefs which he held of the King of France. He was also Governor of Guienne, and he was not without adherents in Normandy and Brittany, while Languedoc was held by the Constable. And yet the position of the Huguenots was discouraging enough. If their party was not confined to those of their religious profession, this only added to the divisions which had always weakened them. The Catholics held by far the greater part of France; in the Netherlands, Alexander of Parma had secured Antwerp (August, 1585), and threatened to carry all before him, and were his task in the Netherlands finished, how should they resist the united forces of the League and of Philip II.? What wonder if many apostatised or fled, and that the beard of Henry of Navarre turned white with anxiety. Already Philip dreamed of overthrowing Elizabeth of England, of placing Mary Queen of Scots on the English throne, and of subjugating France under his lieutenant, the Duke of Guise. Fortunately, however, the King of Spain as usual procrastinated, and preferred to work his end by diplomacy and by bribes, rather than by arms. The Guises were not in complete accord with him, and Henry III. himself daily grew more impatient of the yoke. To these causes, and to the personal ability of the King of Navarre, the salvation of France must be attributed.

Henry III. hoped, in the war which now broke out, to humble the Huguenots, and yet curb the ambition of the Guises. He accordingly gave to the Duke of Joyeuse, his favourite, the command of the army which was to advance against the Huguenots, while he himself opposed the German 'reiters' whom Casimir, brother of the Elector Palatine, had sent to the assistance of the Protestants. Unfortunately for the King, Joyeuse was defeated and slain by Henry of Navarre at Courtras on the Isle (October 20, 1587), and although the 'reiters' were forced to retire, the Guises succeeded in gaining the credit of their retreat. 'Saul,' cried the fanatics of Paris, 'has slain his thousands, but David his ten thousands.' Philip was anxious at this moment to prevent any interference with his schemes for the Armada. His envoy, Mendoza, therefore urged the Duke of Guise to make further demands on the King; and on his hesitating to comply with these, the Duke entered Paris in defiance of the royal command (May 12). The attempt of the King to reassert his authority by ordering the Municipal Guard and the Swiss to secure the important points of the city was answered by the 'barricades'; and Henry III., finding himself no longer master of his capital, retired to Chartres, never again to enter Paris. Forced for the moment to submit to the League, the feeble monarch next tried to outbid the Guises with the deputies of the States-General, which assembled at Blois on September 16, 1588. But so extreme were the views adopted by the League at this moment that this proved impossible. Accordingly, the King turned to the last expedient of the coward, and ordered the assassination of Henry of Guise in his royal palace of Blois (December 23, 1588). The Cardinal of Guise the

Marginal notes:

Eighth Civil War. War of the three Henries. —— 1585- April 30, 1589.

Battle of Courtras. Oct. 20, 1587.

The Barricades. Aug. 12, 1588.

Assassination of Henry of Guise. Dec. 23, 1588.

brother of the Duke, was executed the next day, and the Cardinal
of Bourbon was held a prisoner. 'Now at last I am King,'
said Henry. The illusion was soon to be dispelled, for the
assassination of the Duke led to the open revolt of the
League. Supported by the decision of the Sorbonne, it
declared that the crown was elective; and when the 'Parlement' resisted, its more obstinate members were imprisoned.
The Duke of Mayenne, the eldest surviving brother of the
murdered Duke, was made Lieutenant-General of the realm,
and ruled Paris with a Council of forty, formed of deputies
from the affiliated societies of the League. The example of
Paris was followed elsewhere, and the League secured most
of the important towns of the centre and south of France.
Meantime, the failure of the royal army in Guienne destroyed
the last chance of maintaining an independent attitude, and
the King at last did what he should have done four years

Ten years
Truce.
April 30, 1589.

before, and threw himself into the arms of Henry of
Navarre. A truce for a year was made between the
two Henries (April 30, 1589). The King promised
to leave the Huguenots undisturbed, and Navarre engaged
to oppose the Duke of Mayenne. The armies of the two
Kings shortly after advanced on Paris, which seemed doomed,

Death of
Catherine,
Jan. 5;
Assassina-
tion of
Henry III.
July 31, 1589.

when the dagger of the Dominican, Jacques Clé-
ment, an emissary of the League, avenged the
assassination of the Duke of Guise (July 31).
The death of the last Valois King had been
preceded only a few months by that of Catherine
de' Medici, his mother. She died (January 5,
1589), with the reproaches of the Cardinal of Bourbon ringing
in her ears: 'If you had not deceived us and brought us here
(to Blois) with fine words, the two brothers (the Guises) would
not be dead, and I should be a free man.'

§ 6. *Henry IV. and the League, July* 1589—*May* 1598.

By the assassination of Henry III., Henry of Navarre became
the legitimate King of France. The question was, whether he

would make good his claim. Had he now been willing to declare himself a Roman Catholic, he would have at once won over the more conservative of the people, for the League was daily becoming more anarchical; the Cardinal of Bourbon, who was by it acknowledged as King Charles x., was but a puppet of Spain; and the Spanish alliance was ever growing more unpopular. But conversion would have probably lost him the support of the Huguenots, while it would not have gained the more fanatical members of the League. Accordingly, Henry refused. He offered to recognise Catholicism; to grant to the Huguenots no privileges beyond those they had hitherto gained; and to submit 'to the instruction' of a National or General Council. In thus acting he was guided by policy, not by conviction; and the interpretation he would put on his favourite phrase 'receiving instruction' would depend on his success in the field.

Not feeling strong enough to attack Paris itself, Henry determined to hold Picardy, Champagne, and Normandy, whence the capital drew her supplies. The Duke of Longueville was therefore sent to Picardy, the Marshal d'Aumont to Champagne, while Henry himself dropped back on Normandy, and occupied Dieppe, the most important of the Norman ports, and valuable on account of its proximity to England. The attempt of the Duke of Mayenne to dislodge him was foiled at the battle of Arques (September 21). In the following March, 1590, the still more brilliant victory of Ivry, near Dreux, conclusively proved the superiority of Henry over his antagonist. Henry perhaps 'committed the bravest folly' that ever was in staking the fate of a kingdom on a single battle, in which he had far inferior forces; but at least his intrepidity won for him the admiration of his countrymen. Possibly if he had pressed on at once, Paris might have been taken; but Henry had not the faculty of making the best of a victory, and preferred to continue his more cautious policy of starving the city into submission. He

9th and last Civil War. 1589-1595.

Battle of Arques, 5 Sept. 1589; and of Ivry, March 1590.

occupied Corbeil, Lagny, and Creil, which commanded the upper Seine, the Marne, and the Oise, and by the end of August, Paris was reduced to fearful straits. 'Nothing was

Siege of Paris. cheap except sermons.' As at Sancerre, dogs, cats, rats, and mice were eagerly devoured; some, it is said, even ate the flesh of children; and the people were loudly clamouring for peace or bread, when the approach of Alexander of Parma, from the Netherlands, baulked Henry of his prey, and forced him to retire (September 10). In the year 1592, Parma again entered France, and saved Rouen from Henry's

Death of Alexander of Parma. Dec. 1592. clutches. In December, however, the death of the great commander freed the King from immediate apprehension, and left the League without any leader who could match him in the field. Nevertheless, the war seemed likely to be indefinitely protracted. The party of the League indeed threatened to break up. Mayenne was impatient of Spanish influence, and was becoming daily more disgusted with the extravagance of the League in Paris. In the preceding November, the Sixteen had even dared to execute Brisson, the president of the 'Parlement,' and two other judges who opposed them, and had established a reign of terror. Accordingly, Mayenne had marched into the city, seized and condemned four of the Sixteen to death, and reasserted his authority. Hated, however, as he was by the fanatics, he was in no position to carry on the war with vigour unless with Spanish help, which he wished to do without.

Henry, too, was gaining popularity. Although his sensuality, his lack of real conviction, his cynical indifference, pre-

Position of Henry of Navarre. vent our making altogether a hero of the King of Navarre, his superabundant energy, his splendid courage, his frankness, affability, and genuine humanity, coupled with his caustic wit, had already endeared him to his countrymen. And yet he was not powerful enough to win his country by the sword; the Catholics would not consent to see a heretic on the throne of France; his attempt to settle the religious difficulty by the Declaration of Mantes (July, 1591), which acknowledged the Catholic religion as that of the State, while he himself remained a Protestant, pleased neither party. Too many, like the Marshal Biron and D'O, who had control of the finances, were interested in perpetuating the war, lest a return of peace might deprive them of employment, or of the hope of carving out a fortune for themselves.

Declaration of Mantes. July, 1591.

Meanwhile, France was going to ruin. Trade was at a standstill. Even the more patriotic of the nobles—whether Catholic or Protestant—despairing of peace, were aiming at their own independence, and the enemies of France were taking advantage of her weakness; Philip II. hoped to place his nominee on the throne, and to secure Brittany; the Duke of Savoy was attempting to encroach on her south-east frontier; and even Elizabeth of England was demanding Calais, or some other return for help, niggardly and intermittent though it was. The earnest desire, therefore, of all the moderate Catholics in France who were not sold to Philip, that Henry would 'go to Mass,' cannot excite surprise. In the spring of 1593, the meeting of the States-General, summoned to settle the question of the succession, brought matters to a crisis. The Cardinal of Bourbon had died in 1590; and, according to the Catholic view, the throne had been vacant for three years. Philip II., therefore, instructed his representative the Duke of Feria, to propose that the crown should be conferred on the Infanta (who through her mother represented the House of Valois in the female line). If, however, the Salic Law could not be violated, he was to suggest that the Archduke Ernest, the Governor of the Netherlands, and brother of the Emperor Rudolf, should be chosen King, or, failing him, the young Duke of Guise, who should take the Infanta as his Queen. In all probability, had the Duke of Feria at once proposed the Duke of Guise as King, he would have been accepted; but fortunately for Henry IV. he first

The States-General. Jan. 26, 1593.

suggested the Infanta, and thereby aroused the indignation of the 'Parlement' and of all those who cared for the fundamental laws of the country, and were not wholly sold to Spain. Convinced that delay was perilous, Henry now accepted the

Henry IV.
'receives
instruction.'
July 23, 1593.

offers of a deputation of the Estates-General sent to hold conference with him at Suresnes, and promised to 'receive instruction' within two months, while at the same time he strengthened his position by occupying Dreux. On July 23, Henry IV. recognised the Catholic, Apostolic, and Roman Church as the true one, and promised obedience. On the following February 27, he was anointed in the Cathedral of Chartres, since Rheims, where this ceremony should have been performed, was still in the hands of the League.

In dealing with the justification of Henry's 'conversion' it must always be remembered that, although by no means a disbeliever, he had no strong convictions as to the relative merits of Catholicism and Calvinism, and was a man on whom religious scruples sat somewhat lightly. To him, therefore, the question would necessarily be one to be decided on the grounds of political expediency. But some may be disposed to think that, even if Henry had been convinced of the superiority of the Huguenot faith, it would still have been his duty to guide his policy by the same considerations. Any one in his position, it has been said, would have been justified in accepting Catholicism as the State religion if he had good grounds for believing : first, that there was no other way of giving peace to his country ; and secondly, that he could, while officially recognising Catholicism, secure complete and lasting toleration for the Huguenots. Of the first, it was not difficult to convince himself. He had attempted to win France by arms and had failed. We must remember also that the Huguenots, after all, represented but a small minority of the nation, and that a large number of the Catholics preferred the Duke of Guise with his Spanish wife to a heretic King. Nor is it easy to believe that, if Henry had been willing to efface himself, any settlement which the Huguenots would have accepted could have been arrived at. On the second point, opinions will probably always differ. The danger was that in accepting Catholicism, he would revive the idea as to the intimate connection between Church and State in France which led men to look on heresy as treason. We know that the Edict of Nantes did not last; but whether the Revocation was inevitable, and, if so, whether Henry ought to have foreseen it, may well be questioned.

The King of Navarre was thus at last acknowledged King of France. By his 'conversion' he won to his side all Catholics except the most fanatical of the Leaguers, and those who, like the Dukes of Mayenne and of Mercœur, were intent on their personal interests. While, therefore, Henry restrained as far as possible all hostile operations, he steadily pursued a policy which he had long adopted of buying over those whose opposition was still to be dreaded. The governors of provinces were confirmed in their governorships, or offered pensions ; the smaller nobility were tempted by subordinate offices and money ; the cities were promised exemption from extraordinary taxation and freedom from Huguenot worship within their walls. The wisdom, and indeed the necessity, of this course have been disputed, and certainly the evil results of it—the independence of the nobility, the venality of the government, the serious straining of the finances—long outlived the King himself. Yet at least it must be confessed that the policy succeeded. On March 17, Rouen surrendered, and Henry secured all Normandy. Four days later Brissac, just appointed Governor of Paris by the Duke of Mayenne, accepted the offers of Henry, brought over the Parisian magistrates, and opened the gates. The Duke himself had already left, the Spanish troops were forced to evacuate the city with some sixty of the more prominent Leaguers, and Henry was at last master of his capital. 'That which is Cæsar's has been given unto Cæsar,' said one to the King. 'Given ?' said he, looking at Brissac ; 'No, sold, and for a goodly price.'

Henry secures Rouen, March 17 ; and enters Paris, March 21, 1594.

Henry, anxious to secure his eastern frontier which was always threatened from the Netherlands, next laid siege to Laon, which surrendered on the 2nd of August, 1594. A fortnight later Amiens, and other towns of Picardy, followed its example. The spring of the year 1595 was marked by a far more important event. Henry succeeded in conciliating the Duke of Lorraine and the young Duke of Guise. The former restored the cities of Toul and Verdun; the latter surrendered his governorship of Champagne in exchange for that of Provence, where he shortly proved his loyalty by driving out Épernon, one of Henry III.'s 'Mignons,' who, after joining Henry IV., had played him false. The only important nobles who still held out were the Dukes of Mayenne and of Mercœur, both members of the House of Guise, and the Duke of Nemours. The two first were loth to abandon the ambitions of their family, and hoped, by the aid of Spain, to turn their governorships of Burgundy and of Brittany into hereditary principalities. The Duke of Nemours, with the support of Savoy, threatened the country round Lyons. Henry, therefore, after some futile negotiations with Spain, in which the idea of Henry's marrying the Infanta was entertained, determined to declare open war against Spain. An open war, he held, was far preferable to a continuation of unavowed hostilities; the national enthusiasm against the foreigner might be aroused; all those who continued to resist would incur the charge of treachery to their country; while the English and the Dutch promised their assistance. The war was preceded by the expulsion of the Jesuits. Introduced into France by Henry II. they had made many enemies; the 'Parlement' objected to their extravagant assertions of papal supremacy, and to their attacks on the prerogatives of the crown; the Bishops resented their claim to be free from episcopal authority; the older orders grudged them their popularity, the University their educational success. Although it does not

Marginal notes:

Dukes of Lorraine and Guise come to terms.

Jesuits expelled.
Dec. 1594.
War declared against Spain.
Jan. 17, 1595.

appear that the Jesuits had taken any prominent part in the organisation of the League, and though they were, as a matter of fact, at this time out of favour in Spain, where they opposed the tyranny of the Inquisition, they were nevertheless denounced as the tools of Philip. An attempted assassination of Henry IV. by one of their pupils, though not apparently instigated by them, brought matters to a crisis. They were convicted by the 'Parlement' of attempting to subvert the laws of Church and State, of instigating to rebellion and assassination, and were expelled the kingdom (December 29, 1594).

War was declared against Spain on January 17, 1595. The young Marshal Biron, who had been intrusted with the governorship of Burgundy, succeeded in driving Mayenne from that province. The King, on marching to support him against the attack of a Spanish force under Don Fernan de Velasco, the Constable of Castile, was nearly surprised at Fontaine-Française. He, however, saved himself by his intrepidity; and the Spanish general retreated, much to the disgust of Mayenne. Henry now entered Franche-Comté; but the Swiss who were guarantors of the neutrality of the country, remonstrated, and the King, unwilling to incur their hostility, retreated. His presence was indeed needed elsewhere. The Duke of Longueville, after a successful campaign in Artois, had died in April; and Turenne, the Duke of Bouillon, had suffered a crushing defeat at the hands of the Spaniards under Fuentes, in an attempt to raise the siege of Doullens (July 24, 1595). Doullens fell, and Fuentes laid siege to Cambray, which had been in French hands since the expedition of the Duke of Anjou in 1581 (cf. p. 361). The King, too late to save Cambray, which capitulated in October, besieged La Fère, a fortress on the Oise, which the League had surrendered to the Spaniards, and the siege dragged on through the winter. The success of Henry in the field had not been brilliant. He was more successful in diplomacy. In September, 1595,

The Duke of Mayenne driven from Burgundy.

Fuentes takes Doullens, July 1595; and besieges Cambray.

Clement VIII. at last consented to grant him absolution, and in the following January, the Duke of Mayenne finally made his

The Duke of Mayenne submits. Jan. 1596.

peace. The terms he received were too high. His debts, which were enormous, were paid ; he was made Governor of the Isle de France, and received three fortresses as places of security. Épernon, who soon followed the example of Mayenne, was equally well rewarded. Truly Henry was teaching his people that rebellion, if prolonged, was the way to royal favour.

There now remained no other important noble in arms except the Duke of Mercœur ; and the winning of Marseilles by the young Duke of Guise, which also took place in January, caused Henry to declare 'that God had indeed pity for France.' Yet the outlook was not very promising. The financial straits were severe : Elizabeth would not, and the Dutch could not, render any efficient help ; while the Huguenots were becoming very troublesome. They were scandalised at the desire of Henry IV. to get a divorce from his faithless and hated wife, Margaret of Valois, that he might marry his mistress, Gabrielle d'Estrées ; they were outraged by the delay of the King in dealing with their grievances, while the rebellious Leaguers were receiving all that they could desire, and they even talked of enforcing their claims by arms.

In April, 1596, the new Governor of the Netherlands, the Cardinal Archduke Albert, invaded France and inflicted a

Archduke Albert takes Calais. April, 1596.

serious blow on the prestige of Henry's army by taking Calais. The town might have been saved if Elizabeth had not demanded its possession as a price of her assistance, and higgled till it was too late. In the ensuing month, Henry, in a measure, balanced this serious loss by taking La Fère, and by driving the Archduke across the frontier ; but he was quite unable to dislodge the Spanish garrisons from Calais or from Doullens. If the war was to be continued with vigour, money at least must be found ; and to this object the Baron de Rosny (Sully), who had lately been appointed 'surintendant' of the finances, now turned his attention. New offices were created, which were sold to the highest bidder. Loans were extorted from the rich. Those who had filled their pockets by Sully's frauds on the exchequer were forced to disgorge financial part of their ill-gotten gains, and some attempt was reforms. made to put a stop to such corruption in the future. The tax on salt was raised, and in the autumn an Assembly of Notables granted the King the 'Pancarte,' or duty of 5 per cent. on all goods offered for sale.[1]

Yet what Henry gained with one hand he was, with his usual recklessness, ready to spend with the other. Much of the money thus obtained was being thrown away on Porto expensive festivities in Paris, when the news sud- Carrero denly arrived that Porto Carrero, the Governor of seizes Amiens. Doullens, had seized the important town of Amiens Mar. 11, 1597. by a clever *coup de main* (March 11, 1597). 'Enough,' said Henry, 'of playing the King of France; 'tis time to be the King of Navarre again.' Biron was despatched to besiege Amiens forthwith. In June, the King followed himself with an army, in which the presence of Montmorenci, Mayenne, and Épernon showed that the old factions had been well-nigh extinguished. The English and the Dutch also sent reinforcements, in pursuance of a treaty of alliance which they had made in the previous year (August-October, 1596). On September 3, Porto Carrero died. The Archduke Albert, unable to raise supplies even on credit, owing to Philip's late act of repudiation, could not advance to the relief of the

---

[1] While Sully had been doing something to replenish the exchequer of King Henry, his antagonist, Philip, attempted a more summary method. On November 20, 1596, he publicly revoked all assignments, or mortgages by which the taxes on the royal domain had been pledged for money advanced to him. The pretext for this wholesale repudiation was that his exertions for Christianity had reduced him to beggary, while the money-lenders had been growing rich at his expense. The deed, however, produced a panic. The chief merchants and bankers suspended payment, and the credit of Spain received a shock from which it did not easily recover.

garrison till September 12 ; then, finding himself in the
presence of a superior force, he retreated 'like a priest,' and
Amiens on September 19, 1597, Amiens was at last re-
recovered. covered. Henry now determined to take advantage
Sept. 19, 1597. of his success to negotiate with Spain. Philip did
not refuse his offer. Tortured by disease, knowing that his end
was approaching, that Spain could no longer bear the strain
of war, and that his feeble son was not likely to succeed where
he had failed, he was anxious to leave his country at peace.
Philip agrees He accordingly agreed to a truce, and to hold a
to a truce. conference at Vervins in the following January
for finally settling the terms of peace. The affairs of
Brittany Henry was determined to settle without any foreign
interference ; and this he succeeded in doing without drawing
the sword. The Bretons, despairing of successful resistance
The Duc de now that the aid of Spain was withdrawn, deserted
Mercœur the Duke of Mercœur, who was forced to come to
submits. terms at Angers (March 20). He surrendered
Mar. 20, 1598. the governorship of Brittany, with the hand of
his daughter, to Cæsar, the illegitimate son of the King by
Gabrielle d'Estrées, and received a pension in return. Thus
at last all resistance had ended, and France was once more
united.

The King was now in a position to attend to the grievances
of the Huguenots. On entering Paris he had republished the
The Edict Edict of 1576, with the amendments added thereto
of Nantes. by the treaties of Bergerac and Fleix. Since he
April 15, 1598. could no longer be their Protector, nor allow any
other to hold that position, he had also authorised the Huguenots
to organise themselves into a federative system for defence, and
ten provinces had been formed, each with its elected assembly
and a General Council of ten nominated by the assemblies.
But the Huguenots were not satisfied ; they complained that
these concessions were not sufficient, and that they were often
violated. All members of the League, whether noble or town,
who came to terms were allowed to forbid the exercise of the

Protestant religion within their jurisdiction, and what security had the Huguenots that one who could so lightly change his own religion would care or dare to protect that of others? They therefore had demanded more formal ratification of the privileges already granted them, an extension of the system of 'Chambres mi-parties' to all the 'Parlements' of France, and admission to all offices. The King, in spite of the grave discontent which at times threatened to break out in open war, had hitherto refused to satisfy their demands; until the Catholics were completely reconciled such a policy might be dangerous, and certainly would be futile, since Henry was not strong enough to enforce his promises. Now, however, that he was really master of France, he had neither the excuse nor the wish to delay any longer. Negotiations had, indeed, been going on for some time, and finally led to the Edict of Nantes, which was published on April 15, 1598. The clauses of this famous Edict followed closely on the lines of the Treaty of Bergerac of 1577. The Huguenots were permitted to hold divine service in all towns specified by that treaty, or in which it had been held in 1596 and 1597; and besides this, in one town in each bailiwick and in the fiefs of Protestant nobles. In these privileged towns they were also allowed to found colleges and schools, and to print books. Paris, however, as before, with a circuit of five leagues, was especially exempted till 1606, when the King allowed a temple to be built at Charenton, five miles distant. Huguenot ministers were to be exempt from military service, and the King promised to contribute an annual sum for their support; while the Protestants, on their part, were to pay tithes. In the 'Parlements' of Paris, Rouen, and Rennes, special 'Chambres de l'Édit'—one of the judges of which was to be a Protestant—were to be established to try cases in which Huguenots were concerned; while three 'Chambres mi-parties' at Castres, Bordeaux, and Gap were to exercise a similar jurisdiction in the south. Finally, the Huguenots were to be allowed to hold synods, to have admission to all colleges and schools; all offices were to be open to them, and they were to suffer in no way for their religion. They were to hold the eight cities they possessed for eight years, but to allow the Catholic worship to continue there. Considering that the Huguenots did not number more than one-twelfth of the population of France, the terms they thus obtained were as favourable as they could expect, and all that was perhaps possible in the existing condition of France.

But the principle on which the Edict was based was radically faulty. It can scarcely be called an Edict of general toleration, for no other religion but that of Calvinism was allowed. Moreover, the concession of the privilege of worship to individual nobles, and to congregations in special towns, tended to accentuate the independence and isolation of the Huguenots, and to perpetuate the centrifugal tendencies, both of feudalism and of federative republicanism, which the wars of religion had intensified, and which were yet to give trouble to France. As long as there was a King on the throne willing and able to enforce the Edict, the compromise continued fairly satisfactory. But after he was gone, the chances that the Edict would be permanent day by day became less. The Huguenots, partly in self-defence, partly in pursuance of political aims which the Edict had fostered, attempted to form those towns which had been granted them into a semi-independent federation ; and when, to check this, Richelieu deprived them of these pledges for the fulfilment of the Edict, he left them to fall defenceless before the tyranny and bigotry of Louis XIV.

While Henry was thus removing the last traces of opposition in France, the negotiations with Spain had been going on ; Peace of Vervins. May 2, 1598. and, on May 2, the Peace of Vervins was signed. Spain evacuated all the conquests she had made in France during the last war with the exception of Cambray; Henry, on his part, restoring the county of Charolais. The Duke of Savoy came to terms at the same time ; he surrendered Berre, the only place he held in Provence ; while the question as to the Marquisate of Saluces, which he had seized in 1588, was referred to the arbitration of the Pope.[1] Neither the Dutch nor the English were included in the Peace. The Dutch refused to enter into any treaty which did not recognise their independence, while Elizabeth was not unwilling to see the war continue between France and Spain. She had even attempted to make capital out of the negotiations, going so far as to suggest to Philip that he should cede Calais in exchange for Brille and Flushing, which she still held. Henry accordingly contented himself with securing the right of his allies to become parties to the treaty within six months.

CONCLUSION.

The Treaty of Vervins scarcely made any alteration in the political geography of Europe. Its importance lies rather in the changed conditions which accompanied it, and followed it. A few months after the signing of that treaty, Philip II. died (September 12, 1598) in his seventy-second year, at the Escurial—that magnificent though somewhat strange mixture of 'a palace, a monastery, and a tomb,' which is the chief architectural monument of his reign. Had Philip been a wiser man, he might have retained the obedience of the Netherlands, and profited by their industry and their colonies. He might have developed the resources and the constitutional liberties of his country, and enriched her by commerce with America. He might have turned her arms against the Turk, made himself master of the Mediterranean, and left Spain consolidated and prosperous. Intent, however, on more magnificent schemes, he had failed disastrously. His attempt to lead the Catholic reaction, and to re-establish the unity of the Church on the basis of Spanish supremacy, had ended in disaster. The defeat of the Armada had saved

Condition of Europe at the Peace of Vervins.

Decline of Spain.

---

[1] The Marquisate of Saluzzo in Piedmont had been ceded to France by the Treaty of Cateau Cambrésis, cf. p. 257. Henry IV. in 1601 exchanged it with the Duke of Savoy for Bresse, Bugey, and Gex.

England from both Spain and Rome. The United Provinces had virtually won their religious and political freedom, and Henry IV. had bowed the Spaniard from his doors. Meanwhile Spain, exhausted by the constant drain which the vast attempts involved, and ruined by the disastrous policy pursued at home (cf. ch. vii.), was fast declining. After Philip's death her royal race degenerated rapidly; and with a shrinking population, paralysed industries, and attenuated resources, she was forced to step aside and leave the struggle for supremacy to others.

And yet the Catholic reaction, of which Philip had been the leading spirit, had not been without its successes. If
Successes of England, the United Netherlands, and the Scandithe Catholic navian kingdoms had decisively broken away from Reaction. Rome, Protestantism had been completely crushed out in Spain and in Italy, and in 1587, Catholicism was finally restored in Poland by Sigismund. In France, if the Huguenots had secured toleration, that toleration was not to last; and Catholicism had not only captured the King, but had again been recognised as the religion of the State. In Germany, too, the advance of Protestantism had, since the middle of the century, been arrested. The Jesuits had by this time made their influence felt, not only by their missionary and educational work among the people, but also on the policy of the Princes. In Bavaria, Albert III. (1550-1579) drove out the Protestants, and made his Duchy a stronghold of Catholicism. In 1576, Rudolf II. succeeded his father, Maximilian II., in the most important of the Austrian dominions,[1] and was elected Emperor. Maximilian had been half-inclined towards Lutheranism. Rudolf, educated under the influence of his mother, the daughter of Charles v., and subsequently at the Spanish Court, was strongly Catholic. He dismissed the Protestant preachers from Vienna, and

[1] His brothers, Ferdinand and Charles, received Tyrol and Styria. These were reunited to Austria proper under Ferdinand II., and the Austrian dominions were declared indivisible, 1621.

supported a Catholic policy in the Empire. The advance of Catholicism was also favoured by the dissensions between the Lutherans and the Calvinists, who were respectively headed by the Electors of Saxony and of the Palatinate. Under these circumstances, quarrels over the controverted clauses of the Peace of Augsburg were inevitable (cf. pp. 248-9). The Catholics questioned the right of the Bishop of Magdeburg to a seat in the Diet, and, in 1581, had driven Gebhard Truchsess from his Electoral See of Cologne, because these two prelates had embraced Protestantism.

Day by day the relations between the adherents of the two creeds became more strained. Already the Thirty Years' War was looming in the distance—a war in which Pro- Disorganised testantism was indeed to hold her own, but at the condition of price of the destruction of German nationality Germany. and unity, almost of German independence, and of the crippling of national prosperity and intellectual growth for more than a century.

France, it is true, had suffered severely from her civil war of thirty-six years. Trade and industry had been ruined, and her finances heavily strained. The Condition of venality of her administrative system had been in- France. creased. The Estates-General and the 'Parlements,' the representatives of constitutional life, had been discredited; the former by the extreme views it had at times adopted, both by their subservience to the League. The power and self-importance of the nobles had been increased during the civil wars, and by the system adopted by Henry iv. of buying off their opposition. The desire for federative republicanism had grown with the growth of Calvinism. All these things had been the results of the religious wars. Yet after all, it was the royal power and prestige which in the end had benefited Revival of most from the internal discords. It was Henry the Royal who had given his country peace at last, and authority. thereby earned the gratitude of his people; he it was who chiefly gained by the discredit into which the organs of

constitutional life had fallen, and by the divisions and dissensions of his subjects. The nobles, indeed, were dangerous, but
Henry IV. was successful in defeating their intrigues. His
able, though self-sufficient and egotistical minister, Sully,
reorganised the finances, and did something to check the
venality and corruption which existed. The marvellous re-
cuperative powers of the country came to his assistance ; and
France under the clever, though somewhat cynical, rule of
her great King became once more a first-rate Power. Had
Henry lived longer, or had he been succeeded by a capable
son, the Thirty Years' War would probably not have occurred,
or would have been ended sooner. The House of Hapsburg
might have been humbled to the dust, and France might have
established a dangerous supremacy in Europe. The assassination of Henry IV. in 1610 prevented this ; France, on his
death, became the victim of a weak minority, and a troubled
regency ; and Europe was not threatened with a French
supremacy until the reign of Louis XIV.

APPENDIX I

THE FRENCH CONSTITUTION IN THE FIFTEENTH AND SIXTEENTH CENTURIES.

Cf. Gasquet, *Institutions Politiques et Sociales de la France.*
Chéruel, *Dictionnaire Historique des Institutions de la France.*

I. CENTRAL ADMINISTRATION.—*Conseil du Roi* (King's Council), or *Conseil d'État* (Council of State). The supreme Executive Council of the realm. It also exercised *Legislative* powers through its Ordinances, and high *Judicial* power until organisation of the Grand Conseil.

    1. Sometimes heard ultimate appeals from the Sovereign Law Courts.

    2. Evoked cases from other Courts in which public interests were involved.

    3. Heard complaints against the royal officials.

    These Judicial Powers were subsequently transferred to—

        a. THE GRAND CONSEIL.—Finally organised in 1497, to decide questions of disputed jurisdiction between the other sovereign Courts, but never very important. Composed of the Constable (the chief Military Officer), the Chancellor (the Supreme Civil Officer), the Princes of the Blood, Officers of State.

        β. THE CONSEIL PRIVÉ or des parties.

        A Judicial Committee of the Council erected in the seventeenth century.

A number of clerks (Maîtres de Requêtes) under the Conseil du Roi, worked various Departmental Councils, such as those of War and Finance.

II. CENTRAL COURTS OF JUSTICE.

    A. THE PARLEMENT OF PARIS.—The Central Judicial Court of the Realm, sharing with the Grand Conseil the right of hearing appeals from all subordinate Courts.

    It also (1) issued Arrêts, or Injunctions.

        (2) Registered all royal ordinances, treaties of peace, and other public documents; and,

from the reign of Louis XI., claimed the right of refusing to register—a right which gradually ripened into a right of veto. The King, however, could always override its veto by holding a 'Lit de Justice'—*i.e.* by summoning the Parlement, in solemn assembly, before the Peers of France and the officers of State, and ordering it to register.

Its members held office for life, and were, since the reign of Louis XI., irremovable, unless convicted of some penal offence. As membership was generally purchased from the King, they became saleable, and, after the reign of Henry IV., practically hereditary.

The Parlement was divided into five Courts :—

1. *The Grand Chambre.*—This heard all appeals of great importance, and cases of first instance which concerned the Peers ; cases of treason ; and criminal charges against royal officials and members of the Parlement.

2. *Chambre des Requêtes.*—Decided smaller cases of first instance.

3. *Chambre des Enquêtes.*—Heard smaller cases of appeal, and prepared the more important appeals for the Grand Chambre.

4. *Chambre de la Tournelle.*—Tried less important criminal cases.

5. *Chambre de l'Édit.*—Established after the Edict of Nantes, 1598, to try cases between Catholics and Huguenots. One or two of the judges were to be Protestants.

B. CHAMBRE DES COMPTES.—Exercised jurisdiction in all financial matters dealing with the royal domain, and audited accounts of the Baillis and Sénéschals ; registered edicts concerning the royal domain, and recorded the fealty and homage of tenants-in-chief. Jurisdiction civil—not criminal.

C. COUR DES AIDES.—Exercised civil and criminal jurisdiction over cases dealing with Taxation, and audited
accounts of the Élus who collected the direct taxes.

III LOCAL JUSTICE AND ADMINISTRATION.

    1. *Provincial Parlements,* exercising the same authority as
the Parlement of Paris within their districts, existed
in the fifteenth century at—

        Toulouse for Province of Languedoc, instituted 1443.

Grenoble	„	Dauphiné,	„	1453.
Bordeaux	„	Guienne,	„	1462.
Dijon	„	Burgundy,	„	1477.

And the following were added during the sixteenth
century at—

        Aix   for Provence, 1501.
        Rouen for Normandy, 1515
        Rennes for Brittany, 1553.

Five more were subsequently added—

Pau	for Béarn, 1620.
Metz	„ 3 Bishoprics, 1633.
Douai	„ Flanders, 1686.
Besançon	„ Franche-Comté, 1676.
Nancy	„ Lorraine, 1769.

Most of these Provinces had their separate Chambre des
Comptes, and Cour des Aides.

    2. *The Baillis or Sénéschals* (with Prévôts under them).

        (*a*) Collected the dues from the royal domains (while
the Élus collected the regular direct taxes).

        (*b*) Tried petty cases.

        (*c*) Administered affairs, civil and military, of their
Bailliage or Sénéchaussée.

Their jurisdiction was subordinated to that of the Parlements, and their financial accounts were under the
Cours des Comptes, while that of the Élus were
audited by the Cours des Aides.

Francis I., however, appointed new officers — *the
Lieutenants, Civil and Criminel*—to whom, by the
ordinance of 1560, the judicial functions of the Baillis

and Sénéschals were transferred. After that date the importance of the Baillis and Sénéschals rapidly declined, especially after the final institution of the Intendants by Richelieu.

Francis I. also appointed twelve *Lieutenants-Général* over the frontier Provinces. During the Civil War these were extended to most of the Provinces ; and the *Governors*, as they now were called, made themselves so powerful as to be 'very kings.' Henry IV. did his best to buy off these Governors ; but their power was not finally overthrown till the time of Richelieu.

3. In 1551 Henry II. instituted *Tribunaux Présidiaux* as intermediate Courts between the Parlements and those of the Baillis or Sénéschals.

4. The nobles still retained their Seignorial Courts ; but these, jealously watched by the Baillis and Sénéschals, were confined to questions between the Seigneur and his dependants.

5. The towns enjoyed municipal government, which varied very much, but was usually composed of a General Assembly which elected a Corps de Ville, which in its turn elected a municipality composed of the Mayor and échevins (sheriffs). In Paris the Prévôt des Marchands took the place of the Mayor. The rights of election, however, became day by day more and more visionary. The officials were usually nominated by the Crown, often in return for money. The towns also had their Courts, but the judicial powers, always limited, were finally withdrawn.

In Paris, however, there was a peculiar Court, that of the *Châtelet*, under the Prévôt of Paris (to be distinguished from the Prévôt des Marchands). The Prévôt of Paris had no Baillis or Sénéschal over him. He administered the police of the city, and heard cases on appeal from the Seignorial Courts of the town and district, as well as certain cases especially reserved to the *Châtelet*, such as dowries, rights of succession to property, etc.

THE ESTATES-GENERAL (États Généraux).

Composed of three Chambers, consisting of deputies from the three Orders of Nobles, Clergy, Tiers État (Third Estate).

Mode of Election.—On fixed day, nobles, clergy, and townsmen met in chief town of Bailliage or Sénéchaussée.

Nobles and Clergy by direct Election.—The nobles and clergy drew up their cahiers (petitions), and elected their deputies separately.

Tiers État by double Election.—The townsmen chose a body of electors, who drew up the cahier, and elected the deputy.

After 1484 the peasants of the villages took part in the election of the Electoral Body.

In some of the Provinces a different system prevailed. Thus in Languedoc and Champagne, the three orders elected their deputies in common ; in Brittany, the deputies of one order were chosen by the other two orders.

Procedure.—On the meeting of Estates-General the three orders were summoned to a Royal Séance (Session), in which the reasons for the summons were given.

The orders then separated, and each order proceeded to draw up their general cahier apart. The three cahiers having then been presented to the King, the States-General was dismissed.

Powers.—The States-General were originally summoned not to discuss, but to hear the will of the King, and to present grievances.

These Petitions were of considerable value, for, although the States-General was dismissed without having received the answer of the King, the cahiers often furnished the basis for royal ordinances. At various dates the Estates-General attempted to gain the same powers as those finally secured by the English Parliament :

1. Frequent and regular Sessions.
2. That their petitions should be answered.
3. Control of taxation and of policy.
4. Appointment, or at least responsibility, of ministers.

But in spite of notable attempts, especially those of 1355-1358, 1484, 1561 (p. 398), 1576-7 (p. 423), 1588 (p. 431), the States-General failed in obtaining its object, and after 1614, ceased to be summoned until 1789.

Reasons for failure of the States-General.—It is sometimes said that the States-General did not represent France ; it is more correct to say that it represented France too well—in its want of cohesion, its class divisions, its absence of local government.   Nor were the circumstances of the fifteenth and sixteenth centuries propitious.   During that period, the hundred years' war, and the religious wars, led the people of France to lean on the King ; the privileges of the feudal nobles prevented any unanimity between the upper and lower classes, and allowed the bureaucracy to gain such strength that it was impossible subsequently to overthrow it.

Thus the causes of failure may be tabulated as follows :—

1. The existence of three Houses prevented unanimity, more especially because they represented class divisions which were deep.   The nobility being a caste dependent on blood ; while the upper offices of the Church were also filled by nobles.

2. There was no class of country gentry as in England, from whom the knights of the shire were elected, and who united with the burgesses in the House of Commons.

3. The number of royal officials elected as deputies of Tiers d'État was generally very large.

4. The Estates-General of Orleans (1439), in establishing a permanent army by the Ordonnance sur la Gendarmerie, was held to have granted to the King a permanent tax, *the Taille* ; and this, in spite of several protests, was subsequently increased at the royal will.

5. Since the nobles and clergy were exempt from the Taille—the first because they served in the feudal array ; the latter because of their clerical privileges—the deputies of these two orders did not support the Tiers État in their attempt to control the purse.   Thus the States-General lost the control of the purse.

6. There was no efficient local government like that of the English shire. The real power being in the hands of the royal officials, the Baillis and the Sénéschals, and later, of the Intendants.

PROVINCIAL ESTATES.—It is true that all the Provinces of France originally had their Provincial Estates composed of three orders.

(1) But in many Provinces they were artificial creations.

(2) They were weakened by the same class divisions as the States-General.

Accordingly after the fifteenth century many Provinces lost their Estates, and finally only some four survived the reign of Louis XIV., and even those had but little power beyond that of assessing the Taille.

THE CHURCH.—The Church had its

(1) *Ecclesiastical Courts,* which as elsewhere in Europe had attempted to extend their jurisdiction very widely, not only over clergy but over laity. By the end of the fifteenth century, however, their jurisdiction was confined to offences of clerics or laics against morals, the law or doctrine of the Church, and to cases concerning the marriage and death-bed—*e.g.* divorce, wills, etc. ; any attempt on the part of the Ecclesiastical Courts to encroach on the domain of secular jurisdiction being met by the Appels comme d'abus (abuse), which were presented to the Parlement of Paris.

(2) Its Assemblies, in which, in and after the sixteenth century, the clergy voted 'dons gratuits' (voluntary offerings) to the Crown.

The relations of the Church to the Crown and to the Pope were further defined by the Pragmatic Sanction of Bourges, and the Concordat of Bologna (cf. p. 81).

TAXATION.

The revenue during the fifteenth and sixteenth centuries was drawn from the following sources :—

I. THE ROYAL DOMAIN.
   (*a*) Feudal incidents.
   (*b*) Profits of Justice.
   (*c*) Rights appertaining to the King as Sovereign—*e.g.* of succeeding to property of aliens dying without heirs, and of all bastards ; fines on land granted in mortmain.

II. DIRECT TAXES.
   (1) *The Taille*, which was of two kinds—
      (*a*) In the *Pays d'États* it was generally a tax on the value of land, assessed by regular assessments, under orders of the Provincial Assembly.
      (*b*) In the other parts of France (the *Pays d'Élection*), it was a tax levied on presumed income derived from whatever source, and assessed in a very arbitrary fashion by Élus, who were responsible to the Cour des Aides.

   Exempt from the Taille were Nobles following arms, Clergy, Students at the Universities, Royal Officials, Municipal Authorities. Thus the tax fell practically on the lower classes.

   (2) *Dons Gratuits.*—Taxes on clergy voted by ecclesiastical assemblies.

III. INDIRECT TAXES.
   (1) *Aides.*—Dues levied on the sale of food-stuffs, wine, and other articles.

   (2) *Gabelles.*—Salt was a royal monopoly ; and every household had to buy so much salt for every member above the age of eight. The price was very high, but varied, as well as the amount to be bought, in different Provinces

(3) *Customs* at the frontiers of every Province. These in later days were so heavy that a cask of wine would pay its value before it reached Paris.

(4) *Sale of Offices.*—By the end of the sixteenth century there was scarcely any royal office which was not sold.

The Aides, Gabelles, and Customs were in the hands of farmers of the taxes, who exercised great extortion.

APPENDIX II

CONSTITUTION OF FLORENCE IN THE FIFTEENTH AND SIXTEENTH CENTURIES.

I. Based on System of *Guilds* (since 1282), cf. Von Reumont, Lorenzo de Medici, vol. i. pp. 15 and 67. Villari, *Florence*, p. 312 ff.

> Seven Greater Arti = Popolo Grasso.
> Fourteen Lesser Arti = Popolo Minuto.

Each with its Council, Consuls, and Proconsuls. Number of eligible citizens (Statuali), some 5000 out of 100,000.

II. EXECUTIVE.—The *College*, composed of Signory and Collegi— *I tre Maggiori* (offices).

(1) *Signoría* appointed for two months. Its members (unpaid with exception of its Secretary, and Chancellor), lived in Palazzo Publico at public cost.

Powers.—(*a*) Initiation of Legislation.

(*b*) Supreme Executive power.

(*c*) Right of summoning a Parlamento.

Members.—A. *Gonfalonier of Justice* (first instituted 1293), must be forty-five years of age and a member of one of Arti Maggiori. Presided over all Councils—and could call out the Militia. Originally elected by the Councils, but subsequently appointed by lot. Cf below.

B. *Eight Priori.*—Two from each quarter of the city (originally elected by the Arts), must be thirty years old and members of a guild (six from Arti Maggiori, two from Minori since 1345). Each Prior presided with Gonfalonier for three days, and could put any measure to the vote if Gonfalonier refused. (' Il proposto.')

(2) *The Colleagues* (*Collegi*).

    (*a*) Twelve *Buonuomini* (nine from greater, three from lesser Arts). These acted as a Privy Council and check on the Signory.

    (*b*) Sixteen *Gonfaloniers* of the sixteen militia companies (four from each quarter of the city), under the *Capitano del Popolo*.

    (*c*) Nine assessors of the Priors.

A permanent paid Secretary called ' Second Chancellor.'

Exceptional. Capitani di Parte Guelfa.—These instituted in 1297, for protection of city against Ghibellines, were continued long after danger had passed away. They were from three to nine in number, elected for two months, and empowered to administer proceeds of confiscated property of Ghibellines exiled or condemned, and as these sums were large the Capitani undertook the maintenance of fortresses and defences and public buildings.

By Law of 1358 all who held or had held office might be accused openly or secretly before the Capitani as being no genuine Guelph. No witnesses for defence allowed—and if the accusation was supported by six witnesses worthy of belief the accused could be condemned to fine or death, without appeal.

By the end of the fourteenth century, however, this tyrannical organisation had somewhat lost its power.

III. FOREIGN AFFAIRS were in hands of—

    (1) Dieci di Guerra—called later Dieci di libertà e Pace—first appointed 1423.

    (2) Two Councils, which considered the bills concerning foreign affairs before they went to the ordinary Councils.

        (*a*) *Consiglio del Dugento.*—Two hundred of those who had held the highest offices of State.

        (*b*) *Consiglio Centotrentuno*, 131 (the Signory, Captains of Guelph Party, Ten of War, Councils of craftsmen, Consuls of Guilds, and forty-eight citizens).

IV. LEGISLATION after 1328.

A Law approved by the College went to—

1. The Two Councils of the Capitano del Popolo.

   (*a*) Consiglio di Credenza or del Cento, 100 officials of guilds, sometimes called Senate, often disregarded. Cf. Nardi, 1, 4 (b). Symonds, *Age of Despots*, p. 530.

   (*b*) Consiglio del Popolo, 300 originally chosen from the greater Arts—later from others as well, renewed every four months.

2. The Two Councils of the Podestà.

   (*a*) A special Council of 90.

   (*b*) The larger Consiglio del Podestà or del Commune, some 390. This contained judges and law officers (and therefore nobles, since nobles could hold these offices), as well as popolani, and were renewed every four months.

Finally, a law having passed these Councils had to be submitted to a General Council of them all.

The Signory and the colleagues *ex officio* were members of these Councils.

System of voting. By ballot. Black and white beans. Black = yes, white = no. $\frac{2}{3}$ of black beans necessary to carry a question.

Tenere le fave or il partito	= To vote no.
Rendere le fave or il partito	= To vote yes.
L'autorità dei sei fave	= Majority of $\frac{2}{3}$ in Signory. (6 out of 9.)
Il piu della fave	= $\frac{2}{3}$ of votes.

V. JUSTICE.

1. *Court of Capitano del Popolo*—a paid officer—must be a foreign noble and lawyer. Exercised summary criminal jurisdiction, especially over Plebs.

2. *Court of Podestà*—a paid officer—must be a foreign (Italian) noble and lawyer. Exercised higher civil and criminal jurisdiction.

3. *Executor of Justice*—a paid officer—must be a popolano and a Guelph and a foreigner. Exercised summary jurisdiction, especially over nobles.

All these held office for six months.

4. *Casa della Mercatanzia.* A tribunal for decision of Commercial Cases, which also acted as a Board of Trade.

5. *Otto di Balía e Guardia,* nominated by Signory, held office for four months.

A court of appeal from Court of Podestà and with powers of police.

The Signoria and the Otto had power to execute, banish, or imprison any citizen.

VI. Mode of Appointment to Chief Magistracies.

Originally elected by the Councils, but subsequently this replaced by system of 'lot.'

For each office a purse (borsa), was formed every three or five years of all citizens eligible to said office, and names were drawn out of this purse.

In case of Priors, fifty wax balls, each containing eight names (six from Arti Maggiori, two from Minori), were put in the purse, and then a ball was drawn out.

Eligibility (Benefiziati, the Eligible).—This was decided by a Squittino (Scrutiny) conducted by a board—and persons could be considered ineligible 'messo a sedere,' for the following reasons (the disenfranchised 9000 out of 100,000) :—

1. (*a*) *Grandi.*—By Ordini della Guistizia, 1293, nobles could not be members of the Signoria or of the Collegi or of Consiglio del Popolo until 1434, when Cosimo allowed them to enter Guilds.

   (*b*) The Plebe or Ciompi, all not members of Guilds.

   (*c*) Inhabitants of Contado, country districts.

2. *Ammonito.*—'Warned' for any political offence, *e.g.* being a Ghibelline, and denounced by the Capitano del Parti Guelfa ; disqualification for life or shorter time. This system carried to great extravagance. 'Hast thou no enemy ? Consent to admonish mine and I will do the same by thine.' Cf. Napier, ii. 235.

3. *Moroso di Specchio* (mirror).—One who had not paid his taxes. (*Netto di Specchio*, freed from this ineligibility.) By law of 1421, taxes must have been paid for thirty years by self, father and grandfather.

4. *Divieto* (prohibited).—Even after names were drawn a

man might be disqualified because he or a relation had recently held office—' veduto ma non seduto.'

The members of the board bound to secrecy, but

(1) As the period for which the purses had been made up drew to its close, it became possible to guess who would be the coming magistrates, and there were charlatans who pretended to foretell this.

(2) The members of the boards of scrutiny were bribed to divulge the names who would be drawn.

Legalised Revolution.—At times of crisis the Signoria would summon a Parlamento nominally of the whole citizens, but generally only of party adherents, who granted exceptional powers (Balía) to a certain number of citizens.

The *Balía* (1) could alter the constitution.

(2) Appointed Accopiatori (couplers or joiners) who selected those eligible to office, and sometimes nominated the officials, *i.e.* appointed 'a mano' instead of 'a sorte.'

In 1459 (under Cosimo) a council of 100 was instituted to elect the Accopiatori.

Florence enjoyed political, but *no* civil liberty.

(1) Powers of magistrates unchecked.

(2) No appeal from Law Courts. Arbitrary Jurisdiction.

(3) No liberty of Press.

CHANGES IN THE CONSTITUTION.

N.B. Signory lasted till 1530.

I. UNDER LORENZO.

1472. Burd, *Machiavelli*, 81, 85, 89; Perrens' *Histoire de Florence, Depuis la domination des Médicis*, 1, 362, 445, 523; Armstrong, *Lorenzo de' Medici*.

Arti reduced to 12 by suppression of 9 Arti minori.

1480. After Pazzi Conspiracy.

Consiglio de Settanta (College of 70), appointed by Signoria with power to fill up its own vacancies from those who had held office of Gonfalonier.

Its work (*a*) To permanently nominate to offices (a mano).

(*b*) Appoint the *Otto di Pratica* which superseded the old Dieci di Libertà e Pace.

This College, originally appointed for five years, was continually reappointed.

In 1490. This College intrusted some of its powers to a smaller
Committee of 17, of whom Lorenzo was one ; and
this Committee

(*a*) Appointed Accopiatori to nominate to offices.

(*b*) Supervised every branch of administration.

II. 1494. Savonarola's Reforms. Cf. Burd, p. 94. Guicciardini, *Storia Fiorentia,* iii. 120. Villari, *Savonarola,* p. 257.
Perrens, ii. c. 3. *Cambridge Mod. Hist.,* vol. i. p. 158.

(1) Temporary.—A Parlamento summoned, who appointed 20
Accopiatori (*Governo de' Venti*). These filled up
magistracies for the year and prepared a Squittino for
the future.

(2) Permanent.—Constitution formed in imitation of Venice.
Consiglio del Popolo and del Commune and Parlamento
abolished.

A. *Consiglio Generale,* or Maggiore, formed of all
eligible 'benefiziati' citizens (all those of age of
29 whose father, grandfather, or great-grandfather
had been veduto *or* seduto for one of three greater
offices, about 3000). But if the number of the
'benefiziati' exceeded 1500, they were to be
'sterzati,' *i.e.* divided into 3, and ⅓ of the whole
number were to form the Consiglio for 6 months.
A small number of citizens, above age of 24 and
otherwise qualified, were admitted, and each year
60 eligible but neither veduto nor seduto might
be elected if they received two-thirds of votes.

B. *Consiglio degli Ottanta,* a Senate elected out of and
by Consiglio Generale for six months, must be
40 years of age.

The Senate was to advise *The Signory* (which
remained as before), and elect ambassadors
and commissioners to army.

The Consiglio Generale was

(1) To elect to magistracies by a complicated system of
voting and selection by lot. Cf. Guicciardini,
Storia Fiorentina, iii. 125.

(Subsequently the system of direct appointment
by lot was again introduced. Cf. Guicciardini,
iii. 155, 203, 235.)

(2) To hear criminal appeals from the Signory and Otto
di Balía.

(3) To pass laws. The President *Il Proposto*, one of the
Signory, changed every third day, laid the law
before the Signory and the Collegi. If they
approved it might be submitted to a *Practica* of
selected members of the Consiglio d'Ottanta.
Thence it went before the Ottanta, and then to
the Consiglio Generale. Here laws could not be
discussed, though Signory might call on some one
to speak in support, but were voted on.

C. Dieci di Libertà e Pace (called also Dieci di Balía), again
restored in place of the Otto di Pratica. The Signory,
the Courts of the Capitano and of the Podestà, the
Mercatanzia, and the Otto di Balía remained as before.
The Dieci di Pace e Libertà restored.

In 1498. The Courts of the Podesta and the Capitano del
Popolo were restored.

This Government lasted till 1512, with these exceptions :—

(i) In 1502.

(*a*) The Gonfalonier to be elected for life, by a double
system of nomination and election. Piero Soderini
elected. (Guicciardini, iii. 281 ; Villari, *Life of
Machiavelli*, ii. 102 ; Perrens, *Hist. Flor.* ii. 408.)

(*b*) Courts of Podestà, of the Capitano del Popolo, and of
Mercatanzia abolished. Instead, the *Ruota della
Justizia* composed of five Doctors of Law with civil
and criminal jurisdiction. These to be foreigners
elected by Signory and the College for three years, and
paid, one of whom was to be Podestà. The Mercatanzia, however, continued as a Board of Trade.

(ii) 1506. A militia instituted at suggestion of Machiavelli.
All males from 15—50 years of age to serve, but only
from the city and country district (contado) of Florence.
Not from her subject cities. (Burd, 126.)

The militia placed under a new board of nine, *Nove
della Milizia*, which however was under the Dieci di
Libertà e Pace in time of war.

III. 1512. RETURN OF MEDICI.

The constitution restored as it was before the revolution of
1494, although nomination to offices lay practically in hands of
the Medici, Giuliano, and Lorenzo. (Burd, 145, 148.)

The Quarantia appointed to expedite cases. (Guicc. 329.)

IV. 1527. Re-establishment of the constitution of Savonarola, 1494, except that Gonfalonier was to be elected for 13 months.

V. 1530. **Final overthrow of the Republic.** Perrens, *Hist. Flor.*, iii. 368.

Alessandro de Medici appointed Grand Duke.

12 Reformatori elected in a Parlamento to 'reform' the State.

    1. Signory abolished.

    2. A Council of 200 elected for life.

    3. A Senate of 48 elected for life from the 200, with powers of legislation and taxation, and appointment to offices.

    4. A Privy Council of four Councillors elected for three months by 12 Accopiatori chosen out of the Senate.

        These with the hereditary Grand Duke fulfilled duties of the Signory.

The Otto di Pratica
The Otto di Guardia } to be nominated by the Senate.
The Buonuomini

All distinction between higher and lower 'arti' abolished. The offices paid.

TAXATION.

See Napier, iii. 117. Von Reumont, i. 30. Ewart, *Cosimo de' Medici.* Armstrong, *Lorenzo de' Medici.*

I. Indirect Taxes. Import and Export Duties. Monopoly on Salt.

II. On Real and Personal Property. (Guicc. 328.)

III. *Prestanze.*—Forced loans on the estimated property. In theory these were to be repaid and interest paid meanwhile, but this was rarely done ('tenere i luoghi' (shares) = to withhold the payment of interest), so much so that most took advantage of the law, that where the amount did not exceed two golden florins they might pay one-third down and forfeit all claim to interest or repayment.

    The system led to great abuse. The influential got repaid, not so the poor. Hence speculators connected with Government bought up claims on the State for small sums, and then got the loan refunded.

The Assessment (estimo) of citizen's property for II. and III. was originally managed thus—

    1. A Balía appointed who assigned to each ward their *quota*.

    2. In each ward. Seven Boards of seven each (Sette Settine) made seven schedules of assessment on the citizens according to their idea of the property of each individual.

3. These seven schedules were sent to some of the best reputed monasteries, which rejected the four schedules which differed most widely, and then, adding up the amounts assessed to each taxpayer by the three remaining schedules, divided the total by 3.

But under this system numerous exceptions had crept in ; indeed, the rich were largely exempted on the plea that they served the State by taking office.

Hence the reform of the *Catasto,* 1427 (*Accatastare,* to heap up). A valuation made every five years of all property subject to taxation. (Lands, movables within or without city, rents, profits of business.)

From this sum capitalised at the rate of 7 per cent., *i.e.* 7 florins income = 100 florins capital, deductions for necessary expenses were made. The remainder, which was looked upon as a surplus, was liable to be taxed either for direct tax or for loans at the rate of $\frac{1}{2}$ per cent. on the capital.

From the time of Cosimo the Assessment was made by officials instead of representative Committees, and the principle of graduation was introduced. This became perpetual in 1480, when the tax was thrown on land only at $\frac{1}{10}$th of annual value (the *Decima Scalata*). In 1482 the tax on movables and professions (*Arbitrio*) was reintroduced.

Under Savonarola, 1494, the system of graduation was abolished and the Decima was levied on land only, but shortly after the old system was re-established.

In 1503. The Arbitrio, a tax on Professions established.

IV. Poll Tax from $1\frac{1}{4}$ to $4\frac{1}{4}$ florins per head between ages 17-70. In cases of large young families only one member taxed.

SUBJECT TOWNS AND DISTRICTS of two kinds.

1. *Somissio* by conquest or compact. The relation of Florence to these differed ; but, generally speaking, the Podestà was appointed by Florence, and an appeal lay to Florentine Courts, while the dependent city kept its own government and laws, and more or less freedom of taxation.

The trade relations were peculiar. Both mother city and dependent cities maintained protective duties against each other.

2. *Accomandigia.*—Under a Protectorate, the town then called *Raccomandato.* This did not amount to much more than acknowledging the Florentine supremacy, and following her lead in war.[1]

[1] Guicciardini in his *Ricordi* says : ' The subjects of a Republic are in worse

Causes of instability of Florentine Government—
1. Conflict between idea of equality and desire of families to rule.
2. Jealousy of the Executive.
3. No adaptability in the Constitution.
4. Weakness and partiality of Justice.
5. Taxation the sport of parties, except when regulated by the Catasto, and that only for a short time.
6. Turbulent character of its citizens.
7. Oppressive government of its subject cities.

APPENDIX III

VENETIAN CONSTITUTION IN THE FIFTEENTH AND SIXTEENTH CENTURIES

AUTHORITIES.—Daru, *Histoire de la République de Venise*, B. xxxix.
Brown, *Venice*, pp. 163, 177, 398; *Venetian Studies*, p. 178.
Cambridge Modern History, vol. i. p. 263 ff.

I. THE GREAT COUNCIL (Maggior Consiglio).

Confined by law of 1296 to the families of those who were *then* members (*Serrata del Maggior Consiglio*). The eligible had to be elected, but were, as a matter of fact, always elected. No one could take his seat until the age of twenty-five, with the exception of thirty who were elected every December, and a few specially allowed to do so, in return for loans lent to the State.

Its functions were chiefly *Elective*. All officials, and magistrates elected by it, except a few of the highest officers, *e.g.* the Savii Grandi, the Savii di Terra Firma, and the Admiral.

System of Election.—Nominators, chosen by lot in the Council, elected candidates—sometimes two, sometimes four—for the vacant office. The names of these candidates were then submitted to the Council, and the one who received most votes was declared elected.

The Great Council also originally enjoyed (*a*) some legislative powers, but these were gradually absorbed by the Senate; (*b*) judicial powers. On presentation by the College they tried commanders accused of negligence or incompetency.[1]

case than those of a Prince. A Republic grants no share of its grandeur to any but citizens of its chief city while oppressing others. A Prince considers all equally his subjects.'
[1] The College decided whether the offender should be tried by the Council or the Senate. If he was accused of treason, the case went to the Council of Ten.

II. THE SENATE (Pregadi, *i.e.* the Invited), 246 in number :—

    (*a*) Sixty elected in the Great Council for one year.

    (*b*) Sixty (the Zonta, *i.e.* addition) elected by the outgoing Senate and confirmed by the Great Council.

    (*c*) *Ex officio.*—The Doge, his six Councillors, members of Supreme Court of Criminal Appeal, and members of financial and judicial departments.

    (*d*) Fifty minor officials, who had a right to debate, but not to vote.

  Its Functions.

    (*a*) *Chiefly Legislative.*—It passed laws on the proposal of the College.

    (*b*) *Elected* a few of the higher officials.
        The Savii Grandi.
        The Savii di Terra Firma.
        The Admiral.

    (*c*) Sometimes tried commanders accused of negligence or incompetence.

III. THE COUNCIL OF TEN (Consiglio de' Dieci).—After 1310 this Council absorbed some of the functions of the Senate. Brown, *Venice*, p. 177.

  How elected.

    For one year, by the Maggior Consiglio, out of a list of twenty, of which ten were elected by the Consiglio, ten by the Doge, his Councillors, and the Chiefs of the Supreme Court of Justice. No member to be re-eligible for a year after holding office. The Doge and his six Councillors were *ex-officio* members. Subsequently, twenty additional members were elected in the Maggior Consiglio for each important case.

    Functions.—(*a*) It looked after urgent questions of finance, public policy, and military organisation.
    (*b*) Tried cases of treason, and other cases removed from the ordinary courts by the College.

IV. THE COLLEGIO proposed measures to the Senate, and was the *Supreme Executive Authority.*

> *Members.*—(*a*) The Doge, six Councillors, three Presidents of the Criminal Court of Appeal.
>
> (*b*) Six Savii Grandi, elected by the Senate for a period of six months. • Must be 38 years old.
>
> > These superintended the action of the boards below them, and fulfilled the work of the responsible ministers of State.
>
> (*c*) Five Savii di Terra Firma, elected for six months. Must be 30 years old.
>
> > 1. Savio alla Scrittura. Minister of War.
> > 2. Savio Cassier. Chancellor of Exchequer.
> > 3. Savio alle Ordinanze. Minister for Native Militia.
> > 4. Savio ai da mo. Minister for execution of urgent matters.
> > 5. Savio ai ceremoniali. Minister for ceremonies of State.
>
> (*d*) Five Savii da Mar, or agli ordini.
>
> > The Board of Admiralty, elected for six months, worked under direct superintendence of the Savii Grandi. Had a vote, but no voice in the College. Filled for most part with young men, who here received their political education.

V. THE DOGE.—Elected for life, by forty-one electors, themselves chosen by ballot, and vote in the Great Council (cf. Brown, *Venice,* p. 150). His position ornamental. He, with his six Councillors, who were elected for eight months in the Great Council, presided over the Council, the Senate, the College, and all State affairs were conducted in his name. But he had no power without his six Councillors, and little even with them.

VI. JUSTICE.—This was administered by four Supreme Courts formed of judges elected out of its own members by the Great Council, who held office nominally for one year, but were usually re-elected.

(*a*) *Criminal.*—The members of this Court sat in the Senate, and its three presidents in the College.

(*b*) Three Courts of Civil Jurisdiction: of which one heard appeals from the inferior Courts in Venice, the other two from the Courts in the dependencies.

No decision of the appellant Court was valid unless it confirmed the decision of the inferior Court ; and in the event of their decisions differing, the matter was constantly referred backward and forward until the Court of first instance and the Supreme Court could agree.

VII. TAXATION.—Venice always objected to permanent direct taxation, and it was not till 1530 that she resorted to an income tax.

The chief taxes were :

1. Forced loans, redeemable or not, on which the State paid regular interest. This system, adopted in 1171, is perhaps the earliest instance of a national debt.

2. Each member of a guild paid—

(*a*) The *Taglione*=capitation fee for belonging to a guild.

(*b*) The *Tansa insensibile*=tax on profits of his work.

3. Duties on imports and exports.

4. Trade in salt, which was a State monopoly. The profits of this trade at home and abroad amounted at times to one-tenth of the gross revenue.

5. Profits of the State Bank, which did business often with foreign princes.

6. In days of her decline Venice also resorted to the system of selling public offices.

VIII. GOVERNMENT OF DEPENDENCIES.—Aim to leave as much independence as was compatible with maintenance of Venetian supremacy, and to assimilate the government of the dependent towns as closely as was possible with that of Venice. This wise policy she accounts for the way in which her dependent towns returned to her after the League of Cambrai. Contrast the policy of Florence.

The representatives of the Venetian Supremacy were, in the larger towns, the Rettori.

That is—

1. The Podestà—the supreme civil officer, with control over the police, the fiscal, and other administrative work.
2. The Capitano—who looked after the local levies and other forces.

Both these officials were in immediate communication with the Venetian Senate and the Ten, but were bound by oath to respect the local privileges.

Under the Rettor stood the Free Municipal Government, which varied in every town, but was always presided over by a Podestà—an elected officer, who was sometimes a native, sometimes a Venetian, sometimes the Rettor himself.

The smaller towns were governed by a Podestà, a Capitano, or a Proveditore.

Each town had its statuto dealing with details of municipal and even of private life. Octroï duties, roads, bridges, water, lighting, doctors, nurses, guilds, sanitation; which the Rettor swore to observe. Education, primary and secondary, was charged on the municipal revenues.

Reasons for stability of Venetian Government—

1. Coincidence of theoretical and practical Sovereignty in the same hands.
2. Adaptability of the Constitution, *e.g.* gradual assumption of power by Senate, and then by the Ten.
3. Strength of the Executive which excited no jealousy.
4. Impartiality of Justice.
5. Provision made for nobles in Government of Dependencies, for the middle class in civil service and commerce, for the lower classes in the fleet.
6. Large alien Population who did not want political power, but to be judged fairly, taxed lightly, and find employment.

For the Imperial Institution, see pp. 106, 145.
For the Spanish Constitution, see pp. 92, 299.

APPENDIX IV

Page 20, last paragraph. Alfonso's attempt to buy the support of the Sultan Bajazet by the surrender of Otranto and Brindisi had failed.

Page 21, first paragraph. Louis Duke of Orleans had driven off the Neapolitan fleet at Rapallo, and the seaboard was therefore in the hands of the French.

Page 23, line 2. The French fleet was, however, shortly after captured by the Genoese at Rapallo.

Page 23, line 18. The attack on the centre and rearguard was led by the Marquis of Mantua.

Page 43, last paragraph. D'Aubigny was popular owing to his conciliatory policy during the occupation by Charles VIII.

Page 64, line 12. In this campaign the infantry for the first time were mainly French. Hitherto the infantry had been mainly foreign mercenaries.

Page 74, line 13. The character of Julius II. is well illustrated by his remark to Michael Angelo when he was at work at his statue : 'Why talk to me of books ? Give me a sword.'

Page 167. Between the tables of Wittelsbach and Welf insert : There were two other branches—that of Ingoldstadt, which was united to that of Landshut in 1445. On the death of George the Rich, 1502, the Landshut branch also became extinct.

Page 238, line 11. These two men were members of the Hohenzollern family of Brandenburg.

Page 245, line 9. Albert also attacked Duke Henry of Brunswick. Henry of Brunswick, a violent and eccentric man, had been driven from his Duchy by Philip of Hesse and John Frederick of Saxony in 1542. Cf. p. 213.

THE POPES, 1494 TO 1598

Alexander VI. (Rodrigo Borgia), August 1492 to 1503.

Pius III. (Francis Piccolomini), September to October 1503.

Julius II. (Julian della Rovere), November 1503 to February 1513.

Leo X. (Giovanni dei Medici), March 1513 to December 1521.

Adrian VI. (Tutor of Charles V.), January 1522 to September 1523.

Clement VII. (Giulio dei Medici), November 1523 to September 1534.

Paul III. (Alexander Farnese), October 1534 to November 1549.

Julius III. (Giovanni Maria del Monte), February 1550 to March 1555.

Marcellus II. (Marcello Cervini), April 1555.

Paul IV. (John Peter Caraffa), May 1555 to April 1559.

Pius IV. (Giovanni Angelo dei Medici), December 1559 to December 1565.

Pius V. (Michael Ghislieri), January 1566 to May 1572.

Gregory XIII. (Hugh Buoncompagno), May 1572 to April 1585.

Sixtus V. (Felix Peretti), April 1585 to August 1590.

Urban VII. (Giovanni Baptist Castogna), September 1590.

Gregory XIV. (Nicholas Sfondrati), December 1590 to October 1591.

Innocent IX. (Giovanni Antony Facchinetti), October to December 1591.

Clement VIII. (Ippolito Aldobrandini), January 1592 to March 1605.

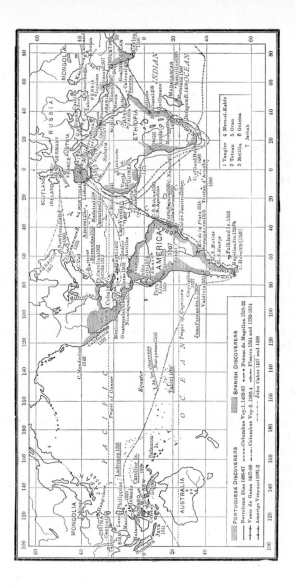

GENEALOGY OF THE HOUSES OF VALOIS AND BOURBON.

CHARLES V.

CHARLES VI.

Louis, Duke of Orleans.

CHARLES VII.

LOUIS XI.

Charles, Duke of Orleans, *ob.* 1467.

John, Count of Angoulême.

Charles, Count of Angoulême = Louise of Savoy.

Charles of Vendôme, descended from Louis IX

CHARLES VIII., 1483-1498 = 1. Anne of Brittany

1. Jeanne = LOUIS XII., 1498-1515. 2. Anne of Brittany. 3. Mary, d. of Henry VII.

Anne = Peter, Duke of Bourbon.

Susanna = Charles, Count of Montpensier, Constable, *ob.* 1527.

1. Claude = FRANCIS I. = 2. Eleanora sister of Emp. Charles v. 1515-1547.

Margaret = Henry d'Albret, King of Navarre.

Margaret = Emanuel Philibert, Duke of Savoy.

Catherine de Medici = HENRY II., 1547-1559. *ob.* 1589.

Jeanne d'Albret, Queen of Navarre. = Antony, Duke of Vendôme, *ob.* 1562.

Charles, Cardinal of Bourbon, *ob.* 1590.

Louis, Prince of Condé, 1569. *ob.*

Henry, Prince of Condé.

FRANCIS II., 1559-1560 = Mary Stuart.

CHARLES IX., 1560-1574 = Elizabeth, d. of Emp. Maximilian II.

HENRY III., 1574-1589 = Louise of Lorraine.

Elizabeth = Philip II. of Spain.

Hercules Francis, Duke of Alençon and Anjou, *ob.* 1584.

Margaret = HENRY IV., 1589-1610.

THE HAPSBURGS IN GERMANY AND IN SPAIN.

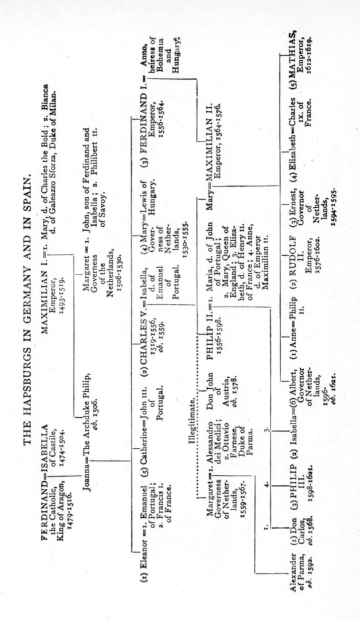

HOUSES OF LORRAINE AND GUISE.

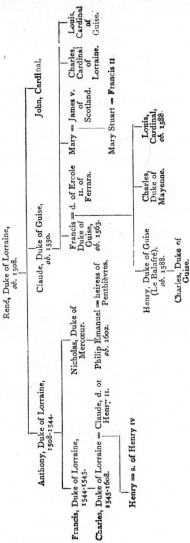

INDEX